Bubbles

Bubbles

An Encore

by

BEVERLY SILLS

GROSSET & DUNLAP

Publishers/New York

To Mama, Papa, Peter,
Muffy and Bucky

Acknowledgments

This book would not have been possible without the superb editorial assistance with both text and pictures of Milton Orshefsky.

My husband Peter was consistently helpful and jogged my memory on most of the events.

James G. Burke was responsible for much of the picture research.

Contents

9

Bubbles

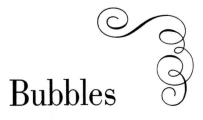

1

"That's no seven-year-old! She's a midget"

Me at three, "The Most Beautiful Baby of 1932"—in Brooklyn.

When I was only three, and still named Belle Miriam Silverman, I sang my first aria in public. The stage was Tompkins Park, in Brooklyn, New York; the occasion, a contest to proclaim "Miss Beautiful Baby of 1932." I wore an outfit with a deep *décolleté* and I had no doubt I would win the title for Body. My song was a catchy little number entitled "The Wedding of Jack and Jill"; it won me the award for Talent, too. When the master of ceremonies for the event asked me my name, I replied, "Chewpee Bow Sipperman," which was as close as I could get to Cutie Pie Silverman, a pet name my father called me. That is, when he, my mother and my two brothers were not calling me "Bubbles," an endearment forced on me at birth because I was born with an enormous bubble of spit in my mouth. "That's an omen," the doctor said. "We *have* to call her 'Bubbles.' " The name has stuck.

I wish I could say that Tompkins Park was the start of my career. It wasn't, of course; there were no plans then for me to have a career. But my mother had, and still has, an intense passion for music and she passed it on to me. Among her collection of phonograph records were eleven old Madame Galli-Curci records—seventy-eights. She would play them even before she made coffee in the morning, and they would echo throughout the house all day long. Before I was seven, I had memorized all twenty-two arias on the recordings, and could sing them in phonetic Italian. My mother felt strongly that all little girls, whether they go on to college or not, should learn to sing, to tap dance, and to play the piano. Every Saturday morning I was schlepped downtown to a school and there, for a dollar, I was given singing lessons, dancing lessons, and elocution lessons. The last curriculum I did not really need; I was then, as I am now, a compulsive talker. I probably taught the elocution teacher a thing or two.

The school had a weekly Saturday morning local radio program on Station WOR called "Uncle Bob's Rainbow Hour," on which the more talented little pupils would get to perform. At four, I was not a sensational singer, piano player, or tap dancer but I did have a precocious tongue and vocabulary. They got me on the show. I would say some funny things with Uncle Bob Emory on the air and then he would allow me to sing. My big aria was still "The Wedding of Jack and Jill," which ended with the words "ding, dong, ding." Once, the live audience applauded before I finished the song, drowning out the ending. "Wait a minute!" I shrieked over the air waves. "I haven't finished my ding-dong!" That plaint became a kind of password with Uncle Bob and me; we still giggle over it.

Just before one of my scheduled appearances on the radio show, I was told by our doctor that I might be coming down with mumps, but I insisted on being taken to the studio for my regular "do" with Uncle Bob. On the air he said to me, "How do you feel today?" hoping to start a nice, funny conversation. "Not so good," I replied. "I have the mumps." Every male in the studio raced out in panic—except for Uncle Bob, who was saddled with me and the mike. He allowed me to finish my song and then I was taken home. I did, it turned out, have the mumps.

Uncle Bob gave his kids, including me, maximum public exposure. Once he rented Town Hall to present the talent and I got to sing a coloratura aria that I had picked up from Galli-Curci's records—*"Il Bacio."* My performance moved one New York columnist to accuse Uncle Bob, half-seriously, of misrepresentation. "That's no seven-year-old!" the columnist wrote. "She's a midget."

When I was seven, and renamed Beverly Sills (a friend of my mother's thought that some day it might look better on a marquee than Belle Silverman), Twentieth Century-Fox made one attempt to make a movie star out of me. In American cultural history we were at the beginning of the *Wunderkind* era. Shirley Temple was at her peak, Bobby Breen was making it big with Eddie Cantor, and Deanna Durbin and Judy Garland were about to check in. I, meanwhile, had been heard singing my Italian arias in the Queen Mary Restaurant in New York City by a studio director and asked to sing something in an educational-type film called *Uncle Sol Solves It,* starring Willy Howard.

I sang in the movie but I did not conquer Hollywood. My mother wasn't a stage mother pushing, pushing me into a career and at that point I still had no formal voice training—I was simply singing imitations of Galli-Curci. But the experience at least made my parents think that perhaps there *was* something to this little girl who was singing all those arias at such an early age. My mother decided that the time had come to have someone listen to me who could make an honest evaluation of my talent.

One day, as we were walking along Fifty-seventh Street, in Manhattan, we noticed on a newsstand near Carnegie Hall a magazine called "Musical Courier." On its cover was a picture of Estelle Liebling captioned "Coach to the World's Greatest Voices." My mother had already determined that if I was going to be anything, it would have to be the greatest; she called Miss Liebling and made an appointment. When we arrived at her studio, Miss Liebling took one look at this beautiful lady, my mother, and said to her: "Leave the little girl with the secretary. I'll hear you sing right now." "Oh, no, no," my mother said. "The audition is for my little girl." "But I don't teach children," Miss Liebling replied. Then, after a pause, "In fact, I don't even *know* any children."

That could have been the end of Beverly Sills right there. But when my mother explained that we had come all the way from Sea Gate—which is past Coney Island—and that we had been traveling for an hour and a half on one bus, one trolley, and two subway trains, Miss Liebling agreed to listen to me. Heretofore, every time I had done my little vocal routine for adults they had gone crazy with applause. Now, when I finished singing my *"Il Bacio"* for Miss Liebling, she burst out laughing. *I* burst out crying: *nobody* had ever laughed at me before. Much later she explained to me what had set off her laughter. My Italian, learned phonetically from old records of dubious quality, came out so funny that it was nonexistent. At the same time she was bowled over by the idea of a seven-year-old imitating the famous Galli-Curci trill.

In any event, Miss Liebling must have been impressed: she agreed to teach me one day a week for fifteen minutes. That, she said, would be quite long enough for my still-fragile young voice. Every Saturday my mother and I would travel three hours portal-to-portal so that I could sing fifteen minutes of scales. It must have been quite a chore for Miss Liebling, too. Like all seven-year-olds, I was extremely wiggly. I had to stand in the middle of a big circular pattern in the Oriental rug in her studio and try not to fidget while singing for fifteen minutes. It wasn't easy.

Miss Liebling was an incredible teacher. She had been an opera singer, making her debut in *Lucia di Lammermoor* with the Dresden Royal Opera Company. She had studied with Mathilde Marchesi, one of the great voice teachers of all time. Madame Marchesi had numbered among her pupils Emma Calvé, Emma Eames, Mary Garden, and Nellie Melba. Miss Liebling taught the Marchesi method; when she died in 1970 she was, I think, the last surviving pupil of Mme. Marchesi. Her own pupils had included Galli-Curci, Frieda Hempel, and Maria Jeritza. She had a marvelous technique: even in her eighties she could occasionally sing beautiful tones. She is the only singing teacher I have ever had on a continuing basis. Our association started in 1936 and lasted until her death—thirty-four years!

Miss Liebling was more than a teacher to me, she was a second mother;

and as she was older than my real mother, she was even more matriarchal. I was married in her studio. When she died, at ninety-two, she left me in her will a beautiful Sèvres china cup. It was the same cup in which she would have hot chocolate waiting for me when I showed up in her studio in the middle of winter, freezing from that long commute from Sea Gate. I have never been more touched.

After my first two years with Miss Liebling she decided it was time to display my new, polished singing voice to the public. She was a good friend of Major Bowes, who at that time had a very successful weekly radio program on CBS called "Major Bowes' Amateur Hour," and she set up an audition for me. I was accepted, appeared on the show singing *"Caro Nome"* from *Rigoletto,* another aria I had learned from a Galli-Curci record, and I won the amateur contest. As a result, I became a regular member of Major Bowes' Capitol Family Hour show, which broadcast nation-wide every Sunday from the old Capitol Theater Building in New York City.

The Major and I got along famously. On the air we would chat, as I had done with Uncle Bob. I was less funny now but I used more and bigger words. Then I would sing. What I didn't realize at first was what an enormous audience the program had; it went into millions of homes. The first time I appeared on the Capitol Family Hour Major Bowes gave me a tiny glass elephant. When he announced over the air that I was clutching the elephant for good luck when I performed, I began receiving in the mail hundreds of elephants—to supplement the lovely jade and ivory ones the Major kept giving me. I eventually wound up with a huge collection of elephants. Once on his program I made the mistake of saying on the air that I would love to have a sled because it was snowing outside; I received twenty-five sleds from listeners, all of which we distributed to various orphanages and schools except one, an all-chrome job from the Kalamazoo Sled Company, which I was allowed to keep. And when I told on the program how my mother made all my clothes for me and how I was hoping, now that I was ten, that she would allow me to wear a long dress, dozens of long dresses streamed at me through the mails. It was wonderful.

My father took a rather dim view of theatrical children, but he went along with my extracurricular activities because he believed enthusiastically in education in any form and I was certainly getting that. In addition to my singing lessons, I was studying piano—at Miss Liebling's insistence—with Paolo Gallico, father of the writer Paul Gallico. He was a great teacher—and a hard taskmaster: I had ten red knuckles at the end of every lesson because he would bang a ruler across my knuckles if I had not practiced enough or done as well as he felt I should. It was affectionately done—I think. He gave me books to read and introduced me to all kinds of interesting literature about famous pianists. I was also, at my father's insistence, learning foreign languages. I already spoke French because shortly after I was born a French maid had come to live with us. There we were, my brothers and I—three little kids from Brooklyn running around the house talking French! By the time I was ten I could speak Italian too, and I had already learned *Rigoletto.* Gilda was the first role Miss Liebling taught me.

It was all fun. Public school on weekdays, then to Manhattan on Saturday for piano lessons, language lessons, singing lessons, lunch with my mother at a Horn and Hardart Cafeteria, the Roxy Theatre to take in a movie, to Chinatown for supper with the whole family, and then back to Brooklyn. Sundays I would be taken to my regular stint with the Major. My original twenty-two Galli-Curci arias had expanded into some fascinating new repertoire and I was enjoying every minute of it.

Through Major Bowes' Capitol Family Hour came an offer to me to appear in a soap opera called "Our Gal Sunday." I signed on for thirty-six weeks, at $67.50 per fifteen-minute broadcast, playing the role of Elaine Raleigh, a little mountain girl whose drunken father continually abuses her, forcing her to take refuge in song and in the hills. One guest star was Esther Ralston of silent screen fame; she played a famous opera singer from New York who happens to visit, hears this young mountain gal singing in the hills, and takes her back to the city—never to be heard of again.

Probably a good thing, too, because I had just turned twelve and my parents decided that I was ready for retirement and a more normal existence.

To tell the truth, I was ready for retirement myself. I was beginning to look a little awkward. I had already done a number of exciting things—soap opera, Major Bowes, a Rinso White commercial. I had been one of the first children ever to be telecast on NBC for a program called "Stars of the Future." Then, too, Major Bowes had become seriously ill and the Capitol Family had been replaced on the air with a program called "The Cresta Blanca Carnival," a program of music played by the Morton Gould orchestra. Now instead of my regular talking-and-singing visits with Major Bowes, I was a soloist with Gould, along with a young man who had, and still has, one of the most beautiful baritone voices I have ever heard. He was then called Merill Miller; his name is now Robert Merrill.

Even in retirement I was to continue all my lessons, going to the City by myself every Saturday on subways, then judged safe, with four dollars pinned inside my bloomers for the various lessons and two nickels in my pocket for all the transportation. The rest of the week I was an ordinary Brooklyn teenager. We lived in an all-Jewish neighborhood in a house much like all the others in that Sea Gate area—two stories, detached, six rooms (three of them bedrooms on the second floor), and a little Victory Garden at the back. Our front yard was the Atlantic Ocean. I had a "steady," a boy named Sandy Levine, aged fifteen, who used to drive my father out of his mind. Sandy would never come into our house to fetch me; instead he would hang around outside all day long, and when he wanted to summon me he would whistle the tune of my Rinso White commercial—"Rinso White, Rinso White, happy little washday song." "Are you going out," my father used to ask me, "with a boy or a bird?"

I was attending P.S. 91, an elementary school in Brooklyn, and was an associate editor of the school newspaper, the *Herald*. When I was graduated in 1942, the paper published its annual Personality Poll. I was voted Prettiest Girl, Most Likely to Succeed, Fashion Plate, Most Talented, and Most Personality. I was *not* voted Smartest or Wittiest or—surprise!—Most Talkative.

The dream at that early age of my eventually becoming an opera star was mine, not my mother's. But it was she who made me believe that the impossible dream was possible. In her eyes, anything that her three children wanted to be, they could be—and she would support them all the way. Even though my father's attitude at the time was that there was no place in *his* family for a theatrical child, he continued to rationalize his reluctant approval of what my mother and I were doing: at least I was getting a good musical education. I was already a good enough pianist for Mr. Gallico to urge my mother to allow me to concentrate solely on the piano. And my father loved the fact that I was becoming multilingual; the idea of my eventually sitting at a dinner party conversing in several languages would have appealed to him. That is probably what was in the back of his mind— not the idea that, oh goody, she'll be able to sing opera in three different languages. At that time my mother never really considered the possibility of my becoming a famous opera singer either. I think that what delighted her most, given her own passion for music, was that what delighted *me* most was singing.

They were happy times, and to me, at least, quite normal. I never thought that I was doing anything special. I was doing something I loved with the backing of both my parents—though admittedly for different reasons, with different goals in mind.

Bubbles at five months.

The Silverman kids—
Sidney, eight, Bubbles, three, Stanley, six.

Papa—in his mid-forties.

At P.S. 232 in Brooklyn in 1935,
our first grade put on a play called
Sur le Pont d'Avignon. The boy
is Albert Silverstein. Forty-one
years later we bumped into each other
on Beverly Sills Day in Brooklyn.

The show must go on. It did, at Uncle Bob's Rainbow House program in 1936—although the studio was evacuated in panic except for Uncle Bob and me when I broke the dreaded news: I had MUMPS.

My professional pose at age ten. Note how little it has changed since that Tompkins Park contest.

Celebrating with Major Bowes on his Capitol Family Hour in 1939.

2

*Thank God
Pons had a light, high voice!*

Lily Pons in Lakmé.

My mother took me to see my first opera when I was eight years old. It was Delibes' *Lakmé* at the Metropolitan, with Lily Pons in the title role. Miss Pons, a little Dresden doll, came on stage in a costume that had a brief halter top and a lot of bare midriff. It was, for those days, an extremely *risqué* outfit. I got so excited that I yelled at the top of my lungs, "Mama, Mama, her belly button is showing!"

I was hooked. I became an instant Pons fan, so overwhelmed by her performance that I wrote her a letter about how beautiful she was and how beautifully she sang. She wrote back inviting Mama and me to a concert she was giving at Carnegie Hall. I began to collect her recordings—*The Daughter of the Regiment, Rigoletto*—and I fell in love with the bell-like quality of her voice. Not only was her voice remarkable; she also *looked* all her roles. That was not the case then for most opera stars; it was still the era of the singer, not the singer-actress. Lily looked so much like Lakmé, so much like Gilda, so much like the little girl in *The Daughter of the Regiment* that I began to get interested in the actual stories of operas and the characters in them. I asked my mother to buy me a book of opera stories, and that Christmas I was given a large yellow volume entitled *Operas Every Child Should Know*. It was a Bible for me; there is no other book that I have reread as often.

When I studied my first role, Gilda, with Miss Liebling, she made me translate the entire opera from Italian into English in my own words, without using the libretto. The idea, of course, in addition to helping my Italian, was to teach me what the story meant in my own terms. (I had no idea at that young age, for example, that Gilda was abducted and raped by the Count, and I kept asking Miss Liebling, "What's she so excited about? What's the big deal? Here she is in this beautiful castle and she's got this handsome Duke . . ." I thought it was all pretty terrific!)

I credit Pons, in a way, for getting me interested in characterization on stage, which later became an integral part of my singing. I realize now that often she looked the part more than she actually portrayed it. In *Lucia*, for example, her performance was much more vocal than dramatic. During the Mad Scene she wore a beautiful white satin nightgown with a red velvet stole that made a kind of slash across her costume. She was very stage-wise and costume-wise, yet she barely moved during the scene. To me, though, she looked like Lucia, she *was* Lucia.

Although I was in forced withdrawal from public performing, I attended a good many musical functions. Miss Liebling was always giving me tickets to operas, and she opened a whole new world to me. She used to invite my mother and me to dinner at her home. We would sit at table surrounded by famous singers—Maria Jeritza, Jessica Dragonette, Grace Moore, Lauritz Melchior, Lucy Monroe, and many others—and after dinner I would be asked by Miss Liebling to sing a little song or two for the evening's entertainment. Miss Liebling knew that I loved soufflés, and whenever I came to dinner the dessert was chocolate soufflé or one of the courses was cheese soufflé. Della, the cook, would say, "I knew you were invited tonight because Miss Liebling told me to make lots of soufflés."

At her parties Miss Liebling would stand up and deliver funny speeches. I was always amazed that she was so much at ease on her feet, and I think that I have unconsciously copied her style, because I feel very free and easy now when I talk in front of large groups. She taught me to talk to people as though on a one-to-one basis, and she had a kind of funny twinkle in her eye, so that even when she was saying something that was rather unpleasant it was said in good humor.

For a girl in her early teens those glamorous evenings at Miss Liebling's were heady drink. They gave me a taste of a kind of life I thought might be great fun—the life of an opera star. Miss Liebling may even have had the Metropolitan Opera in mind for me; she often told me of her excitement when she performed at the Berlin Opera, and of how she used to tour all over the United States giving more than a thousand concerts with John Philip Sousa. So far, *my* longest traveling had been from Brooklyn to Manhattan plus an occasional journey to New Jersey for summer camp. I was dreaming of travel, of long train rides, and the kinds of experiences I was hearing about only made me want more and more to be a singer.

Over those years I built up a large repertoire; by the time I was fifteen, I knew twenty operas. Miss Liebling was extremely shrewd in her choice of repertoire for me—she kept it very light and very high. She had published books of ornamentation for the coloratura voice, and as I was still learning to sing by imitation, she would sing for me and I would try to duplicate the sound. She had a fantastic trill; I learned to trill simply by listening to her and imitating her. The main thing that Miss Liebling gave me was a solid technique. She stressed breath control and my whole technique of singing is based on it. As a result, I know how to sing. Even when I have laryngitis and cannot speak, I am almost always able to sing.

By then I was traveling from Brooklyn to Miss Liebling's studio in the city three or four times a week and my lessons had expanded to 45 minutes or an hour, depending upon what we wanted to accomplish. (I could never have afforded her usual fee—about $25 per hour. Although my father was an assistant manager in a Metropolitan Life Insurance office and we were not poor, we were more in the $2 per hour bracket than the $25. But Miss Liebling refused to take a penny for any of my lessons in all the years I was with her, even when I was able to afford it. By that time I was a member of her family, she of mine, and the question of money was naturally never broached.) She piled music on me and I absorbed it like a sponge. Everything in the *bel canto* repertoire delighted me. Primarily because of my worship of Lily Pons, I wanted to sing everything she sang—*The Daughter of the Regiment, Rigoletto,* Rosina in *The Barber of Seville.* Thank God Pons had a light, high voice! Heaven help me if I had worshiped Kirsten Flagstad instead. But even that would not have stopped me; I would have memorized Flagstad's repertoire too, because I was just plain nuts about opera. I have even memorized about ten operas that I never want to sing and never will sing. I learned them because I loved them. When, for example, I saw the debut of Ljuba Welitch in *Salomé* at the Met in 1949, I became a Strauss buff. I learned Salomé but I don't want to sing her. I've learned Elektra too, but I will never be able to sing her—it requires a totally different voice from mine.

In 1944, when I was fifteen, I decided to come out of retirement. I began reading theatrical publications for announcements of chorus auditions for Broadway musicals. You must understand that for a fifteen-year-old-girl who dreamed of being an opera star, the starting possibilities then were nil. The New York City Opera had not yet been established. There were fewer opera companies than there are today, and no regional companies. Miss Liebling thought it was a good idea for me to begin auditioning around because it would give me opportunities to sing before live audiences. (I had sung before large numbers of people only a few times in my life—on Major Bowes' Amateur Hour; at an amateur contest in junior high school, where I won ten dollars and a policeman had to escort me and my enormous earnings home; at the première of my movie at the Savoy Theatre in Brooklyn when I was seven, attended by about half the Metropolitan Life Insurance Company; and at Miss Liebling's dinner parties for twenty-five people.) But she did not like the idea of my auditioning for Broadway choruses; *no* self-respecting would-be opera star, she felt, should take a job as a chorus singer, much less in a chorus line.

Nevertheless, I went auditioning. I had turned into a tall, statuesque fifteen-year-old with very long blond hair. I must have looked like a show girl because I was offered every chorus job I ever auditioned for. I turned them all down. But at one chorus audition for a Broadway show that J. J. Shubert was producing—it was called *Love in the Snow*—I was offered the job of understudy to Anne Jeffreys, the star. When I raced home to break the news, my father, who was not aware that I had been auditioning, hit the ceiling. Out of the question, he said. I was going to get a college education first, and *then* if I wanted to go on stage, fine. But I was going to have a college degree in my pocket in case things didn't work out for me on the stage.

That was that. In our house, as in most Jewish middle-class households of the time, the father's word was law. And my father was a very positive man; every sentence he spoke had a period at the end. When I was about thirteen, for example, he said to me, "Listen, your mother doesn't smoke and she doesn't drink and you're not going to either and that's the end of the discussion." And it was. I never smoked and I still do not drink, except wine. There was never a question of my rebelling against my father's decision about the Shubert offer, or of running away from home. Besides, I loved my father.

Once more unto the breach, dear Miss Liebling. She knew J. J. Shubert well and arranged for me to have an audition with the great man himself. It was love at first sight. I guess that I was the baby girl J. J. had never had and perhaps he was the grandpa I had never had. We read scripts together, both of us playing all kinds of parts and he trying hard to get rid of my Brooklyn accent. He brought people in to teach me how to wear makeup. Frequently we would have dinner in his apartment and do jigsaw puzzles. Then I would subway back to Brooklyn, doing my homework on board, so that I would be home—as agreed—by nine o'clock.

I was enjoying myself tremendously—making new friends, exploring

Greenwich Village (whose life style then was considerably different from what it is now). I discovered the art film, mostly French, and was suddenly aware that there was a Europe on the other side of the ocean. Would I ever get to France, I dreamed, where everyone must look like Lily Pons?

I remember standing room at the Met, holding an armful of school books, wearing bobby socks and brown-and-white saddle shoes and a big Sloppy Joe sweater, listening to the opera and wanting it to go on forever. The war was on and we lived in terrible fear because both my brothers were in combat service. From Norton Point, the farthest tip of Sea Gate, we could see the ships being loaded with soldiers leaving for Europe and the wind would bring back the sounds of their voices—the saddest sound in the world.

It was a crazy-mixed-up time in my life—I was growing up. Musically it was an incredibly exhilarating period. What J. J. was cooking up for me was a Gilbert and Sullivan repertory tour that would enable me to sing roles in seven different operettas. But first there were my parents to convince. My father was dead against it—I was too young, he said, he didn't want my mother to travel with me, she belonged at his side, and so on. But J. J.—and my mother—finally won. Mama found a chaperone for me, a nice, religious girl in the cast. She was to room with me, see that my clothes were packed properly, that I made all the trains, was taken to the theater and brought straight home afterwards. And off we went on tour. My chaperone was also supposed to do my hair, using a recipe my mother had invented to keep it a lovely golden color. The recipe called for two parts of gold bleach to one part of red rinse, plus peroxide. The chaperone got it backwards—two parts red to one part gold. That's how I became a redhead. I liked it and I have remained a redhead ever since.

The only trouble with my chaperone was that she had a tendency to entertain her men friends in our room until the wee hours. When Mama learned of this, through a letter a chorus boy in the cast wrote her, she promptly fired the girl chaperone and appointed her informant my chaperone for the rest of the tour. (*That* chaperone later served a term in jail for murder. We corresponded all during his term and he sent me the most gorgeous needlepoint pillows he had made. A week after he was paroled, he died of a heart attack and my husband and I helped bury him.)

It was 1945 and I was sixteen. My salary was $100 a week—which seemed an enormous sum at the time—out of which my father insisted that I buy a twenty-five-dollar war bond. By that time I had transferred from Erasmus High School in Brooklyn to the Professional Children's School in Manhattan. While on tour I finished that school's curriculum via a correspondence course. My father couldn't bear the idea of my graduating with a correspondence-course diploma; to him it was a waste of my brain. He was even more upset when Frank Fay, who handed out the diplomas at graduation, patted me on the fanny as I went by and said, "Boy, they didn't make them like you when *I* was graduating!"

My father was very worried about my future. To show him that I was

still his smart little baby girl, I won a mathematics scholarship in Fairleigh Dickinson College. He was overjoyed and kept urging me to take advantage of the scholarship. But I had other ideas. I had returned from the Gilbert and Sullivan tour with a fistful of marvelous reviews. I had learned a good deal about stagecraft. I had learned how to project my speaking voice on stage. (Although my accent has always remained New York, I did at least manage to get rid of a good bit of the Brooklyn tinge. You just don't perform Gilbert and Sullivan sounding as though you came from the Ebbetts Field bleachers.) I had worked very hard with my music, I was a very disciplined young girl, and my desire to perform in front of an audience had become insatiable. Fairleigh Dickinson? Not a chance. I was going to be an opera star—and a very serious one. Period.

The Mikado, *as done by Camp Lincoln and Laurel in New Jersey in 1940. The star in the center is me, eleven, "Yum-Yum" Silverman, in a costume made by my mother. The handsome boy on my left is Buddy Israel, playing Nanki-Poo. Buddy went on to become Jules Irving, formerly director of the Vivian Beaumont Theatre in Lincoln Center and now a Hollywood TV producer. Buddy gave me my first kisses—offstage and on, both memorable.*

Graduation from P.S. 91. I was twelve. I made the dress myself—the first and last sewing I ever did. My brother Stanley took the picture and gave it to me as a graduation present; maybe he should have destroyed the negative.

Below, left, J.J. Shubert, the theatrical producer who launched my career by sending me on a Gilbert and Sullivan tour in 1945. At right, on that tour, that's my fifteen-year-old, grown-up-woman smile.

Miss Estelle Liebling, for thirty-four years my one and only voice teacher, in a portrait done in 1939.

3

"No, Morris,
this one will be an opera singer"

And then, suddenly, I'm nineteen.

In 1946, when I was seventeen, J. J. Shubert bought me my first pair of high-heeled shoes and sent me out on tour again. This time out we were a repertory company of three shows. My two were *The Merry Widow* and *Countess Maritza;* a lady named Blanche Chanson—which I thought was the best stage name in the whole world—did *Rose Marie.* With my first high heels, my first strapless gown, and my first upswept hairdo, I didn't know what to hold up first on stage—the gown, the feet, or the hairdo. My very handsome leading man was Frank Melton. My salary was $150 per week and I was saving $37.50 of it in savings bonds, per my father's new instructions. I was billed as "The Youngest Primadonna in Captivity."

Playing The Merry Widow was fun (through the years I was to do the role several hundred times). In Gilbert and Sullivan I could always simply play myself; in *Patience,* for example, I played myself with a crisper accent. *The Merry Widow* was the first time I had to take on somebody else as a character and I loved it.

Even though I had no part, even as understudy, in *Rose Marie*, I used to watch every performance. One night I walked into the theater to find pandemonium backstage: a ballet dancer who played the part of Wanda, the Indian girl, had ptomaine poisoning. Would I do the part? Would I! At the moment my hair was very curly, set for the next day's matinée of *The Merry Widow*, and the makeup crew had only fifteen minutes to try to braid it so that I would look a little more like an Indian girl. Somebody raced next door to the grocery store and came back with six milk bottles, whose wire caps were then roughly fashioned into six stays to try to turn my hair into flat pigtails. Fat chance—by the time I got to the famous Indian Totem Tom-Tom Dance my pigtails were curled in great hooks at each end. My favorite line in the operetta was, "You come to my cabin later, huh?" Still all-absorbed in the Widow, I made it: "You come to my *castle* later, huh?"

The Shubert tour was invaluable experience for me, and the love Mr. Shubert bestowed on me is something I shall never forget. I had been around long enough to know what the name Shubert meant in the world of the theater and here was J. J. grooming *me* to be a star of the musical theater. It was somewhat off my original dream of being an opera star, but at the time it seemed the logical road to my eventual destination.

My parents, however, saw it differently and threw a roadblock. I remember a conversation the family had had during dinner one night when I was fourteen. I had been urging my mother to please tell Papa that I wanted to be an opera star and that he really ought to have a more positive attitude about it. As she served him his favorite dinner she said, "Listen, Morris, the child wants to be an opera star." He never looked up from the soup and replied, "The child will go to college and be smart." Mother: "No, Morris, the two boys will go to college and be smart. *This* one will be an opera singer."

My father was now reconciled to that dream of his two ladies, but he disagreed with my notion that through Broadway I would wind up in the opera. So did my mother. They told me firmly that I had to settle down, not spend three months on the road doing tours, without singing lessons, without piano lessons, without adding to my repertoire. That would get me nowhere. Either aim for a serious career, they ordered, or go back to school and become a music teacher.

And so my whole career with the Shuberts ended. To J. J.'s credit, he agreed with my parents' decision. He had felt when I first auditioned for him that for a young American artist eager to be an opera singer there was too little opportunity. Hordes of American singers, especially men who had just come back from the service, were returning to Europe to sing because there was no opportunity for them here. The Metropolitan was called an international house but the handful of Americans on its roster were treated like poor relations compared to the European singers. The whole country at the time was Europe-oriented as far as culture was concerned. If a singer's name was unpronounceable, why, of course, she was a great opera singer; if her name was pronounceable, how could she be great? We still had an inferiority complex toward the arts. J. J. was much more aware of that cultural syndrome than my family and I were at the time.

Reluctantly, I quit show biz and returned to serious study with Miss Liebling. By the time I was nineteen I had a repertoire of fifty or sixty operas. I was beginning to speak German. Not well—I have never been able to speak it well—but my accent is good and I can converse in it although not with the fluency of Italian or French. Miss Liebling was working hours with me on my repertoire, my style of singing, my coloratura technique. It was a period of intense training—and of very little employment.

But I did, finally, make my operatic debut. I played the role of Frasquita, one of Carmen's gypsy gang, in a Philadelphia Opera Company production in which Winifred Heidt and Eugene Conley, who were then married to each other, played Carmen and Don José. Giuseppe Bamboschek, the conductor, was a good friend of Miss Liebling's and he allowed me to understudy many roles with the company. I knew, because the Philadelphia was strictly star-oriented, that I would never be allowed to fill in even if a star singer did get sick, but at least I was able to watch great artists at work. I got to know Armando Annini, a fine stage director; he would tell me wonderful stories about Grace Moore, Jan Kiepura, Ezio Pinza, Lucrezia Bori, and about how Claudia Muzio would do the letter scene in *Traviata*, all of which further stirred my imagination and my desire to be an opera star.

Annini also taught me the Italian approach to stage acting. It was a kind of *verismo* approach, very much the style in those days—posy, blood-and-gutsy, featuring highly exaggerated makeup, especially for the eyes, and extensive overacting. When I saw my first *Thaïs*, done by the Philadelphia Company, I was struck by Florence Quartararo, a beautiful girl with a beautiful voice, who played the title role in a highly individualistic manner, not at all in the *verismo* style, and I realized that there must be another style of acting. Annini explained that the French school of acting was entirely different from the Italian. That is when my affinity for French opera began. I went through a passionately French period and in a very short time learned *Manon, Louise, Thaïs, Sapho, Faust,* and all the roles in *The Tales of Hoffmann.* I just couldn't get enough of French repertoire.

In 1948, Miss Liebling, wanting to find some employment for her young singers, formed a group called the Estelle Liebling Singers. We were five girls and one baritone and we toured university and college towns. We had a good time, and each of us took home about $75 per concert, after expenses, but I was not getting any closer to being an opera star and I felt thoroughly frustrated.

In the latter part of the year my father had to undergo a series of operations. Only he and my mother knew how ill he was. He was in the hospital in August 1949 when I was offered a three-week tour to South America on a Moore-McCormack Line ship to do two concerts down and two back. My parents thought I should go and told me my father's condition was not serious. What they didn't tell me, of course, was that he was dying of lung cancer; he had been a four-packs-a-day man. My father, I think, preferred that I not see him physically deteriorate, and so, unknowing, I went off to

South America. The day I returned my mother met me at the pier, dressed in black: my father had died five days earlier.

Those were bleak times. At the beginning of my father's illness we had moved into Manhattan and taken a large apartment in the Stuyvesant Town complex, so that he could have treatments at Bellevue Hospital, which was nearby. When he died, my mother and I moved into a one-bedroom apartment in the same building and began what was a very lonely, close existence. My brothers were off at school—Sidney in medical school and Stanley at a teachers' college. My father had left us enough money to live on, although not in the same style as before. Life was manageable, but I was twenty years old, going nowhere, and very, very down.

One day, after my lesson with Miss Liebling, I was walking down Park Avenue looking into store windows. I must have been humming. Suddenly, next to my reflection in the window appeared that of a very distinguished-looking man in his sixties, wearing a derby and pince-nez. In a very clipped accent he asked me, "Are you a singer?" I said yes. He gave me his card; a member of a very prominent family in New York City, he ran an after-hours club open only to a very select membership and the club was looking for a woman who could sing and entertain the members. He hired me at $125 a week to sing at his club, which was on the East Side between Park and Madison. I would sing twenty minutes at a stretch and accompany myself on the piano, doing popular music as well as operatic if I liked, and then I would sit in a nearby lounge for forty minutes, reading a book. The hours were terrible, from ten P.M. to three A.M. but I was picked up in Stuyvesant Town and driven back every night. The first night I sang there I realized that this was not your average clientele; there were some of the biggest names in politics and business, names I had been reading in the newspaper. It was a private club with its own chef, where customers and clients could eat, drink, and be entertained without being seen by people they did not want to be seen by.

I was quite shocked one night, after having done my twenty minutes of song for a well-known name in the jewelry world, when the head waiter, who was very protective of me—always making sure that no one got too near me or said anything unpleasant—brought me back a hundred-dollar bill. "The gentleman you sang for," he said, "liked you very much and wants to give you a present." "I don't sing for tips," I said. My friend the head waiter replied, "Oh, yes, you do. Don't be ridiculous. You take that hundred dollars and enjoy it. You earn every penny you get." I took it.

Miss Liebling knew I had taken a job singing in a private club, but I never told her that the hours were ten to three. She felt that the best time to take a singing lesson was ten o'clock in the morning, and I could never persuade her to make it any later. The result was that I would stagger into bed at about four A.M. and stagger out again at nine to get to her studio on time. There were times when I was a bit groggy. My mother was not enthusiastic about my job, but she sensed my need to become somewhat independent and to feel that I was making a contribution to our existence. I think she also felt that my seeing that kind of after-hours life-style was in some way good for me: it certainly made me grow up quickly. Until then I had led a rather sheltered life within the bosom of my family. I had had boy friends, of course, but as the youngest child and the baby girl of the family, I was always extremely protected by my parents and my two brothers. My brothers believed, I think, as my mother did, that I would eventually become what I wanted to be, but during that growing-up time they treated me very much as the baby sister. We were inseparable as children. If one went to the movies, the three of us went. If Sidney wanted to see the Brooklyn Dodgers at Ebbetts Field, the three of us had to go. We always sat in the bleachers and to this day my mother is convinced that what cleared up my bad sinus condition as a child was the hours we spent under that baking Ebbetts Field sun. She may be right: whatever the reason, I did lose my sinus problems in the bleachers.

I continued to work at the after-hours club until I was twenty-one. By then I had made enough money to quit and take my mother to Europe. A fellow passenger on the ship, the *De Grasse,* was a lady named Gypsy Rose Lee. Aboard ship she and I would do benefit performances for the Seamen's Pension Fund. A lovely, bright, witty gal, she was a joy to be with. When the time came at those benefits to collect the money from the audience, she would say, "If you pay to hear Beverly sing, I'll let you stuff the dough down my bosom. She has her thing, I have mine."

Armed with a letter of introduction from Miss Liebling, I was accepted by Max de Rieux of the Paris Opéra into his acting class. There were eight singers, I the only American. Max taught me *Louise* and we went through *Manon* together. All the instruction was entirely in French and my accent improved tremendously; I was now as at home in French as in English. My mother and I had a marvelous time that summer. We stayed at a lovely small hotel, did the Louvre, the Lido, the Bateaux Mouches. We saw Paris the way I had always dreamed of seeing it and I had no desire to visit any other European city.

When we returned to New York at the end of summer, Miss Liebling was excited by the progress I had made and by my fascination with French repertoire. My mother was also very much involved in what I was doing. She still sewed all my clothes and did my hair, whipping up the ingredients with an eggbeater and brushing the result into my curls with a toothbrush. She is a remarkable lady and was a most unselfish mother—she always put her own life's desires second to those of her children. That's why, I think, she never married again. She was still a beautiful and talented woman and she certainly had lots of opportunities. But she always felt that as long as any of her children—in this case, me—was still at home and needed her she would not marry; she could never bring a strange man into the house while she had children living with her. Then by the time I had married she was so caught up in her grandmother role—my oldest brother had produced an heir and my other brother was married—that she apparently didn't feel the need to share her life with anyone other than the family she already had.

We still had some money and my spirits were high but I was once again in the familiar position of having no place to go. Regional operas were in their infancy and jobs were hard to find. The New York City Opera was going strong but I did not audition for them at the time. Why not is still a mystery to me. I suppose I felt, as a great many people still feel, that it is impossible to get into the New York City Opera. Actually, it is the easiest thing in the world to get an audition with them. In one way I'm happy that I didn't even try then—I had absolutely no experience in opera, simply a huge repertoire that nobody had ever heard me sing publicly.

Miss Liebling must have felt the same way: she never suggested that I try the City Opera. Instead she moved me into more repertoire. I was learning German songs. I went through books and books of Schubert *lieder*. She taught me the role of Sophie in *Der Rosenkavalier*, my first German role. She and my mother would always talk as though they were sure that some day, when the moment was absolutely right, everything good would begin happening to me. I was younger and more impatient. I knew that I was a rather attractive young woman. I felt somehow that *something* should begin to click soon. But nothing seemed to be happening and I did not want to return to the after-hours club. I wanted to get opera offers. I began to nag Miss Liebling to arrange an audition for me at the Metropolitan.

On tour in 1947 in The Merry Widow. *I'm the Widow in the center with my first strapless gown, my first upswept hairdo. Decorously holding hands with me is the leading man, Frank Melton.*

In her studio Miss Liebling puts the female contingent of the Liebling Singers through their 1948 pretour paces. I'm the blonde in the center. The gal on my left is Susie Yager Cook, my oldest, dearest friend and my daughter Muffy's godmother.

4

*Tired, hoarse,
running a high fever,
I can always sing Violetta*

*My first Violetta—on tour
with the Wagner Company, 1951.*

Miss Liebling, I must say, didn't take long to come up with something—through another great and good friend, of course. Désiré Defrère, a stage director at the Metropolitan Opera, was then preparing to take on tour an opera company organized by Charles Wagner, one of the all-time great impresarios, who launched the careers of so many artists that it would be impossible to list them. Wagner's touring company was the only one of its kind in the United States at that time; in nine weeks it used to do a series of sixty-three one-night stands with a thirty-piece orchestra and two alternating casts.

Miss Liebling got Defrère to come to her studio to hear me sing, he got Mr. Wagner to let me audition for him, *et voilà!* I was launched. To my amazement, Mr. Wagner offered me the role of Violetta in *La Traviata;* he was the first impresario to tell me, "Miss Sills, you are going to be a star." Many years later, in 1975, when I made my debut at the Met, Francis Robinson, the assistant manager, gave me an opening night gift of a photograph showing Charles Wagner with one of the other artists he had once handled—

Amelita Galli-Curci. Robinson knew how great an influence they both had been in my life.

That tour in 1951 began my operatic career. I sang more than forty Violettas. I have sung more than three hundred Violettas since but the basis of my characterization is still the one Defrère taught me on the tour. I would experiment with the character, never playing her the same way twice, and when I finished the tour I could sing Violetta standing on my head or doing somersaults. To this day, sick, tired, hoarse, or running a high fever, I can always sing Violetta. She has been trained into my vocal chords.

Defrère was with us on all sixty-three nights. Every morning after a performance he would call me to the front of the bus we traveled in—he had a double seat to himself while the rest of us shared—and for an hour we would discuss my performance the day before, why I had done this or that, try it this way tomorrow. Once he gave me a pair of rhinestone earrings that he had bought in the previous town. "Put these on tomorrow in the first act," he said, "but do the third act with no jewelry at all." "After all," he explained, "the invitation Violetta receives for the party in Paris comes *after* she has already sold all her jewelry to support Alfredo and herself in the country." Defrère challenged me constantly on my characterization of Violetta.

On that tour we would travel three hundred miles a day on the bus, arrive at a town, race through dinner, get into costume in a dressing room if there was one or in the bus if there was not. Alfredo was sung by a then unknown tenor named John Alexander. To while away the time on the bus John taught me to play poker. He considered himself a real shark, but by the time the tour was over he owed me $132. We were inseparable; that is, when he wasn't writing love letters (he wrote a lot) to his fiancée, Susie, whom he later married. We were earning only $75 per performance. The first order of business in any new town was to search out the cheapest café. We would insist on seeing the most expensive steak in the joint, usually about $1.50. If it was big enough to split two ways, we would order one; if it wasn't, we would complain about the steak, send it back, and order something cheaper. Everything that came with the dinner we gobbled up; whatever we weren't able to eat on the spot we would take back to the hotel. Everyone on the tour traveled with his own portable cooking equipment. You would walk down the halls and smell the most delicious garlic butter sauce. Sometimes there were spaghetti parties: we would each chip in twenty-five cents and somebody in the chorus would run out to buy spaghetti, cheap red wine, and Italian bread.

John Alexander is my oldest, dearest tenor friend. I think I have sung more performances with him than with any other man. In March of 1976, when we sang *Traviata* together at the Met, the audience tossed confetti and flowers at us and I turned to John on the stage, kissed him, and said, "We've certainly come a long way from the Wagner tour!" We both got teary-eyed right there.

I came back from that first Wagner tour a far more sophisticated singer than when I had left. My voice was still that of a twenty-one-year-old girl but the performer, the actress, had matured a great deal. I now had an idea of who I was on the stage and a passionate urge to make the public pay attention to me. It had been a kind of evolutionary process—finishing off with people like Annini in Philadelphia, Max de Rieux, in Paris and now Defrère on tour.

Defrère was a very amusing, charming man. He believed in my talent. He also loved my mother. He thought she was the most beautiful woman he had ever seen and he would constantly tease her to marry him so that I would have a permanent stage director and never have to shop around for one. He was extremely thoughtful and generous. He bought me the first illustrated classic I had ever read, Anatole France's *Thaïs*. More important, he emphasized to me that whenever one plays a role based on a figure in literature, it is wise to read the literature first. I have always followed that advice—going back to the original Lucia, the original Traviata, the original Manon. I have found it the ideal way of gaining insight into a character that is perhaps not so obvious in the treatment given it by the composer. Defrère gave me two other pieces of sound advice: Eat steak and salad at four P.M. on the day of a performance (I still do). And don't worry about short tenors: that's not your problem, he would say, it's the tenor's (I don't worry any more).

I still have a great many opera scores bearing little scribbled sketches by Defrère. Some of the operas I had never seen performed and in his drawings of the stage sets for them he would always draw, right in the middle, a caricature of me with very curly hair looking like Harpo Marx. I loved to telephone him just to hear him shriek my name. He pronounced Beverly as though it had ninety-six syllables.

When I was married, Defrère was the only person from my theatrical world, other than Miss Liebling, whom I wanted at the ceremony. He was then quite old, still playing the nice-dirty-old-man role. He toasted my mother: "Shirley, you're not losing a daughter today, you're gaining a husband, ME." The day Miss Liebling and I learned that he had died, we looked at each other without a word. A bright color had gone out of our lives.

After that Wagner tour I had to struggle again. I did a few recitals early in 1952. I acquired an agent and was invited to sing with the St. Louis Symphony. John Alexander and I did a concert version of *Traviata* in Vermont —$100. I began singing on the Borscht Belt; the Concord Hotel in the Catskills had opera nights every Tuesday and many famous opera singers would appear there. I would do several arias backed by Sholom Secunda's orchestra and I would come home with $90, which went a long way in those days. The huge rooms were packed with appreciative Jews, the food was fantastic, and I got to sing a lot of my high notes—not a bad way to spend an evening.

In September of that year I went on tour with Mr. Wagner's company again, this time as Micaela in *Carmen*. I wound up doing sixty-three Micaelas on the tour, and even the money—$100 per performance—did not entirely make up for the loss of my sanity. Micaela is *not* one of my favorite roles; it is limited and frustrating, a bore.

Still, aside from the money, there were compensations. I took up the classical guitar. I learned every role in *Carmen*; I can sing the opera from the first note to the last and could even conduct it, I think. I did a lot of reading—Oscar Wilde, Hemingway, loads of plays. Reading was a very costly hobby for me—in those days there were few paperbacks. I used to buy a hardcover book in one city, read it all day on the bus, sell it in the next city to a used-book store, and with the money buy another new book. I learned to play chess—Defrère taught me but he was a terrible cheat—and bridge—my brother had taught me that game the year before and I began to read books on the subject.

When the tour was over, I was twenty-three years old, had more than

A scene from my first Traviata *with the Wagner Touring Company. My tenor friend John Alexander, playing Alfredo, is seated at the table behind me. In 1975, when I went to Memphis to sing* La Traviata, *a girl from the chorus walked on stage wearing that same dress; it had been preserved and refurbished from the time I wore it when I was twenty-one and had been in use for twenty-five more years. I recognized it because it still had the red thread I had used to sew on the turquoise velvet fringes. The fan dangling from my wrist is the same fan I use today in the role.*

a hundred opera performances under my belt—and was out of a job again. The Wagner tour the following year would be *Madama Butterfly*, an opera that was not and is not in my repertoire. It is too heavy a role for my voice and I have always felt that someone with my figure would look ridiculous trying to play a little Japanese girl. I would probably be billed as "The Biggest Butterfly In Captivity." Besides, I felt that two tours with Wagner were enough. I wanted to move on to something new.

Désiré Defrère (above) was my mentor on those two Wagner tours. For my third-act Violetta (right) his instructions were formal: painted eyebrows, dark red lips, but no jewelry and no false eyelashes. He thought false eyelashes changed the entire look of a face. I do wear them in the role now but whenever I do, I think, Oh, D.D. wouldn't like this.

As Micaela in Carmen *during the second Wagner tour, in 1952. You can tell from the sweet boredom on my face how I feel about Micaela.*

About to embark on my first opera tour with the Wagner Company in 1951. My outfit was made, like all my things then, by my mother. That handsome purse I'm clutching was bought for fifty cents in Rio de Janeiro when I was on that Moore-McCormack trip. The little ring on my pinkie was a good-luck present from my mother; I still have it. The white-haired gentleman holding my hand is impresario Charles Wagner. Standing over him is tenor John Alexander and next to John is baritone Ed Dunning.

5

*I was still saying "yes"
to everything*

My first Manon, 1953.

Maestro Bamboschek, my old friend from the Philadelphia Opera Company, had nothing for me when I phoned, but *his* old friend, Rosa Ponselle, was forming a company in Baltimore with *Manon* in the repertoire and maybe, he said, she might have something. He arranged an audition for me and Miss Ponselle sent her chauffeur to drive me from the railroad station to her home, the Villa Pace. When I saw it I said to myself, *That's* the kind of home a prima donna should have. It was an Italian villa that she had had brought over from Italy brick by brick. It had oodles of poodles yapping all over the property, lots of servants, a swimming pool, acres of landscaped grounds. At the doorway stood Rosa herself, robed in a stunning caftan.

When I walked through that door we became instant lifetime friends; the chemistry was incredible. She threw her arms around me, gave me a big bunny hug and a glass of wine. I had come prepared to stay one day; I stayed five. I walked into a house that had all the atmosphere of glamour and wealth, everything I had dreamed of, yet here was this simple, down-to-earth, warm lady with an enormous ringing laugh. In her closet were fur coats as far as the eye could see, and she would ever so casually stick her hand inside, pull out a mink, and drape me in it; then we would walk through the woods in the stinging cold.

Rosa would sing for me anything that came into her head—Isolde, Manon. Although I have always been very skeptical when people say you should have heard so-and-so sing in the so-called "Golden Age," her voice *was* still in its golden age. I have never heard another voice like it. Her face is extremely broad between the cheekbones—the area that singers call the "mask"—and her whole voice seemed miraculously to sit up in that mask. It was spine-tingling, hearing that voice in her great villa.

I sang parts of *Manon* for her and she was a most considerate listener—more than that, a most considerate colleague. I was, after all, just a kid of twenty-three; nobody knew what hole in the wall I had come out of. And she was the famous Rosa Ponselle. Yet the relationship between us was that of two colleagues and she made me feel unique. Three hours after my arrival we were chattering away about the characterization of Manon, arguing over it. (Needless to say, I got the part!) Everyone I had ever worked with on Manon before—people such as de Rieux and Defrère—had always discussed the role as played in the French light style. But Rosa, who was the artistic director for the new Baltimore Opera and had much to do with working on characterizations, especially with new young people, saw Manon differently. For her, the role should be played much more in the exaggerated Italian *verismo* style. We quarreled and quibbled over the interpretation; I had envisioned Manon in a totally different way. But ours was a very stimulating collaboration and it served to rid me of some of my inhibitions. What I had learned from Defrère on any interpretation was never really the result of mutual give-and-take; it was simply instructions from him and I had never challenged them. Rosa had never portrayed Manon but she was a performer, and so our tug-of-war was a creative exercise for me.

Whatever the reasons, *Manon* was a huge success in Baltimore. I played her in the early scenes as though she were a little girl from the countryside who had got caught in the hayloft a few times too many by her parents and as a result was being rushed off to a convent, a girl with a voluptuous figure who had not yet learned how to show it off, who exuded a lot of sex appeal but no polish. My entrance was, and still is, in flat-heeled shoes as a kind of flat-footed country bumpkin with a knack for attracting men. Not till later in the opera did I turn Manon into the graceful, beautiful courtesan.

After that Baltimore engagement I was somewhat depressed because I had not realized completely the Manon I had wanted. But I knew now that I was a good actress and I felt I had finally made it. After my first Charles Wagner tour I had expected that all New York would be waiting for me; I thought that everyone knew about my triumph in Athens, Georgia, and how the critic in Kansas City had called me "The Singing Bernhardt." I had assumed that all doors to the operatic stage would be open to me. They were not, of course. But now, after Baltimore, my getting to know Rosa Ponselle had made me a part of the real scene. I was very aware that unlike Mary Garden and Geraldine Ferrar, who had built their reputations abroad before singing here, Rosa was an all-American girl from Meriden, Connecticut, who had made it big here right from the start. And she was my friend, my Rosa. I began to feel that, finally, I belonged to the world of opera. There were a handful of people, at least, who knew what a Beverly Sills was.

Soon after I did *Manon* in Baltimore, Charles Wagner wrote a letter about me to Gaetano Merola, music director of the San Francisco Opera Company. So did Miss Liebling. The twin salvo may have seemed to Mr. Merola a tactical bombardment, but it wasn't planned that way. I didn't even know about the letters. In any case, when Mr. Merola came to New York early in 1953, I sang for him. He went into shock when I told him the number of operas I knew and how many performances I had already done. The upshot was that he invited me to come to San Francisco that summer and live with him and his wife while he coached me in the roles I would do that fall in repertory. My debut was to be as Elena (Helen of Troy) in Boito's *Mefistofele,* but my big plum would be the role of Donna Elvira in Mozart's *Don Giovanni.* I was, as you can imagine, terribly excited; I had the world on my string.

Mr. Merola had written me that I would be met at the San Francisco airport and taken to his home, but when I arrived with my two suitcases there was nobody there to meet me. I couldn't reach him by phone, the line was always busy. When I finally made it to his home by public transportation, I found chaos: Mr. Merola had died the night before, while conducting a performance. His wife was not to be seen, of course, and nobody seemed to know who I was or that I was expected. I took my two suitcases and went to the opera house. There they knew who I was but not what to do with me. I wound up at a terrible hotel on Market Street but at least it was cheap; I didn't have much cash on me because I had been expecting to move in with the Merolas, and I did not want to impose on my mother to send me money. I figured that I could last it out until I went into official rehearsal and on the payroll the following week. I knew no one in town and I didn't eat very much for several days. It was the loneliest week I have ever spent; for a long time afterwards, whenever I heard the name San Francisco I would feel cold shivers up and down my spine, remembering.

But finally rehearsals began (Kurt Adler having been appointed acting artistic director), and I found a little apartment in a hotel. We began to plan for my mother to come out to live with me. Things were looking up. The conductor for *Mefistofele* was Fausto Cleva. At the first rehearsal he asked me if I spoke Italian. When I said yes, he laid me out in lavender—in Italian— for having agreed to do a role meant for a dramatic soprano voice when I was a lyric coloratura. The best careers, he yelled, were the result of learning to say no, I should never have accepted the role. But as soon as I explained to him that it had been Mr. Merola's idea, not mine, he relented. Later, when anyone in the cast became sick and he felt that I could substitute in the role, he would call on me. He would continue to yell at me, of course, that I wasn't doing it correctly, do this, do that, picky-picky-picky. But underneath it all I think he really liked me; he became a great pal and helped me a good deal.

My debut as Helen of Troy was extremely successful. So was my appearance as Donna Elvira, although the production was a little disappointing for me. The conductor was Tullio Serafin and I had looked forward to working with him, but I think that I came into his life a few years too late. He was by then old (seventy-five) and tired; he conducted as though he didn't care very much.

One night, on very short notice, I was thrown into a performance of Wagner's *Die Walküre* as a substitute for a singer who had left the company because her father was ill. The role was Gerhilde, one of those eight lady Valkyries dressed in robes, shields, breastplates, and helmets shouting "Hoyotoho, Hoyotoho" from the balcony. In the excitement of my being a last-minute replacement on opening night, nobody remembered to try the helmet on me for size—although everything else including the great breastplate (you should pardon the expression) had been altered to fit me. Naturally, during the performance my helmet fell off and clattered to the footlights. I should have left it there, but instead I darted over to retrieve it while the audience clapped its approval. Seventeen years later, when I returned to the San Francisco Opera to sing again, there was my helmet filled with fruit, nuts, a big bottle of wine, and a card that said "Welcome Home." Kurt Adler had dug up the old helmet; it still said "Sills" in it. Now it sits in my living room in New York, a plant holder.

San Francisco was good experience for me. It was, and still is, one of the finest opera companies in the United States. I got to do four different roles—including the fifth slave girl in *Elektra*. I came away with wonderful personal notices. I met a great many famous people and sang with them. On evenings when I wasn't singing I would listen to others: Cesare Veletti and Guilietta Simionato in *Werther*; Simionato again in *Barber of Seville*. I heard Albanese's Butterfly and wept and wept and wept. I heard Inge Borkh's Elektra—hair-raising.

And I made more lifetime friendships. One I especially cherish was with Italo Tajo, who sang Leporello with me in *Don Giovanni*. Before my mother got to San Francisco, Italo knew how lonely I was. He helped me find my apartment and made sure I never had to eat lunch or dinner alone. He took me to Fisherman's Wharf. He was the perfect escort, amusing and cultivated. Today he and his wife, Inelda, live in Cincinnati, where he is Professor of Voice and Opera at the University of Cincinnati Conservatory of Music.

Even if years go by without our getting together, when we do meet we pick up the conversation right where we left off in mid-sentence. The warm affection that we felt in San Francisco I still feel—for him and Inelda.

When I returned to New York in December of 1953, Maestro Bamboschek introduced me to Carlo Vinti, who was then producing a television show on Dumont Television called "Opera Cameo." The sponsors were Progresso Foods and Gallo Wines, and in addition to singing three operas I did commercials for antipasto, minestrone, and Gallo's California Tawny Port. If you think that last item is easy to say, try it a few times. I sang my first *Tosca*, with Giovanni Martinelli narrating the story act by act for the TV audience. Probably no one understood his English but it didn't matter, he was such a presence with that shock of white hair, like the King of the Beasts. I did *Traviata* with the great baritone Ettore Bastianini; he courted me with parakeets that he had trained to say *Bella, Bella, Bella*. I also sang *Thaïs*; how *that* French dish got into all that Italianate fare I do not know. I wound up with barrels of Gallo wine and cases of Progresso food. I'm not sure that I ever got paid any money but the exposure was fabulous—all the television time plus reams of publicity in the Italian-language newspaper *Il Progresso*. And after every show Mr. Vinti, whose whole family seemed to be working on the program, would take me home, where his wife Rosa would put out a spread of Italian food that could have fed the whole Italian army. *Bella, bella, bella,* indeed!

That summer, 1954, I went to Salt Lake City to sing, of all things, *Aida*. I had not yet accepted Maestro Cleva's advice—that the best careers come when one learns to say no. I was still saying yes to everything because I needed to earn a living and because I felt that the more people who heard me sing, the better. Besides, Salt Lake, although a huge outdoor stadium, had lots of microphones, which meant I would not have to strain my voice. All I had to do was look the part. Perhaps I did, and I sang Aida well, I think—no Leontyne Price but it was musical and I enjoyed it.

All in all, I was beginning to get somewhere. At least I was singing a good many performances. The time was now right, Miss Liebling decided, to make a serious assault on another bastion—the New York City Opera.

Opening night of Manon, Baltimore, 1953. At left, backstage with my mother, who made all my costumes for the opera, including the ones hanging behind us. Above, Rosa Ponselle and I, radiant at the post-opera party. Below, Mama and I flank Maestro Bamboschek and his wife.

56

Playing a scene with Italo Tajo at the San Francisco Opera's 1953 production of Don Giovanni—he Leporello, me Donna Elvira. Nicola Rossi-Lemeni was Giovanni and Jan Peerce was Don Ottavio.

In the summer of 1953 I sang Traviata *and* Naughty Marietta *in Brigham Young Stadium with the Salt Lake City Orchestra, conducted by Maurice Abravanel. This is a dress rehearsal of* Traviata *with me, Violetta, greeting my guests. The stage was so big we needed twenty-four microphones to be heard.*

In 1954, my days of wine and minestrone—singing opera and doing commercials for Progresso Foods and other Italian outfits on a TV program called "Opera Cameo." At left, whipping up a salad commercial. Below, left, dressed up for my role as Tosca with leading man Jon Crain; we were to sing together later at the New York City Opera. Below, discussing my Tosca role with producer Carlo Vinti. And finally (bottom, opposite page) my interpretation of Thaïs—and my mother's (she made the costume).

*Me as Aida, believe it or not,
in Salt Lake City, 1954.*

*At my San Francisco Opera debut in 1953 as
Helen of Troy. I am congratulated by an admirer.*

6

Mama, Mama,
I think I've met a man
I could marry!

No personality, Dr. Rosenstock said.

At twenty-five I was a rather *zaftig* redhead and I liked to show off my figure by wearing very low-cut gowns. But for auditions I felt that my image as a serious opera singer called for a more sedate, proper look—the simple black dress, long red hair tied in a tight bun, hands clasped demurely beneath ample bosom, et cetera. That is the look I adopted when I began auditioning for Dr. Joseph Rosenstock, who was then the general manager of the New York City Opera in the old City Center on Fifty-fifth Street. Since 1952 I had auditioned for him seven times and got nowhere. When my agent asked me to do just one more audition for him in 1955, I said, Why keep going back, why not just ask him what's wrong? "I did," my agent said. "He says, 'She has a phenomenal voice but no personality.'"

I nearly exploded. I went to that final audition, in the spring of 1953, with an enormous chip on my shoulder. I wore black lace stockings and a dress cut nearly to the navel, and I let my hair hang all the way down. When I walked on stage, Dr. Rosenstock, who I later learned was a long-time aficionado of ladies' legs, came down the aisle, looked closely at me, and said in his heavy German accent, "Vell, vell, and vat are ve going to sing today?" "Well, Dr. Rosenstock," I replied, rather icily, "you've already heard *my* entire repertoire so I think I'll start on somebody else's. I will sing '*La Mamma Morta*,' from *Andrea Chenier*."

To sing an aria for dramatic soprano in my high, light coloratura voice was, of course, ridiculous; I was a guppy pretending to be a whale. When I had finished, Dr. Rosenstock just smiled and asked, "Vat else do you vant to sing?" "Actually," I replied, "I don't really want to sing anything for you, but if you want more, I'll do '*Vissi d'arte*,' from *Tosca*"—another dramatic soprano role.

"Okay, Sills," Dr. Rosenstock said after my second number, "upstairs to my office, you've got yourself a chob." It must have been the black-laced legs. He offered me a debut the following season in the role of Rosalinda in *Die Fledermaus* and also an understudy role in Tchaikovsky's *The Golden Slipper* (later affectionately called by the cast *The Golden Schlepper*). I was ecstatic—not only at the $75 per performance but at the prospect of a New York debut and the chance to be part of a company that included Norman Treigle, Cornell MacNeil, Frances Bible, Eva Likova, Virginia Haskins— some pretty damned good singers! And there was also Julius Rudel, then Rosenstock's assistant—"Chulyuss," he would scream at the top of his lungs. During all my auditions at the City Center Julius was the friendly face in the back of the house, and he always had something pleasant to say to me before I went on.

My debut in *Die Fledermaus* in October 1955 was, thank God, a great success. The role of my on-stage lover, Alfred, was played by Jon Crain, with whom I had done a TV "Opera Cameo" production of *Tosca;* he was the funniest Alfred I ever saw or sang with in my life. Coley Worth, who played the jailer, was always up to some unscripted mischief on stage and you had to be on guard when you played a scene with him. I was wearing a low-cut gown and high heels and to heighten the glamorous look I was carry-ing a king-sized, filter-tipped cigarette that had just been introduced on the market. Coley looked at me, then turned to the audience. "King-sized, eh?"

Then, looking down the front of my dress, "And filter-tipped too." The audience broke up and so did I.

Later in that first season I got a chance to sing Oxana in *The Golden Slipper*. The company was committed to do three performances of the Tchaikovsky work, and after the first two—not very successful—Jean Fenn moved out of the role and I was pushed in for the third. The lead tenor was Richard Cassilly, who later became the leading tenor of the Hamburg Opera. (He left the United States because he couldn't support his family as a singer here; the Hamburg Opera at least had a medical and pension plan, unlike opera houses in this country.) I was delighted to be singing with Cassilly: he was six feet four, and despite Defrère's advice I was still worrying about playing opposite short tenors. So much so that I had earlier written a poem to Julius Rudel:

> I'd like a tenor taller than my ass-illy.
> Please, Chulyuss Darlink, can I have Dick Cass-illy?

Since all the rest of Miss Fenn's costumes for the part of Oxana fitted me, I hadn't bothered to try on her golden slippers. That was a mistake. At the climax of the opera, the tenor brings in the slippers—all I can remember about Oxana is that she keeps singing about four million times, "Bring me the golden slipper and we shall be married"—and puts them on Oxana's feet; the couple does a lovely dance, sings a marvelous duet, and lives happily ever after. Jean's feet, it turned out, were slightly larger than mine; the slippers went on very easily but they came off the same way. I danced right out of the shoes. When the curtain came down, there I was barefoot while the golden slippers sat prominently on stage with no feet in them.

It was one of my less triumphant evenings in the theater. Dick Cassilly and I never stopped laughing until it was time for curtain calls. But backstage I could hear that familiar Rosenstock shriek—SILLS!—and I knew I was in for it. Rosenstock refused to take my hand during curtain calls and it was a long time before he would even speak to me again. Nevertheless, he rehired me for the 1956 season. I have been with the New York City Opera ever since.

Dr. Rosenstock was a very volatile man with a difficult job and I learned a great deal working with him. We later became good friends, although he never called me anything but SILLS! When anyone in the company was too ill to go on, he would always say, "Get Sills, Sills will do it." He knew exactly the type of voice I had and tried to find the right roles for me in the coloratura repertoire. Not an easy task: the City Opera in those days chose the operas first and the singers for them second, not the other way round.

Dr. Joseph Rosenstock hired me in 1955 to sing with the New York City Opera and I made my debut in October as Rosalinda in Die Fledermaus.

As Rosalinda (left) in my City Opera debut. My mother made the gown (in those days the opera was more than grateful if a singer could provide her own costume!). The fan I picked up for a dollar at the Paris flea market. The earrings were the same rhinestone jobs that Defrère had given me on that 1952 Traviata *tour. I also wore a white stole Mama and I found at a thrift shop. At far right, a scene from the opera, with Jon Crain playing the part of my lover, Alfred.*

In 1964, when the New York City Opera revived Die Fledermaus, it was in good enough financial shape so that Mama didn't have to make my costumes. At right, that's John Reardon as Alfred; I've sung a great many operas with him and he later joined the Met. Below, Jon Crain (in the stocking cap) is Alfred and Lee Cass is the prison warden.

In the summer of 1955, while awaiting my City Opera debut that fall, I sang the lead in the Cleveland Music Carnival's production of Rosalinda, *a sort of Broadway version of* Die Fledermaus.

In those days, too, the City Opera did only a fall season, no spring; instead, the company would tour the provinces. One night, while we were on tour in Cleveland, the company threw a party for the local press. I did not want to go—I wanted instead to see a movie entitled "The Man Who Loved Redheads"—but Julius Rudel insisted that I attend the party. So I did—in a very low-cut dress indeed. At my table was a handsome blond man who began winking at me. Well, *that's* a novel approach, I thought. Then the man passed me a book of matches on which he had scribbled his telephone number and a note saying that if I had any free time he would like to see me. Come to the party being thrown for me tomorrow night, I said, after my performance in *Die Fledermaus*. I can't, he said, I have another date. That's too bad, I said, and left the party and went to the movies.

The next night the big handsome blond man showed up at the party; he had got rid of his date, he said, because he wanted to see me again. His name was Peter Greenough, he was an associate editor of a local newspaper, the *Cleveland Plain Dealer*, which was then owned by his family, and would I have dinner with him tomorrow night—Sunday? Can't, I said, I'm going beagling during the day and then back home; my mother expects me.

While beagling—in Cleveland they do it on horseback and I felt like Auntie Mame—I must admit that I thought about Peter a great deal. I was supposed to catch a six P.M. flight to New York. What possessed me I don't know, but instead of taking that flight I phoned the big handsome blond man and said that dinner would be fine. Then I phoned my mother to break the news that I was going to spend the night in Cleveland; I was tired from horseback riding, and so on. I think she suspected something but she didn't pursue it on the phone.

When I came down to the hotel lobby to meet the big handsome blond man, he had two cute little girls with him. One was Lindley, aged nine, the other was Nancy, six. They're mine, he said. Where's the mama? I asked. Right at the moment, he said, I don't know. We dropped the subject, what with the children standing there, climbed into his station wagon, and drove to his home—which seemed miles and miles and hours and hours away. Later, when we were married and I had moved into that home, I realized it was only about eight minutes from downtown Cleveland but at the time I thought that he was taking me into the wilderness. Why in hell did I ever agree to *this?* I began thinking. Who is this guy, anyway, what is this with his kids, he doesn't even know where his wife is, and this is the dumbest move I have ever made.

Peter's home was a beautiful twenty-five-room French château on Lake Erie in a community called Bratenahl. Inside the house were two lovely ladies and a Chinese supper. One lady served supper and disappeared and afterwards the other lady disappeared with the two nice children. That left Peter Greenough and little Beverly Sills sitting in this living room, which was probably forty-five by thirty feet, in front of an enormous fireplace. Well, dummy, I said to myself, you've finally done it.

In his best Rudolph Valentino manner Peter put a Frank Sinatra record on the hi-fi—"One for My Baby, and One for the Road." Then he asked, Shall I light a fire? It seemed logical—this was Cleveland in November. But Peter had just moved into the house, the fireplace had never been lit before, and he forgot to heat up the chimney first to induce a draft. What was supposed to be a rather romantic production turned into an unromantic asphyxiation; the smoke that poured from the fireplace almost choked me to death. We wound up opening all the windows and retreating to his kitchen, where we talked for hours. Peter was originally from Boston, a direct descendant of John Alden, one of the Mayflower's passengers; another ancestor, the first Peter Bulkeley here, had founded the town of Concord, Massachusetts. He was in the process of divorcing his wife and trying to get custody of their three children. He asked me if he could come to New York to see me and I said yes. Then he took me to the hotel and picked me up again several hours later to take me to the airport for the nine o'clock flight to New York.

When I got home, the first thing my mother asked was, all right, why the delay in coming back? "Mama, Mama," I said happily, "I think I've met a man I could marry." My mother was ecstatic—at first; I was, after all, twenty-six years old and in Jewish families mothers have long since begun to despair when their babies reach that age unmarried. (Not that I had been a shrinking violet: I had so many dates between Sandy Levine and Peter Greenough that they all now seem one big blur. My brothers used to fix me up with college friends of theirs, both Jewish and non-Jewish; some of them were even *doctors!* I was the kind of girl that men seemed to get serious about quickly, but until Peter came along I never got really serious about any of them.)

Back to Peter.

"There's a small problem, though, Mama," I said. "What is it, sweetheart?" "He's still married," I said, "he has three children, he's thirteen years older than I, and he's not Jewish." Mama burst into tears: "Why does everything have to happen to my baby?"

Peter was very clever. He knew that there would be tremendous resistance from my family, especially from my mother, and so he set about to make her an ally. Whenever he came to New York, he wooed both of us, bringing Mama flowers and books. We became a sort of *ménage à trois:* it was always Mama, Peter, and Bubbles because Mama was not about to allow her baby girl to be seen in public, unchaperoned, with a married man. We had wonderful times together—the three of us. One night Peter and I had a terrible row, much to my mother's embarrassment and discomfort, and he turned to me and said, "You know, I think I'm gonna marry your mother instead, she's so much nicer."

My mother and I were still living in that tiny two-room apartment in Stuyvesant Town, and once Peter overdid the flowers-for-Mama bit. He bought her an azalea tree that kept growing and growing. It stood in the middle of the living room, so big that it was impossible for two people to sit at opposite sides of the room and see each other without moving the tree. Whenever Mama and I wanted to talk, we had to huddle together on the sofa or else keep moving the tree around. It didn't survive all that schlepping but to this day my mother has refused to get rid of the pot it came in. The pot is now an umbrella holder—which gives you an idea of how big the thing was.

On New Year's Day, 1956, I received a phone call from Maestro Bamboschek in Philadelphia: Vivian Della Chiesa was scheduled to sing Montemezzi's *The Love of Three Kings* but she was ill, could I learn the opera in eight days? Could I! I could have learned it in eight hours, it was such an opportunity. The role of Fiora is a beautiful one—Lucrezia Bori had made it one of her jewels—and to sing with the tenor Ramon Vinay was a soprano's dream. Peter was visiting the apartment when I got the phone call and the next day he bought me a recording of the opera. By dress rehearsal time on January 7 I had memorized the role and two days later I performed it.

The production attracted a great deal of attention because the opera was rarely performed, and I received an excellent reception from press and public. Fernando Corena sang the basso role of King Archibaldo, Fiora's father-in-law. In the opera Corena had to lift my "dead" body from a bench and carry me across the stage of the Philadelphia Academy of Music to an upstage exit. Corena, though a well-built fellow, was not very big. To this day, when we spot each other on a street he will yell, *"Ciao, Bella,"* then grab his side and double over in pretended agony. He tells everyone that I caused him the one and only hernia of his life—jokingly, of course.

That summer I was engaged by the Music Carnival in Cleveland to sing Carmen, *not* Micaela but Carmen, a role I had never sung before. It was ideal timing, not only because of the cast—Norman Treigle as the toreador, Lloyd Thomas Leech as Don José—but also because Peter lived there. I sang eighteen Carmens on eighteen successive nights, which must be some kind of record. I took all the high endings Bizet had written and loved every minute of it. In my interpretation I used a good deal of the "business" Defrère and I had discussed during those long bus rides on the Wagner tours. For example, when Carmen is tied up and left in Don José's custody, he throws her into a chair and she casually crosses her legs. At this point Defrère would have Carmen, whose hands are tied behind her back, bend over and with her teeth pull up her skirts to expose more of her legs and further excite Don José.

Treigle, too, had invented a piece of business. When, as the toreador, he sees Carmen for the first time, he is eating an orange. He would swagger over to me, look insinuatingly at my bosom, and say, "I'd like to be a friend of yours." "You already have enough friends," Carmen would reply. He, still staring at the bosom, replies, "Yes, but I want to be a *very* good friend." And then he would take a big bite of the orange. The audience loved it, as did Norman.

Norman and I, both new to the New York City Opera, were already good friends, very eager to work together. We were both riding high in those days, having the time of our lives. I had promised my mother that Peter and I would not be seen alone together in Cleveland, so Peter, Norman, and I soon became a trio. The two men got along so well that occasionally they forgot I was there. I spent a lot of time with Peter's daughters, Lindley and Nancy. Peter and I felt that it would be good for me to get to know them better because it was beginning to look as though he would get them in the divorce settlement. His third daughter, Diana, his youngest and a retarded child, was away at a special school and I didn't meet her until after Peter and I were married.

We became formally engaged shortly after Peter got his divorce in early October. Mama had insisted that we wait six weeks before we got married; what that magic number was supposed to mean I do not know, but she seemed to feel that it wasn't right to marry any sooner after Peter's divorce. We settled for a big engagement party in Cleveland.

When Peter was courting me, my mother used to tease me. "How big an engagement diamond are you getting?" she would ask. "How big did you have?" I replied. "Three carats." "Okay," I said, "so I'll have three carats too." Until the day Peter gave me my engagement ring he and I had a kind of a game. Every time we separated he would hold up two fingers—one for each carat—and I would hold up three. Then one day he stepped from an airplane and held up three fingers.

The announcement that a nice middle-class Jewish girl from Brooklyn named Beverly Sills was engaged to a rich Boston Brahmin named Peter Bulkeley Greenough must have puzzled a good many people. One of them was a little Jewish shopkeeper who lived in our Stuyvesant Town neighborhood. Originally from Odessa, Russia, where my mother was born, he would always chat with her in Russian; his only English came from a diligent reading of every word of the Sunday *New York Times*. When he read my engagement announcement in the paper he said to my mother, "Nu? I read she's getting married. Greenough? Greenough? What kind of name is Greenough?" "He's a wonderful boy," my mother said. "Greenough?" the little Jewish shopkeeper continued. "He must have changed his name from Greenbaum." Now, whenever I get angry with Peter I say, "Look here, Peter Greenbaum."

I was then under the management of National Concerts and Artists Corporation and not very happy about it. They had swallowed up my two former agents and I felt like a small fish in a large pond. They were not paying much attention to my career (there were so many more famous artists they were already handling), and so I decided I needed a change in management. At the time Leonard Bernstein was conducting a concert performance of *Der Rosenkavalier* with the NBC Symphony Orchestra in New York. I auditioned for the role of the Marschallin; Lenny offered me Sophie instead and he was absolutely right. *Time* magazine gave me a rave review complete with photograph, but the caption indicated that I was more interested in a career than in marriage. Naturally, that made Peter tremendously angry with the NCAC people, who had apparently been interviewed for the *Time* story. Although Peter has always made it a policy not to interfere in my career matters, I knew he was offended. Then at our engagement party an executive of NCAC asked my mother, Why does she have to marry him, why doesn't she get engaged to him for a few years and then she can get engaged to someone else?—implying that anything permanent at this point in my life could mean the end of my career.

That did it: NCAC had now made two enemies, my husband-to-be *and* my mother. I left them. Julius Rudel then recommended me to Columbia Artists Management; they kept me waiting in an outside hall for two hours and finally a man said, "Well, we have a stableful of sopranos already just like you. *I* said, "I'm not a horse, and even if I were, I still wouldn't want to be in your stable." At various times in my career I had noticed a gentleman named Ludwig Lustig, an agent who used to come backstage to wish his clients luck. I thought that very sweet. I went to see Mr. Lustig; we signed and have been together ever since.

That season with the City Opera I repeated Rosalinda but I was also given two new roles. One was Madame Goldentrill in *The Impresario*, Mozart's one-act opera. That gave me my first chance really to sing coloratura, with several high Fs to negotiate. It was also a very comic role and I enjoyed it thoroughly. For the first time my picture was published in a New York newspaper—a very exciting first.

By then Dr. Rosenstock and I had a kind of teasing relationship. He was small, I was large, and he did not like to stand next to me too often. He would tease me about my size and because he was the boss I could never tease him back. But *The Impresario* gave me an opportunity. In it, two sopranos, one an established primadonna (Mme. Goldentrill) and the other a young poopsie (Mme. Silverpeal), vie to prove who can sing higher. When I was ready to begin my aria I was supposed to pull out a large purple handkerchief and wave it at the conductor, Dr. Rosenstock, to cue him and the orchestra. Every time I played the role, I kept delaying the cue, always finding more stage business to prolong it until Dr. Rosenstock was a nervous wreck. When I finally gave him the cue, he would look up at me with an expression that said, "Vait, I'll get you ven this opera is over."

The other new role I sang that season was Philine in Ambroise Thomas's *Mignon*. For the first time in New York I felt that I had a role ideally suited to my voice and temperament—a glamorous part in which I could both speak and sing in French. It was a very difficult opera to do, particularly with an all-American cast (Frances Bible was Mignon and Donald Gramm, Laertes). Jean Morel, the conductor, coached me in the role; he was so pleased that I could speak French with him that whenever I made a mistake during the staging or did anything to displease him, he would look at me and say, "Et tu, Philine," as though I were Brutus and had just betrayed his Caesar. When I sang my coloratura showpiece, "*Je Suis Titania*," it brought down the house, the first time I had caused *that* to happen. Because of the audience reaction, the excellent reviews, and Mr. Morel's enthusiasm about my contribution to *Mignon*, I thought that this was, finally, it—the successful turning point in my career. It was not. Nothing very spectacular resulted.

The 1956 season over, I was supposed to go to Detroit with the company and then return to New York to be married—the six-weeks waiting period was up! It must have been all the excitement: I got the worst case of laryngitis I have ever had and I never made it to Detroit.

On November 17, 1956, Peter and I were married in a civil ceremony. The ceremony, conducted by State Supreme Court Justice James McNally, a friend of Miss Liebling's, took place in her apartment studio with Peter and me taking our vows standing in that same little circular design on her Oriental carpet where I had first sung for her when I was seven. It was a terribly stormy day. My side of the family was represented by my mother, my two brothers, their two very pregnant wives, and my Uncle Sydney, my father's baby brother and my favorite uncle. On Peter's side were his father and stepmother and his sister and brother. The only "outsiders" were Sue Yager, my oldest friend, who had been one of the Liebling Singers, and Désiré Defrère. My wedding gown had been made by my mother, as was my entire trousseau.

I had not met my father-in-law until that day. He had felt that the proper time to meet was when everything was signed, sealed and delivered. We hit it off right away. He put his arm around me and said, "I'm glad you're pretty at least. Call me Dad." He was a great old man with a fine sense of humor, and he was fiercely protective of every member of his family. At the wedding breakfast, in the Cottage Room of the Hampshire House, I asked him, "Well, Dad, what was your reaction when Peter told you he was going to marry a Jewish opera singer?" He looked at me, eyes twinkling, and replied, "Well, I'll tell you, dear. Peter and I were off Martha's Vineyard at the time, fishing in my boat, and I had two choices—I could throw myself overboard or I could go on fishing. Being the intelligent man that I am, I went right on fishing and said to Peter, 'Tell me about her.'"

Peter and I honeymooned in Nassau in a rented house. So that I could go fishing with Peter, my mother had made me a most stylish fishing ensemble —matching hat, jacket, and pants to wear with sneakers. The only trouble was that I got seasick while our boat was still tied to the pier. Peter must have had a lot of second thoughts about his new bride, who had laryngitis and was seasick most of the time. The laryngitis lasted for months and Peter maintains that it was the quietest period he has ever spent with me. I claim that he's the one who made me speechless.

When we returned from the honeymoon and drove up the driveway to our house in Cleveland, there pasted on the front door was a huge sign Lindley and Nancy had made. It said: WELCOME HOME, MAMA AND DADDY!

My first proposition from my husband-to-be, Peter Greenough,
written on a book of matches. 912 was my hotel room.

At the Cleveland Music Carnival, in August 1956, I sang my first Carmen. At right, I'm surrounded backstage by the men in my opera life: on my right is Norman Treigle, the toreador; on my left, Lloyd Thomas Leech, Don José. Below, Carmen takes a breather during rehearsal.

A last-minute substitute for Vivian Della Chiesa, I sing the role of Fiora in Montemezzi's The Love of Three Kings, *in Maestro Bamboschek's production at the Philadelphia Opera. With me is Frank Guarrera, singing the role of Manfredo, my husband.*

Relaxing with Lenny Bernstein during rehearsals for the concert version of Der Rosenkavalier *he conducted in 1956. I wanted to sing the Marschallin role; he said Sophie. Sophie it was and he was right.*

In the New York City Opera production (above) of Mozart's L'Impresario, in 1956, I, as Madame Goldentrill (second from right), give what-for to my rival, Madame Silverpeal (extreme left).

As Philine in Thomas's Manon at the New York City Opera in 1956. The costume I'm wearing showed up on a chorus girl in a 1969 production of Manon with my name still sewn on it.

At our first home, in Cleveland,
Peter and I with two of his daughters—
Lindley (at left) and Nancy.

Mr. and Mrs. Peter B. Greenough, after our wedding in Miss Liebling's studio.

En route to Nassau for our honeymoon Peter and I checked in at the airline ticket counter. This picture was published in the Nassau newspaper with a caption that read: "Newspaper editor Peter Greenough with his wife, Jackie Searles." Jackie Searles was a male comedian. Peter was upset.

7

"Miss Sills,
you are *Baby Doe"*

Alias Baby Doe

My two little stepdaughters must have thought that strange woman their father had married was really a traveling salesman, I was on the road so much of that first year of my marriage. Three weeks after the honeymoon I was in Texas for a three-city concert tour (including a place called Palestine, Texas, which Texans pronounce Palest*een* but I always called Palest*ine* to make myself feel more at home) and then on to Miami for a concert with the Miami Symphony Orchestra. It was difficult to explain to my husband, and indeed to myself, why I went on these trips, because, after expenses, I would probably come home owing somebody ten dollars. But at that stage of my career I had signed up for concerts a year in advance.

I did get home for Christmas and it was lovely. My mother came out from New York—a perfect grandma to the girls, laden with goodies, and always teaching them to make things with their hands. At that time I was completely useless in the kitchen: my mother had never taught me any culinary accomplishments, and when Peter and I were married we had a cook and other help in the house. Peter himself is a graduate of the Cordon Bleu and on special holidays he likes to do all the cooking. When he knew his mother-in-law was coming, he turned out Oysters Rockefeller, turkey stuffed with chestnut dressing and truffles, and Cherries Jubilee. All I did was set the table. After dinner my mother turned to me and said, "The dinner was just delicious. I knew you could do it if you set your mind to it." "Oh, Mama, *I* didn't cook any of this." "Well, did your cook make it?" "No, Mama, Peter did it, Peter did it all." She looked at me and said severely, "In *my* house your father never even knew the color the kitchen was painted." Later she gave me a long lecture: if you can read, she said, you can cook, so get cracking. Eventually Peter taught me to cook; I could turn out a fancy Hollandaise sauce before I knew how to boil an egg.

After Christmas I had to hit the road again. A concert in Jamestown, New York, so cold that only a hundred people showed up, and then on to another concert in Athol, Massachusetts. The best thing to be said about that junket was that I got to spend a weekend at my father-in-law's farm in Concord, in a farmhouse whose *newest* part dated to 1710. The farm, about three hundred and fifty acres, nineteen miles from the center of Boston, was a real gentleman's farm, the kind where the price of milk and the price of champagne are the same. My father-in-law's chauffeur, James, drove me to Athol in a limousine that was longer than the hotel's entrance. There I met my accompanist, Armen Boyajian. It was twenty degrees below zero. The concert took place in the school auditorium, and while the crowd assembled Armen and I waited in a classroom, he with his fingers in warm water and I vocalizing with steam gushing out of my mouth. The "crowd" was thirty people. I began to wonder what this career of mine was all about and why I was not at home with my nice, warm, handsome husband. I was even more depressed at what was facing me—something called a Johann Strauss Tour, which would keep me away from home for almost two solid months. Peter joined me as often as he could on that tour. Once he met me in Tampa, a convention town so overbooked that we had to stay in a "hot-pillow" joint: all night long sailors and their dates kept checking in and out of the "hotel" at very short intervals.

By then I had made up my mind to have a baby as soon as possible, but as that involves two people being in the same place at the same time, I was less than successful. Instead, that year I sang with the Memphis Symphony and the Jacksonville Symphony. I sang at the Brevard (North Carolina) Music Festival. I sang on the Woolworth Hour with Percy Faith's orchestra. I sang my first and only Gilda in a concert performance of *Rigoletto* in Chicago, conducted by Julius Rudel. My career was not exactly skyrocketing, but the reviews were all lovely and despite the long absences from home and family, my marriage was increasingly happy. I was having a marvelous time just learning to be Mrs. Peter Greenough.

That summer of 1957 I appeared again at Cleveland's Music Carnival, this time in a modern-dress, updated version of *Tosca*. By weird coincidence, at exactly the same time in Buenos Aires a young stage director named Tito Capobianco was also doing a modern version of *Tosca* at the Teatro Colón. Both productions were written up in *Time*. I had never heard of him before and he obviously had never heard of me. Later our careers were to mesh, with great consequences for both of us.

In the Cleveland *Tosca* there was one very colorful scene. In the second act, I, as Tosca, pick up a knife and stab the wicked Scarpia. He, played by William Chapman, had a small celluloid capsule between his fingers which he was supposed to slap across his white shirtfront to simulate blood when I "stabbed" him. Unfortunately, he held the capsule upside down, so that when he slammed it against his chest it squirted all over my face, my hair, my teeth; it must have held a gallon of thick, red "blood." The audience started to giggle and Bill, lying on the stage, was shaking with laughter. I had worked very hard to build up and sustain the tension that would climax in the actual stabbing and I was damned if I was going to let it all evaporate in giggles. So I kicked Bill—that stopped his laughter *and* the audience's.

We finished the act without incident but we needed a half-hour intermission to get me cleaned up for Act III.

Meanwhile, back at the New York City Center things had changed. Dr. Rosenstock had left, to be replaced for one year by Erich Leinsdorf. The company was in serious financial trouble. I went to the Yale Club with Cornell MacNeil, Norman Treigle, and Michael Pollack to beseech Newbold Morris to help save the company. He and a great many other people did come to the rescue and Julius Rudel was named artistic director. The eventual greatness of the New York City Opera dates from his arrival on the scene; Julius, in addition to being one of the world's finest conductors, is an administrative genius.

The 1958 spring season of the City Opera, Julius announced, would be devoted to contemporary American operas, sponsored by the Ford Foundation, the first season of its kind in New York City. The showpiece opera was to be *The Ballad of Baby Doe,* by Douglas Moore, which had been given its première in the mid-50s in Central City, Colorado. The rumor was all over New York music circles that Moore, Rudel, and Emerson Buckley, who was to conduct the opera, had auditioned scores of women singers for the role of Baby Doe but none had met with the approval of all three men. Nobody had asked *me* to audition; I had heard that whenever my name was brought up, the general reaction had been that I was simply too large for the role.

The New York première was scheduled for April 3. Walter Cassel was set for the role of Horace Tabor and Martha Lipton for Augusta, but by January 1 there was still no Baby Doe. One day Julius called me in Cleveland: how about auditioning? I'm not interested, I said. If Moore and Buckley have this preconceived notion that I'm too tall, there's no point in my auditioning just to be turned down. "Bubbela," Julius said soothingly, "let me at least send you some of the music, see what you think of it." He sent me the Willow Song and the final aria, both of which I loved immediately. I phoned Julius: Of course they're ideal for my *voice* but obviously the role is not ideal for me.

I was being very defensive at that point because I was irritated at being told that I was too large for something. I was simply not going to New York to be turned down. Then Emerson Buckley called me: Come on, come on in and audition. Buck, I said, there's no point if you think I'm too big for it. I won't be any smaller when I get to New York. "Get in here and sing," he said. Actually, he said something more vulgar than that.

I went to New York February 6, Peter's birthday, rationalizing my decision to audition by saying we were coming anyway to celebrate his birthday and see some shows. For the audition I wore the highest-heeled pair of new shoes I could find at Bergdorf's and a white mink hat of my mother's—I must have looked nine foot three. "Mr. Moore," I said to the composer, "this is how tall I am before I begin to sing for you and I'm going to be just as tall when I'm finished. We could save your time and my energy if you'd tell me now that I'm too big to play Baby Doe."

Douglas was such a dear sweet man, such a perfect gentleman, that I think he was thoroughly taken aback. He walked down the aisle to the stage and in a gentle voice said: "Why, Miss Sills, you look just perfect to me." I sang The Willow Song. Douglas walked down to the stage again. "Miss Sills," he said, "you *are* Baby Doe."

I loved the role. I read everything that had ever been written about her. I copied her hairdos from whatever photographs I could find. I absorbed her so completely in those five weeks of studying the opera that I knew her inside and out. I *was* Baby Doe.

At every performance Walter Cassel, as Horace, made me cry. When Horace was dying he would look up at me and sing "You were always the real thing, Baby" and I would sing, in reply, "Hush, close your eyes, sleep." Then I would take him in my arms and bawl like a baby. It was difficult to do the final aria after that scene. Walter and I lived those roles when we were on stage; there was never a moment during the performances when I didn't believe he was Horace Tabor. And even offstage he never called me Beverly or anything else, just "Baby."

The morning after opening night I grabbed the *New York Herald Tribune* from Peter before he had a chance to look at it. But there was no review on the regular review page. "Look at that," I said to Peter, "they didn't even cover it, can you imagine?" "Well," Peter said, "do you mind if I read the rest of the paper?" He turned to the front page and there—on the front page!—was the review.

The Ballad of Baby Doe is one of the great contemporary American works and should, I think, be a permanent fixture in the opera repertoire. I will always be grateful to Douglas Moore for having written it and for the opportunity it gave me to play opposite someone like Walter Cassel. Baby became an integral part of my operatic experience; it was difficult to shake her off even after I left the opera house. If I have ever achieved definitive performances during my career thus far, Baby Doe is one of them. The other three would be Manon, Cleopatra in *Julius Caesar,* and Queen Elizabeth in *Roberto Devereux.* They have been the only times in my entire career when I have walked out of the theater feeling that I have done everything I wanted to do with a role and that nobody else could have done it better.

In the New York City Opera fall 1957 season I
was given two new roles. One was Violetta in
La Traviata, *with baritone Igor Gorin singing
Germont. Good reviews but no handstands.*

*Walter Cassel as Horace and I as Baby Doe
locked in joyful embrace in Douglas Moore's
opera at the City Opera in 1958.*

My other new opera in the City Opera fall 1957 season—The Merry Widow. My second-act costume here was certainly put to good use. I wore it for the first time as Micaela on the Wagner tour in 1952. Later I wore it as Carmen at the Cleveland Music Carnival in 1956. Here it is the third time around.

The up-to-date version of Tosca I sang at the Cleveland Music Carnival in June 1957. Scarpia, played by Bill Chapman, is wearing a uniform strongly reminiscent of that of a Nazi storm trooper.

8

Tragedy at home—
Not why me? Why them?

Peter and I decided that it was time to have a baby. I was six months pregnant when I appeared at the New York City Opera in April 1959 to play the character of The Prima Donna in the world première of Hugo Weisgall's *Six Characters in Search of an Author,* based on the Pirandello play. The opera was rather interesting and a personal success for me but it was not very well received.

The real hero of the production may have been Edgar Joseph, head of the City Opera's costume department, for the imaginative lengths he went to conceal my pregnancy. He redesigned a copy of a Dior dress I owned, gathered it high in front, and draped me in an enormous mink cape that Peter had bought me or in large stoles or shawls. I was never allowed on stage without a prop—usually a hatbox or an umbrella. One night the stage director, William Ball, had the brilliant idea of my entering carrying a tiny French poodle; it would not only effectively cover my tummy but would also be the kind of item my character would normally own. On opening night, the

With my daughter Muffy at the Central City, Colorado, Music Festival, summer of 1959.

lady who lent us the poodle was very nervous that the poodle would be nervous, so she gave it a tranquilizer. As a result the dog looked dead, but at least, I thought, he'll be quiet. Suddenly, during one of my arias, I felt a warm trickle down the front of my dress; the dog, naturally, was peeing all over me. When I pulled him away from the dress, he woke up, startled, and howled at the top of his lungs throughout the whole aria, off-key. The audience was hysterical, and as far as I was concerned, *that* poodle's operatic career was finished. I never sang with a dog again.

Back home in Cleveland that summer, awaiting the birth of my baby, I got a call from Julius Rudel: Leopold Stokowski is opening our fall season with *Carmina Burana* and it would be nice if you could be in it. I went to New York to audition for Mr. Stokowski. I was very pregnant and he asked me if I were practicing breathing exercises. With his accent, it sounded like "breeding" exercises, so I replied, Obviously I practice breeding exercises. It was an Abbott and Costello routine—he said "breathing" and I thought "breeding." He offered me a role in *Carmina Burana* provided my baby was born on schedule, by July 25. She was not and I was never able to take that job with Stokowski.

Meredith "Muffy" Greenough was born August 4, 1959, and I became an asterisk on the City Opera roster—"On leave of absence." Except for two one-night stands with the company in 1960, I was to remain an asterisk because of family responsibilities for more than two years. Staying home with my little girl was a source of great joy, as was the feeling of settling in in Cleveland. I now had three girls to take care of and a twenty-five-room house with servants to run; I even had monogrammed towels for the first time in my life—most of the towels in our New York apartment had borne the label "Beth-El Hospital" (my brother Sidney interned there).

The whole family spent that first summer at the Central City, Colorado, Music Festival—my stepdaughters, Muffy, Nurse, and I—and Peter would fly in for weekends. I had accepted a summer engagement from Emerson Buckley, the music director. *I* thought I had agreed to do Lucia; he thought I had agreed to do Aida. Aida it became, and I enjoyed it; I think that I probably was the first Aida to wear an Afro in the role, spraying black dye into my curly hair. Living in Central City was very much like a kibbutz: part of your fee for singing was housing and a food allowance. It turned out to be a wonderful summer and I sang a lot of Aidas.

That fall my husband announced that we were moving to Boston: he was leaving the *Cleveland Plain Dealer* to write a financial column for a Boston newspaper. We settled in a nineteen-room house in Milton, Massachusetts, about ten miles south of Boston, and decided to have a second child. In April of 1961, when I was seven months pregnant, the phone rang and a deep voice said: "This is Sarah Caldwell." I had never met Sarah but I knew, of course, who she was. Even though her opera company was still young, she had begun to put her personal stamp on every production she did. I had once attended a production of her *Traviata* and was fascinated by how much she did with so little; she literally did it all with sheets and things made out of paper, yet it all worked and was truly distinctive. I was very much impressed with her work.

Sarah was planning a production of *Die Fledermaus* with Arthur Fiedler conducting. Would I play Rosalinda? "I'd be delighted," I said. "When?" In a few weeks, with rehearsals beginning in a few days. Wonderful, I said, and we hung up. My husband, who had been listening to this, asked dryly: "What are you planning to wear?" "Oh, costumes," I said airily. Then I looked down and realized what a shape I was in. I called Sarah back and said, "Miss Caldwell, I'm terribly sorry but I can't do your *Fledermaus* because I'm pregnant." There was a pause and then: "Weren't you pregnant five minutes ago?"

Our son, Peter Jr. (Bucky), was born June 29, 1961, weighing nearly ten pounds. We were on Cloud Nine: he was the first boy to be born into the Greenough family in forty-seven years and we at last had someone to carry on the name. A month later we suffered a tremendous shock: we learned that our daughter Muffy, who was then twenty-three months old, was deaf. We had suspected that something might be wrong with her hearing when she was only nine months old, but the doctors had convinced me that I was just being a worried first-time mother. She was such a bright child that she deceived us all. She would spend happy hours with picture books and she seemed to understand what they were saying. One day she moved close to a hot stove and I grabbed her just in time, screaming HOT! HOT! HOT! She spent the rest of the day wandering around the house saying hot, hot to everyone, her face lit up with a smile. It was the first word she had ever spoken. That near-miss with the stove forced us to have Muffy's hearing tested; it took only nine minutes to determine that she had a profound loss of hearing. "This is the worst day of my life," I said to Peter. "At least," he said, "it's over."

But it was not: shortly after the discovery of Muffy's loss of hearing, we learned that Bucky was mentally retarded. When he was two months old we asked a baby photographer to take some pictures of him. The photographer, trying to get Bucky's attention, suddenly looked startled. "Hey, lady," he said. "There's something wrong with your son—I can't get him to look at the birdie." There is no way of describing my initial desolation.

The discovery of our children's problems seriously altered our lives. In order to make Muffy as verbally communicative as possible we enrolled her in the Sarah Fuller School, a special nursery school in Boston. The process of teaching a deaf child to read lips and to speak is a frustratingly difficult one. What pulled us all through was the unfailing cheerfulness of my baby girl. She never stopped smiling, never stopped laughing. Even the most tedious sessions never seemed to tire her. She, her teacher, Merl Sigel, and I would crawl on the floor together for hours trying to get her to blow out a candle so that she would know how to pronounce the "wh" sound. The first candle she blew out was probably the most triumphant moment of her life— and of mine. When she saw how excited it made me, she couldn't wait to return home so that she could show her father too; she kept bringing out all the candles in the house for me to light and for her to blow out. She was always so proud of her accomplishments in learning. She has had many since and I hope will have many, many more.

During that period Sarah Caldwell and I became great friends. She knew of Muffy's condition, of course; she came to the house for dinner many times and Muffy fell in love with her. In February 1962, Sarah and I did our first opera together—*Manon.* The cast included John Alexander and Norman Treigle and in the orchestra pit was the Boston Symphony Orchestra; that ain't chicken liver! It was an exquisite production—once more what Sarah Caldwell did on a shoestring was nothing short of a miracle—and the reviews were raves. More important, for me, was the audience reaction; I had not provoked such enthusiasm anywhere before. I realized how much I needed opera now as a kind of refuge from personal problems.

Not that I felt much like singing, and especially if it meant going to New York and being separated from Muffy and Bucky. When I told Julius Rudel about the new developments in my life, he began to write me funny little "Dear Bubbela" letters signed "Julius Darlink" to get me to return to the City Opera. Once he phoned: "Listen, I have this marvelous Russian opera for you, *Boris Godunov.* You know how much I love you: you can play either Boris or Godunov." When I continued to resist, Julius turned stern: he insisted that I return to New York to sing Baby Doe in April—I owed it to him, he said: I had a contract to fulfill and he could no longer keep me on leave of absence status. Besides, he added, I was behaving foolishly.

I did sing that one performance of Baby Doe and then told Julius, That's it, I can't sing any more, I have too many other things on my mind.

The next month, on my thirty-third birthday, Peter gave me fifty-two round-trip tickets on the Boston–New York shuttle: I was to go to New York once a week, have my singing lesson with Miss Liebling, and see my mother. It was the best present he could have given me and he knew it; it was the kind of therapy necessary to force me out of the house and make me begin thinking about something besides family problems. Julius Rudel helped, too. He wrote me an order that fall on official stationery. He was tired of my excuses for not returning to work, I was to come to New York and sing and that was the end of it. He had a new opera for me to do—*Wings of the Dove,* by Douglas Moore, composer of *The Ballad of Baby Doe*—and he had also scheduled me to do *Louise*, with John Alexander as my lover and Norman Treigle as my father. I obeyed Julius.

Douglas had had me in mind when he began composing *Wings of the Dove*, but when I became pregnant with my son, he changed the role. The opera proved to be less successful than *Baby Doe*. But the *Louise* I sang on October 31, 1962, was one of those performances I will never forget. The *New York Times* the next day said it was "bland"; the *New York Times* didn't know what it was talking about. Alexander never sang better in his life, and Treigle and I gave the first of many performances together that made us walk out of the theater so moved that we were unable to speak. In the final act of the opera, when Louise decides to forsake her father for her lover, Treigle, caught up in the father's role, got so furious with me that he picked up a chair and threw it at me. I ducked (the chair hit the scenery) and then ran off the stage with Treigle sobbing out after me at the top of his voice: "Louise, Louise." When it was over, we were both crying. Jean Morel, the conductor, put his arms around us both, kissed us, and we three walked out on stage to take our bows, bawling our heads off. Bland performance—bull!

That night, in his hotel room, Norman wrote me a "Dear Bev" love letter: "...Watching you and hearing you just now in the aria and duet filled me with such beauty, admiration and emotion that I could hardly stand it. There are only a few people who have ever made me feel this way on stage and you are one who is on top of them all..."

Norman and I did our first *Faust* early the following year for Sarah Caldwell in Boston, at my suggestion. Sarah ran out of money before all the sets could be completed and we had to do the prison scene on a bare stage, but I never felt the need for scenery less. The starkness of that stage, Treigle in those black leotards as Mephistopheles looming ominously over my Marguerite—I felt for the first time that I had to fight for my stage life. Norman was always a great challenge to me; I like to think we brought out the operatic best in each other. Certainly we were never as inventive alone as we were on stage together and I never enjoyed operas as much as those in which we appeared together. It is a great credit to the City Opera that they recognized his talent and a great loss to the Metropolitan that it never put him on its stage. That voice, that temperament, that acting talent should have graced every opera stage in the world.

At about that time I was asked by Leopold Stokowski, who had never forgotten our pregnant audition, to sing four arias in a performance of Bach's *St. Matthew Passion* that he was to do with the American Symphony Orchestra in Carnegie Hall. I accepted but wrote him that I resented a cut he was making in one of my arias. He wrote back: ". . . From your delightful letter I fear you are not satisfied with these four inspired pieces of music by Bach. When I meet him in heaven, I will tell him about your 'frustration' and I am sure he will be deeply sorry, because he is such a nice man (although a genius). I hope you will pardon him and me." (Signed) "Always with friendly thoughts." I pardon him and Bach—wherever they are.

I was now only thirty-four, but a very mature thirty-four. In a strange way, my children had brought me an inner peace. The first question I had asked when I learned of their tragedies was a self-pitying "Why *me?*" Then gradually it changed to a much more important "Why *them?*" Despite their handicaps they were showing enormous strength in continuing to live as normal and constructive lives as possible. How could Peter and I show any less strength? After all that had happened, I felt that we could survive anything.

9

*All an "iron lung" needs
is comfortable shoes*

*As Olympia, the mechanical doll,
in* The Tales of Hoffmann.

My career seemed to be moving along at a faster clip; at least my fees were higher! And I was "singing around" quite a bit—at the Philharmonic opening of the 1963 Promenade Concert Series with André Kostelanetz; at Lewisohn Stadium, a Musetta in *La Bohème;* at Robin Hood Dell, a *Merry Widow* with Franz Allers; on to Honolulu with André Kostelanetz for a musical Viennese Night. Then in the fall back to the New York City Opera.

I sang *La Traviata* that season. I cannot say that the public suddenly felt they had discovered a new star, but I *can* say that people had begun to pay attention when I sang. The conductor was Franco Patane. He was very concerned with the musical values of an opera but didn't seem to care particularly about how it was staged or what was happening dramatically, probably because he was accustomed to opera in Italy, where the singers plant their feet and stare straight at the conductor.

Because I had a character to portray, I never looked directly at him although he was always in the periphery of my vision. After that opening night performance, Patane congratulated me on the fastest and cleanest coloratura that he had ever heard. Then he complained that I never looked at him when he was conducting. "I never look at you," I said, "but I always *see* you, Maestro." "I don't believe it," he said. During the second performance of *Traviata,* when we came to the *"Sempre Libera"* aria, Patane began the tempo like a bat out of hell. I had never heard it played that fast before; I whirled around to look at him and on his face was a triumphant smile: he had forced Beverly to stare at him. And I dared not stop staring because the tempo was so unbelievably fast. I had not planned to sing the aria that way but it did make for a pyrotechnical virtuoso display that the audience loved. After that, whenever we got to the *"Sempre Libera,"* Patane and I had a joke going: I would whirl around and stare hard at him until he set the tempo. Then I would go about my stage business. "I can sing it," I once told him, "as fast as you can conduct it."

On the winter tour of the company that year I had the chance to sing my first Donna Anna in *Don Giovanni,* a role I had coveted and now consider one of my best. Julius Rudel and I have always had a special, unspoken understanding—no extravagant compliments, please. We always knew when a performance had that special quality; the look on our faces during and after a performance was enough to tell us how pleased we were with the way things had gone. But on that tour, after my first Donna Anna, when Julius came on stage to take bows with me, he blurted out, "My God, you sang like a goddess tonight!" I was so unprepared for that kind of hyperbole from Julius that I didn't even thank him; I just looked at him and said, "Yeah!" To this day, whenever we talk about my singing Donna Anna again, I always kid him. "How can I go back to singing her again? I can't sing it any better than a goddess. I should quit while I'm ahead."

On December 9, 1963, the New York City Opera celebrated its twentieth anniversary. I sang the Willow Song from *The Ballad of Baby Doe* at the celebration, then caught the flu and canceled a performance for the first time in my career. I have been nicknamed "The Iron Lung" because of my attitude that even if I had to be carried on stage feet first, I should sing a scheduled performance. It always devastates me to know that someone else is up there in *my* place. Thus when I cancel I am very, very sick. I figure that, even functioning a little bit less than at full potential, I still deliver a first-class performance—and I try very hard to do that.

I had recovered enough in the next few weeks to sing, in January of 1964, in Boston, my first Queen of the Night in Mozart's *The Magic Flute*. I wish it had been my last, and if I had a brain in my head it would have been. No role—not even Micaela—has ever bored me more. No role has given me less anticipation or less feeling of involvement; at one performance Peter and I backstage managed to address 250 Christmas cards between my first and second act arias! The role consists of five high Fs. If all five come out beautifully, you're a fabulous hit; if not, forget it, even though you may have sung all the rest of the aria beautifully. The only perfect performance I ever gave, by my own standards, was a Queen of the Night I did at the Tanglewood Music Festival conducted by Erich Leinsdorf. When I walked on stage to do the arias, Erich had a look in his eye that said, Don't-you-dare-miss-one-of-those-high-Fs. I didn't, by God, and because the performance was broadcast I know that there is a historic record attesting to my one perfect Queen of the Night.

Actually, I think my average for the role was four out of five high Fs, which I consider damned good. I know women who have made careers out of that Queen who had a worse batting average.

In February, for my debut with the New Orleans Opera, I sang for the first time all the lead female roles in *The Tales of Hoffmann* with Norman Treigle. It was the first of many *Hoffmanns* we were to do together and I think it was our greatest collaboration, vocally and histrionically. The concepts we created in the roles as we went along were totally original, more imaginative than anything else we had ever done together. In March I sang my first and only Adina in Donizetti's *The Elixir of Love* with Sarah Caldwell's Boston Company. Glynn Ross, who heads the Seattle Opera Company, had advised me against singing Adina because he considered the opera strictly a tenor's opera. I bet him five dollars that I could turn it into a soprano's opera; I won and he paid off. In April I sang with the Fort Lauderdale Symphony Orchestra, Emerson Buckley conducting, and a critic for the *Miami Herald* called me a "red-haired tomato." Other music critics around the country were also beginning to notice me. When I returned to New York in the fall to sing Donna Anna there for the first time, as well as Constanza in Mozart's *The Abduction from the Seraglio*, Winthrop Sargeant, the *New Yorker*'s music critic and one of the most respected in the country, called me THE *prima donna* of the New York City Opera. He was the first to bestow that title on me and I loved it.

The year ended on the road—a Marguerite in East Lansing, Michigan, a double-header in Chicago (*Die Fledermaus* in the afternoon, *The Merry Widow* in the evening); and a debut with the San Antonio Opera in Howard Hanson's *Merry Mount*, in which the first line I had to sing was, "Unhand her, you dastard."

That whole year reminded me of a story about Birgit Nilsson, the great Wagnerian soprano. In *Tristan and Isolde* she is on stage for most of the opera's four hours. After one of her usual magnificent performances, another soprano visited her backstage and said, "Really, Birgit, it's not so difficult, I don't understand why everybody makes such a fuss over it." "You're absolutely right," Birgit replied, "all you need is a comfortable pair of shoes." By the end of the year I felt the same way: it had been a good, busy year, my throat was in fine shape but my feet hurt terribly.

The year 1965 began on an unpleasant note. Sarah Caldwell and her Boston Company were doing the American première of an opera entitled *Intolleranza* and Sarah asked me to sing in it. The opera was written by Luigi Nono, son-in-law of the composer Arnold Schönberg. Mr. Nono is a very talented man but he has an unpleasant disposition. He is a member of the Italian Communist Party, or was at the time: perhaps he has since come to his senses. He came to Boston dressed in overalls and a worker's cap but he stayed in one of the city's most luxurious hotels (with the bill, I understand, being picked up by the opera company).

From the start of the production he raised havoc. The English translation of his opera, he complained, had lost all its poetry. The production itself was multimedia—huge slides were projected on a screen behind the performers, depicting man's inhumanity to man. Mr. Nono felt that man's inhumanity existed only in the United States. He had chosen slides of black men being lynched, for example, but refused to allow any of the Russian invasion of Hungary. At one point in the opera I had an aria entitled "Ban the Bomb," which contained a phrase "the screaming voices of Hiroshima," On the "shi" in "Hiroshima" I had to hit a high C-sharp. I tried to explain to Mr. Nono that on a note that high the text would be indecipherable and so it would be better to sing the word "Hiroshima" on a lower note so that people could understand. "No," he said, he wanted the high C-sharp to sound like the screaming of the bomb itself. When I said that I did not think I could bring it off, he began to yell, accusing me of acting this way because I did not want to admit my country's guilt in dropping the bomb.

The conductor was Bruno Maderna, who had a genius for difficult modern music. He was in total sympathy with the singers who had worked so hard to learn the music, and we all agreed to protest Mr. Nono's one-sided slide projections of man's inhumanity; they didn't *all* have to bear a made-in-America label. After a tremendous struggle we wound up with a kind of sixty-forty breakdown in the choice of slides as between the United States and the rest of the world.

On opening night there was one picket from the Polish Freedom Fighters outside the theater, protesting the very idea of Mr. Nono's opera being performed. Even the picket got bored and left at the end of the first act. In all fairness, Mr. Nono had written some intriguing music in the twelve-tone idiom, but most credit should be given to Sarah Caldwell and the cast of American singers who stuck it out for what, we felt, was as fine a performance of his opera as Mr. Nono could ever hope to have. Mr. Nono thought differently. He complained later that the reason his opera had not been a huge success in Boston was because the orchestra couldn't play the music—it was the Boston Symphony in the pit!—and in a letter to a newspaper he denounced the whole performance. I shall never sing another note of Nono's music—ever.

Another less than notable event in 1965 was my appearance as Mimi in the Seattle Opera's production of *La Bohème*. For me, Mimi has always looked exactly like Licia Albanese or Lucrezia Bori. I have always prided myself on knowing, or thinking I know, exactly what I look like on the stage; not even in the wildest leap of my imagination could I ever see myself looking like Mimi. I simply never got the hang of her. I love her, I cry when I see her performed. I also give thanks that I don't have to sing her anymore. I still look at the score from time to time, trying to figure out what eludes me about the character. Maybe it's because she is really a French heroine lost in the *verismo* of Italian opera; if she is supposed to be an Italian heroine, what's she doing in a French garret? The problem is mine alone, of course, because a great many famous sopranos have sung Mimi very successfully. But I was only too happy when, after my third performance of Mimi in Seattle, she was dead forever for me; not even mouth-to-mouth resuscitation could bring her back after that last dying gasp. I feel the same about Musetta in *La Bohème*, which I have sung only a few more reluctant times than Mimi. Musetta is a royal pain in the A. When I put Mimi, Musetta, Micaela, and the Queen of the Night to bed forever in my repertoire, they well deserved the rest.

Marguerite in *Faust* is something else. That year, when I sang the role for the first time in New York with Norman Treigle as Mephistopheles, the reviews were so overwhelming that Julius Rudel had them blown up and, for the first time in the company's history, displayed in the lobby of the City Center.

Norman and I were involved in another memorable performance that summer at—of all places—the Cincinnati Zoo Opera, so called because the theater had a roof but no sides and was smack in the middle of the zoo. (I remember a performance there, years later, of a *Traviata* which should have been billed "Starring Beverly Seals": throughout my entire "*Sempre Libera*" aria you could hear nothing but the barking of seals.) The Zoo Opera's artistic director was that same Tito Capobianco who had done the modern *Tosca* in Buenos Aires. Norman had met him in Mexico City. When Mr. Capobianco invited Norman to the zoo that summer of '65 to sing *The Tales of Hoffmann*, Norman agreed, but only if he could bring along his pal Beverly, with whom he had sung the opera before and who could sing all three soprano roles, so that Tito wouldn't have to hire any more sopranos, and so on. Tito was very intrigued and hired me sight unseen.

What Norman had neglected to tell him was that his pal Beverly stood five feet eight-and-a-half inches tall and weighed a hundred and fifty pounds. Tito had already decided that Olympia, the mechanical doll, should weigh in at about five feet and a hundred pounds, give or take a little—more or less like his wife, Elena (Gigi) Denda, who had been the prima ballerina at the Teatro Colón, in Buenos Aires. When I walked into rehearsal in Cincinnati, Tito's face fell; I figured that I had done something to upset him but inasmuch as I hadn't even said Hello yet, I couldn't imagine what it was. When I was introduced to Mrs. Capobianco, Gigi, she kept staring at me, and I thought something terrible must be happening. After the musical rehearsal I asked the Capobiancos what the trouble was. Gigi asked me what dress size I wore. I said, "Fourteen." Gigi said, "You see, we thought you were a Toddler Two." Our friendship dates from that first meeting: Gigi is my "sister" and Tito is my director.

The Cincinnati production of *The Tales of Hoffmann* was a sensation. The Petrouchka ballet originally planned for the doll in the first act was changed to take into account my size fourteen; the doll became a funny, Charlie-Chaplinesque walking doll with huge eyelashes that literally clicked when the eyes closed. Gigi did my makeup, and instead of painting on the red cheeks she cut out little circles of red masking tape and pasted them on my face. When we removed them after a performance, we would paste them on top of one of my pancake-makeup boxes. Unconsciously, we began to save all my "cheeks"; we did so many performances of *Hoffmann* that in a year every makeup box I opened had two little red masking tape cheeks pasted on it.

I got to show my legs on stage for the first time (other than that City Opera audition for Dr. Rosenstock) in *Hoffmann*. In the second act, as Guiletta, I was supposed to wear a long skirt with so many open slits that every time I moved the audience would get an unobstructed view of my legs. I balked at the costume at first; "I'm a singer," I complained, "not a strip teaser." But Tito convinced me I should wear the costume and, as usual, he was right: I got smash reviews for my voice *and* my legs.

Julius Rudel had agreed to do *Hoffmann* for Norman and me in New York at the City Center. But because there was no money for a new production, he was planning to use a mishmash of sets from four different operas. At the time Norman and I had agreed to the mishmash because we wanted so much to do our characterizations on stage, but when we realized that for a few thousand dollars we could bring the whole Cincinnati production to the City Opera Company, with Tito as director and Gigi doing the choreography, we began to badger Julius at every opportunity. One day when we were in Palo Alto to do a *Don Giovanni* with the City Opera, Norman came into my dressing room and said, "I want you to sing so that man on the podium (Julius) will just be sick to his stomach at the idea he can't give us the *Hoffmann* we want. Make him want to throw up in the orchestra pit." Julius was absolutely bowled over by our *Don Giovanni* that matinée; at the first-act curtain call he was in tears. *Giovanni* is, I think, his favorite opera; he conducts it as if Mozart were whispering in his ear. When Norman and I came off stage, Julius said to us, "What are you two guys doing to me? I'm absolutely limp." So Norman said, "Okay, Julius, you want a second act to match or you want a lousy one?" Julius looked at him quizzically. Norman: "Do we get the *Hoffmann* or don't we?" Julius: "You've got the *Hoffmann*, you've got the *Hoffmann*. Now leave me alone and finish this opera the way you started it."

Julius kept his word: he raised the money and brought *Hoffmann* to New York with the Capobiancos, who became permanent members of the company. Tito had separate triumphs of his own, of course, but he staged *all* of mine: *The Tales of Hoffmann, Julius Caesar, Manon, Roberto Devereux,*

Maria Stuarda, Anna Bolena, I Puritani. I work with the Capobiancos better than with any other director and assistant. They have studied every gesture I make, every reaction; they know how to deal with me when I am having difficulty with a character and how to leave me alone when I think I have caught on immediately. Gigi does my makeup and is always backstage with me before a première. She is an extremely calming influence. She knows what places in the opera are bothering me, and while she is putting on my makeup she will talk quietly about how we had decided to resolve the difficulties.

Tito has one of the most fertile minds in the business. He can think of fifteen different ways to do a scene until he finally finds the one that you are most happy with. If you are still unable to make up your mind at that point, he will decide for you. His taste is impeccable. I have total trust in anything Tito tells me to do and he, I think, feels the same about me. He likes to say I am a diamond that needs a magnificent setting and that he will always try to provide it for me. He always has.

As Giulietta in The Tales of Hoffmann, *1965.*

My first, and unfortunately not my last, Queen of the Night in Mozart's The Magic Flute—*Boston, 1964. What a bore she is!*

But Marguerite in Faust is something else. When I sang her for the first time at the New York City Opera (below, left) in 1965, the reviews were so favorable that Julius Rudel broke house tradition and displayed them, blown up, in the lobby.

Constanza in Mozart's The Abduction from the Seraglio *(below, right) was another new role I took on at the City Opera in 1965. I was now singing so many different key roles in the repertory that the* New Yorker *critic referred to me as the prima donna in the company.*

A scene from the Boston Opera
Company's 1965 production of Luigi
Nono's opera, Intolleranza. He *was a
no-no!* I'm singing twelve-tone
music against a backdrop of smoke
and other curses depicting man's
inhumanity to man.

Donna Anna in Mozart's Don
Giovanni *is a role I had always
coveted. This scene is from the City
Opera's production in 1965, with
Norman Treigle as Giovanni and
Donald Gramm as Leporello.*

A scene from Sarah Caldwell's 1965 Boston Opera production of The Abduction from the Seraglio *with me, Constanza, third from left. It was an exquisite production, with the Boston Symphony in the pit.*

My first of only three performances in my life of Mimi in La Bohème—*all in a production of the Seattle Opera Company in 1965. It wasn't Rodolfo's fault, here played by tenor Luciano Saldari. I simply never got the hang of Mimi and so I have never sung her again.*

Julius Rudel and I share a hot dog after some opening or other. We've been sharing for more than twenty years at the New York City Opera.

Gigi Capobianco and me—she's the Toddler Two.

Tito Capobianco and me. He was my director and provided me with many perfect settings.

10

If I don't get Cleopatra, I quit!

Cleopatra—the turning point of my career.

Early in 1966, the New York City Opera moved from the ancient City Center on West Fifty-fifth Street to its shiny, glamorous new home in the New York State Theatre, part of the Lincoln Center complex. The first season that spring, devoted to contemporary works (I did *Baby Doe* again), was not considered the official opening; that was scheduled for the fall, with the première to be Handel's *Julius Caesar*. Norman Treigle was to be Caesar and Julius Rudel had invited Phyllis Curtin to return to the City Opera (she had left its roster to join the Met) to sing Cleopatra.

Julius' decision to use Phyllis annoyed the hell out of me. There was nothing personal in it: Phyllis had been my friend for more than twenty years, still is, and as an artist she is without peer. But I felt that asking her back to do Cleopatra implied that no one in the City Opera company could sing the role and that just wasn't true—*I* could sing it. I had already sung several of the arias in my recitals and I felt that the role was ideal for me. Besides, as the *New Yorker* critic had written, I was now the *prima donna* in the company; my repertoire included key roles—Constanza in *The Abduc-*

tion from the Seraglio, all the roles in *The Tales of Hoffmann*, the Queen of the Night, Donna Anna—and it would be difficult to replace me in those roles. I decided to talk turkey with Julius: either I get the Cleopatra role or I resign from the company.

I discussed it first with John White, the extraordinary managing director of the company, and the pal to whom I gave the final wave at all my curtain calls. He felt that I had a valid beef. Then at breakfast with Julius in his home I made my case: "If you gave Cleopatra to anyone else already with the company," I said, "I would not protest. But going outside the company to find another soprano was a public admission that nobody then in the house could sing the role. Well, how about me?" Julius said my arguments seemed reasonable. Then he looked at me mischievously and said, "You're not really going to resign from this company, you're too much a part of it and it's a part of you, just the way it is with me, and besides, you know how you love to come to New York." "True," I replied, "but I feel so strongly about this that if I don't get the Cleopatra, I *will* resign, and then I'll hire Carnegie Hall and sing five Cleopatra arias just to get her out of my system, because, by God, I'm going to sing Cleopatra in New York!"

Julius is an extremely fair man. To his everlasting credit, he said, "Yes, the part is yours." What arrangements he had to make with Phyllis I do not know. In any case, there has never been any bitterness between Phyllis and me over the matter.

That summer, while I was working on Cleopatra, I received my first offer from the Metropolitan Opera Company—to do a performance of Donna Anna at Lewisohn Stadium in New York with my old friend Dr. Rosenstock conducting. Robert Herman, Rudolf Bing's assistant manager, who tendered the offer, told me that everyone at the Met was very happy to have me finally make my debut with them. "To me," I replied, "a debut in an opera house takes place on the stage of that opera house, *not* in an open-air stadium." I would be delighted, I continued, to be a guest in the performance, but I would not consider it my debut at the Met nor consider myself a member of the Metropolitan Opera Company. I signed the contract, they paid my fee. Then

I was informed that the big Donna Anna aria, *"Non Mi Dir,"* in the second act was to be deleted. When I protested that I would not do the performance under those circumstances, the aria was restored. It was a show stopper. Mr. Bing did not attend the performance and it was another six years before the Met nibbled at me again.

By sheer coincidence, the Met had scheduled for the opening of its new Lincoln Center home in 1966 the world première of Samuel Barber's *Anthony and Cleopatra.* The Met's Bob Herman said to me at the time that the City Opera was foolish to open with *Julius Caesar* against the Met's *Anthony.* My answer was that inasmuch as Mr. Handel had got there first we had a perfect right to do *Caesar* on our opening night. And so it was a head-to-head competition. As it turned out, it was really no contest. Despite Barber's gorgeous music and the incredibly beautiful singing of Leontyne Price as Cleopatra, the Met opening, rumored to have cost three quarters of a million dollars, was a disaster—overproduced, overdirected, over-everything, a Hollywood extravaganza in which the opera got lost. Our opening, quite simply, was a complete triumph—a sixty-thousand-dollar authentic Handel, duplicating the way the opera had been performed in the composer's time. The women from the neck down were dressed in baroque gowns; from the neck up they wore headdresses that would suggest the character—Cleopatra in one scene, for example, wears a headdress with an asp in it. The men wore togas. Some people believe that in Handel's time singers used to make up their own ornamentation—the flowery vocal embellishments to a melody—on the spot during a performance. I do not believe it: it was a great period for show-offish singing, for trying to outdo one another, and the ornamentation must have had to be well-prepared and rehearsed in advance. In any case, we tried to stick with what we thought was authentic and tasteful Handelian ornamentation.

The cast was inspired and memorable. Norman Treigle as Julius Caesar looked and acted like John Gielgud in the role and sang like a Roman god. The rest—Beverly Wolff, Maureen Forrester, Dominic Cossa, Spiro Malas—were equally awesome. When the performance was over, I knew that something extraordinary had taken place. I knew that I had sung as I had never sung before and I needed no newspapers the next day to reassure me. Julius came to my dressing room and we shared what I think was the most intimate moment in our more than twenty-five-year friendship. He put his arms around me and said, "God takes care of people like me. I'm very lucky that I shared such an evening with you." Then he turned and walked out of the room.

Of all the nights in my performing life, including the night I made my debut at the Metropolitan nine years later, none will remain in my memory as long as that opening night of *Julius Caesar*. It was—and I don't mean to be immodest, but after all these years I *am* a pretty good judge of performances—one of the great performances of all time in any opera house. It was the kind of night when the audience was so caught up in the general euphoria that it never even noticed a bizarre piece of stage business. As Ptolemeo, Spiro Malas had a small band of soldiers—nonsinging, spear-carrying extras paid a couple of dollars per performance just to add physical presence to the staging. Their instructions were simple: when Mr. Malas goes on stage, follow him and stand behind him; when he exits, exit with him. On opening night, while on stage, Spiro suddenly could not remember the opening words of his next recitative. While someone else was singing an aria, he quietly and with great dignity marched off to the wings to consult the score. What he did not notice was that his soldiers were dutifully following him off stage and then back on. The audience apparently did not notice anything awry either. We in the cast thought it was hilarious: the two opening words that Spiro had forgotten were—"Julius Caesar."

Julius Rudel and I have talked often about reviving the opera, but you can't go home again. Without Norman Treigle around (he died in 1975) it no longer has much appeal for me and I doubt that I will ever sing it again. When you feel that you have done a definitive anything in your life, it's best to leave it at that.

The day after the première of *Julius Caesar* I flew home. There was an excellent review in the *New York Times*, but I didn't see any other reviews until I returned to New York four days later for my next performance. They were fabulous: all the critics, national and international, had been in New York for the opening of the Met, and as we were only a few hundred yards away across the plaza, it had been no great chore for them to come to our opening, too. There were five hundred fan letters in my mail box at the theatre; before, I used to average about ten a week.

Needless to say, *Julius Caesar* was the turning point of my career. But strangely enough, that success, when it came, meant less to me than it might have if it had occurred five years earlier. Let me try to explain. Once, during rehearsals for the opera, when I was singing for Julius, he said to me in awe, "Where the hell did you learn to sing like that?" An interesting question. My voice had not changed; *I* had. Now, instead of using my singing just to build a career, which is what I had been doing up to that time, I was singing for pure pleasure. I was singing not because I wanted to be Beverly Sills Superstar, but because I needed to sing—desperately. My voice poured out more easily because I was no longer singing for anyone's approval; I was beyond caring about the public's reaction, I just wanted to enjoy myself.

At the same time, as I indicated earlier, I had found a kind of serenity, a new maturity as a result of my childrens' problems. I didn't feel better or stronger than anyone else but it seemed no longer important whether everyone loved me or not—more important now was for me to love them. Feeling that way turns your whole life around: living becomes the act of giving. When I do a performance now, I still need and like the adulation of an audience, of course, but my *real* satisfaction comes from what I have given of myself, from the joyful act of singing itself.

This all may sound a little Pollyannaish and I don't consider myself a Pollyanna. But it is the only explanation I can give for the way I sang in *Julius Caesar* that night—and for the way the audience, sensing my own joy, responded.

Norman Treigle as Julius Caesar and I as Cleopatra.

11

Manon—
"Think Lolita, think Lolita"

Swinging away as Manon.

When our little boy Bucky was six, Peter and I had to face the sad realization that he could no longer live at home with us. He was a beautiful big boy, brown eyes, brown curly hair, a dead giveaway for his mother. But he was autistic, could not speak, and was showing signs of epilepsy. I was against sending him away to a special school but Peter and my mother convinced me that he needed the teaching and the therapy that only a special institution could provide; keeping him at home would deny him whatever help was possible. We decided to put him in the same school in Massachusetts where my stepdaughter Diana had been since 1959. At least we could visit them regularly.

It was, of course, a particularly tense, highly emotional period for me and I sought out Julius Rudel to find me some challenging, absorbing project that would help me through it. We decided that I would sing *Il Trittico*, Puccini's trilogy of one-act operas. No soprano in New York, to my knowledge, had ever sung the leading roles in each of the three one-acters on the same night; I decided that would be my challenge.

The week my son was to leave home, I sang a scene from Strauss's *Daphne* in a concert with the Boston Symphony Orchestra conducted by Erich Leinsdorf. By that time Erich and I had become close friends, and of course he knew about Bucky. While the orchestra was playing a long orchestral interlude, I looked at Erich. He had tears in his eyes; so did I. When the performance was over, we took no curtain calls. Hand in hand, we walked off, he to his dressing room, I to mine. We did not speak. We felt, I think, that we were sharing a rare moment of intimacy. We have never talked about it but I know he remembers that moment as well as I do.

Il Trittico opened March 8, two days after my son had gone away to school. I don't remember much about my performance but it must have been memorable. *Suor Angelica,* one of the three operas, is the story of a young noblewoman who has become a nun in expiation of a scandal in her life—she is an unwed mother. In one scene the Sister (my role) is told that her son, whom she had been forced to abandon, had died two days earlier. I had considerable trouble getting through that scene, breaking down in tears several times. The conductor was Franco Patane, and many years later I learned from his son that Franco had also wept uncontrollably as he was conducting that scene. He too had difficulty finishing the opera. When *Suor Angelica* was over, I vowed that I would never sing her again, because of the painful associations it had for me, and I never have.

Singing all three roles in *Il Trittico* was purely a stunt; the roles are written for three different types of voices. One critic asked afterwards why I, with a voice like peaches, had to be every apple in the orchard. She was absolutely right, of course, and I will never repeat the stunt. But at the time it served its purpose: it certainly occupied my mind.

For the 1967 fall season of the New York City Opera, Julius Rudel was mounting a new production of Rimsky-Korsakov's *Le Coq d'Or.* Norman Treigle was to play King Dodon and I the Queen of Shemakha. The Capobiancos, who were to direct it, were very busy at the same time working on a new production of *Tosca,* and when we started rehearsals for *Le Coq* they were not paying any attention to me. Other people seemed to be moving around carrying palm leaves back and forth but I would just be standing there in the center with no stage business plotted. It was totally unlike the usual Capobianco operation and with only a week left before the première I finally complained to Gigi: "What am I supposed to *do* in this role? Why am I just standing still and where is my costume?" Gigi said, "We've been somewhat afraid to tell you but you have to dance throughout the entire role." "Dance!" I shrieked. "I barely can do social dancing. And what do I wear?" The Capobiancos produced what looked like three and a half veils. Those, together with a five-story, fragile, bejeweled crown like a French spun-sugar concoction, were to be my entire costume. Then Gigi, a former ballerina, demonstrated the dance I was to do—a thirty-five-minute belly number. I just stared at her. "Impossible," I said. "I can't wear this bikini with my belly button showing, I can't wear this flimsy bra, I can't dance. Out of the question." "Look," Gigi said soothingly, "I'll work with you, and if you still feel you can't do it, then we'll change it."

By the end of the first three hours of dance rehearsal I was bruised, battered and charley-horsed but you could not have taken that dance away from me for all the money in the world. I was into the belly-dancing bit literally up to my navel and I loved it. The dance also helped me define the role which up to that point had eluded me; I decided the best way to play Queenie was like Mae West, poking fun at her own sexiness. It was such a complete change of fare for Norman and me from *The Tales of Hoffmann* and *Julius Caesar* that we had a ball. So did the audience: the ticket lines around Lincoln Center fountain were the longest in the company's history. Even our version of the opera on television brought a huge rating. Bless the public's taste: it *was* a knockout of an opera.

After the success of *Julius Caesar,* Julius Rudel had called me into his office: "We're going to do *Coq d'Or* for Norman in 1967 and then, in 1968,

we'll do a special one for you. Start thinking about what you'd like it to be."
Manon, I said immediately, and just as quickly Julius said yes. He was as excited about the project as I.

Our *Manon* was a Fragonard painting come to life—his famous painting of the lady on the swing. Gigi bought me a whole new case of makeup for the part—it was all pink, pink, pink. The sets alone created an atmosphere that tore your heart out; Julius Rudel said that the second act apartment of the Chevalier des Grieux reminded him of the small Paris hotel he had stayed in as a young man after World War II. The tenor who sang Des Grieux was Michael Molese, a young American who had done a lot of singing in Italy. We used to fight terribly during rehearsals, not because Michael didn't understand the role—he did—but because he was trying so hard to do it all exactly right. I had considerable trouble with my own role at the start. You look too innocent, Tito would say to me, Manon isn't that innocent. In the bedroom scene in Act II, when Manon is reading the letter that Des Grieux is about to send to his father explaining their love, one line goes: "Yesterday she was sixteen." I burst out laughing during rehearsal and asked Tito, "What the hell am I supposed to do with *that* line?" "Think Lolita, think Lolita," he replied, and suddenly the whole character fell into place for me.

Everything in the production was perfect, but I remember especially the scene in Act III that takes place in the Seminary of Saint Sulpice. Des Grieux has gone there to become a priest and Manon tries to entice him out of that decision. I was wearing a beautiful lace gown and carrying a chiffon scarf. As I circle and circle De Grieux, he suddenly seizes the scarf and buries his head in it as though he can no longer hold out against my perfume. Every night the public would go wild after that scene.

Whenever I was to sing Manon, I couldn't wait to get to the theater. I would come in two hours early and spend a half-hour on Manon's swing, swinging slowly back and forth. I think that was the real beginning of my schizophrenic personality; I suddenly felt as I was walking into the theater that I was no longer Beverly Sills but the lady I was about to portray. For those three hours at least I was totally divorced from myself and my problems.

After *Julius Caesar*, offers began pouring in from all over the world. I was still the girl who couldn't say no, too excited at being invited to all those places every soprano dreams of. In a period of three weeks I sang on three different continents. Norman and I did a *Tales of Hoffmann* in Santiago, Chile, and a *Julius Caesar* in Buenos Aires. Tito Capobianco, for political reasons, was not allowed to accompany us to Argentina, which annoyed me and I made my unhappiness clear to the authorities. The conductor of that performance was Karl Richter, who never believed in cuts; as a result, I sang my last aria at 12:40 A.M. I went to Vienna to do three Queen of the Nights and three Violettas at the State Opera. Because of a badly infected ear I had to cancel all but the first Queen. It was rather unpleasant: the opera director threatened that if I canceled he would make such a *scandale* that I would never again be invited to sing in Europe. I was foolish enough at the time to believe him. I have been invited many times since to sing in Europe and even with the Vienna Opera—now under new management.

My second trip to Vienna was to do a record for ABC of Donizetti and Bellini arias. I had stalled ABC in 1967 when they first made the offer because I wanted to ask my friend Roger Hall, then head of artists and repertoire at RCA, if he was interested in my recording those arias for him. What street does your mother live on? Roger asked. Fifty-ninth Street, I said. Well, Roger said, it'll sell three records on Fifty-ninth Street and your mother will buy them all. Roger, I said, one day you're going to have to eat that record. I should have insisted on it—the recording has sold more than 100,000 copies.

Between engagements at the City Opera, in Europe, and in South America I was still taking my show on the road here. I did *Traviata*s in Cincinnati and Texas; *Hoffmann*s in Los Angeles and San Antonio; a *Faust* in Orlando. And I got to do my first *Lucia*—in Fort Worth, Texas. Somebody asked me how come I had never done a *Lucia* before. Because nobody asked me, I replied. When *Time* did a cover story on me in 1971, they called me "The Fastest Voice Alive." That was a reference to Thomas Schippers's statement that I could move my voice faster than anybody else alive. But it could also be applied to another of my strengths: I am a quick study. I can learn almost any part quickly and usually can be talked into going anywhere to sing it. Indeed, I was the work horse at the City Center ("Need someone to sing three nights in a row? Call on old Beverly") and I was very proud of it. When I am gone, if my career is ever discussed, I hope it will be in terms of the kinds of performances I gave in repertory all those seasons at the City Opera. I'll settle for that.

"Bucky," Peter Greenough, Jr., at five.

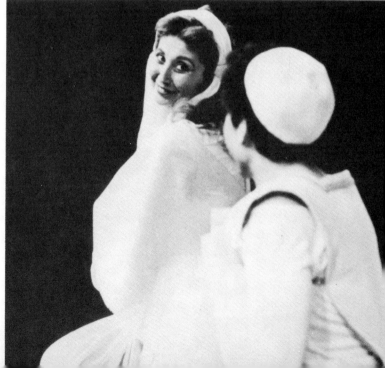

*When I learned that our son Bucky had to be
sent off to a special school in 1967, I decided
I needed something especially challenging to
help me during a difficult period. And so I
sang all three roles in Puccini's* Il Trittico *in
the same evening: Suor Angelica (top left),
with Frances Bible in the role of my aunt;
Giorgetta (top right) in* Il Tabarro, *with
Placido Domingo playing Luigi; and Lauretta
in* Gianni Schicchi *(right).*

At the San Francisco Opera production of the same opera in 1971, Tito Capobianco, who directed both productions, gives me a helping hand during rehearsals.

At Tanglewood in 1968 I sang a concert with Erich Leinsdorf conducting the Boston Symphony Orchestra. This was only a few days before my son Bucky was to leave home permanently for a special school and Erich knew it. When he began to conduct the orchestral interlude from Strauss' Daphne, we were both moist around the eyes.

*"Chulyuss Darlink" Rudel and me
laughing it up—as usual.*

*When it's apple-throwing time in San
Francisco. The invisible target is
Luciano Pavarotti, who had just
pinched my behind during a
rehearsal break.*

127

Queens,
madwomen,
country girls,
army mascot
—I sing'em all

As Cleopatra in the New York City Opera's 1966 production of Handel's Julius Caesar.

*As Marie
in Donizetti's*
The Daughter
of the Regiment.

12

La Scala—
"Well, Bubbles,
now we've done it all"

Every career, when it begins to take off as mine did after *Julius Caesar*, needs a mentor—one person who will make decisions based not on personal gain but on an honest love for the individual whose career he is involved with. There are always a great many people ready to come backstage to tell you how wonderful you were when you really were not. There are also many people—thank God, not as many—ready to tear you apart after even your best performance. I have always felt that I was the person best qualified to judge my own performances. I have lived with my talent, such as it is, longer than anyone else. I know its capabilities and its limitations. I know when I have done a crackerjack job and when I have not. But it is still invaluable to have someone who can come backstage after a performance and render a completely sincere cold assessment of what you have done right or wrong —even if *he* is wrong!

I found my mentor in Edgar Vincent, who runs what is probably the most successful public relations firm for the classical performing arts in the country. Even before we knew each other Edgar had helped push my career: he was instrumental in introducing me to André Kostelanetz, and whenever Erich Leinsdorf, then musical director of the Boston Symphony, needed a soprano Edgar would always recommend me.

One day Edgar got a phone call from Thomas Schippers, the American conductor then living in Rome. Schippers was desperate: he was to conduct a new production of Rossini's *The Siege of Corinth* in April at La Scala to commemorate the centenary of Rossini's death, and his soprano, Renata Scotto, who was to sing the leading role of Pamira, would be too pregnant to perform. Did Edgar know *anyone* who was proficient in Italian, could learn a long, difficult role in four months, and could fly to Rome to spend some time learning the role with him? "Call Beverly Sills," Edgar said, and hung up.

And that is how I came to make my debut at La Scala. First I had to get out of several previous conflicting engagements. I phoned Julius Rudel: "By all means," he said, " so long as you're back at the City Opera for the opening of *Manon.*" I phoned Erich Leinsdorf, with whom I was scheduled to do several concerts: "Go, you're released." I wrote to Eugene Ormandy (I didn't know him well enough at the time to phone): he wrote back a funny, tongue-in-cheek letter saying he could think of no reason in the world why I would consider La Scala more important than doing three performances of *Elijah* with him, but, of course, if that was the way I felt about it, fine.

At the beginning of February I flew to Rome to begin work on the score with Mr. Schippers. We had never met before—I doubt that he had even heard me sing. I was very nervous. In the score he had sent me was insert after insert because the version of the opera he was planning was a rough combination of three different Rossini operas—the original Italian version of the *Siege* and scissored-in excerpts from an earlier Rossini opera called *Maometto II* and from the rewritten version that Rossini had done for the *Siege*'s first successful performance in Paris in 1826. The vocal score was extremely complex. It had so many notes that I wish I had been paid by the note rather than by the performance.

At Tom's apartment, his wife Nonie, sensing how nervous I was, suggested a spot of tea. Great idea. While she was in the kitchen Tom explained to me that what I regarded as a hodgepodge of versions of several operas was actually the way the opera was performed in Rossini's time. When Nonie came back with a tray, she promptly tripped over the rug—tea, cookies, lemons, and Nonie went all over the room. She looked up. "How's *that* for making a nervous guest feel at home?" My nervousness had already gone. Everything seemed to jell between Tom and me once we started work. It turned out we were both bridge nuts. "Okay, fifteen-minute break," he would say during our first rehearsals, and then we would talk bridge. He was so enthusiastic about the opera, as was I, that we eagerly awaited the debut. *The Siege of Corinth* had last been performed at La Scala in 1853.

On March 8 I arrived in Milan and rented an apartment in a hotel. Marilyn Horne and her little girl were living in the same hotel, and when my mother, Peter, and Muffy came over to join me, we all became one big happy family. The street our hotel was on, we learned later, was famous for its colorful retinue of "ladies of the evening." Every night they would line up about a foot apart, heavily made up and dangling the inevitable enormous handbags. Muffy, who was ten, thought they were absolutely gorgeous; every evening as we passed the ladies on the way to the theater or to dinner, her eyes would pop. One day she asked me, "Mama, how do you say 'beautiful' in Italian?" "*Bella, bella,*" I told her. The next night Muffy went up to one of the more colorful ladies, put a great smile on her face, and said, "*Bella, bella.*" The woman was so touched that she reached into her handbag, pulled out a piece of chocolate, and gave it to Muffy. *Grazie.*

Marilyn Horne had already made her debut at La Scala, in *Oedipus Rex.* She knew her way around at the opera house and was a great help to me. She had already learned that at La Scala you don't say please, you always talk in loud, booming tones, and you play *prima donna* twenty-four hours a day. Otherwise nobody pays any attention to you. It took me a while to learn. One day the woman who was making the costumes came to me with a big tape measure, measured me, and then showed me the design of the costume intended for Madame Scotto. It was in gold and I felt that with my hair, silver would be much more suitable. Even though the original costume had already been cut and sewn, Nicola Benois, who designed both the sets and the costumes, agreed that silver was better and we both instructed the costume lady to redo the gown. *"Non si preoccupa, Signora,"* she said. "Don't worry about it." At the first dress rehearsal parade, a custom at La Scala, the ladies of the Costume Department marched across the stage holding up the costumes to spotlights to determine if there were any problems; there was my costume—still in gold. I reminded the lady—silver. *"Non si preoccupa,Signora."* On the day of the first piano dress rehearsal I walked into my dressing room and hanging on a hook was my costume—in gold. I took the costume, walked on stage, and asked the Technical Director to summon the costume lady. "Did I not tell you to make this costume in silver?" *Si, Signora.* "Did I not tell you four or five times to make this costume in silver?" *Oh, si, Signora.* I took the gold costume, folded it very carefully into a square, lifted a pair of scissors the costume lady had dangling around her neck, and slowly and deliberately I cut the costume in half. Then, with a smile, I said, "Now you go back upstairs and make the costume in silver."

The chorus broke into wild applause; they cheered as though I had just sung the most divine aria in the world. After the dress rehearsal I went upstairs to see Signor Luciano Chailly, who was then artistic director of La Scala. He smiled: "Well, we were all wondering when it was going to happen." "When what was going to happen?" "Well," he replied, "you're always so cheerful, you speak so softly, we kept wondering when is this lady who is so famous for her acting temperament, when are we going to see some of her temperament? Now we've seen it." "No," I said, "you haven't seen my temperament, you've just seen me temperamental. There's a big difference."

Marilyn Horne and I lived in excited anticipation of opening night of *The Siege of Corinth:* the opera suited us both vocally to a high C—of which we had plenty. I do not remember even being nervous, but Gigi Capobianco, who had accompanied me to Milan for the opening, says that I was—I forgot to wear my false eyelashes and played the whole opera without them. I don't think that any two female American singers performing together at La Scala ever equaled the success we had; the ovations were endless and I shall never forget them. Not that the public at La Scala is any more discerning than operagoers in the United States, who, I think, make up one of the most discriminating, intelligent audiences anywhere. But there is an undeniable unique mystique about singing at La Scala; the house has, after all, given world premières of, among other operas, *The Love of Three Kings, Andrea Chenier, La Gioconda, Madama Butterfly, Mefistofele, Otello, Turandot.* It is the historic "golden theater." I was very conscious of all the great singers who had appeared there before me; I was more than pleased to have joined their ranks. And I picked up three new names given me by the Milanese: *La Sills, La Fenomena* (which is self-evident), and "Il Mostro." The last title made me laugh: it means "The Incomparable One" but it can also mean "The Monster."

We gave six performances of the opera at La Scala. The production became known as The Siege of the Americans because the three leads and the conductor were all Americans—Marilyn, Justino Diaz, and I, and Tom Schippers. So triumphant was our reception by the Italian public that, probably for the first time in La Scala history, we even managed to beat the claque. The claque at La Scala is an evil, archaic bit of nonsense; with audiences as knowledgeable as they are today, I am amazed that all the great singers who have appeared there have not simply banded together and told the claque to go to hell. We had been warned by colleagues in the United States that the claque would make serious financial demands on all of us in view of the fact that we were Americans singing in *their* house. Sure enough, as soon as we arrived the head of the claque paid a visit to Maestro Schippers to make his pitch. Tom and the rest of us decided that the way to beat them was to join forces: each of us made a contribution of lira, put it all together in the same envelope, and handed it over as a group. It worked: it cost us each $25 for the entire run of the opera and after the opening night truimph the head of the claque knew that it was pointless to try to dun us again.

While we were still in Milan, *Newsweek* appeared with a cover story on me, pegged to the La Scala debut. During a five-day break between performances, when Peter and I were visiting Venice, a newspaper vendor, hawking the latest wares in the Piazza San Marco, recognized me from the picture on the *Newsweek* cover. Everywhere we went that afternoon the vendor followed, screaming at the top of his lungs, "Here's the woman on the cover of *Newsweek*, here's the woman." He peddled a lot of magazines and I made a lot of new friends; there were a great many Americans in the Piazza that day. It was my first experience with a phenomenon my husband has referred to many times since, my "recognition factor." I have, for example, Peter will say, a high recognition factor on the first floor of Bloomingdale's. That day in Venice he said, "You've certainly a high recognition factor in the Piazza San Marco."

On the plane returning home, Muffy, exhausted, was asleep across the aisle in Peter's lap. My mother and I were seated next to each other. "Well, Bubbles," she said, "now I feel we've done it all." That is exactly the way I felt.

In my dressing room at La Scala making up for my debut. On the table to my left is a small decorated egg that Miss Liebling, too ill to make the trip to Italy, gave me as a present.

Nervous? Who's nervous? In my hotel room in Milan I tootle away between rehearsals of
The Siege of Corinth.

Between performances at La Scala, Peter and I toured the countryside and, like all tourists, had our picture taken.

13

*Lucia,
or how to go mad
all over the world*

As a result of my La Scala success, and the *Newsweek* cover, I quickly received two more foreign assignments—one in the Philippines, the other in Naples, Italy. The sponsor of the six concerts I was booked to sing in the Philippines was Eugenio Lopez; he owned the Manila Electric Light Company as well as several newspapers and his brother was vice-president of the country.

I must say that Mr. Lopez and all those Filipinos know how to make a gal feel good. They booked the whole first-class section of an airplane just for Mama, Muffy, Peter, and me. When we arrived in Manila, there were eleven bodyguards waiting, our permanent escort. "Eleven bodyguards!" I marveled to Peter. "This is really the big time." Peter said: "Has it ever occurred to you that they feel we might actually need them?" At which point I grabbed Muffy and said, "You hold on to Mama's skirt and don't let go for the entire time we're here." The poor child was frightened half to death.

In addition to the bodyguards we had a large retinue—Mama and I were given our own hairdressers and private secretaries. The Filipinos have an interesting custom: if you admire something they are wearing, or anything in their homes, they will present it to you, usually right on the spot. It is a part of their natural generosity. Before we learned that custom we picked up quite a number of items! When I mentioned that I liked a particular fruit called a mangosteen that had been served on the plane, five hundred mangosteens were at our hotel door within a half-hour. When my husband admired a hand-embroidered shirt, he received twelve the next day. When I suggested to Mrs. Lopez that maybe I ought to have some gowns designed in Philippine fashion to wear for my concerts, she sent over her dress designer to make four beautiful beaded gowns for me—with shoes to match—and I was not permitted to pay for any of them. I admired a plate from the Ming Dynasty; I went home with it. My mother admired somebody's pearl ring; she went home with it. We had arrived in the Philippines with eight pieces of luggage; we left with seventeen, the additional nine pieces having been made to order for us.

At a dinner at the Presidential Palace given by the President and Mrs. Marcos, I decided to wear one of my Filipino gowns as an act of courtesy. Mrs. Marcos decided to wear one of her European gowns as an act of courtesy. Guess who looked prettier? Filipino styles are not meant to be worn by ladies as well endowed as I.

That entire stay in the Philippines was so luxurious, so surrounded by kindness that none of us will ever forget it. When it was time to leave, Muffy cried. Back in New York (we had moved there from Milton that summer) we were greeted by eighty-four cartons sitting on the white carpet in the middle of our empty apartment waiting to be unpacked. It was a hot August day and the air-conditioning was not working. I sat down on one of the cartons and cried and cried and cried, remembering all that luxury in the Philippines. The doorbell rang; it was my upstairs neighbor, Isaac Stern, with his fiddle. "Can I do something for you?" he asked. "Sit down with me on the carpet,"

I said, "and listen to me cry." We drank some wine together, I got over my doldrums and unpacked all those damned cartons. Peter, Muffy, and I had become New York apartment residents.

Not that I was ever there for any length of time. Early in 1970 I was invited to the Teatro San Carlo, in Naples. I was delighted: San Carlo has an even older tradition than La Scala and the opera would be *La Traviata*, with Alfredo Kraus singing Alfredo and Aldo Ceccato conducting.

Even the rehearsals were fun in the Neapolitan manner. The bass players were lined up against the back wall and Ceccato kept picking on one very fat one claiming that he wasn't playing neatly, not playing the right notes, and so on. This irritated the fat man no end: Italian musicians, the old saying goes, may not play all the notes right but they play the wrong notes with such heart. Finally the fat bass player could no longer stand Ceccato's criticism. He hoisted his enormous bass fiddle and stomped out, knocking down men, music stands, and music; it looked as though a tornado had swept through the orchestra pit. I burst out laughing. "What are *you* laughing at?" Ceccato asked me angrily. "I just feel sorry for him," I said. "Why couldn't he have played the flute, been skinny, and been nearer the door?"

Italians watch familiar operas like *Traviata* the way we watch soap operas: they know every word, every character, and they become as much a part of the performance as the singers themselves. After my second act plea, "*Amami, Alfredo,*" I left the stage as the audience applauded and went to my dressing room. It had been very hot and I was perspiring in rivulets. I took off the belt of my dress and my shoes and dabbed huge globs of white powder all over myself to try to dry off. Suddenly the door of my dressing room burst open and in rushed the head of the opera company. "Hurry, hurry, you've got to take a bow!" "What already? Have Alfredo and Germont finished the *Di Provenza* scene?" "No, no, the audience is still applauding your '*Amami.*' You've got to go out or they'll think you don't like them."

Taking bows *during* an act, stopping the action, is ridiculous. It will be the end of my career, I said, if I do. "Aha, Signora," he said, "*here* your career is just beginning!" So out I went, clutching my beltless dress, covered with great patches of white powder, and scrunching down so that the audience would not see that I was barefoot. Of course they saw and went wild. Next day the newspapers reported with a flourish: Before, I had owned La Scala, *now* I owned San Carlo. I am not usually a quoter of my own reviews but one in particular tickled me. "It took an American to teach us Italians how to sing *Traviata*."

Even the claque was a pleasant surprise. Its leader had come to visit me before the performance to make sure that I would remember his face and he had hovered around the opera house during rehearsals. But after the dress rehearsal, which was attended by the press as well as certain privileged citizens, he came to me and said, "Look, you're going to have such a big success I will just put on my dinner jacket and take some of my friends out for coffee after the performance." "Fine," I said, "my treat."

Lucia di Lammermoor had entered my repertoire at the City Opera in 1969 and in the next few years I found myself going mad all over the world —New York, London, Boston, Shreveport, Mexico City, Milan, San Francisco, Buenos Aires. It took me quite a while to work out my interpretation of Lucia. I went back to the original source, Sir Walter Scott's novel, *The Bride of Lammermoor.* As I play her now, she is not twenty-five, from a good family; she is more like a slightly older Juliet, vulnerable from the start, unaware of what is happening around her, a manic depressive entirely withdrawn from the real world. When we first began rehearsing the Mad Scene in New York, Tito Capobianco had a completely different idea from mine: he thought Lucia should exhibit more physical signs of madness— shakes, head rolling, and kicking feet. I tried it and fell to the floor, hysterical with laughter. So did Tito and that was the end of *that* version. It was Gigi Capobianco who made the suggestions to Tito for the Mad Scene in the successful City Opera production.

In Boston, Sarah Caldwell had ideas of her own for *Lucia*. In Sir Walter's novel Lucia stabs her husband thirty-eight times, so Sarah had my costume looking considerably more bloody than usual. For the Mad Scene she had built a ramp around the orchestra; she called it her "Hello, Dolly" ramp. Lucia's lucid moments were spent on the actual stage, but when she went mad she took to the ramp. It was a very effective production.

Opera, Rossini once said, is voice, voice, voice. He was wrong. Opera is music *and* drama. I'm prepared to sacrifice the beautiful note for the meaningful sound any time. Lucia, for example, has to sing a phrase, "This bloodless hand beckoned me into the well." What kind of noises, I wondered, would she be likely to hear from the specter? Normally it would be a wail with an embellishment. I took out the embellishment and substituted a chromatic scale, thus turning the sound into a short, not-very-musical wail. I did the same thing with Queen Elizabeth in *Devereux* when I felt the dramatic action called for her to shriek. I can make a pretty tone as well as anyone but there are times when the drama of a scene demands the opposite of a pretty sound. Take Tosca. In the first act she's consumed by jealousy; in the second act, by loathing. If the voice remains the same to portray both jealousy and loathing, then all the singer has done is let loose four thousand notes, got paid, and gone to bed.

I had opened the 1970 New York City Opera Season on February 19 with *Lucia di Lammermoor* and repeated it three days later. In the two nights between, I was in Boston singing *The Daughter of the Regiment* with Sarah Caldwell's company. It was a crazy marathon—commuting back and forth between New York and Boston, singing four performances in five nights of two different operas in two different cities. My Mad Scenes in Lucia were very, very realistic!

Poor Sarah! she was still looking for an opera house of her own. We performed *The Daughter of the Regiment* in the gymnasium of Tufts University. While we rehearsed, the track team was racing around the gym track doing its own rehearsing. The main dressing room was the women's locker room; mine was the men's locker room, and I made my entrance on stage through a back wall behind the basket on the basketball court.

Still, Sarah created another miracle. She turned the back wall of the gymnasium into a little village; all the locker-room doors became houses at different levels. Because there was no way of entering or exiting without being seen by the audience, Sarah used the audience as part of the action. People in the bleacher seats were given sheets of colored paper with instructions to please hold the sheets up when Miss Sills makes her final exit in the carriage up the center aisle. Everyone did so, right on cue, and all those sheets of paper added up to a most colorful French tricolor flag.

When I went to Milan to go mad again in *Lucia* later in 1970, it turned out to be the strangest engagement of my career. The *Lucia* that La Scala was doing was not a new production; it had been mounted the year before and was done with scrims, no scenery. The conductor, Maestro Nino Sanzogno, believed that every cadenza in the score La Scala was using had been written by Donizetti himself. Whenever I would sing a cadenza I had used somewhere else in the role, he would say, *Non è scritto cosi,* It's not written like that. If I asked to have a certain cut in the score restored, he would say, No, no, it is *tradizione* to make that cut. I have always found that when someone uses the word *tradizione* it means simply that about thirty years ago there was a singer who was unable to handle certain passages and so they were cut. And those sacrosanct cadenzas in the La Scala score, supposedly written by Donizetti himself, had actually been written, I learned later, by my teacher, Estelle Liebling, and had been brought to La Scala by Toti Dal Monte when she sang Lucia there. So much for *non è scritto cosi* and *tradizione.*

I did three performances of Lucia at La Scala—with three different tenors. Opening night, the tenor felt ill during the performance but finished up. I was not informed that he would be replaced the second night. When I walked on stage, going about my business, out came a dark-haired gentleman I had never seen before. He shook my hand on stage, introduced himself, and began singing. On the third night a new tenor emerged, wearing a red wig. He was so short that a good deal of his singing was aimed at my navel. On that night, too, I looked into the orchestra pit for the white-haired conductor of the first two performances; there instead was a bald head. No one had told me of the sudden switch in conductors—a dangerous move for *Lucia,* in which the conductor must be familiar with the singer's particular ornamentation and cues.

That whole experience at La Scala made me realize one thing: When La Scala puts on a special production (such as *The Siege of Corinth*), in which a great deal of care and love go into the selection of singers, conductor, stage designer, director, etc., they are unbeatable. When it does its regular repertory, however, it seems just an ordinary, rather provincial opera house, certainly not up to the overall quality of New York repertory opera. When I returned to New York, for my final Lucia of the season at the City Opera, it was like returning to paradise.

On April 15, 1970, at Philharmonic Hall in New York, I was asked to sing at a memorable occasion, the Salute to Pablo Casals, honoring his first visit to New York since 1964. During the first half of the program, while Rudolf Serkin was playing the piano and Leopold Stokowski conducting the orchestra, I sat next to Casals; his beautiful wife, Marta, had generously relinquished her seat so that I could chat with the Maestro. Suddenly I felt Casals patting me on the knee, then the thigh. "Look at that Stokowski," he said. "Look how young, how attractive, how strong he is." Then he smiled at me. "That's what happens," he said, "when you marry a young wife." I smiled back.

When Mr. Casals went on stage to conduct a piece he had written for one hundred cellos, Mr. Stokowski sat down next to me. Suddenly I felt *his* hand patting my knee, then my thigh. "Look at that marvelous Casals," Stokowski said to me. "So young, so strong, so virile. That's what happens when you marry a young wife." Stokowski, then eighty-eight, had married Gloria Vanderbilt in 1945 when he was sixty-three, she twenty, and the marriage lasted ten years. Casals was then ninety-three, his wife thirty-three; he had married her when she was twenty and he was eighty. I have often wondered whether those two incredible senior citizens had rehearsed the routine they did for me.

I was forty-one myself. What a late bloomer: that was the year I made my debut in New York as a recitalist. Miss Liebling was in the hospital and terribly disappointed that she could not attend. Actually she had been in failing health and unable to teach for several years; I visited her whenever I could, and she knew and approved of the fact that I was working with Roland Gagnon, an excellent voice coach. She would insist on attending all my premières. Peter would pick her up in a chauffeured limousine, tuck her in with a woolen blanket, and get her to the theater on time. I remember one night when she came to hear me do Marguerite in *Faust*. She was then ninety-one. Next morning at seven o'clock my telephone rang. It was Miss Liebling. "Beverly," she said sternly, "that trill in the Jewel Song was very sloppy and slow. I expect you over here by ten o'clock." I had to agree—the trill *had* been sloppy and slow. Exhausted as I was that morning after the performance, I got dressed, went to her studio, spent forty-five minutes with her, trilling, and when I walked out I had a damned good trill.

At the end of my debut recital in New York I gave a little speech to the audience: how fortunate I was to have had only one singing teacher in my entire career, to have been with Miss Liebling for thirty-four years. I explained that she was ill and that as a get-well present I would sing a Portuguese folk song that she had arranged and given me as a birthday present when I was ten.

Miss Liebling died September 25 of that year, eight months after the debut recital. Ever since, I have ended all my recitals with a brief eulogy to her followed by the little Portuguese song, whose last verse goes:

> Tell me why you bid me leave you,
> There are tears in your eyes.
> Tell me why you wish our parting.
> Is not my love worth more than sighs?

She was a remarkable lady. I miss her a great deal. I miss her humor, I miss the funny luncheons we used to have. And I miss her calling me "My Bev."

A considerably more bloody than usual Lucia, I take my bows with the rest of the principals in Sarah Caldwell's production of Lucia di Lammermoor. *Sarah is the lady on my right.*

Muffy and me in our dressing room at the New York City Opera after our performances in Lucia *in 1971. Muffy was making her debut as one of the candle bearers at my funeral in the final scene. When my "dead" body was being carried across the stage, my view of Muffy was blocked by one of the singers. "For God's sake," I hissed at him, "move your ass, I can't see my kid." He jumped and I was able to see Muffy. When that story was published, my mother phoned. "You didn't really say that, did you?" "Yes, I did." "I don't believe it," Mama said. "My baby doesn't use dirty words."*

154

Luciano Pavarotti and I pour it on in a scene from Lucia *at the San Francisco Opera.*

On our trip to the Philippines Muffy and I shoot the "rapids."

Rehearsing with Miss Liebling in her apartment-studio not long before her death at ninety-one.

Opposite: Those two virile senior citizens, Pablo Casals and Leopold Stokowski, at the Salute to Pablo Casals concert in New York in April 1970.

14

*Off on a Queen kick—
a Bette Davis
with high notes*

As Queen Elizabeth I.

Queen Elizabeth I in Donizetti's *Roberto Devereux* first entered my consciousness as a possible role in 1965, when Tito Capobianco showed me a score of the opera. I was not familiar with it, and when Julius Rudel asked me after *Julius Caesar* to start thinking of what else I would like to do, Donizetti's Queen didn't cross my mind—I wanted to play Manon and Lucia too badly. But two years later, while on a trip to Europe, I found a score of *Devereux* in the Donizetti Museum in Bergamo, Italy, and on the plane home I read the libretto. At one point in it Queen Elizabeth says to Devereux, Earl of Essex: "It would have been better for you to incite the wrath of the gods than to incite the wrath of the descendant of the terrible Henry VIII." I got goosebumps and I said to Peter on the plane, "This is really a Bette Davis role with high notes. Now, if I could only find a tenor who looks like Errol Flynn!"

Julius Rudel had agreed that he would mount a new production of

Devereux for me. "By the way," he asked, "have you looked into any of the other Donizetti operas?" "Like what?" I asked. "Well, take a look at *Anna Bolena* and *Maria Stuarda*." "What are we going to do," I asked, "go on a queen kick?" Fateful words: that is exactly what we went on.

Roberto Devereux kicked off the trilogy of queens in October, 1970. The cast was phenomenal. Placido Domingo played Essex, and he did look like Errol Flynn; I played Bette Davis. Louis Quilico was Nottingham and Beverly Wolff was Sara. Julius conducted and the production team was the same as for those other memorable premières—*Julius Caesar, Le Coq d'Or, Lucia*—with the Capobiancos, Jose Varona doing my costumes, Ming Cho Lee the sets. All the ingredients were right.

My preparations for the role of Queen Elizabeth were enormous. I like to play characters who really lived because so much has been written about them. I read extensively about Elizabeth's life, about her physical appearance, from my own quite large collection of books on the Elizabethan period. She was a multifaceted lady and consequently, fascinating to play.

Gigi Capobianco created my makeup. She fashioned a bald pate made of latex to go over my own hair and painted my face chalk-white, slashed with heavy dark lines. The whole effect was remarkable, especially when lighting turned the black lines into the cracks and crevasses of an old woman's face. Because Elizabeth had been extremely vain about her hands and gesticulated with them a great deal, Gigi painted my hands with white paint, outlining the fingers in black to make them look slimmer. Originally I played the role with a putty nose—Gigi thought my own nose was too small for Elizabeth's—but when I perspired during the performance the nose would always fall off by the end of Act II, a most unregal sight. We decided instead to make my nose bigger with shadows.

My costumes were designed after paintings of Elizabeth in the National Portrait Gallery in London and in Woburn Abbey. The costume I wore in the second act weighed fifty-five pounds and was much too heavy to be lifted over my head, which already bore a wig and attached crown. Instead, the costume would be spread out in the middle of a room, held upright by its own beaded weight; then I would step into it and two people would hoist it to my waist and hook it on. After the dress rehearsal my shoulders were covered with great bruises from the weight of the gown. My friend, Grace Miceli, of Grace Costumes, then devised a system of supporting strings inside to transfer the weight from my shoulders to my waist.

Converting me from Bubbles into Queen Elizabeth took more than two hours. In the years when I was playing both her and Manon in repertory I liked to point out that it took two and a half hours to make me up as Elizabeth in her sixties and only a half-hour to turn me into a seventeen-year-old Manon. Now it's the other way round: half-an-hour to make me a sixty-year-old, and two and a half hours to become a teenager. That's the way the cooky crumbles.

Tito Capobianco's staging was brilliant. Elizabeth's throne dominated the opera and he had designed it to be a haven for her. Whenever she felt threatened, whenever Essex was behaving in a displeasing way, she would retreat to her throne, heavily, an embittered old woman. The weight of my costume was a great help in getting the proper walk, and Gigi and I spent hours working on gestures. In one scene Elizabeth takes Essex's hand, points to the ring she has given him, and reminds him imperiously that the ring bears words spoken by kings. Elizabeth's attitude when she lifts Essex's hand and points to the ring with royal insignia, Gigi said, must convey to Essex Elizabeth's implied warning: Don't behave like a beggar. The key to the success of my characterization of Elizabeth lay in small touches of that kind.

There were times during performances of Elizabeth when I got completely carried away. In Act II, the Queen, in anger, slaps Essex's face. Gigi was always in my dressing room to remind me at the last minute that, before whacking Essex, I must make sure I switched rings from my right to my left hand; otherwise I would murder the tenor. One night she forgot to remind me and I forgot to remember. As I approached Essex to slap him, he noticed the big knuckle-bending rings still on my right hand—and he became the most frightened tenor who ever strode a stage. At the last minute, I remembered the rings and slapped him with my palm rather than the usual back-of-the-hand. He was so relieved that he claimed later he never felt the slap. Another tenor said that he was unable to hear a thing for two days after I had slapped *him*. And a third I once hit so hard that his mustache almost wound up as a third eyebrow. There were nights when Act II was so exciting that I completely forgot there was a tenor in front of me; I thought he was Errol Flynn and really wanted to let him have it.

The role of Elizabeth, I think, done properly, is the most taxing in the entire soprano *bel canto* repertoire. (Donizetti must have realized that too: although he keeps the Queen on stage throughout Act II, he at least provides scenes in other acts that do not involve her, so that she gets a chance to recuperate.) One cannot sing the role and come out of it unscarred vocally and emotionally. At least I cannot: I have lost as much as eight pounds during performances of Elizabeth.

They have been worth every pound. On opening night, when I came out for my bows at the end of Act II, the audience rose and applauded—the first time in my career that I had been given a standing ovation in the middle of an opera. I was very touched; no, more than that—I was ecstatic because I felt that the audience and I had just shared a marvelous experience.

Although Cleopatra in *Julius Caesar* was the turning point in my career, I think that Elizabeth is my finest accomplishment. I am proud of her, the first of my three Donizetti queens. To complete the trilogy—*Maria Stuarda* and *Anna Bolena*—would take another two years. But for now I was Queen Elizabeth and I hoped to continue to portray her to the end of my career. I really love that old lady.

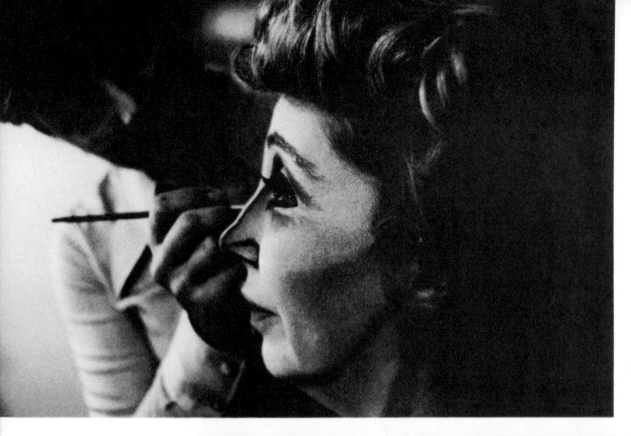

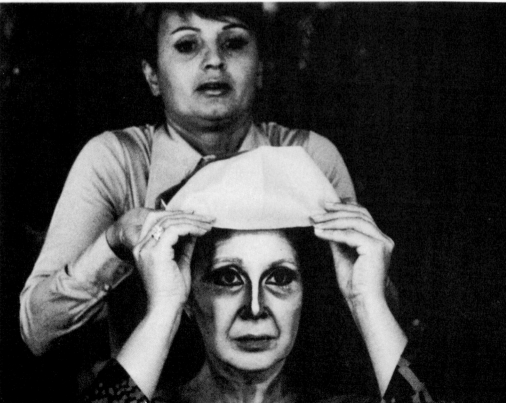

162

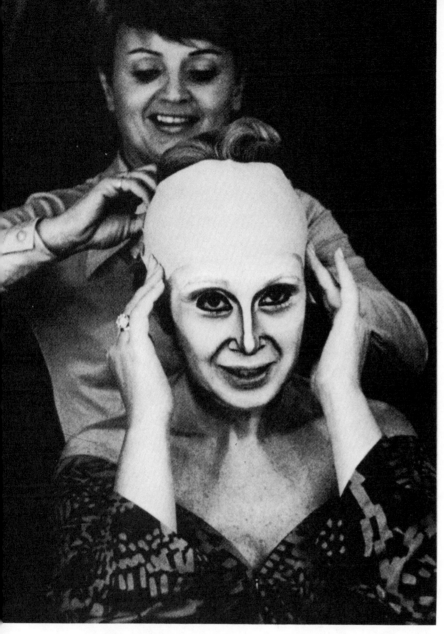

Gigi Capobianco goes to work to turn me into a sixty-year-old Queen of England. First she brushes in the black streaks to age my face (opposite, top), then carefully stretches a bald pate made of latex over my own hair (left and above). Add a wig, costume jewels, and crown and the transformation (right) from Beverly to Elizabeth Regina is complete.

Roberto Devereux, *Act II: Queen Elizabeth*
stands before her throne to denounce
Devereux, Lord Essex (Placido Domingo,
right foreground). In close-up above,
Elizabeth is just about to whack Essex's face
for his craven behavior.

15

Nicolai Gedda and me in Manon.

*Moments when I deserve
to be where I am*

For a gal who had not sung outside the United States until 1967, I was certainly making up for it now. In January 1971 alone I sang three times in London, Berlin and Paris. I made my debut at London's Royal Opera at Covent Garden in *Lucia di Lammermoor* over the Christmas–New Year holidays of 1970. Three hundred twenty-four friends of the City Opera chartered a flight to attend that debut, and when the Mad Scene was over the stage was covered with congratulatory flowers. This antagonized some of the British press; they took great pleasure in referring to me as "Miss America, Superstar." But the British public liked me and the Covent Garden management was very solicitous.

With some reason: conditions for *prima donna*s were rather spartan, to put it mildly. The dressing rooms were small, the backstage chilly, and there was no heat in the bathroom, or the "loo" as the British call it. Birgit Nilsson, Margot Fonteyn, and I were alternating nights, and whenever I opened the closet of our common dressing room there, hanging up would be three simple woolen bathrobes; all that was needed to complete the picture was felt slippers. When you open your dressing room closet at the Met, say, or the New York State Theatre, it contains elaborate silky caftans in which you greet your fans after a performance. One night John Tooley, general administrator of Covent Garden, came backstage to inquire if there was anything they could do for me. "Yes," I said, "you can warm up the seat in the loo. It is the coldest thing I have ever put my backside on." He thought it was funny —I guess—but the seat never was warmed up.

Between performances of *Lucia* at Covent Garden, I flew to Berlin to sandwich in a *Traviata* at the Berlin Opera. Berlin was a very sad city. When I toured it with Egon Seefehlner, the head of the Berlin Opera (he is now head of the Vienna State Opera), he said, "You know, I'm probably the oldest thing in Berlin today." I understood what he meant: the city had been so destroyed during the war and then so rebuilt that everything in it seemed new. There was no stage director for my Berlin engagement; the management figured that this was just a revival, I was to do a *Gastspiel* and all I had to manage was my regular Violetta. Even Lorin Maazel, the conductor, felt at first that because we both knew the opera so well we needed no real rehearsing. "Let's have a good time," he said, "and see what happens."

As much as I admire spontaneity in a performance, I felt that we should have *some* rehearsal time, so we spent a delightful half-hour putting our *Traviata* together. It made me realize that "instant opera" exists in Europe, even in the important houses, as well as in the United States. Opera stars would be flown in on a few hours' notice to be plunked into a performance without preparation, without rehearsal. In our country, fortunately, that is now being done away with. Impresarios are demanding, and rightly so, that sufficient preparation time be allowed for their productions. Some are even fining artists for arriving late for rehearsals—up to $500 per day. That is a marvelous idea. I have always been a fanatic about showing up on time for rehearsals and I resent being kept waiting by late-comers.

On to Paris from Berlin for my debut there—an orchestral concert at the Salle Pleyel, conducted by John Pritchard, who was conducting my Lucias at Covent Garden. If I do say so myself, I tore Paris apart—audience, reviews, everything was *formidable*. It helped, of course, that I was very much at home with the language; I announced my encores in French. The French they are a funny race, but they do prefer people who can speak their language well.

Covent Garden, Berlin, Paris—they had all been satisfying, but my prevailing feeling had been that of homesickness. This was, after all, the holiday season, and even though my mother, Muffy, and Peter had come over for my London debut, it was not the same as spending the holidays at home. I made a promise to myself that never again would I be working away from home and family during the holiday season. Since then I have also made a promise to Peter never to sing in Europe again, because I don't want to be separated from my family for long periods. If I have any regrets about that decision, it is not being able to sing in Paris.

Shortly before that European tour, President Nixon had appointed me a member of the Council on the National Endowment for the Arts, and in February I was invited to sing at the White House. In the middle of the concert the zipper on my gown broke. Luckily Mrs. Nixon had suggested that I wear a dress with a matching cloak, because the room in the White House was rather drafty. When the zipper popped, I walked off to find the matching cloak to cover my gaposis. "My Walter Mitty dream," I apologized to the audience, "just popped in the form of a zipper on the back of my dress." Then I finished the program. The whole audience had seen the zipper popping and the talon flying. The papers, naturally, had a good time with it the next day.

Mr. Nixon was a solicitous host and I enjoyed Mrs. Nixon immensely. She invited me to bring my daughter Muffy for a private tour of the White House and Muffy and I did go back. Rather than disturb Mrs. Nixon, I phoned her secretary and asked her *not* to tell her that we were coming. But just as we began our tour, Mrs. Nixon spotted us and insisted on being our tour guide. When it was over, Mrs. Nixon gave Muffy a piece of her daughter Tricia's wedding cake, all wrapped up. Muffy will never forget that day.

I have lost my temper on stage in public only once in my life—in San Francisco on April 30, 1971. I had been invited to sing a recital, not in the opera house but in the Masonic Auditorium. The acoustics were impossible: when I turned my head to the left, Charles Wadsworth, my accompanist, could not hear me, but I had to turn my head to the left because the sound of the piano bouncing off the right side of the auditorium was driving me crazy. Seats had been sold on stage for the concert, and in the middle of one of my Handel arias a little old lady had to go to the bathroom so off she went, down the stage stairs and out of the auditorium. I had prepared a very elaborate, difficult program. Six months' work shot to hell, I began thinking, and just popped my cork. I made a speech saying that it was the worst hall I had ever sung in and that I would never sing in it again. The press, of course, chastised me severely; *other* singers had appeared there and managed. Nevertheless, I have kept that promise. Neither singer nor public should be subjected to such atrocious conditions.

Up to that point in my career I had never sung Bellini's *Norma*. Then, in June of 1971, I gave my first performance of the role in Boston, in a production directed and conducted by Sarah Caldwell. I felt at the time, and still do, that Norma is not a very difficult role. The vocal range is not particularly high, the makeup is easy, the costumes light. Physically, then, it is not exhausting; as Birgit Nilsson would say, all you need is a comfortable pair of shoes. Indeed, I perform Norma in my sandals.

The production was a huge success. Sarah's theory was that one of the reasons the Druids had made Norma their priestess was that she looked different and behaved differently from the rest of them. She decided that I would play Norma as an albino, with a pure white wig. At her first entrance she was to go into a kind of trance.

I was quite concerned about that first entrance—how to convince the audience immediately that Norma was subject to epileptic seizures and different from the rest of the Druids in that way too. I practiced for days trying to get it right. One night after rehearsal I went back to the hotel, kicked Peter out of the bedroom, and practiced epileptic fits until two A.M. I must have done something right: at the rehearsal the next day the fit I threw was so convincing that several stagehands, thinking I was really ill, rushed over to help me stand up.

There are some lines in *Norma* that always make me want to giggle. Here is this woman who has betrayed her people by falling in love with the enemy, a Roman proconsul, and secretly having two children by him. At one point her lover, Pollione, turns to the chorus after Norma has confessed her treachery and sings, "Don't believe her, don't believe her." Norma sings back, "Norma never lies." That's one of my favorite lines. In another scene she tells Adalgisa, her rival for Pollione's affections, that she, Adalgisa, must take Norma's two children to Pollione and marry him. Well, what about you? the rival asks. Norma: You marry him and I will just kill myself. Instead of reacting in horror to the idea of Norma committing suicide, Adalgisa says, You want *me* to marry him? For me it is one of the classic funny moments in operatic drama.

I returned to London later that year to record *Maria Stuarda*, the second queen in Donizetti's trilogy. In the cast were Eileen Farrell, Louis Quilico, and Stuart Burrows—three singers with the same propensity for uninhibited laughter that I have. No recording session went by without some moment of hilarity. To sing with Eileen is one of the great joys of my life. We have exactly the same attitude toward singing: have a good time, otherwise stay home in bed. She had brought her daughter Kathy with her, I had brought Muffy, and we used to spend every singing and nonsinging hour together. My husband took his harem—Eileen, Kathy, Muffy, and me—all over London, wining and dining, and I have never enjoyed the city as much. Eileen's laugh and mine echoing through the restaurants and museums of London is still mind-boggling; we must have attracted a lot of attention. I wish that Eileen and I could find more projects to record.

Seventeen years after I made my first appearance with the San Francisco Opera, I returned to sing another opera—*Manon*, with Nicolai Gedda as Des Grieux. I was high with anticipation: to appear in an opera I considered my own in a production made to order for me by my director, Tito, and surrounded by all the glamorous brouhaha of a triumphant return— what a way to erase all those sad memories of my first visit in 1953! It *was* a beautiful *Manon*. In the St. Sulpice Monastery scene, where Manon persuades Des Grieux to renounce the priesthood for her, a hush fell over the audience, that unique silence which occurs when people hardly dare breathe. When we finished the final *"Je t'aime"* duet, a roar went up unlike any I had ever heard before. Oh, perhaps at the end of an opera filled with blood and guts, but this was a quiet scene with just two people on a dimly lit stage. Nicolai and I ran off stage together, locked in embrace. My feet never touched the ground. Moments like these are what have made my career important to me. These are the moments when I return to my dressing room and say, "Okay, I deserve to be where I am."

Two scenes from my first Norma, *a Sarah Caldwell production of the Boston Opera Company in June 1971.*

With the Nixons at the White House in 1971—
scene of my zipper-popping incident.

My first concert—1971—with The Chamber
Music Society of Lincoln Center, which is headed
by my regular accompanist, Charles Wadsworth.
I don't know why Charlie is holding his head;
he says it's because of me.

174

My return—after seventeen years—to the San Francisco Opera Company to do Manon with Nicolai Gedda as Des Grieux. I know that I will never sing Manon with a better tenor than Nicolai, and that's no mean compliment.

The hours
are long,
but there are
fringe benefits

Getting stitched up in the Metropolitan Opera costume department for my debut as Pamira in The Siege of Corinth

Scenes from my Met debut, April 8, 1975. Harry Theyard (who plays my father), I as Pamira, and Justino Diaz as Maometto, who wants to marry me, sing a trio at the end of Act I (above). At left, Shirley Verrett, who plays the male role of Neocle who also wants to marry me, and I watch the rehearsal from off stage. The dress rehearsal (without wigs) of the scene in which I agree to marry Maometto is at the top of the opposite page. And at right, in actual performance, I'm singing my second-act aria.

Rehearsing the final scene of The Siege of Corinth. *Behind me on the right is director Sandro Sequi and the chorus.*

Upstaging my friend Bob Merrill in the Met lobby. When I was eleven and he twenty-one, in 1940, we sang on a radio program with the Morton Gould Orchestra.

Relaxing off-stage with some of the on-stage men in my life: Tenor Harry Theyard munches an apple and listens to me at the same time (above) during a rehearsal break at the Met. Top left, Norman Treigle and I dressed in our Julius Caesar *outfits backstage at the New York City Opera. Left, Justino Diaz and me in my dressing room during* The Siege of Corinth.

A typical off-stage pose—hunched on the bed in the master bedroom of our New York City apartment overlooking Central Park, phone at my ear, my five-year-calendar book at the ready for further entries. The tapestry on the wall is a Siamese one that Peter bought me.

◀ The Greenough dolls, Beverly and Muffy, do their mechanical-doll number during a visit Muffy paid me at the City Opera during a performance of The Tales of Hoffmann.

At home confronting my bedroom mirror:
"Mirror, mirror on the wall,
Is this my favorite role of all?"

16

*"When will you stop
this marathon?"*

My father was a Romanian Jew who emigrated to this country with his family when he was a baby. My mother was a Russian Jew, born in Odessa. There she went to a school run by nuns, the only school in the village, and she likes to recall the many times that the nuns, who specialized in making and selling pickles, used to stuff her and the other Jewish girls into empty pickle barrels to protect them from marauding Cossacks. She came to the United States, via Yokohama, when she was fourteen.

In Brooklyn, we Silvermans were a typical middle-class American Jewish family. I had never considered myself anything but an American Jew, but, like most Jews, I had considerable curiosity about Israel. When I was invited to sing there in 1970 for the first time, with the Israeli Philharmonic Orchestra, my mother said, "Fine, but do the concerts for free. No nice Jewish girl takes any money out of Israel." The manager of the Philharmonic, Abe Cohen, was naturally delighted at the news that I would contribute my services. I was supposed to sing eight performances of a concert version of *The Abduction from the Seraglio,* with Julius Rudel guest conducting. While strolling through the streets of Tel Aviv, I kept noticing program posters announcing my concerts—my name in English, all the rest in Hebrew, which I cannot read. My name seemed to be showing up more times than eight. "Abe," I asked, "what's with all these concerts? I agreed to sing eight." "Don't worry about it," he said. "It's fourteen." "Fourteen! How come?" "Well," Abe replied, "the price was right."

Fourteen it was—I wound up singing every other day for a month. The Israelis had provided us with a chauffeur as well as a lovely guest house, and on my nonsinging days we all went sightseeing—Mama, Muffy, Peter, and I. It was Christmas–New Year's again, 1971; if we could not be in our own home at least we would be together. It turned out to be the best of all possible worlds. Our cast included a black tenor, George Shirley, a WASP soprano, Pat Wise, and an Armenian bass, Ara Berberian—a nice mixture of races, colors, and religions. The children got presents on Chanukah and on Christmas, and two holiday feasts with appropriate ethnic meals to match. They loved it.

One night Peter and I went to the Wailing Wall, the sacred wall in Jerusalem where men pray at one end, women at the other. Peter moved closer to the men's section of the wall to get a better view. I didn't know what to do—join the ladies or just stand there. It had begun to drizzle. Then I felt a tugging on the Spanish cape I was wearing. It was a tiny old lady. In a thick accent (I learned later she was a United States citizen who had settled in Tel Aviv) she said: "Nu? You're not going to pray? You've got nothing to pray for?" "Yeah," I said, "I've got something to pray for." "Then come, I'll show you a spot, you rub the spot, talk to God, and you'll walk away from the Wall laughing."

As we were walking to the women's section of the Wall, she stopped and looked at me again. I had no hat and Jews at prayer must have some sort of covering on their head. "Nu?" she said. "You've got nothing to cover your hair?" Then she dug into her shopping bag and pulled out a facial tissue about four inches square. "Here, cover your head with this." At the Wall she took my hand, placed it on a particular stone, and said, "Now rub, talk to God. You'll see, you'll walk away laughing." I rubbed the stone, said a few personal things to God, and suddenly I burst out laughing. There I was, standing in the rain with a piece of paper on my head, draped in a long black Spanish cape, wearing high boots, standing next to a four-foot-tall old lady, rubbing an ancient stone and talking to God. It *had* to be the funniest sight in the world and so I had to laugh. The little old lady looked up at me, in triumph. "See?" she said. "I told you you'd walk from here laughing."

I still consider myself an American Jew but now I feel a strong emotional tie with the Israelis. They are an incredibly brave people living in a wonderful country. While we were there we visited some of my father's relatives who had moved from Romania to Israel and that gave me a feeling of having roots there too. I made up my mind then that I would do everything I could to help Israel survive. And I told Peter—teasingly—that if he should ever convert to Judaism, it will have to be before the highest menorah in history.

After that Israel trip I returned to the United States to do some more *Norma*s and then, in Philadelphia with Luciano Pavarotti, my first *I Puritani*. I decided, before Luciano and I went on stage, that we had better straighten one thing out. I get intensely involved dramatically when I sing; Luciano has a glorious golden-toned tenor but is inclined to be somewhat less involved dramatically. He has been known on occasion, after an aria or a particularly successful duet, to bow and acknowledge the applause of the audience. In *I Puritani* the characters Luciano and I were to portray—Arturo and Elvira—are so difficult to make plausible to the audience that I felt any break in the flow or mood would be disastrous.

"Luciano," I said, "*no* bows during the acts. When we finish our Act III duet, that Philadelphia house is going to come down and the applause will go on and on. But NO bows." "Oh, Bevelina," he said, "one little bow doesn't hurt." "NO bows," I said. "*I'm* not going to break to bow, and if I see you start to break, I'll walk right in front of you and throw my arms around you."

The house, of course, did go nuts at the duet. Luciano and I were standing in a kind of semiembrace. He was looking at me pleadingly: A little bow, just a little bow. As he started to break, I threw my arms around him. He, not to be cheated out of his moment, pushed the sleeve of my gown off the shoulder, buried his head in my neck, and began nuzzling. He was having a good time nibbling at my neck, I was giggling because he was tickling me, and the audience ate it up. They applauded for fifteen minutes.

It is a joy working with Luciano. He is a big teddy bear of a tenor, always cheerful. He wears tiny French berets and enormous wide ties. On the road he always takes a hotel apartment with a kitchen; he loves to cook for parties, and if he invites you and four other people for dinner, he always has enough food for thirty and, sure enough, thirty show up. We did a *Lucia* later that year in San Francisco which the newspapers called "historic." But it is that first night of *I Puritani* in Philadelphia I will remember. Which of us won the battle I don't know, but we certainly knew each other better after that performance!

Maria Stuarda premièred at the New York City Opera on March 7, 1972. I now had two of my three Donizetti queens in repertoire. Of the three, Mary Stuart is easiest to sing—she appears in only half the opera, the first half being dominated by Elizabeth I—and I enjoy her the least. Donizetti did not portray her the way I feel Mary Stuart must have been. Unlike Elizabeth I and Anne Boleyn, she supposedly was a woman who ruled with her heart rather than her head. And yet Donizetti never wrote a single love scene for her; he makes Leicester more a friend and adviser than Mary's lover. As a result, you never feel that Mary is a truly passionate woman. Too bad, because John Stewart, who played Leicester in the City Opera production, is a very tall, handsome tenor.

Tito Capobianco staged the opera beautifully, especially Mary's death scene. I wore a red gown as I knelt at the chopping block. The masked executioner raised his sword, and as it swished down the stage went completely black. It was very effective: on opening night the audience gasped and one woman yelled out, "No, no!"

It was a relief to play Mary Stuart in my own hair and with my own face. It was also fun to portray Elizabeth one night and Mary a few nights later. In between, just to keep my sense of humor, I would fly to Shreveport or to San Antonio to bat out a fast *Daughter of the Regiment.* That same touring production of *Daughter* has played in more than fifteen cities and is always successful. The time has come: unless regional opera companies begin to share their productions, they are likely to go bankrupt. Opera companies should get together, agree on a single opera to do, and then have one stage designer prepare a production suitable for all their houses. It would save them all a fortune and opera would not be the expensive art form it is today, with every house trying to design its own production of the same operas. More and more companies in this country are beginning to work this way, starting with Houston and San Diego. It has worked with *The Daughter of the Regiment* and it has worked with Sarah Caldwell's production of *La Traviata.*

By now I was beginning to realize that I no longer enjoyed traveling so much, especially abroad. My life was turning into a rather lonely existence, the separations from my family longer and longer. Muffy, thirteen, was in school and even during summer vacations she didn't really want to travel with me; she preferred camp. My two stepdaughters were in college, leading their own lives. Even Peter was not particularly keen on following me around the world. He had his own interests, his own business projects, his own friends. He enjoyed going to Martha's Vineyard and urged me to agree to his buying land there and building a house. I felt it would be a waste of time and money—we would never be there enough. "Why not?" Peter would argue with me. "Why will we never be there? Why shouldn't we be there? When will you begin to slow down? When will you stop this marathon?"

The questions went unanswered, the property went unbought, and the marathon continued.

That year I was invited by the March of Dimes to become the National Chairman of the Mothers' March on Birth Defects. Theater people are always being asked to be honorary chairman of this or that; you're assured that it will not take your time or money, just your name on a letterhead. That approach, frankly, has always turned me off: if I cannot participate in an organization, giving either time or money, then why bother? Peter and I had long since decided that we would participate only in causes that directly concerned retarded or deaf children. When the March of Dimes approached me to help raise funds, to make speeches, and to talk to mothers with similar problems with children, I agreed.

Birth defects are very democratic: they strike everyone alike, irrespective of race, color, religion, and social or financial status. But *having* children with birth defects is a unique experience. Someone who has not shared that experience might put his arm around you and say, "Well, I know exactly how you feel." But he does not and he cannot. Only the parent of a child with a birth defect can talk nose-to-nose with a parent of a similarly afflicted child. I had never really talked much publicly before about my own children. It is the kind of situation in which you're damned if you do and damned if you don't. Some people think that if you talk about birth defects in your children you are trying to capitalize on their tragedy; others think that if you don't talk about your children you must be ashamed of them. I happen to be very proud of my children, and I felt that if by talking about them, I could help other parents in similar situations, then speaking out for the March of Dimes would definitely be worthwhile.

I also feel strongly that it is every child's birthright to be born healthy. We are so busy worrying about our future—men on the moon, solar energy, atomic energy—but our future is really our children and the simple truth is that we do not yet know how to guarantee a pregnant woman that her child will be born perfectly beautiful and beautifully perfect. If I could encourage people to give more money so that children in the future would no longer be born with congenital defects, that too was worth my time.

The job with the March of Dimes has been one of the most rewarding in my life. I have visited child-care centers and hospitals where I saw scores of children with birth defects. I have talked with their mothers. I have met people whose lives are devoted to helping mothers produce healthy babies. As National Chairman of the Mothers' March on Birth Defects since 1972, I am proud and gratified that I have helped raise more than fifty million dollars. It has been as satisfying as anything I have done in my opera career.

Peter and me on our first trip to Israel, in 1970. We are standing in front of the huge menorah that dominates the landscape opposite the Knesset, Israel's parliament.

On a Mike Douglas show in 1971 Burt Lancaster and I yack it up. I was co-host on the show.
Earlier, when I was in Los Angeles doing a Manon, *Burt, a great opera lover,*
came backstage and invited me to lunch. He wanted to make a movie of me as Manon.
"No way," I said, "I'll never let a camera close in on these wrinkles." "Don't be ridiculous,"
said Burt. "We could photograph you through gauze." "Gauze?" I replied, "You'd have to
photograph me through linoleum *before I'd consent to make a movie!"*

At the JFK Center for the Performing Arts, in Washington, Tito Capobianco and I relax during the intermission of Handel's Ariodante, *in September 1971. When Julius Rudel first proposed the unfamiliar opera to me, I suggested that we should call it* Oreodante, *since the two key roles were to be played by black singers and I felt like an Oreo cookie. The casting was changed: my lover in the opera was played by Tatiana Troyanos.*

Two dramatic scenes from Maria Stuarda: *Mary Stuart calls Queen Elizabeth a bastard. Whether that confrontation ever took place is doubtful but it certainly was an exciting moment histrionically. Below, Mary Stuart's execution, beautifully staged by Tito Capobianco. In front of me is the chopping block. The executioner raises his sword, starts to swing it down, and then—*BLACKOUT!

In April 1972, as National Chairman of the Mothers' March on Birth Defects for the March of Dimes, I visited that organization's Birth Defects Center at the University of Washington Medical School, in Seattle, Washington.

You ain't never sung with an exciting conductor unless you've sung with Zubin Mehta—as I'm doing here in November 1971 at a Celebrity Pops Concert in Los Angeles. That man can whip an orchestra—and a singer—into an unbelievable frenzy and he almost knocked me off the stage. We had the time of our lives, that moment when two artists meld into one.

17

God save the Queen— with Duco cement

As Anne Boleyn in Donizetti's Anna Bolena.

*A*nna Bolena, my third and final Donizetti queen, went into the City Opera's repertoire in the fall of 1973. It almost did not: the musicians were on strike, and by the time the strike was settled we had exactly six days to mount the production. Some critics have written that the opera is one of those neglected masterpieces that deserves to be neglected. I don't agree. When I play Anna, I bear in mind that she was the mother of Elizabeth I (who appears briefly in the opera as a child). For me, Anna is like a high-strung thoroughbred horse, skittish, independent and unpredictable. Not until the final marvelous Mad Scene do I allow her to become soft and vulnerable. In one scene I give Henry VIII a resounding whack in the face. During rehearsal someone suggested that that was wrong, that Anna would never dare slap the face of her sovereign for fear of being beheaded. Well, I replied, she *was* beheaded, wasn't she? I won the right to slap the king. It may not have been historically correct but it was certainly dramatically sound.

Bizarre things are always happening on stage during opera performances, but I think that one mishap during a performance of *Anna Bolena* made some kind of history. As a result of an automobile accident in my teens, two of my side teeth had caps on them. One night as I was singing the two caps flew out. Henry VIII (Bob Hale) was just about to step on them (which would have meant the end of *my* performance, at least) when I grabbed the caps from beneath his heel. It was such a close thing that he skinned my knuckles. He, of course, was unaware of what had happened and when I pushed him back he could not understand why I had suddenly become so violent. Turning my back on the audience, I jammed the caps back on and finished the first act. During the intermission, Gigi Capobianco came up with Duco cement and we cemented the two caps in place. It worked fine. The only problem was that the next day the dentist had to use a hammer and chisel to remove them so that he could replace them properly.

Earlier that year my husband Peter had won his argument about Martha's Vineyard; we had bought some property and were building a summer home. One morning when I was in San Francisco to sing *Traviata*, the phone rang in the hotel. It was Peter: "Honey, something terrible has happened." My God, I thought, the children! Then Peter went on to report that our new house on Martha's Vineyard, which we were scheduled to move into in two days, had just been burned down by arsonists. I was so relieved, I began to giggle. It was only seven o'clock and I was still groggy. I knew that was not the reaction he was expecting so I said, "Listen, let me wash my face and brush my teeth and I'll call you back." When I did, I explained the giggle—the overwhelming relief I felt that the bad news was not the children but just the house. Houses, after all, can be rebuilt; we rebuilt ours in nine months—making all the same mistakes. But it is our dream house and we love it.

January 1974 was a typical month in a singer's life—at least this singer's. Recitals in Pittsburgh, Hartford, New Rochelle, Chicago, San Francisco, Denver, Columbus; three *Traviata*s in Houston; a benefit concert in Albany, New York, for the Lake George Opera Company; a couple of concerts with the Milwaukee Symphony. I was still a gal who couldn't say no; I could shake my head north-south with no trouble, but east-west was a problem.

We opened the New York City Opera Spring Season in February with the new production of *I Puritani* that we had premièred on tour in Los Angeles a month before. I have always maintained that opera productions do not have to cost hundreds of thousands of dollars; all they really need are imaginative directors and stage designers. We had them. Tito Capobianco came up with the idea for, and Carl Toms designed, three ramps that moved on a trolley carrying the assorted painted backdrops, and every time there was a scene change the audience applauded their ingenuity. Toms's costumes were also a vision. My own reviews were unqualified raves, almost as though I had written them myself.

It seems unbelievable to me now, considering all the *Traviata*s I had sung all over the world, that I had not sung a Violetta with the New York City Opera since 1963. Eleven years later I got another completely unscheduled chance. On March 20 the scheduled opera was to be *Medea* but the soprano who sings Medea was ill and Julius decided to substitute *La Traviata*. The only trouble with that decision was that Patricia Brooks, who usually sings Violetta, was off on another engagement. At one P.M. that day, Julius Rudel phoned: would I do it, just for him? He knew that I had sung two Anna Bolenas the week before and was due to sing *I Puritani* the next night. "Let me see if my curls are set," I replied. By three o'clock they were set and my costumes pressed; by five, I was in the opera house.

The 1974 City Opera production of *Traviata* had premièred the same year (1966) as *Julius Caesar* but I had never seen it. Only the first act was set in place, of course, when I arrived, and while I was familiarizing myself with it I told the kids in the chorus just to wing it. What a remarkable group they were: every bit of improvisation I did that night—about ninety-nine percent of the entire performance—they went right along with. When I picked up my skirts to do a can-can, even the boys joined in.

Julius was conducting, and although we had never done the opera together before, it was as though we had done it thirty times. I wore my own costumes (Patty Brooks's were much too small for me). They were a totally different period from those of the rest of the cast, but nobody seemed to mind, though at one point in the first act I was startled by a chorus girl dressed as

Georges Sand. It was, all in all, an "interesting" performance—nobody knew what was coming next. But I was delighted. And it was certainly better than having a dark night at the City Opera.

Rosina in Rossini's *The Barber of Seville* entered my repertoire that year in a Sarah Caldwell production in Boston. It was a typical Sarah production. Rosina wore bird feathers all over her costume to indicate that she was really a bird in a locked-up cage; Figaro, the barber, wore a red-and-white-striped costume and looked like a barber pole. A month before I went up to Boston for rehearsals, Sarah asked me to stop in at Rita Ford's antique music box shop on Madison Avenue and pick up a couple of mechanical birds in cages. "The birds," she said, "must have a good chirp and one that you, as Rosina, can imitate." "How will I know which one will please you?" I asked. "Audition them," she replied, "and when you find a couple you like, phone me and we'll listen to them on the telephone." So there I stood in Rita Ford's magnificent shop singing into the telephone to Sarah while the birds chirped away. We finally agreed on one. The production was such a success that after considerable urging from me, Julius Rudel agreed to bring it lock, stock and barrel, including Sarah as director and conductor, to the City Opera.

At all Silverman family functions, my mother used to trot out a favorite joke. "I'd like you to meet my two sons, the *doctors*," she would say, and then, introducing me, "and this is my daughter. Period." No more, Mama: that June at the Harvard College Commencement I, too, became a Doctor—of Music. It was a special thrill for me. The Greenough family had sent its sons to Harvard since the 1700s, and I had hoped to continue the tradition by sending my son there. When that turned out to be impossible, I kept the tradition going; I accepted my honorary degree not as Beverly Sills, but as Beverly Greenough. Mstislav Rostropovich, the Russian cellist, was given a degree at the same ceremony. We had never met before but I felt as though we had been friends for a hundred years. He is the dearest, huggiest man—we spent a lot of time that day at Harvard being huggy-kissy. When we were awarded our honorary degrees, the students gave us both standing ovations —it was a marvelous moment. I now have honorary degrees from Temple,

New York University, the New England Conservatory of Music, the California Institute of the Arts—and Harvard. That should be enough.

That fall season at the New York City Opera I sang *Lucia*, the entire queen trilogy—Bolena, Stuarda, and Devereux—and *I Puritani*. Looking back on that repertoire, even I don't know how I was able to do it. Still, I took on another new role, Donizetti's *Lucrezia Borgia*, in a new production in Dallas, Texas, mounted especially for me, with Tito Capobianco directing José Carreras and Tatiana Troyanos in the cast. I never got to sing it then. While in Dallas, rehearsing, I got a call from my brother the gynecologist. Come back to New York right away, he ordered; those routine physical tests turned up a cancerous growth in the pelvic region that has to be removed. So I missed *Lucrezia*. But a fast healer, I was back on stage in three weeks, doing *The Daughter of the Regiment* in San Francisco and *I Puritani* in Los Angeles. I didn't want people to think I was dead!

In January of 1975 I was invited to sing at the White House at a State Dinner honoring the Prime Minister of Great Britain and his wife. President Ford introduced me in a most charming fashion. There is no more beautiful instrument, he said, than a well-trained human voice—and even though I was from Brooklyn, I had "made it." Danny Kaye, another old Brooklynite, who was also at the dinner, was so tickled that in the tape the White House sent me of the evening you can hear Danny whooping it up in the background.

Also in the audience, of course, were Mrs. Ford and Mrs. Happy Rockefeller, both of whom had recently undergone, as I had, highly publicized "female" operations. During the course of his introduction President Ford wanted to say that Beverly Sills was as equally at home in a Verdi ballad as a Strauss operetta. Instead, the words came out "Strauss operation." I guess it was the presence of the ladies. We all began giggling and he joined in; he is a great sport and a friendly man. Then he turned to me and said, "I'm not going to belabor this any longer." At which point he broke up, I broke up. "Mr. President," I said, "I'm going to see that you come along on all my tours to introduce me."

As Elvira in Bellini's I Puritani *at the New York City Opera, February 1974.*

At a playback session during the Angel/EMI recording of The Barber of Seville. *Standing at left is Sherrill Milnes. Seated next to me is Christopher Bishop, the producer of the album. The jolly curly-haired man is James Levine, the conductor, and at far right is tenor Nicolai Gedda. It looks like fun but actually I hate recording. On records a character gets built in pieces—not my way of working. I need to act and to use facial expressions, and I need an audience desperately so that I can communicate directly. I like to leave a performance emotionally* drained *and I never do after a recording session.*

Sarah Caldwell's Boston production of Rossini's The
Barber of Seville *in 1974 was a typically imaginative
Caldwell success. The big bird in the big gilded cage
is me, Rosina; the smaller bird I'm chirping to in the
smaller gilded cage is a mechanical canary I
auditioned for Sarah in New York City. She got the
part. Below, the quartet is made up of Donald
Gramm as Bartolo, Fred Teschler as Don Basilio,
Alan Titus as a barber-poled Figaro, and Rosina.*

As Anne Boleyn I tell Henry VIII (Bob Hale) off.

The Daughter of the Regiment *is an opera I've done for many years and in a variety of cities and productions. In 1970 I did a performance for Sarah Caldwell in a university gymnasium (above), with Spiro Malas as Sulpice, the sergeant of the French regiment of which I was the "daughter." Three years later I sang the same role of Maria in the San Diego Opera production. There I met my childhood idol, Lily Pons, for the first time. She came backstage (left) with the manager of the opera company and said to me in that marvelous French accent:* "My dear, next *time you must demand a white horse for your entrance. That's how I came onstage at the Met when I played the Daughter."* When Miss Pons died a part of my childhood died with her. I'm so pleased that I finally got to meet her and that she turned out to be everything I thought she would be—friendly, talkative, and so French!

Holding hands with President and Betty Ford at the White House in January 1975, when I sang there at a state dinner for Prime Minister Harold and Mrs. Wilson of Great Britain.

Like my brothers, Sidney and Stanley, I am now a Doctor—of Music. Harvard gave me an honorary degree at its June 1974 commencement. My citation reads: "Her joyous personality, glorious voice, and deep knowledge of music and drama bring delight to her audiences and distinction to her art." That's a long way from P.S. 91!

209

18

I meet the Met—1975.

Sir Rudolf Bing and I—
"star-crossed lovers"

On the night of April 8, 1975, I made my debut at the Metropolitan Opera —twenty years after my debut at the New York City Opera, six years after La Scala, five years after Covent Garden. What, I am still asked, took you so long? In three words: Sir Rudolf Bing—who ran the Met from 1950 to 1972.

Mr. Bing had a thing about American singers, especially those who had not been trained abroad: he did not think very much of them as singers or of their ability to "draw" at his opera house. He made exceptions, of course, but only when he was in desperate need of a particular voice, usually a tenor or a baritone. One is never desperately in need of sopranos! I certainly do not blame Mr. Bing for not paying much attention to me in the fifties or early sixties—at that point not many other people were paying much attention to me either. But after my success in *Julius Caesar* in 1966, he could no longer claim that I could not sell tickets; all of my performances were sell-outs.

After my successes in *Julius Caesar* and at La Scala and Covent Garden, Mr. Bing came under increasing pressure from his Board of Trustees to find something for me to sing at the Met. He invited me to make my debut in *Lucia* and offered me the choice of three dates. The first, October 15, 1969, I was already scheduled to première *Roberto Devereux* at the City Opera. The second, December 24, 1969, I was scheduled to make my debut at Covent Garden. The third, January 8, 1970, I was scheduled to make my debut at the Berlin State Opera. It is common knowledge that opera dates are fixed long in advance; Mr. Bing must have known that I could not accept any of his suggested dates—even for the Met. I sympathize somewhat with Mr. Bing in his dealings with me. He used to say, "Not every singer can sing at the Met." I agree, but not every singer wants to—unless the role, the production, and the date are right, all of which I intended to insist on.

Mr. Bing and I were to have one other "misunderstanding." On the Dick Cavett TV talk show he made a few incredible statements about singers in general and Mr. Cavett invited me later on another program to answer back. Mr. Bing, seriously or otherwise, had said that singers are not really gifted, they simply have a disease: vocal cords. Most singers, he added, were uneducated and could barely read or write. My answer was that if you bought Mr. Bing's premise that talent is simply a kind of disease, it would mean that Isaac Stern, the violinist, has diseased fingers and Joe Namath a diseased throwing arm. As for singers being uneducated, I said that most singers *I* knew were educated enough to be able to sing in three or four different languages, and that they could read well enough to figure out the fee on their checks and write well enough to endorse them.

In an odd way, Mr. Bing made my career by keeping me out of the Met so long. Nothing infuriates the American public quite as much as the notion of a haughty, foreign-born aristocrat being mean to one of its native-born girls for some personal reason. And Mr. Bing had a part in my doing the Donizetti queen trilogy. Julius Rudel had originally planned for me a new production of *The Daughter of the Regiment*. That made Mr. Bing furious because he had already bought the Covent Garden production of the same opera for the Met. Julius and I decided that *Daughter* was not a vehicle worth fighting over. If it had been *Devereux* or *Lucia* at issue, I would have fought Bing to the death. Instead, Julius and I said, "To hell with it, let's find something more interesting." That's how those three Queens were born— and I wound up on the cover of *Time*.

In his book about his adventures as an opera impresario, *5,000 Nights at the Opera*, Mr. Bing mentions me only once. He describes how annoyed he was that the City Opera had scheduled my Donizetti trilogy at the same time as he was planning to produce it at the Met for Montserrat Caballé. "We finally accepted the fact," he writes, "that Beverly Sills of the City Opera, having been born in Brooklyn, was entitled to priority in the portrayal of British royalty." Enough said.

One day in 1973 in San Antonio, where I was singing *Traviata*, there was a knock on my dressing room door. It was the usher: Miss Sills, he said, Sir Rudolf Bing would like to come backstage after the performance. "By all means," I said. Sir Rudolf praised my performance and could not have been more charming. He was on tour publicizing his book and he had just made his debut in a nonsinging, nonspeaking role at the New York City Opera in an opera called *The Young Lord*, by Hans Werner Henze. "Mr. Bing," I said, "I understand you've just made your debut at the City Opera." "Yes, indeed," he said, "and I had a lovely time." "Well," I said, "I always knew we'd both be working for the same opera company sometime." He had the good grace to laugh. The usher, who already had got Mr. Bing's autograph, then asked me for mine and I signed. "Young man," Mr. Bing said, "that's an historic document you have. It's the only piece of paper in the world bearing the signature of both Rudolf Bing and Beverly Sills."

We met again in 1976, in the radio studios of WQXR in New York, where he was the host for a series of programs about opera singers. When he came to my apartment to discuss the program, we spent a delightful two hours talking. He has great wit and charm. On the radio I said to him, "Mr.

Bing, I feel that you and I are like star-crossed lovers—we came into each other's lives at the wrong time." I regret all the years that Mr. Bing and I were not friends; whether or not I sang at the Met was immaterial, but not being friends was a great loss to me. I'm so happy now that we've made up.

Sir Rudolf retired from the Metropolitan in the spring of 1972. One day early that year his successor, Göran Gentele, invited me to lunch. "Before we leave this restaurant," he said, "you are going to make me very happy and I am going to make you very happy." "I wonder," I said, "which will be the harder job." Mr. Gentele invited me to sing at the Met and he wanted me to make my debut in *I Puritani*. I told him that I would have to discuss it with Julius Rudel because I had already promised to do *I Puritani* for him. "How many years," Mr. Gentele asked me, "will you have to work for me before I get that kind of loyalty?" "It doesn't have anything to do with working," I replied, "it's because Julius has been my friend for twenty years." But at the end of the lunch Mr. Gentele and I were both happy: we had agreed that my debut would take place in 1975. That would be the first season that he would produce on his own. And I wanted to get the three Donizetti queens and other various City Opera projects out of the way first. I wanted my Metropolitan debut to be an isolated event.

Julius was reluctant to stand in the way of that debut, but at the same time plans for his own *Puritani* were advanced: he had an "angel" to pay for the new production and he had a tenor, Enrico di Giuseppe, who had the high Ds necessary. No problem, I said, Mr. Gentele will just have to spring for another lunch.

At that second lunch Mr. Gentele seemed vastly relieved when I broke the news to him. What he had not known at the time he offered me *Puritani* was that Joan Sutherland had been after Mr. Bing for years, with no success, to produce *Puritani* for her. If Mr. Gentele gave it to me first, it might create all sorts of problems later. It turned out for the best: I got my production of *I Puritani* at the City Opera in 1974, Joan got hers at the Met in 1976, and both were extremely successful.

It was my mentor, Edgar Vincent, who came up with the brilliant idea to make my debut vehicle *The Siege of Corinth*. Why not, he suggested, reunite Tom Schippers, Marilyn Horne, Justino Diaz, and me in the Benois production, have Sandro Sequi stage it, and show New York exactly what had set La Scala on its ear? That's just what we did—with Shirley Verrett replacing Marilyn Horne (she had decided not to do any more "pants" parts, our term for girls-playing-boys roles), and Harry Theyard, an American, replacing an Italian tenor. It was, once again, The Siege of the Americans.

The rest, as they say, is history. It is impossible to describe the tension, the excitement before my Metropolitan debut. I could not open a magazine or a newspaper without seeing my picture. I was welcomed at the Met like a long-lost child: everyone bent over backwards to be kind and accommodating. Schuyler Chapin, who had taken over the Met when Mr. Gentele was killed in an automobile accident in 1972, fulfilled every promise that Mr. Gentele had made me. During a break in one rehearsal, when Shirley Verrett, Justino Diaz and I were alone on stage, I muttered that I certainly hoped we could live up to all the hoopla that was being made over this. "How can we miss?" Justino said. "I'm a Puerto Rican, Shirley is black, and you're a Jew. We've cornered the market on minorities. Who would *dare* criticize us?"

Peter and I have always had a routine. When I leave home for the opera house to get ready for a performance, he always says, Have a good time. I reply, I'll probably sing like a pig. That opening night at the Met I found on my dressing room table when I arrived a gift from Peter—a little gold pig from Tiffany's, mounted on a chain. Outside the Metropolitan, Lincoln Plaza looked, my mother said, like St. Peter's Square on Easter Sunday. When I made my first entrance on stage to sing my opening line, *"Che mai sento?"* ("What do I hear?") I heard nothing but a tremendous roar from the audience. After my first aria the applause lasted so long that I got teary-eyed and had to walk upstage to compose myself. The curtain calls at the end of the opera were seemingly unending. Muffy, who couldn't hear anything, of course, but noticed all the people standing and clapping, kept tugging at Peter: "Was Mama good? Was Mama good?" Someone in the audience let loose several screeching whistles and yelled, "Speech, speech!" It was my "claque" and fellow Brooklynite Danny Kaye.

I had already proved my revolutionary point: that one can become an international opera star *without* the Metropolitan. Nevertheless, I had grown up at a time when, if you wanted to see the really great baseball players you had to see Di Maggio and Gehrig at Yankee Stadium, and if you wanted to see an opera *star* you had to go to the Met. It is hard to shake that kind of indoctrination. Now, I had sung at the Met and I was the compleat opera star. On opening night the ladies and gentlemen of the chorus chipped in and bought me a gold charm bearing a replica of the Metropolitan Opera House. It made me cry—again.

*My debut at the Metropolitan Opera:
as Pamira, with Justino Diaz as Maometto,
in a scene from Rossini's*
The Siege of Corinth.

Sir Rudolf Bing and I—star-crossed lovers no more—at the studios of WQXR in New York City, where he was the host for a series of programs about opera in 1976. Below, chatting with Schuyler Chapin, head of the Met when I made my debut.

Taking curtain calls after my Met debut, April 7, 1975.

The clan gathers at the Met. Peter and Mama, holding hands, chat with Joel Grey. Left, at the party after my Met debut the Silverman kids from Brooklyn whoop it up, brother Sidney on the left, brother Stanley on the right.

The champagne glasses are raised at my post-debut party.

19

*So what do I do
for an encore?*

Man plans, God laughs. I have always been a kind of fatalist. I firmly believe that what's going to happen to any of us is already written down in a great big book. Someone up there looked down one day, pointed a long finger at me, and said: "That one is going to be a singer with very high notes." I like that notion.

But if God gave me the pipes, I had to play them and it has not been easy. After my success as Cleopatra in 1966 at the New York City Opera, people began calling me an "overnight sensation." Overnight? God is laughing and so am I. There was never a straight line in my career, never a short cut. Some singers make it with ten roles; I had to learn a hundred. I never bought or slept my way into an opera role. If I was an overnight sensation, it was certainly the longest night's journey into day that anyone has ever seen.

On May 25, 1981, I was fifty-two years old and I had been singing since I was three. I had a repertoire of more than a hundred operas and I had sung fifty or sixty of them, in opera or concert form. I had sung in every major opera house in the world. For the previous five years I had averaged about a hundred performances a year. If not the highest-paid opera singer in the world, I was certainly among the top three. So what could I do for an encore? More.

I may have slowed down a bit—I say may!—but I have no intention of quitting yet. It is *not* the money—although there is certainly nothing wrong with making a lot of money out of one's talent. My husband Peter and I have always had an understanding: we would live on *his* money, and mine would be all mine to do what I like with. All the money I earn now goes into a trust for Bucky and Muffy.

The last few years of my performing career were busy with many projects. I brought *Louise* back into the New York City Opera repertory, and I considered more French opera. I had another Bellini work in mind. I planned an American premiere. And a world premiere: in San Diego in 1979. I did *Thaïs* at San Francisco and at the Metropolitan in 1978, and another new production was planned for me at the Met in 1979.

What was to happen when my voice would finally give out? I did not want to coach or teach singing: once I stopped singing I intended to turn off all the voice knobs. But at that point I knew I wanted to help run an opera company; I knew a good deal about all the artistic phases involved.

It is very difficult to know when to quit. Peter said you quit when you can't do today what you did yesterday. I always thought it was much more subtle and more complicated than that, more like watching yourself getting a new wrinkle every day and thinking that *this* is the last one until you finally shriek, "My God!" and say, "That's it. Enough." I have been in the public eye nearly all my life, and it is not easy to give that up. It's like hitting a home run and hearing all those cheers from the crowd—it gets in your blood. I have hit lots of home runs, and when the cheering finally stops, I will certainly miss it.

Once a long time ago, when I was still growing up in Brooklyn, I came home from Manhattan very late at night. "You must have had a marvelous time," my father said, "you were out so late." "No," I said, "I had a miserable time; I had no money for a taxi and the subway took more than two hours." "You mean," my father said, "you sat there being miserable just because you didn't have taxi money?" He gave me a twenty-dollar bill and said, "Now you'll always have money enough to get out of doing what you don't want to do."

That's what I have now—the moral equivalent of a twenty-dollar bill. I no longer have to do anything professionally or personally that I don't want to do. And as long as I am having a good time, I don't intend to stop. Papa, who didn't live long enough to share my triumphs, would approve, I know. My mother says that she never goes to the theater alone: my father, she claims, is always seated next to her. We tease her that the woman actually sitting next to her must find it uncomfortable with a man sitting in her lap. But I agree with Mama: everything my brothers and I have accomplished *has* been witnessed by our father.

In January of 1976 Sarah Caldwell made her
debut at the Metropolitan, the first woman
conductor in the house's history. The
production was La Traviata with me singing
Violetta. Above, at dress rehearsal Sarah and I
get together in my dressing room. Below,
tripping the light fantastic in one of the
opera's party scenes.

At the annual San Francisco Opera fund-raising ball in 1973, Joel Grey, the master of ceremonies, and I do a tap-dance-soft-shoe routine. That was after we sang a duet from Mozart's Don Giovanni, "Là ci darem la mano." I told him he was the sexiest Don Giovanni I had ever danced with. He captioned this picture: "Bubbles and the Bantam." We've known each other only about five years, but from the first day we met—accidentally, in a museum with our children—we've been old friends.

Three days after my debut at the Metropolitan, I was back on the Met stage, this time with Danny Kaye in a show for children to introduce them to the world of opera. We too did a soft-shoe number and the kids loved it. Danny's rapport with children is second to nobody's.

With Johnny Carson on his TV talk show, 1974. He's Nelson Eddy, I'm Jeannette MacDonald and we're about to do our "Indian Love Call" number.

Carol Burnett and me doing song-and-dance routines in our Thanksgiving Day TV special, in 1976. When we were taping an eight-minute tap-dance number, Peter, who was in the audience, turned to my mother and said, "Hey, Ma, she's not doing so bad for forty-seven years old!" "Don't be silly." Mama replied. "She could do that when she was five years old."

The Greenoughs—alone at last! Muffy, now seventeen, is a junior at a regular private school for girls in New York City. She even speaks Latin!

I was Belle Silverman at three in Brooklyn.
Now I'm Beverly Sills at forty-seven.
Plus ça change, plus c'est la même chose.

Epilogue

by

Harvey E. Phillips

Epilogue

"So here I am living 'the best.'" Beverly Sills smiles that magic smile. It is five years later, and the changes have been enormous. The soprano has retired, and yet she is working harder than ever. Every retirement occasion—a final operatic appearance, a last recital, the great benefit gala of October 27, 1980, steppingstones on the path to definitive withdrawal from singing—seemed to end with the heartening assurance from Beverly, as if she were more concerned about her public's state of mind than about her own, that "the best is yet to come." And now, ensconced in her basement office at the New York City Opera, the company she heads as General Director, Beverly puts in endless days making good on her promise.

Approached from any direction, it's a tough promise to keep. For one thing, the administrative duties of the New York City Opera are awesome and often wearing, encompassing not only artistic matters but the nitty-gritty of labor relations, scheduling, contracts, public relations, and fund-raising. Hardly areas that fall naturally within the purview of an individual whose operatic experience has been gained under the lights and in front of adoring audiences. For another, Beverly's active performing career until that night in 1980 had been as lively, as interest-provoking as ever. This was exactly how the singer would have had it. "I wanted to end my singing career while I was still selling out and people could say, 'Why *aren't* you still singing?' rather than 'Why *are* you still singing?'"

The last years of the Sills career were studded with new productions, a world premiere, and, inevitably, those landmark farewells. For example, *Thaïs* at the Met. It arrived January 18, 1978, a production donated in her honor to the San Francisco Opera by Cyril Magnin in the fall of 1976 and transferred free of charge at her insistence to the Metropolitan Opera in New York. While certain elements of this revival proved controversial in both cities, Beverly won plaudits for her contribution. "Her voice had a wealth of color, was immensely expressive and big and brilliant when needed," wrote Harriett Johnson in the *New York Post*. Harold C. Schonberg in *The New York Times* added, "Her artistry remains undiminished, and she was able to create an appealing characterization of Massenet's cardboard figure." "The unquestioned star of the revival is Beverly Sills, and on opening night she was in sumptuous voice, bringing incredible sensuosity to the seductive Massenet music, a vibrant physical presence and sensitive acting to the courtesan-turned-saint" (Byron Belt, Newhouse papers).

It was perhaps the all too convincing quality of the portrayal that got Beverly into a bit of trouble. One disturbed person sent the star a furious note because she was portraying a "whore seducing a priest." The message went on to predict that Sills' and baritone Sherrill Milnes' souls would go to Hell. The writer ominously predicted that Beverly's role-playing would get her there faster. One post-*Thais* night as she was leaving her dressing room, accompanied by her friend, the regal-looking chairman of the New York State Council on the Arts, Kitty Carlisle, and the Met's Artistic Administrator, Charles Riecker, an unusual-looking young man, along with other fans, was waiting in the backstage switchboard entrance area of the theater. Suddenly he unleashed a doomsday tirade at the singer. Met security guards, already alerted to such a possibility, overwhelmed the youth and whisked Miss Sills and Miss Carlisle ("Our feet never touched the ground.") into the back seat of a waiting limousine.

With typical humorous candor Sills today recalls other, lighter adventures with the Alexandria femme fatale. "I wish I had done the part five years earlier when my figure was better. Maybe then people wouldn't have called the piece 'Thighs,'" she says, chuckling. ("Thighs" notwithstanding, the opera brought an unprecedented rush to the box office in Minneapolis during the Met spring tour, a rumor having been circulated that Beverly would assay her role in the nude.) She remembers, too, how she sympathized with Milnes who, during rehearsals, New York and tour performances, was required to lift his leading lady an aggregate of thirty times and carry her across the stage. At one point she apologized for those weighty artistic duties, but a cheerful Milnes assured her they didn't really bother him. "After all," he said, "I was a farm boy and accustomed to hoisting 500-pound bales of hay." "Somehow," she says, "our love scene that night lacked its usual ardor." Later during an interview, when asked how he felt about Beverly, he said, "When you lift a gal like her thirty times, you've got to love her a little!"

Beverly's Met career had been scheduled for many years ahead. Indeed, a new *Rigoletto* was in the works for the 1979-80 season, but gradually she began to withdraw from those extended tours. (The only clue to what that *Rigoletto* might have been like is to be found in the Angel recording intended to complement the new production. It is Beverly's last full-length operatic venture on disk.) Her retirement during the fall of 1980 was announced the very month of *Thaïs'* successful arrival at the Met. Along with this news came word that the closing of the vocal career would also mean the beginning of a new and challenging one: co-director, with Julius Rudel, of the New York City Opera.

Beverly had commitments well into 1984 when she announced her retirement. Such long-range arrangements are commonplace in the music business—certainly at the Sills superstar level. She would have had to announce her retirement five years in advance to avoid canceling those contracts.

By default, then, the Metropolitan's new production of *Don Pasquale*, unveiled December 7, 1978, became a Sills good-by to the Met. "It was a farewell Valentine," says Beverly, and once again every scheduled performance sold out. In John Dexter's Edwardian updating of the Donizetti comedy's action, the singer-actress was hailed for once more giving a lesson in how to fuse musical and dramatic values. Commented one critic: "She used her star energy for the purpose of the work as a whole. Gaily brandishing her cigarette holder, she performed her characteristic feat of turning her own delight at tossing off her feats of coloratura singing into the character's delight in her own independence and resourcefulness, and thus, not for the first time, showed us a heroine of *bel canto* opera not as a silly ninny, but as a feminist *avant la lettre.*"

What Beverly remembers most about this *Don Pasquale*—she is uncharacteristically hazy about the warm and extended applause, the shredded programs raining from the Family Circle heights that greeted her curtain calls after a matinee performance, her last moments on the vast Met stage— is its legacy of, of all things, tobacco. As a "new woman," Norina was discovered in her first scene indulging a taste for little cigars. Today, Sills confesses, she is lightly addicted to mentholated cigarettes. "When the going gets rough I close the office door, make myself a cup of espresso and light up a cigarette. That's a new luxury for me."

Earlier that same season of 1978-79, Beverly Sills had made her last New York City Opera foray into comedy as Fiorilla in a new Tito Capobianco production of Rossini's *Il Turco in Italia.* Her work was described by Donal Henahan as "consistently witty . . . as well as wonderfully fresh of voice." Few who saw this *Turco* will ever forget the delicious potpourri of tragic attitudes. In a kind of loving burlesque of her greatest triumphs in the serious repertory, she knowingly incorporated mock-melodramatic staging into Fiorilla's grand *scena* of contrition.

The vehicle of her final appearance at the New York City Opera was, in contrast, a totally serious one, in fact one of the most thematically grim operas she was ever to be associated with—Gian Carlo Menotti's *La Loca.*

The world premiere took place in San Diego, June 3, 1979, and it came to New York a little more than three months later, September 16, 1979.

This was a fiftieth birthday present to Sills from the late Lawrence Deutsch, a devoted Los Angeles patron of both the singer and the New York City Opera. Menotti, the composer, chose as his subject the descent into desolation and insanity of Juana, a sixteenth-century queen of Spain. Far from finding the somber subject matter inappropriate for a celebratory occasion, Beverly is glad her last City Opera assignment was a real "meat and potatoes" role. In spite of widespread criticism of the work, it was never considered anything but a triumph for her. "Miss Sills brought all her redoubtable musicianship and acting ability to the role, and at the end was rewarded with cheers" (Schonberg in the *Times*). "She perhaps scored the greatest triumph of her long, distinguished career" (Bill Zakariasen in the *News*). "Sills still has plenty of ammunition with which to lay out the audience. All the royal temper tantrums, vengeance scenes, love scenes, mad scenes, farewell scenes, and death scenes that have lighted her stairway to superstardom seem recycled into this one opera" (Leighton Kerner in *The Village Voice*).

For Beverly herself, however, *La Loca* always held intrinsic merit. "I love the opera," she insists. "I believe that someday it will emerge as a great work. The farewell scene to the daughter is the most beautiful operatic scene written in the last thirty years. It's theatrically perfect. The audience was in tears. Gian Carlo is a great craftsman, but keeping appointments and meeting deadlines are not among his great strengths." The soprano recalls that the orchestra score had not been completed by the time of the dress rehearsal and that the important aria for the lead baritone was not ready until ten days before the premiere. "Menotti likes to work and work and work. He's not terribly concerned with dates. There's still, as far as I know, no approved published score."

Sills brought more than her interpretive talents to *La Loca*. She argued long and hard about the opera's ending. Menotti wanted the heroine's final word, "Promise," sung. Sills resisted. She felt that Juana's desperate demand for reassurance from the priest that God exists—should be spoken, indeed screamed. Sills won the argument, and the effect in the theater of that inchoate cry proved hair-raising.

The "lasts" were now mounting up. There were farewell Norinas in Houston, a farewell *Fledermaus* in Miami, a farewell, again *Fledermaus*, to Boston and the conductor, Sarah Caldwell, thus ending one of opera's most extraordinary collaborations. A last recital with piano in May of 1980 unrolled in the labyrinthine and somewhat unlikely confines of the Philip Johnson-designed Crystal Cathedral in Garden Grove, California. (A last New York recital—with the Chamber Music Society of Lincoln Center—had come more than a year and a half earlier.) A *Daily News* headline forlornly queried, "Is There Life After Sills?"

The honors also came thick and fast. If Shreveport, Louisiana, could carve out a Beverly Sills day, then New York was sure to present its famous daughter with the key to the city. The American Symphony Orchestra League came up with its Gold Baton Award, Harvard University with a Hasty Pudding Club Woman of the Year citation. The White House conferred the 1980 Medal of Freedom.

And yet there was still one more set of full-length operatic appearances to go, and by any standard it was certainly unusual—a series of October 1980 *Fledermaus* performances in San Diego shared . . . with Joan Sutherland. At last the two greatest coloratura sopranos of their time were to appear together.

Originally it had been decided the ladies would alternate in the roles of Rosalinda and Adele, but limited rehearsal time and Beverly's increased responsibilities as General Director of the New York City Opera made this impractical (Julius Rudel had resigned as co-director as of June 1979). Sutherland would do all the Rosalindas, Sills all the Adeles.

Martin Bernheimer in the *Los Angeles Times* reported on the comedic success of their partnership: "The Bubbles and Joanie show turned out to be fun because the divas seemed to be having fun. . . . Sills oozed savoir-faire: Sutherland smiled and popped push-button high D's. . . . She [Sills] is fun, she has fun, and she provides Sutherland with a splendid, elegant, charming counter-force. No foiling."

Sills remembers the collaboration with pleasure. She and the Dame from Australia got along famously, and Sutherland even attempted, not too successfully, to induct Sills into the mysteries of needlepoint. "Joan was down to earth, as I expected. More of a surprise was Richard Bonynge, who conducted. I had heard he could be more difficult, but we hit it off immediately. He has an urbane wit and a dry humor I loved, and he was extremely supportive. I was exhausted most of the time because during the rehearsals and the performances I had to make eight or nine round trips to New York where *Attila* was about to open. I remember one night during the "Laughing Song," when I was particularly tired, how well he accommodated me. I have enormous respect for him. He's his own man, extremely well prepared and musicians love playing for him. I'm regretful I hadn't worked with him before. He's a real singer's conductor. I've invited him to the New York City Opera to conduct *Mignon,* and I wrote him that if his wife 'happens to be free,' she can come too, and do the Philine!"

In addition to getting the coming season in shape, Beverly was also planning her farewell scheduled for the end of October. It was to be a benefit for the New York City Opera and, in the context of the second act of *Fledermaus,* a host of luminaries were to make appearances. Opera world greats such as John Alexander, Placido Domingo, Eileen Farrell, Donald Gramm, Sherrill Milnes, Leontyne Price, Renata Scotto and Tatiana Troyanos were set to participate, as were flutist James Galway, Beverly's longtime accompanist Charles Wadsworth, dancers Cynthia Gregory and Peter Martins, conductor Zubin Mehta, and, from the world of show business, Carol Burnett, Helen Hayes, Mary Martin, Ethel Merman, Burt Reynolds, Dinah Shore and Bobby Short. These were all friends and colleagues, a reflection of the varied nature of the Sills career, the enormous, universal appeal of her talent, the warmth engendered during her many collaborations over the years.

The gala, suitably enough dubbed "Beverly! Her Farewell Performance," took place two days short of the twenty-fifth anniversary of her New York City Opera debut as, of course, Rosalinda. There was, therefore, pleasing symmetry to *Fledermaus* and Rosalinda serving as a finale. Actually Beverly's dream retirement program would have been made up of the final acts of the three Donizetti "queen" operas, but she feared her stamina, the real victim of her 1974 operation for pelvic cancer, would not be sufficient for such an undertaking. (She admits, though, she was surprised at the plentiful physical energy she was able to summon up for the demands of the heavy Menotti role.)

Certainly, the *Fledermaus* framework provided an overwhelmingly joyous mood to the occasion, a fête far more than a sorrowful leavetaking. It was a party, too, for which elegantly dressed enthusiasts paid as much as $1,000 for a ticket that included, as well as the events onstage, a cocktail party, dinner and the post-performance ball, to the music of Woody Herman, in a 165-foot-long blue and white striped tent set up in Damrosch Park just west of the New York State Theater.

The high jinks and merriment of the evening were to a great extent the province of Carol Burnett who, in an up-to-date sheath, put a stop to the scripted happenings in Prince Orlovsky's ballroom (Orlovsky, by the way, was played by Kitty Carlisle) and signaled the beginning of the special vaudeville. Mary Martin gave out with "My Heart Belongs to Daddy," Ethel Merman "There's No Business Like Show Business," Dinah Shore "Blues in the Night," and the years rolled away. James Galway offered a typically twinkling "Danny Boy," Scotto and Price, very untypically, "Somewhere Over the Rainbow" and "What I Did for Love," respectively. Gramm devised new lyrics for "I Want What I Want When I Want It" that testified to Sills' recently developed capacity to run an opera house according to her own very independent lights.

And there were unprogrammed surprises, too—the appearance of Lady

Bird Johnson, Joan Mondale, Governor Hugh Carey and Walter Cronkite, with whom the honoree danced a brief waltz. No surprise, though, was the ending: Beverly Sills alone onstage with Charles Wadsworth at the piano singing the little Portuguese folk song, taught to her as a child by her teacher Estelle Liebling, with which for so many years she had closed her recitals.

Sills recalls the moment: "I had said jokingly that I wanted to go out with confetti and balloons. It was really just a joke. I knew everything was planned, and I had agreed to finish with the folksong. I did, but I walked offstage feeling maybe we should have had a reprise of 'There's No Business Like Show Business.' Maybe this was too quiet. Somebody said go out for a solo bow. I did, it seemed like the right thing to do . . . and there they were—the balloons and the confetti. It was fitting, the touch I had been waiting for."

Beverly Sills was in her office the next morning at 8:30, pleased that her gala had netted over a million dollars for her company. Still, by nine, she was trying to raise more.

She has not sung a note in public since October 27, 1980.

The retirement of a diva. *Tremenda cosa*, to paraphrase a dire operatic pronouncement. One would think so. And yet Sills, through a combination of well-defined career ideas, a ready acceptance of immutable reality, humor, a keen understanding of the place of her career in the overall scheme of things and certainly through her new role in administration, has managed to reduce that *cosa* to a thoroughly *piccola* one.

"It's true," she reflects, "my singing discipline is gone. I haven't performed since the gala. I miss singing—but I don't miss performing. Maybe sometime I'll get out some Schubert songs and call up Charlie (Wadsworth) and ask him to give me an hour. I'll need privacy."

"No, I don't miss 'the career.' I had no need to go on doing the same thing. Oh, maybe I'll do a straight play sometime, maybe sing on television, just for fun, but I'll never appear in opera or concert again."

Beverly insists that she has no regrets about not being onstage. Unlike so many other performers for whom operating in the spotlight means some mysterious kind of fulfillment, a completion, an act without which the individual is somehow not totally alive, she has never used her singing as a substitute for reality.

"I never depended on the performing experience for anything like that. There are no holes in my life. I have a rich life, a rich family life, and I enjoy it. I think the only interesting psychological note about my retirement is that I haven't tried to sing since that last night. I'm really waiting to see what this crazy mind of mine will do about not performing anymore." (Sills hints that one reason she hesitates may stem from the death of her longtime friend and coach Roland Gagnon. She had appointed him Associate Music Administrator of the New York City Opera, and she describes his sudden passing—he was still in his early forties—as the biggest jolt she has suffered since her retirement. Beverly feels Roland is the greatest loss to her of a musical talent since the death of Norman Treigle.)

Beverly never refused to think about retirement. It was not a bogeyman lurking in the background ready to pounce on the ill-prepared. In fact, she and her husband had set 50 as an ideal retirement age, and the reason that figure actually became 51 was her involvement with the Menotti work.

"Fifty is a young woman, but not a young singer, especially for someone with my kind of voice," Beverly explains. "I was someone who sang a repertory of young women. It might have been different if I had been a Wagnerian or a Straussian soprano."

But Beverly Sills would be the last person to refuse to face up to the fact of the vocal problems she began to encounter during the last years, problems she traces to that postoperative loss of stamina.

"I had trouble getting rested between performances. That had never happened to me before. I remember one season when I did twenty performances of *Manon*, the three queens, and *Puritani*. That's real stamina. But toward the end I was doing the cream-puff roles—Adele, Rosalinda, Rosina —because my stamina was not there for the heavier roles. The compromises I had to make made it unpleasant to contemplate what the future would have been like."

Still, is there not a single role or a single operatic bastion whose unconquered state leaves a pang? The answer is an emphatic no. Even the Marschallin, which had been rumored as an assignment for her, is not regretted—despite Sills' proclamation of her love for the music of Richard Strauss. (Her infrequent forays into this repertory were often among her most extraordinary. One thinks especially of an appearance with the Boston Symphony as Zerbinetta in the fiendishly difficult—for Zerbinetta—unrevised version of *Ariadne auf Naxos*.) No, not even the Marschallin. "I would have had the chance," she reasons, "to do it only five or six times.

It would not have been satisfying."

In her last years before the public, and often to the consternation of her Lincoln Center fans who wanted her all to themselves and feared for the effort it cost her, Beverly continued to appear with a host of regional companies. To counteract any impression these engagements might have been the inevitable and unavoidable legacy of overeager booking, she relished the particular pleasure they gave her. "I needed to go to places like Omaha. I had had plenty of San Francisco, Chicago, Washington—all the major music centers. But everything in those smaller cities was fresh and terrific. People gave parties for you in their homes instead of in the ballrooms of big hotels. In Omaha, I opened a newly renovated theater, and there was a party afterwards in a restaurant, and they named a dish for me. Those personal touches were very appealing. I remember the warmth of people in San Antonio, where the ladies baked my favorite cookies and took me sightseeing."

Almost as proof of what she experienced and so much enjoyed, she points to a quilt hanging at the far end of her office, a series of squares, each depicting a scene from a Sills-associated opera. The materials for this came from the actual costumes she wore in those operas. "The women in San Diego made that, and in San Diego there was a man who brought me fresh strawberries from his garden, people who found old copper—I'm an avid collector—for me to buy or brought presents for my daughter, Muffy. There was a lady who volunteered to drive me anywhere I wanted to go and used to present me each day with a rose in a cute little jar. In the big cities I'd be given a chauffeur and a limousine. So what? I have a chauffeur

In a role that has meant as much to Beverly Sills as any in her performing career, National Chairman of the March of Dimes Mothers' March on Birth Defects, she visits the Cornell Medical Center, New York Hospital.

This snapshot from a family album shows Beverly about to bubble forth, as described by a family member.

*Madame General Director during the first weeks of her directorial position
with the New York City Opera.*

Mayor Edward Koch honors New York's favorite native opera singer.

A thoughtful General Director of the New York City Opera is about to announce an important decision.

*This sculpted work honors one of Brooklyn's most successful daughters and
is on display in the Brooklyn Museum's Hall of Fame.*

*Beverly Sills listens to a young singer audition in the spring of 1981 during
her cultural exchange visit to the People's Republic of China.*

Beverly Sills with her husband, Peter Greenough, and her mother.

and a limousine. No, those regional engagements were very special, and I didn't shortchange them. I did the same Lucia I did everywhere else, and I also got to work with a lot of young talent."

Her choice to personally reach audiences in communities across the nation, like undertaking roles which demanded so much, may have worked to shorten her performing life, but Beverly Sills has often stated her preference for a career of twelve remarkable years rather than for a longer, more prosaic one. For her, what's done was done with great success, and there is no reason to look back with sadness. Surely there's no grain of sadness evident in the incident that took place shortly after her retirement. When someone approached her on the street and asked excitedly, "Aren't you Beverly Sills?", "I used to be," was the giggling reply.

Not only has Sills been spared the dilemma faced by a majority of retiring singers of what to do with their new-found leisure, she has also not had to make any kind of financial adjustment. By her own admission, she accumulated a fortune (her New York City Opera fees, of course, barely figuring in such a reckoning), but it is a fortune that has been set up as a trust for her children. "I have been lucky. I was lucky in my husband. I never had financial needs."

But relinquishing a way of life that meant constant travel and continual preparedness has brought significant alterations to both her personal and family life. Even with the increasing demands made on her to be a spokesperson for the arts, to spearhead fundraising drives for the New York City Opera, and, principally, to act as its guiding spirit, she finds she has increased time for herself and for her family. For one thing she is able to spend more of any given month in New York. Even on the busiest in-season day she at least gets home to her Central Park West apartment for dinner. She is delighted she can read more or relax on the beach at the Greenough summer home in Martha's Vineyard without being plugged into a cassette on which the rigors of a new role unroll. Now, when she gets on an airplane she need not worry about drafts from the air-conditioning system or about taking along three scores for in-flight perusal. She can savor, as well the occasional cigarette, a glass of wine with dinner. She looks forward to accompanying her husband on trout fishing excursions or on long wished-for trips to the wine country of France and through the fjords of Norway. The Greenoughs also contemplate buying another home in a warm climate. "I'm still thinking about what to do. It's all so new."

A source of particular satisfaction now in Beverly's nonoperatic world is her daughter. Muffy is hard at work for a New York publishing house in a training program concentrating on book jacket design. She also attends art school. Being out in the world, and with people not used to her speech, has forced Muffy to articulate more clearly. The adjustments she has made, her intelligence and the pride she obviously takes in her appearance add up to one more happy daily reality for the ex-diva to contemplate.

Perhaps, in an ironic sense, the chief benefactor of Beverly Sills' retirement is the New York City Opera itself. True, it no longer has her voice and presence to sell out the house, but it does have her undivided professional attention as a conscientious administrator. She, in a way, felt relief when her singing career ended, for at least now she only had one operatic area clamoring for her talents.

The introduction to her new job in 1979 could certainly be characterized as a baptism under fire. No sooner was her first season under way than a labor dispute, centering on the orchestra, broke out. It was, fortunately, only of ten days' duration, and Beverly is pleased by the small number of ruffled feathers. Similarly, two years later, just after the gala, when she was indulging herself in a brief vacation in Barbados, word arrived that the new production of Janáček's *Cunning Little Vixen* was running $100,000 over budget. Forsaking the Caribbean, she rushed back to New York and brought in "to the dollar" a critically acclaimed show.

Long experience in the business, albeit from a totally different point of view, furnished the new General Director with an unsuspected wealth of preparation for the job. "I surprised myself how much I knew in terms of production," she comments. "I guess over the years I had accumulated a good deal of knowledge. I had absorbed a lot. When you went on those regional tours, you needed, for instance, to know about lighting to make sure you didn't end up in the shadows. But now I had to approach everything differently; not personally. It was a challenge. I became a constant student of stagecraft. I gave myself a crash course in all aspects of running this house."

Indeed, Beverly now appears to be everywhere. She not only determines casts but also sits in on auditions for replacements for the orchestra. She makes sure she attends all production conferences and she is certain to be present at rehearsals. ("If I see something incorrect, I make a suggestion—unsolicited.") She also supervises New York City Opera's jazzy ad campaigns that seem to have as their goal the total demystification of the operatic experience. She has reorganized the administrative staff, and redecorated the director's office to reflect her taste for Victorian coziness and clutter. Performance memorabilia, posters, her personal library, souvenirs of her trip to China, pillows with slogans ("Support the arts, kiss a soprano"), even an autographed photo of Miss Piggy regretting her absence ("without *moi*") from the gala—all give the windowless room just the ambience Sills needs to command. The only thing she refuses to do is to negotiate fees. She leaves the negotiating to others.

There is the day-to-day operation of the theater that is, of course, her responsibility, but there is also long-range planning. It is only now—in 1981—that the public is beginning to see a reflection of the Sills taste in repertory. For example, the great success of the fall 1980 season, *Les Pêcheurs de Perles*, had a cast handpicked by Sills, and the hit of the spring 1981 season, *The Cunning Little Vixen*, was an all-Sills project. She makes clear repeatedly that the repertory bread-and-butter staples— *Carmen, Bohème, Traviata, Butterfly*—will always be there. At this juncture they are still, with the possible exception of the greatly popular preseason operetta revivals, New York City Opera's most dependable box office draws. (The standard core repertory is the only place Sills feels the Met and New York City Opera may legitimately duplicate one another.) Yet, risky ventures, the sort of thing the company has always been credited with hazarding, will not be avoided.

"Risk? Everything's risky. My three queens were risky. Believe me, I'd like to find a new Beverly Sills to sell the house out."

With or without a new Beverly Sills, the revivals of the less well-

260

known Verdi operas, begun with *Attila* and *Nabucco*, will continue with *I Masnadieri.* Beverly characterizes the fall 1981 *Freischütz* as a challenging venture, and she does not turn away from such works as part of what she calls a Baroque festival (*Alceste* in 1982, *Alcina* in 1983, and something of Rameau for 1984). Thomas' *Hamlet* comes into the repertory in the fall of 1982 and will, incidentally, bring back Sherrill Milnes to the New York City Opera. Tito Capobianco, whose name, at his own request, has been removed from his old New York City Opera productions because his work with the San Diego Opera prevented him from being on hand to supervise them, remains, along with his wife, Gigi, one of Sills' closest confidants. "They're like family. We talk at least three times a week. If I ever had to run somewhere, it would be to them."

Something fundamental about Beverly's repertory planning is that it is not based on the operas identified with her. As a real student of opera, she knows thirty or forty roles she never sang in public. The parochial taste often encountered in other successful opera personalities has never been part of her make-up.

Beverly, as General Director of the New York City Opera often speaks of her commitment to the American singer. But does the soprano who achieved one of her earliest successes in *The Ballad of Baby Doe* feel a similar responsibility to the encouragement of new American lyric composition? Today she looks at the question from several angles: aesthetic, vocal, and financial. She acknowledges that her taste could be described as conservative, but one deduces her restrained response to the avant-garde also comes from fear of what its practitioners can do to the singer's voice as much as from what it can do to the listener's ear.

"The American singer should not be penalized by having to sing things not well written for the voice," she contends. "I am interested in contemporary works written with the human voice in mind. No singer here at New York City Opera will have his vocal cords ruined in the name of contemporary American opera."

A new American work, in fact, has been commissioned (she is adamant about commissioning only American composers) for 1983, or 1984 at the latest. *An American Trilogy*—three one-act operas unveiled in 1980—was a Sills inspiration and she rates it now as "partially successful." The public, of course, stayed away in droves. She thinks a large part of the problem is creating an audience for the new and unknown, and that this can be done if the potential loss is underwritten. This would grant the opera company latitude to keep a new work on the boards until, with any luck and if it merits it, it creates its own audience.

When Beverly discusses contemporary opera and the New York City Opera, her initial instinct is to worry about how it might affect her singers' welfare. She has cast herself as the singers' foremost ally, and as such has been applauded. The unique situation of a singer actually running an opera company has considerably boosted morale in the troupe, for the performers look to her as their front-office ally. There is, as well, a spirit abroad in the company that mirrors her brand of down-to-earth humor. "I'm a cheerful, outgoing woman, so this office has become Grand Central Station," she reports. "The singers know they have a sympathetic colleague, someone they feel they can talk to. After all, I've sung with many of these people.

They know, too, this is a house that doesn't welcome prima donnas of either sex. It's a house where opera is collaboration. No one here tries to walk away with the show."

She obviously finds nurturing careers a wonderful occupational dividend. She recognizes that the public indeed wants new opera personalities to adore, that the public yearns, in fact, to feel it has come, on its own, upon an ineffable, treasurable talent, just as it did with Beverly herself. "I was the public's opera star. The public made me, I was their very own." So she welcomes seeing some glimmers of this happening again.

What has been fascinating to watch is the progression of sopranos—June Anderson, Ashley Putnam, Gianna Rolandi, Diana Soviero, Carol Vaness—who have been worked into roles so closely identified with Beverly: Anderson in *The Tales of Hoffmann*, Putnam in *Daughter of the Regiment*, Rolandi in *Lucia*, *Julius Caesar*, and *Puritani*. Soviero in *Traviata* and *Manon*, Vaness as Donna Anna in *Don Giovanni*. She has encouraged these young women, not only with advice based on her experience, but also through her decision to let them develop their own characterizations both musical and dramatic.

"I give them advice only if they ask for it. I encourage them singer to singer. It was a good omen, I thought, when Ashley Putnam was able to walk right into my *Stuarda* costume, but she had her own interpretation of the part and rightly so. These productions are altered now to suit them. Rolandi isn't a blonde in *Puritani*—I don't even remember why I wanted to be a blonde—and she uses different vocal ornamentation in *Julius Caesar*. Carol Vaness is going to do her first Anna Bolena." The big hit that Barry

McCauley scored in *Les Pêcheurs de Perles* has planted the seed for a "discover your own superstar" ad campaign.

Decisions may ultimately lead to applause, but they can also induce the hurling of critical brickbats. Beverly's leadership of New York City Opera has had to weather occasional criticisms by the press. Does the transition from performer to administrator also allow her to make the necessary mental and emotional adjustment to the change in the direction of critical aim? Her attitude, she says, is unchanged. She has always relied on herself to be critical of her own work. That appraisal is still what counts. "Now that I have two hundred vocal cords, plus lights, to worry about, I'm still stuck with my own taste. If the critics don't like something, I won't change it if I believe in it. And it works the other way, too. If they like something that I don't, it's still going to get changed."

Equally fundamental to her approach to everything New York City Opera will undertake is the conviction it must reflect American input, American talent. She is fighting for recognition of the company, whose roster is indeed 98 percent American, as *the* national American opera company. And she wants it made official, hoping for government acknowledgment that only the New York City Opera has the right to make this claim. It is a status in relation to the Metropolitan that would be equivalent to the English National Opera in relation to Covent Garden.

To bolster this position and also to give some young promising performers experience in leading roles, a National Opera Touring Company, under the aegis of New York City Opera, was instituted in 1980 with an extensive tour of *Traviata*. This dependent company is now booked by

Columbia Artists, and plans, at this writing, an equally ambitious future schedule. Beverly says that "it would be horrendous for a young soprano to do her first Violetta on our stage and face the New York critics. Instead, she gets fifteen Violettas under her belt out of town. Then I'll bring her in, maybe not as Violetta right away, but introduce her as Musetta or Micaela."

In discussing all these projects, aspirations, and great belief in the future of the New York City Opera and that of the American way with opera, Beverly is filled with enthusiasm. "I'm committed to this company. I've had offers elsewhere, but I love it here. It feels good, even if it's a terrific challenge to my stamina. It's what I want to do now. Everything I've ever done is what I've wanted to do." She is determined to do well as General Director, but there is no do-or-die dimension in this. She will continue as long as she feels her contribution is the one the company needs and as long as the act of making that contribution pleases her.

Working for New York City Opera, Beverly has found, does not only require keeping her hand on the controls in the administrative basement from early morning to the dropping of the 11 P.M. curtain in the auditorium. It also means raising money—everywhere, anywhere, and at any time. Although she says its a tough job, anyone who has picked up the telephone to hear on the other end the delighted greeting of "Hi, this is Beverly!" knows she probably deserves her reputation as the surest "toucher" in town. Perhaps the only really hard part for her is getting down all those extra breakfasts and lunches that seem to be indispensable to the money-gathering process. She laughingly calculates twenty-two extra pounds directly attributable to the eating-for-bucks routine. Actually she is a good fund-raiser, and she's prepared to give ample testimony to the fun she gets out of this aspect of her work.

"It takes a lot of time. Those breakfasts and lunches go on for hours. And you sometimes deal with the wives first who want to know all about Johnny Carson, Carol Burnett, Dinah Shore, and Barbara Walters. Once when this was going on for quite some time, I said to the woman that I really had to speak to her husband about money. She patted me on the hand and said, 'Don't worry, honey. Just finish your lunch. He'll give you what you want.'"

Beverly is known for her persistence, and she is not really bothered by the mechanics of fund-raising. She takes a no with as much equanimity as she does a yes. More importantly, she is convinced of the seriousness of her mission. Also, she recognizes that as a spokesperson for New York City Opera and for the arts in general, she deploys credibility that those she addresses, in turn, complement with a good deal of support.

"I'm a middle-aged woman they can identify with. I've had family problems, just the way everyone else has, and I've been married to the same man for twenty-five years. Besides, they know I can speak with authority, that there's never been any self-promotion in my career. They trust me. They know I won't take advantage of them."

Some of her "marks" seem in the long run to get as much of a kick out of the financial tug of war as she does. She relates the tale of Milton Petrie, a businessman whom she first met at a dinner party in New York. She had been encouraged by mutual acquaintances to ask him for a contribution to New York City Opera. When the two were seated next to each other at table and she steered the conversation to her favorite charity, describing its all-American character, Petrie interrupted her. "Look. You're my dinner partner. I'll give you ten thousand dollars and we won't have to talk about it anymore." Beverly, nothing daunted, replied, "My husband gives ten thousand dollars. That's ridiculous. I'm out for something much bigger, so you're not going to get rid of me for ten thousand dollars. Tonight we won't talk about money at all. We'll talk about you and me and we'll make another dinner appointment."

When Beverly was invited to the Petrie home in New York for dinner, she asked if this was the "ask for money dinner" or was she just supposed to enjoy the food. She could solicit only during the first half, Petrie chuckled. And so again began a fervent pitch about the opera company with the all-American complexion. And again came the interruption. "Okay, how much do you want?" "A half million," was the ready answer. Without losing a beat, Petrie nodded, smiled another okay, and inquired, "Now, what do you want to eat?"

Beverly, understandably, seems to love all New York City Opera backers, and they obviously love her right back. When Lawrence Deutsch died, his business associate and co-founder of Adolph's Meat Tenderizer, Lloyd E. Rigler, took up exactly where Mr. Deutsch had left off. On trips to New York, he spends entire days in the New York City Opera offices, offering its employees the benefits of his business acumen.

Leslie R. Samuels has been a committed supporter of all the various parts of Lincoln Center for some time. When Beverly took the reins of New York City Opera, he had already endowed $250,000 for a conductor's chair for the company. Mr. Samuels turned out to be a figure from Beverly's earlier years. When it was suggested she make early and quick contact with him, Beverly did so, not realizing that this was a friend from the past. She telephoned his office, was put through and a voice said, "Hi, gorgeous!" Her mouth fell open. "Instantly forty years dropped away. It all came back. When I was a youngster, Miss Liebling and Mama used to take me once a year to the Samuels' beautiful apartment where I would sing 'Happy Birthday' and one or two arias for his wife, Fan Fox. I used to do her birthdays until I was sixteen or seventeen. It was a wonderful reunion. He's been very special and generous, and I was happy I was one of the people Fan, who died this year, wanted to see at the end."

Director Sills can still frequently be found, as she could in her peak performing years, working at some distance from the opera stage. The television appearances continue—hosting the "In Performance at the White House" series which will feature a Christmas broadcast starring members of the New York City Opera, or the Carnegie Hall Gala of Stars on PBS, which, if any doubt ever existed, gave stunning proof of her consummate poise as a mistress of ceremonies. She regrets that the *Skyline* for PBS, as well as *Lifestyles* for NBC—interview shows with personalities in almost every field—could not go on. But the demands of taping a regular show made severe inroads on her time. "It was a case of too much success," she comments. "They wanted to expand the show, and I just couldn't do it." However, she may again fill a regular stint for PBS. She has also signed with a cable company to shepherd twelve "mega-events." And her thirst to do comedy—to follow up on that enormously successful 1976 Thanksgiving special with Carol Burnett—has not been slaked. "I would drop everything to do a show with Carol, maybe something with Carol, Dinah, and Eydie Gormé. Danny Kaye and I late one night—or was it early one morning?—got giggling about doing something called 'Two Redheads from Brooklyn.' Who knows?"

And she is prepared to go much further afield than television. The spring of 1981, at the invitation of the People's Republic of China Minister of Culture, Beverly, her husband and daughter, accompanied by the one-time Met impresario Schuyler Chapin and his wife, flew to Peking and Shanghai for a series of master classes and meetings with officials avid to learn how a people's opera company worked. It seemed they believed the New York City Opera deserved this designation better than the Met, and therefore was closer to an imitable model for them.

As Beverly tells it, the trip was a combination of rigors and rewards. Very careful to leave her jewelry (her "clunkers," as she calls them) behind, she equipped herself with a half-dozen proletarian shirt dresses from Neiman-Marcus and espadrilles. Fortunately, she also took with her a plastic bottle of Fantastik, for the palatial accommodations the Greenoughs were assigned in the Peking Hotel proved to house equally palatial roaches, minimally functioning plumbing, and to be innocent of regular chambermaid attention. The master class schedule never seemed to end, a fierce heat wave descended, and a tired, not very well-washed Beverly Sills gradually noted she was losing control of her chopsticks. She began dotting the front of her six N-M uniforms with spots her amused, if not sufficiently sympathetic, travel companions nicknamed "Beverlies." Perhaps the worst of it was that at the apex of her discomfort, who should show up in the Peking Hotel dining room but a be-diamonded, be-pearled, utterly unflapped, and evidently China-proof Kitty Carlisle. "She looked gorgeous," Sills remembers, shaking her head.

But the master classes themselves turned out to be enormously interesting for her as well as for the Chinese, who jammed the halls where they took place. Sills came upon an incredible degree of raw talent and, more than that, energy, a general will to accomplish, which she predicts will enable the Chinese in the near future to astound the Western world with what it can do in both arts and handicrafts.

Contacts with Chinese officials were extraordinarily candid. Beverly suggested liberalizing control so that Chinese musicians—especially would-be opera singers—could travel abroad to acquaint themselves with international standards and accomplishments. "If you make life in China attractive enough," she told the ministers, "they won't want to defect." They sat back in those strange, upholstered, fat-armed chairs and stared at her impassively, but Beverly hopes the substance of her "let your people go" speech registered loud and clear.

It is now the fall of 1981. Beverly Sills has been long back from China. Her fifty-second birthday was celebrated in Shanghai, and not on the Côte d'Azur or Martha's Vineyard, as she had originally and self-indulgently hoped. The New York City Opera season has begun—a spanking *Nabucco* featuring Grace Bumbry, in her debut with the company, and Justino Diaz—after a financially upbeat run of *The Student Prince* and *Song of Norway*. The future, as always, is uncertain. Will the new *Traviata* equal the old Corsaro production? Will *Freischütz* attract an audience? Will *Puritani* conquer as it did in former years? Will there be enough money? Will the patrons continue to come through? Will the company weather Reagan cutbacks? Beverly is in her office, and she worries about these matters and many more—from the most mundane to those with the greatest imaginable trajectory. But the conquering, incomparable smile never deserts her. The phone rings and the radiant "Hi!" echoes through the room. She's having the time of her life, at this, a very new and decidedly fascinating time in her life.

Credits

A great many of the photographs used in this book came from my personal albums. For permission to publish the others I gratefully acknowledge the photographers and organizations listed below.

Abresch, James: page 32, 47 right, 48
Angel Records: 204
Bagby, Beth: 125
Bergman, Beth (Copyright): 86 bottom, 105 bottom right and left, 108 bottom, 109, 116, 123 (all), 127 top, 129, 130 (all), 133, 134 left, top right, 154 bottom, 163 right, 174 bottom, 181 top left, 195 top, 198, 227 top
Birnbaum, Jesse (Copyright Time Inc.): 127 bottom
Boenzi, Olga, 218 top
Bruno of Hollywood, NYC: 21 bottom left, 60, 63 bottom left
Classic: 40
Drake, Fletcher: 194
Dunand, Frank/Metropolitan Opera Guild: 132, 134 bottom right
Fehl, Fred: 63 bottom right, 64 (all), 77 bottom, 80, 86 top, 96, 104, 105 top, 106 bottom, 115, 124, 164, 165, 195 bottom
Garrison Recording Company: 50, 56 (all)
Grossman, Henry: frontispiece, 135, 136, 157, 177, 178 bottom, 179 top, 180 (all), 181 top right and bottom, 182, 183, 184, 203, 206, 210, 216/217, 220 top, 221, 225 (both), 230, 231
Hagmann, Mark: 46, 76 top
Heffernan, James: 178 top, 179 bottom, 251
Howard, Ken: 166, 175 bottom
Jones, Carolyn Mason: 226
Le Blang, Sedge: 77 top

March of Dimes: 196
Marcus, Helen (Copyright): 218 bottom

Marshall, Margaret: 107 bottom
Mazelis, V.: 76
McCombe, Leonard (Copyright Time Inc.): 156 bottom
McDowall, Roddy/Lee Gross: 158, 162 (both), 163 left
Meola, Eric: 131
Metropolitan Opera Guild: 132, 134 bottom right
Murphy, Mary/New York City Hall: 252
Opera Company of Boston Inc.: 106 top, 107 top, 154 top
Opera Company of Boston Inc./Milton Feinberg: 205 (all), 207 top
Pan American World Airways: 79 bottom
Peres, Louis: 172, 173
Photo Emka Ltd.: 192
Pote, Louise: 89
Rebman Photo Service: 75 top, 87 bottom
Rubinger, David/Time Inc.: 249

Saxon, Reed: 197
Schwartz: 49
Seligman, Paul (Copyright): 219, 220 bottom
Seymour, Maurice: 22
Smith, H. S.: 21 top
Specht, Edward John: 207 bottom
Time Inc. (Copyright): 127 bottom, 156 bottom, 249
UPI: 47 left, 63 top left
The White House: 174 top, 208
Whitestone Photo: 126
Reg Wilson/Angel Records: 204

Index

Page numbers in italics refer to photographs.

Epilogue Index

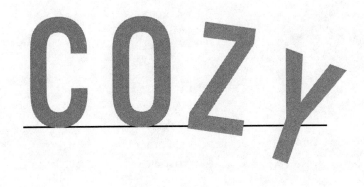

ALSO BY PARNELL HALL

THE STANLEY HASTINGS NOVELS

Detective
Murder
Favor
Strangler
Client
Juror
Shot
Actor
Blackmail
Movie
Trial
Scam
Suspense

THE STEVE WINSLOW COURTROOM DRAMAS (as J. P. Hailey)

The Baxter Trust
The Anonymous Client
The Underground Man
The Naked Typist
The Wrong Gun

THE PUZZLE LADY CROSSWORD PUZZLE MYSTERY SERIES

A Clue for the Puzzle Lady
Last Puzzle & Testament

COZY

A STANLEY HASTINGS MYSTERY

PARNELL HALL

An Otto Penzler Book

CARROLL & GRAF PUBLISHERS, INC.
NEW YORK

First Carroll & Graf edition 2001

Carroll & Graf Publishers, Inc.
A Division of Avalon Publishing Group
19 West 21st Street
New York, NY 10010-6805

Library of Congress Cataloging-in-Publication Data is available.

ISBN: 0-7867-0874-3

Manufactured in the United States of America

FOR JIM AND FRANNY

ONE

"I MISS HIM already."

Oh, dear.

It was not five minutes since we'd dropped Tommie off at sleep-away camp, and Alice missed him already.

Which is not surprising. This marked the first time Tommie'd been away from home. Oh, he'd been to camp before, but that was day camp in Riverdale, not ten minutes out of New York City. Camp Keewaydin was a good six-hour drive, and he was staying eight full weeks.

The camp was located on Lake Dunmore in Vermont, and a more idyllic setting would be hard to find. Tommie's platform tent, in which he would be living with a counselor and three other campers, was just behind the backstop of a baseball diamond. Right across the lawn were the clay tennis courts and all-dirt basketball court, which would become mud holes the first time it rained, doubtlessly to the delight of all; the outdoor boxing ring, which I hoped Tommie would have the good sense not to enter; the wooden footbridge over the road to the riflery and archery ranges, which we had been assured were supervised with great caution; and of course the dock with swimming raft, canoes, kayaks, and windsurfing. By all rights, Tommie was going to have a wonderful time.

We weren't.

Or at least, that was Alice's judgment. Alice felt sending Tommie off to camp was going to make the two of us suddenly feel old and useless. This hadn't occurred to me until Alice pointed it out. The minute she did, I began to feel old and useless. Only I wasn't sure if I really felt that way, or was just very suggestible.

I don't mean to sound cynical. I know Alice is totally sincere. As soon as she began sewing name tags in Tommie's socks, she got a misty look in her eye. Old and useless was just around the corner.

A further extension of Alice's theory was that we should not go home—returning to an empty apartment would only make us depressed. Instead, Alice had planned a vacation for us, hiking in the mountains of New Hampshire. She had done so on her own. It is not exactly the vacation I would have planned. Hiking is not a sport I recognize. Neither is jogging. Basically, for me to move in one direction or another, there has to be a ball involved. Either that or water. I am very happy at the seashore. I can ride the waves all day.

Inland, I do not prosper.

But Alice had her theories, and Alice had her plans. And as they stemmed from an emotional need, I didn't feel it was my place to argue with them.

At any rate, the long and the short of it was, Alice and I were off on an elaborate adventure to make sure that we didn't miss Tommie too much.

Only Alice missed him already.

So did I.

TWO

"WHERE ARE WE?"

I hate it when she does that. There it is, the simplest of questions, but it drives me nuts. Where are we? Well, how should I know? I've never driven these roads either. And I've seen the same road signs she has. So, basically, "Where are we?" is a euphemism for "Look at the map."

And I hate looking at the map. I mean, are we driving through the country to see the country or to see the map? I could have stayed at home in New York and looked at the map. If we're in the car, I would like to look out the window and see the scenery. But, oh no, Alice says, Where are we?, and there I am, fumbling with the map, trying to locate the last recognizable landmark that we'd passed.

And knowing that when I'd found it, the job isn't done. Because Alice will say, What's it near? And then I have to get out the guidebook and look up the nearest point of interest. And read the description so Alice can make a value judgment as to whether it's worth us stopping to see it.

As if that weren't bad enough, we have two guidebooks.

Anyway, we were on our way to the inn, and Alice wanted to know where we were.

The short answer was on Route 112.

I gave Alice the short answer.

She gave me a withering look. Hard to do without taking one's eyes off the road, but she managed. "I *know* we're on Route 112," Alice said. "Where on Route 112 are we?"

We passed a sign for Greely Ponds.

"Greely Ponds," I said.

This did not win her heart.

"Where is Greely Ponds?"

I whipped out my guidebook, located Greely Ponds, and was about to triumphantly impart the information to Alice when I discovered the map had no scale.

"Come on," Alice said impatiently. "Where are we?"

"Well," I said. "We're somewhere between Lincoln and Bear Notch Road."

"What?"

"And it looks like we're a little closer to Lincoln."

"Where is Lincoln?"

"Didn't we go through Lincoln a few miles back?"

"I don't recall."

"Neither do I."

"Then why do you think we did?"

"Because 112 appears to go through Lincoln on the map."

"Appears?"

"This is a hike location map. It doesn't have dots for the towns."

"You're looking at the map in the guidebook?"

4

"Sure."

"That's the wrong map."

"It's the one that shows Greely Ponds."

"You've gotta look at the other map."

I didn't want to look at the other map. It was hard enough dealing with the guidebook. "Wait a minute," I said. "Let me look up Greely Ponds."

"I don't care about Greely Ponds."

"You wanna know where it is. Hang on. Greely Ponds, page 121. Greely Ponds, Greely Ponds. Here we go. Greely Ponds. The parking lot for Greely Ponds is on the south side of Route 112, nine miles east of Lincoln. There you are," I said triumphantly. "We're nine miles east of Lincoln."

"Where is that?"

"Huh?"

"What are we near?"

"Greely Ponds."

"No, damn it," Alice said. "What's next?"

See what I mean?

We were driving along what the other guidebook had described as the state's most popular road for viewing foliage. And it was indeed a gorgeous little mountain road. Only I wasn't seeing any of it. I was reading guidebooks and maps.

"Next up is Champney Falls," I said.

"What's that?"

"I don't know. I have to look it up."

"Well, hurry up before we get there, in case we wanna stop."

I sighed, flipped through the book.

"Champney Falls," I said. "A three-point-five-mile round-trip with a six-hundred-foot elevation gain. It has a wooden footbridge over the brook and rocks to scramble on at the falls."

"So how far is it?" Alice said.

"I told you. Three-point-five miles."

"No. On the map."

"Oh. About a half an inch."

"Stanley."

"Let's see. It's just past Bear Notch Road."

"We just passed that road."

"Then we should be there."

We were. Around a bend a sign announced Champney Falls. We pulled into a parking lot with about a dozen other cars. Alice popped the trunk, took out a backpack.

I shouldered the backpack. Considered what conceivable subterfuge could save me from schlepping it three-point-five miles. Failing to find one, I smiled stoically and followed Alice down the path.

In the beginning it wasn't that bad. The path was relatively wide, and while there was a slight incline, it wasn't steep enough to slow us down. At least to slow Alice down, which, if I may say so, is my main problem hiking with Alice. Though shorter than me, she takes longer strides. Either that or quicker ones. At any rate, wherever we're walking, it's all I can do to keep up with Alice. Throw in a backpack, and I'm really in trouble. So, even though the going was easy, I found myself lagging behind.

We stopped to rest shortly after that, sitting on a tree trunk that was lying beside the path.

"Want some water?" Alice said.

"Just a minute. I want to see where we are."

"Where we are?" Alice said. "We just got started."

"Yeah, but there's a map," I said. I looked in the guidebook. "Did we pass a big boulder with a tree on it?"

"Huh?"

"A great big rock with a tree growing off the top of it. You recall seeing anything like that?"

"No."

"Damn."

"What's the matter."

"It's near the beginning. If we haven't passed that, we haven't gotten anywhere."

"I told you we're just getting started."

"We've been hiking fifteen minutes. We should have passed that."

"We'll pass it soon. What other landmarks are there?"

"Just that. Till we get to the top."

"We're nowhere near there."

"My point exactly."

"So, let's go," Alice said.

And with that she was up and off, with me tagging along behind.

A little farther along we passed another couple coming down. That was fine. But five minutes later another couple passed us going up. Which was okay by me—we were sitting having another rest. I was drinking water this time, having exhausted the information in the guidebook, and Alice was sitting there doing her best impression of a person who didn't mind stopping again so soon.

She did okay until the couple went by. I don't think that pleased her at all.

"Are you ready?" she asked.

I took a breath. "They're younger than we are."

"What?"

"And they've probably hiked before. This is my first time."

"How are we going to hike if we don't ever hike."

"Just a few more minutes."

I got my few minutes. Unfortunately, another couple went by. And this time there was no need to point out they were younger than we were. They were, in fact, straight out of some hiking brochure designed to give the illusion that all participants in the sport were young, tan, and healthy.

Not to mention blonde. This couple could have come from a

Swedish hiking brochure. The boy looked lean and athletic. The girl looked lean and athletic. And fresh. And supple. And limber. And smooth. And soft. And—

But I digress.

The point is, this was an attractive young couple. I say boy and girl but I shouldn't, they were probably in their early twenties, and I'm sure they considered themselves quite mature, despite how adolescent they seemed to me.

At any rate, they breezed right on by us, underlining the fact that I was still sitting down.

So I stood up.

And Alice said, "Who you trying to impress now?"

It took me a moment to figure out what she meant. When I did, it seemed totally unfair.

Yes, indeed, the woman's blond pageboy cut did bob in a casually fetching way along the high cheekbones of a most attractive face. But that was not why I got up. I had not sprung to my feet to chase after my unobtainable lost youth. I had got up so as not to suffer any more of Alice's abuse.

Unlucky there.

There was nothing for me to say that wouldn't make things worse, and sitting back down again wasn't an option, so I gritted my teeth, shouldered my backpack, and set off down the path.

Did I say down the path? I should say up the path, because the incline had just gotten steeper. Of course this didn't bother Alice, she breezed right by me, forging on ahead. I trudged along behind, looking for landmarks and wondering how soon it would be safe to suggest stopping again.

We never found a big rock with a tree on it, but after a while I noticed we were traveling alongside a stream. Which seemed an awfully good sign on the one hand, and a reason for stopping and getting out the guidebook on the other. I did, and discovered the stream was called Champney Brook, and did indeed come from the falls.

And, unless we'd been walking parallel to it for some time without knowing it, we still had an awful long way to go.

I also found out we needed to take a left turn when the path forked. Which stood us in good stead more than an hour later when it finally did. By then we had ascended most of our six hundred feet, and it was just a short scramble over the trail to the base of Champney Falls.

I must admit, it was quite a sight. Water cascading over a series of ledges down to a pool below. There were children wading in the pool, a boy and a girl. Their parents sat on a rock nearby. The older couple that had passed us were there, too, sitting on a rock eating a picnic lunch. There was also a woman with a large dog of indeterminate breed, which was lying in the shade and looking hopefully at the people eating lunch.

The young couple was not there. Not that I looked for them, you understand, but one would have expected them to be. But they were nowhere to be seen.

Alice and I had lunch, which I hadn't even noticed she'd packed, but somehow turkey sandwiches miraculously appeared in a brown paper bag, purchased no doubt the night before while I was watching a ball game in the motel. Their appearance not only startled me, but also attracted the large floppy dog. It came galumphing over, plopped down in front of me, and proceeded to drool.

The woman followed him over. "I'm sorry," she said. "Prince has no manners. I'll put him on a leash if you mind."

"We don't mind," Alice said. "He's a sweetheart."

Easy for her to say. It wasn't her sandwich the sweetheart had his eyes on. Prince was a large, shaggy, golden-brown, floppy-eared beggar, who seemed to have perfected the art of making people feel guilty about whatever it was they were eating.

"What kind of dog is he?" Alice said.

"Oh, the best kind. Golden retriever, labrador, German shepherd, a dash of cocker spaniel, and maybe just a little St. Bernard."

It seemed to me that while she'd been saying this, Prince had somehow inched closer to my sandwich. I don't know how, I hadn't seen him move, but his paws appeared closer, and I could feel hot dog breath on my knee.

"Can I give him some?" I said.

The owner was a chunky woman who seemed to smile a lot. She did so now. "You can if you want to. I have to warn you, though, you'll make a friend for life."

"I'll risk it," I said.

I tore off a crust of bread, tossed it in front of the dog. He scooped it up, held it in his mouth on long teeth, as if reprimanding me for throwing it in the dirt. Then with one sudden huge gulp it was gone, and Prince was back in his begging position, down on all fours, saliva dripping, eyes turned up at me. And this time I actually saw him move, subtly, surreptitiously, scrunching first one and then the other paw forward, very much like a soldier with a rifle creeping forward on his elbows in the tall grass. Before I knew it, he was drooling on my hiking boots.

"I warned you," the woman said.

"Stanley's a sucker," Alice said.

I tore off another piece of sandwich, held it up, and said, "Sit."

His eyes never left the sandwich, but his expression said, "Are you kidding?" He continued to drool on the spot from which I had moved my foot.

I don't know how long the dog and I might have kept it up had there not come a loud snapping sound, like the crack of a whip. It cut right through the background noise of the waterfall, and echoed in the mountain air.

A sharp, slapping sound.

And a scream.

Not a long scream. Just a short, high-pitched cry of surprise and pain.

All heads turned at once.

Saw nothing.

The sound had come from somewhere off in the woods.

"What was that?" the woman said.

"I don't know."

"It sounded like someone got slapped," Alice said.

"Yeah, maybe," I said. "Should we go see?"

Alice looked at me. "Don't be silly. It's nothing. You hear anything now?"

No, I didn't. But whatever it was was not nothing. Someone had certainly screamed. I craned my neck, continued to look around.

For a second I thought I saw something through the trees. A flash of color, like someone's clothes. But I couldn't even say what color it was. Is that strange, to see it and not know? Because that's all it was, just the impression of someone moving through the leaves. I squinted my eyes, trying to pick it up again, and—

I was shocked back to earth by a warm, wet sensation on my cheek, and the sound of laughter.

Alice and the woman were laughing at the sight of me being slobbered on as I got my face licked by the large, sandwich-eating dog.

THREE

IT WAS MUCH easier going down. Which nearly restored my faith in hiking. Going up was an ordeal, but going down, hey, you had gravity in your corner. Just point your feet in the right direction, and let nature take its course. I found myself not only keeping up with Alice, but actually skipping on ahead.

"Take it easy," Alice said. "It's not a race."

Unbelievable, after the way she'd gone pelting up this same path.

"What's the matter?" I said. "Can't you keep up?"

"You're gonna twist your ankle. If you twist your ankle, there goes the whole vacation."

"I'm not gonna twist my ankle."

"You are if you don't look where you're going."

"I'm looking where I'm going."

"No, you're not. You're looking back at me."

"Only because you're talking to me," I said.

But, as usual, with Alice, I knew better than to argue. I stopped, let her catch up.

"Take it easy," she said. "He's not chasing you."

I blinked. "I am not running away from the dog."

Alice smiled. "You looked just adorable."

"I know, I know. I made your day."

"He was a very sweet dog."

"Wonderful. I'm sorry he couldn't have licked your face too."

"I didn't give him my sandwich."

"Right. He knew a sucker when he saw one. Well, I'm pushing off. Would you like a head start, or do you think you can keep up?"

"Don't be a jerk," Alice said. "Just watch where you're going and don't get hurt. I don't want to spend the whole vacation with you laid up in bed."

We continued down the path at what was a moderate pace compared to what I'd been doing, but was greased lightning compared to our pace coming up.

Speaking of which, we passed a number of people who were on their way up, and I could not help feeling smugly superior. After all, I had survived the climb, and was on my way down. And, whether it's psychological or not, I have to tell you, on the way up the people who passed us coming down looked happy, whereas on the way down, the people who passed us going up did not look pleased at all.

I had one other observation I was somewhat amused to find true. In whatever group of people it was that passed us, the grumpiest person was always the adult male. The father, the husband, the boyfriend, whatever. In a family, it was always dear old dad. Unless, of course, Grandpa was there to outgrump him.

But by far, the grumpiest of all was a man who came up alone. He was overweight, and clearly out of shape, huffing and puffing at every step. His bald head glistened with sweat. His shirt was soaked clean through. His shorts had slipped well below his waist, and appeared to be just on the verge of tripping him. He looked angry enough to bite someone's head off.

"See," I said, after he went by, "I am not the world's worst hiker. I am actually pretty damn good."

Alice shook her head. "Sorry," she said. "You score no points at all."

I blinked. "What?"

"That man is alone. No one made him go up the mountain. He's doing it on his own. You, on the other hand, had to be dragged. That man can bitch and moan all he wants about how terrible it is, but the fact remains he's a volunteer."

"Just because no one's with him doesn't mean no one made him do it," I said.

Alice cocked her head. "Are you saying I made you do it?"

And there I was again. *She* was the one saying nobody made him do it. It was *her* premise, not mine. I was an innocent bystander, just trying to hold up my end of the conversation. And suddenly there I was on the hook again.

"Well, for whatever reason he's going up the mountain," I said, "he certainly seemed unhappy."

Before Alice could point out that I'd deflected the question, I said, "Hey, look there."

"What is it?"

"Down there on the path."

"I don't see anything on the path. What are you talking about?"

"I don't mean on the path. Beside it."

"Stanley."

"It's the rock."

"What?"

"The big rock with the tree growing on top of it."

"Where?"

"Right there. That's the one in the guidebook."

It certainly was. I whipped out the guidebook, read the description again to make sure.

"That's it, all right," I said. "That's great."

"What's great about it?"

"Are you kidding. Look at this map. If that's this rock, we're almost back to the road. We made it down in no time."

"I told you you were going too fast."

"Come on. Let's see if it is."

We made our way down the path to what had to be the big rock with the tree growing out of it mentioned in the guidebook. When we got closer, I saw how we'd missed it on the way up. From nearby, you don't see the tree. You have to be farther away, and you have to be looking for it. We had already passed by before I noticed it in the guidebook.

I stood next to it, admiring its beauty, and congratulating myself on how quickly we'd gotten down the mountain.

There came a muffled sound from the other side of the rock. Sort of a stifled, half sob.

Alice and I both heard it. We looked at each other, shrugged. I gave a shall-we-walk-by-the-rock gesture, which Alice and I proceeded to do.

Standing in the trees at the far end of the rock was the girl. The blond girl with the backpack from the Swedish brochure who'd passed us on the way up. Somehow or other she'd managed to pass us again and get back down. She'd also lost her blond boyfriend along the way.

Which might have accounted for her mood. Her face was caked with tears, and it was obviously her sob we had heard.

She saw us, and immediately turned her head and took a few steps away.

I looked inquisitively at Alice.

She murmured, "Leave her alone," took me by the arm, and

led me away, as if I'd been about to intervene. Which isn't in my nature—a stranger's private business is their own.

Alice, on the other hand, might have jumped in, had it been anyone less attractive. That's not fair. I'm sure Alice would have offered aid, had it been appropriate.

Anyway, we went on by as if we didn't see her, and continued on down the path.

I felt bad.

No, not that we didn't help her—my personal opinion is the most help you can be to someone who's upset is to leave them alone. I felt bad for how I felt. I mean the moment I saw her. Saw her crying, that is.

Because I felt good. A sudden flash of elation. It was momentarily, fleeting, immediately gone. But there it was. The least admirable of all emotions, yet one's own.

It's hard to explain. You had to be there. You also had to be me. A middle-aged married man, incapable of winning an argument with his wife, climbing a mountain he didn't really want to climb, and being slapped in the face with the realization of just how old and out of shape he actually was.

And watching the young, perfect couple go scampering up the slope without a care in the world.

It reminded me of the scene in Kurt Vonnegut's *Sirens of Titan* where Rumfoord shows Malachi Constant a painting of his wife as a little girl, dressed entirely in white, the cleanest, most frozen little girl Malachi had ever seen, and Rumfoord says, "Wouldn't it be too bad if she fell into a mud puddle?" which startles Malachi who had just been thinking she looked as if she were afraid of getting dirty.

I realize the example isn't as great as I thought it was. The two young backpackers didn't look like they were afraid of anything. What I'm getting at is, they were so clean, fresh, young, carefree, that you almost wanted to strangle them. At least to say, "Excuse me, you can't go scampering up the mountain so gleefully with wild abandon. There is such a thing as real life, with limits and consequences and responsibilities and cares."

Does that make any sense? I doubt it. The point is, the young couple unwittingly trigger the jealousy that's in us all, and subconsciously one cannot help but long to see them taken down.

So the sight of the woman in tears was actually wish-fulfillment.

For one split second.

Followed immediately by shame and guilt.

Add in the fact my wife was needling me about finding the young woman attractive, and the whole thing was not a pretty picture.

We reached the car in nothing flat, and within five minutes we were safely out of Champney Falls and on the road again.

Still, all things considered, it was just not my day.

FOUR

"IT'S A BED-and-breakfast."

"No, it's not. It's an inn."

"The guidebook says it's a bed-and-breakfast."

"The guidebook is wrong."

"How can the guidebook be wrong?"

"Don't be silly," Alice said. "Guidebooks are wrong all the time."

"It's listed under *Bed-and-Breakfasts*."

"It's listed wrong."

"No, no," I said. "You don't understand what I mean. It's not like they listed it and then said it's a bed-and-breakfast. There's a whole section in the guidebook for bed-and-breakfasts. And that's the section it's in."

"That's the wrong section."

"How do you know?"

"I *know*," Alice said. "Do you really think I don't know?"

"I didn't say that. All I said was—"

"I bet you don't even know what a bed-and-breakfast is."

"Huh?"

"You know what it is? You're telling me this place is a bed-and-breakfast. You know what that is?"

"I'm just telling you how it's listed."

"You don't know what it is, do you?"

"Sure, I do. A bed-and-breakfast is a place that serves breakfast."

"So is an inn."

"Huh?"

"An inn serves breakfast. What's the difference between an inn and a bed-and-breakfast?"

"Ah . . ."

"I don't believe it. Here you are, insisting the place isn't an inn, it's a bed-and-breakfast, and you don't even know the difference."

"What's the difference?"

"A bed-and-breakfast just gives you breakfast. It doesn't serve dinner."

"An inn serves dinner?"

"Of course."

"And a bed-and-breakfast doesn't?"

"That's right."

"So why don't they call it a bed and no dinner?"

"Don't be dumb."

"Is that the only difference?"

"Not at all. A bed-and-breakfast is run by homey folks who introduce themselves to you, and sit on the porch with you, and tell you stories of how they came to buy the place and the tribulations they've had in running it."

"You're kidding."

"It's all right. We're not staying in a bed-and-breakfast. The Blue Frog Ponds is an inn."

"Then why isn't it called the Blue Frog Ponds Inn?"

"It was probably too long to fit on the sign."

"Fit on the sign? Inn has three letters, Alice. I mean, it's not like this was the Blue Frog Ponds University of Psychoanalytic Studies or something."

"Stanley, it's an inn. I booked it. I know. This is a new addition to the guidebook, and whoever added it, added it wrong. Trust me, it's an inn."

Oh, dear.

Those dread words.

I must explain. I'm a private detective, but I don't really see myself as one, it's just what I do to pay bills. I'm also an actor and a writer, and once I even got a screenplay produced.

For anyone who's ever worked in the motion-picture industry, the words *trust me* have a very unpleasant connotation.

So, it was with some trepidation that I watched Alice turn into the Blue Frog Ponds. Was this really an inn, or might it be after all the dreaded bed-and-breakfast?

From the outside it was hard to tell. A circular drive led up to a large white house with blue trim. It was surrounded by grass, and flower beds, and a wooden front porch with table and chairs, suitable for telling guests long stories of how one had acquired the building.

Hmmm.

A sign hanging off the porch said BLUE FROG PONDS. But I knew that didn't mean anything, because after my talk with Alice I had been poring over the guidebook, and not only did not all the inns call themselves inns, but some of the bed-and-breakfasts called *themselves* inns.

I followed Alice up on the front porch, went inside. We found ourselves in a living-room/foyer/hallway sort of deal. In the back right corner was a short wooden bar with three stools, behind which a rather frumpy-looking woman in a print dress was waiting on a middle-aged couple. The man was drinking Bud Light, and the woman was drinking wine.

And they were paying.

That seemed like a very good sign.

Now if we could only check in. But there didn't seem to be a front desk.

The frumpy woman said, "Just a minute, I'll be right with you." She finished making change and came out from behind the bar, which redefined frumpy as plump frumpy. She said, "Can I help you?"

"Yes," Alice said. "We have a reservation. Hastings."

"Of course," she said.

She marched to a breakfront on the wall, flipped down a panel of what proved to be a pull-out desk, consulted a ledger, and said, "Yes. You're in room twelve. You reserved this on MasterCard. You want to pay for it on that?"

Alice produced the card.

I expected the woman to put it in one of those machines you pull the bar across and make an imprint on a form. Instead, she flipped open another breakfront, revealing a computer-and-modem setup, and scanned the card electronically, just as if we'd been staying in some hotel chain.

"There you go," she said, handing the card back to Alice. She bent down, peered at a pegboard in the first breakfront. There were a series of hooks numbered one through twelve. She selected two keys from hook number twelve.

I must say, I found the whole transaction encouraging. First off, we were in room twelve. Surely a house with twelve rooms for rent couldn't be a bed-and-breakfast, could it? No, anything that extensive had to be an inn.

Then there were the two guests at the bar. They were not being offered drinks by a gracious host, they were *paying* for them.

But the payoff was the MasterCard. It was not just a MasterCard, but an *electronically scanned* MasterCard. Surely that had to mean inn.

I was feeling so good I smiled at the woman as she handed me the keys.

She smiled back. "My name's Louise."

Uh-oh.

Bed-and-breakfast.

FIVE

ROOM TWELVE OF the Blue Frog Ponds Inn, Bed-and-Breakfast, or whatever it happened to be, wasn't even in the building. It was out the side door, up the driveway, in a two-story frame house off to the right. It was also white with blue trim, and there was a blue frog on the front door. It occurred to me, at least it wasn't a cartoon, just a simple overhead shot of a frog, accurate in every aspect with the exception of being blue.

To the left of the door, a blue-and-white sign read EAST POND. A sign below that read 9–12.

"Here we are," Alice said. "Rooms nine through twelve."

"Or those are the hours the building is open."

Alice gave me a look, tried the door.

The building indeed had rooms nine through twelve. Nine and ten were apparently on the ground floor, because Alice and I were immediately greeted by a narrow staircase with the sign 11–12 and an arrow pointing up. We went up the stairs to an equally narrow hallway, which also featured a low, slanted ceiling, running as it did the length of the building under the eaves. Alice was able to walk upright, but I had to duck slightly. A small annoyance, but for someone lugging a suitcase, enough to grate.

The first door we came to was room eleven.

I stopped and blinked.

"Oh, dear."

There was a frog on the door. But it was not like the frog downstairs. This frog would have been happy at Disney World. It was a cartoon frog, with big eyes and a big smile, standing on its hind legs and acting human, just like Mickey Mouse or Goofy.

The frog, of course, was blue. He was wearing red shorts and a white T-shirt. Stitched onto the pocket of the shirt was the name Freddie.

Freddie had one thumb and three fingers, just like a Disney character, and with his left hand he was making a big okay sign, with his thumb and index finger curled into a circle and his two remaining fingers pointing up into the air.

He was also winking.

"Uh-oh," I said. "Do you suppose we have our own frog?"

We did. He wore yellow shorts and a white T-shirt with the name Frankie on the pocket. Frankie was standing with his hands in his pockets and his head cocked to one side. He wasn't winking, but his eyes were bright, and he had a sort of enigmatic smile.

"Hey," I said. "I think our frog's better than their frog."

"Don't start with me," Alice said.

"Did you know this when you booked the room?"

Alice didn't answer, just opened the door and went in.

I followed, lugging the suitcase.

It was a simple room. A double bed. A dresser. A chair. A closet and a small bath. The floor was wood, and there was wallpaper on the walls. A simple floral design. The only hanging picture was a landscape. The was a relief. I'd half expected to see poker-playing frogs. But no, the room was simple and spare and—

"Hey," I said. "Where's the TV?"

"Stanley, this is not a motel. It's an inn. They don't have TV in the rooms."

"Sure they do."

"No, they don't. Don't be silly. Nobody goes to an inn to watch television."

"But—"

"Does the guidebook say this place has TV?"

"It doesn't say one way or another."

"There you are."

"But most of the inns have TV. I can show you."

"What's the big deal?"

"Bed-and-breakfasts don't."

"Are you going to start that again?"

"This is listed as a bed-and-breakfast."

"Stanley, what's the big deal about television?"

The big deal about television was I'm a Red Sox fan, and living in New York City all I get are Yankee and Mets games. For me, getting to see the Sox was one of the main attractions of vacationing in New England. They were playing the Blue Jays this afternoon, and I must confess I'd been looking forward to getting up to the room and switching it on.

"Well," I said, "there's a Red Sox game."

"Now?" Alice said.

"Yeah. It's on now."

"So go watch."

"Huh?"

"They'll have a TV in the inn. Go watch the game and stop being such a cranky puss."

"But—"

"Go on, go on. I'll be fine. You go watch the game, and I'll unpack for us."

With Alice being so nice it was hard to point out that a TV in the inn wasn't nearly the same thing as a TV in the room. I was still horribly disappointed with the whole affair, and couldn't shake the nagging suspicion that I had been somehow manipulated into a bed-and-breakfast against my will.

On the ground floor I couldn't resist checking out the other rooms. Unless they happened to have televisions, their main advantage seemed to be that one could stand upright in the hallway outside 'em.

Of course, each room had a frog. For my money, Felix, green pants, room nine, looked rather smug, while Fredericka, pink dress, room ten, looked rather coy.

I let myself out of the front door of East Pond and briefly considered checking out the frogs in the West Pond building opposite.

Very briefly.

I headed for the main pond, or building, or whatever, in quest of the TV.

I figured the most likely place would be the bar. Naturally, I figured wrong. No one actually sat at the bar, it merely dispensed alcohol for people to carry out onto the porch. Not that there were a lot of people out there—in fact, the only ones were the couple that I had observed earlier buying drinks.

While I stood there looking stupid, halfway between the bar and the porch, Louise suddenly appeared behind me, which was a bit disconcerting—I had not seen her make an entrance, and there did not appear to be any door.

"Can I help you?" she asked.

"Is there a television?"

"Oh, yes, of course." She pointed. "Through the living room, and it's the door on the right."

"You have cable?"

"Sure do. Seventy-two channels."

That was a relief. I had been envisioning a worthless pair of rabbit ears, or some ancient antenna on the roof I'd have to climb up and try to turn.

"Do you get NESN?"

"New England Sports Network? We sure do."

"Great," I said. "Thanks a lot."

I went through the living room, which was empty but which featured a number of chairs and couches of which Alice could tell you the period but which I could only classify as old, and into the TV room.

Which was almost empty.

There was one occupant. A young girl, maybe five or six. She had blond curls, a pink dress, and a Barbie doll.

But she wasn't playing with the Barbie doll.

She was watching TV.

Nickelodeon.

The children's channel.

She heard me, turned, looked up. From her expression, I must have impressed her as that man her mother had taken great pains to warn her about.

I smiled ruefully, beat a hasty retreat back to the room, where Alice was arranging clothes in one of the dresser drawers.

"What's the matter?" she said. "No TV?"

"There's a TV. It's being watched by a six-year-old child. I didn't ask her if she might prefer baseball."

"Were her parents there?"

"Not so you could notice."

"Then they can't have left her long. I'd try back in a little while."

"The game'll be over in a little while."

"Don't be a grouch. Go do something else."

"Like what?"

"There's a swimming pool and a putting green."

"How do you know?"

"It's in the guidebook."

"What guidebook?"

"Not the guidebook. The directory. The brochure. The list of services." Alice pointed. "There. On the table."

I picked up what proved to be a two-page booklet, or four-page, if you were counting sides. On page three, or the front of page two, depending on how you figured, was a listing of recreational services. These included a TV room, swimming pool, and putting green.

"There's also shuffleboard," I said.

"Yes, I know."

"Would you care for a game?"

"I'm not sure we're old enough."

"We could use phony IDs."

"I'm still unpacking," Alice said. "Why don't you go swim or putt?"

That seemed better than watching her unpack. I put on my swimsuit, went out to look for the pool. It wasn't near East Pond, and it wasn't near West Pond either. But from there I could see a pool where South Pond would have been, just around the far side of the inn. On my way I detoured past the TV room, but, as expected, Nickelodeon was still on. I gave up on the Red Sox as a lost cause, and headed out to the pool.

It was sunny and warm, and I would have expected the pool to be crowded, but apparently the Blue Frog Ponds didn't have that many guests. Uncharitably, it occurred to me that was probably due to bad word of mouth.

The pool was surrounded by a wooden fence. I opened the gate, went inside.

The pool was not entirely unoccupied. There was one person there. The woman was sunbathing. She was lying on her stomach on one of the lounge chairs.

She was nude.

At least, she looked nude. There was no bikini strap across her back. And that certainly was her bare behind. Good lord, she must have thought she had the place to herself. Maybe I should leave.

Then I saw the string around her waist. She was wearing a thong bikini. At least the bottom of it. And she'd probably just untied the top. So, for all intents and purposes, she was a fully dressed sunbather, and I could just ignore her and enjoy my swim.

I dropped my towel on a chair, kicked off my flip-flops, and pulled off my shirt. Stepped to the edge of the pool and dove in.

When I came up, it was only natural to see if the sunbather had reacted to my presence.

She had.

The young woman had raised her head to see who had joined her in the pool enclosure.

It was her. You know. The young, attractive, Swedish brochure, blond, crying hiker from Champney Falls.

And she smiled and said, "Hi."

I didn't want to talk to her. When we'd found her crying behind the big rock, Alice couldn't help whispering, "Looks like you broke her heart." And here she was, half naked, alone with me in the swimming pool enclosure, not half an hour after we'd checked in, and I could imagine what Alice would make of that.

But I couldn't be out and out rude, could I?

So I smiled and said, "Hi."

"You're new here, aren't you?"

"Just checked in."

"I thought so. I hadn't seen you here before."

The young woman had craned her neck to talk to me, revealing that she was indeed lying on an untied bikini top.

I pulled myself out of the pool and sat on the edge. Not to get a better view, merely to allow her a more comfortable position.

Honest.

"So, you've been here for a while?" I said.

"Since yesterday. It's nice, but there's not much to do."

"Except swim."

"Yes." She smiled, then put on a mock pout. "But, you know what? I don't really like the water. I just want to get a tan."

Oh, dear.

That was my cue, if ever I'd heard one, to compliment her on her body. Which would suddenly, instantly, and irrevocably have transformed the conversation from casual to flirting. Already, I was acutely aware of the fact the young lady had avoided the use of the pronoun *we*. From her conversation, the young man did not exist, and she was staying there alone.

I was even more acutely aware of the fact that I had not mentioned Alice. Which I certainly wanted to do. It just seemed so clunky to say, "Yes, I'm here with my wife."

On the other hand, it would have been easy for me to say, "Yes, we just checked in." Only I hadn't done it. In light of which, it was impossible to deny this girl's allure.

She actually seemed quite innocent. Aside from being half naked. There was a warm, puppy-friendly quality about her.

While avoiding the compliment, I didn't swim off. Instead, I deflected her remark with a joke. "You've been sunbathing since yesterday?"

She giggled at that, feeble joke though it was. "No, I went hiking. At some waterfall or other. I forget the name."

I could have told her. But if she hadn't recognized me from Champney Falls, I wasn't about to remind her. Embarrass her with the realization I'd seen her crying behind the rock.

"Yes," I said, "I'll probably be doing some hiking too. Well, enjoy your tan."

I slipped into the pool and swam off, aware of the fact I'd, once again, neglected to mention Alice. It occurred to me life was incredibly complicated. At least mine was.

I swam to the other side of the pool, pulled myself out, and toweled off. I noticed the young woman was no longer watching me, had gone back to working on her tan. She certainly made lying in a deck chair look desirable. I lay back in my deck chair, closed my eyes.

It was a gorgeous day. The sun was warm, but there was a cooling breeze. Lying there felt great. I was tired after hiking all day. It occurred to me I might fall asleep. I don't think I actually did, but rather drifted in a sort of blissful, semiconscious state, where there weren't any responsibilities, or decisions, or cares, or woes, and everything was kind of lazy, carefree, sunny, and bright.

"Look who's here."

The words snapped me back to reality. I opened my eyes to find Alice standing next to my deck chair.

Great. Look who's here, indeed. I know who's here, Alice. I didn't invite her, I didn't know she was coming, I didn't expect to see her, and I'm not going to take kindly to being blamed for it.

I was mulling over in my mind just how much of that I wanted to put into words, when Alice was suddenly bumped aside by something floppy and brown, and the next thing I knew I was being licked unmercifully again by the large, sandwich-eating dog.

SIX

"SHE'S FROM BOSTON," Alice said.

"Oh?"

"Well, just outside it, actually. She has a house with a yard, which is perfect for Prince. She said she wouldn't want to keep a dog in the city."

"Certainly not that dog," I said.

"She's divorced, runs an antique shop on Boylston Avenue. Her husband left her for a younger woman. He's a doctor, she's a manicurist."

"She runs an antique shop *and* gives manicures?"

"Don't be dumb. The younger woman's a manicurist. The one her husband left her for."

"Uh-huh," I said. "And how long ago did this happen?"

"I'm not sure," Alice said, and looked disappointed at herself at having failed to glean this bit of information in the full fifteen minutes she'd had talking to the woman while I was changing for dinner.

Alice and I were seated at a booth in the dining room of the Blue Frog Ponds. I had been more than a little reluctant to dine there, figuring the menu would be completely inedible on the one hand, or feature blue frog legs on the other, but Alice had told me not to fear. Whatever else the Blue Frog Ponds might be, its dining room was famous, listed in the guidebook as a four-star restaurant. Or, as Alice explained, it wasn't just for the guests, it was a place people actually came to eat.

I couldn't argue with that. There were two booths and about a dozen tables in the dining room, and almost all were full. We owed our booth to Alice's foresight in checking out the dining room on her way to the pool and making a reservation. I could see why she had. The booths were semiprivate, partitioned alcoves for two, with plush, cushioned benches, and a table of some dark wood or other of which I'm sure Alice would know the name. All in all, a very pleasant place to dine.

I looked at my menu. "Any tips on what to eat?"

"Huh?"

"Did the guidebook make any recommendations?"

"It said pay attention to the specials."

"I don't see any specials."

"Of course not. The waitress tells you the specials."

"So where's our waitress?"

"They're busy. I'm sure she'll be right over."

Our booth, though semiprivate, had a clear view of the dining room. Both the waitresses I could see were indeed busy. One of them was young and somewhat pretty, though not in the blond, Swedish, sunbather, hiker category. The other was middle-aged, and looked rather severe.

Naturally, that's the one we got. She strode up, whipped out a pad and pencil, and said, "Would you like to hear the specials?" Her tone implied if we didn't, we would be taken outside and shot.

"Yes, please," Alice said.

Our waitress had black hair streaked with gray, pulled back into a bun. The expression on her face gave the impression the bun was way too tight. "Very well," she said. "Our fish today is maki shark, with the chef's special sauce, mint potatoes, and fresh corn off the cob. We also have prime rib with horseradish. It comes with baked potato and mixed vegetables."

"What do you recommend?" Alice asked.

"The shark is excellent. But if you're really hungry, the prime rib is thick."

"I'll have that," I said.

"And I'll try the shark," Alice said.

"Would you like anything to start?"

"Are there any specials for appetizers?"

She shook her head. "There's a wide variety on the menu. Our barbecued ribs are famous." She cocked an eye at me. "But it's a large portion. You won't want to order it with the prime rib."

Damn. I'd been about to, and now I couldn't. I had half a mind to order it, just to show her. But I wasn't going to win Alice's heart by picking a fight my first night there.

"Maybe just a house salad," I said.

She nodded. "Good choice. Now, you, with the shark, might want something more substantial."

"I'll try the scampi."

"Fine. And a house salad?"

"Sold."

"Can I get you anything to drink?"

Alice ordered a white wine, and I ordered a Diet Coke. From the look on the waitress' face I might as well have ordered poison, but she wrote it down and went away.

"Cheerful," I said.

"I'm sure she's perfectly pleasant," Alice said. "They're just very busy."

"Even so."

"I bet she smiles when she brings us the drinks."

She didn't, but I scored no points in the matter, because our drinks were actually brought to the table by a boy who looked too young to be doing it. Whether he was a waiter, or a busboy, or even the bartender, I had no idea, but if he'd shown up in my bar I'd have carded him. Anyway, he brought the drinks to the table, asked which was which, and at least had the decency not to sneer when I claimed the Diet Coke.

Alice took a sip of wine, said, "So anyway, she seems very nice."

"The waitress?"

"No, not the waitress. The woman with the dog. You know, that dog likes you."

"He liked my sandwich."

"You never should have given it to him."

"I didn't expect to see him again. What is she doing here?"

"Hiking in the mountains."

"No, I mean *here*. At this bed-and-breakfast."

"It's an inn."

"Fine. What's she doing at this inn?"

"What do you mean, what's she doing here? She's staying here."

"Yeah, but why here? Did she follow us?"

"Well, of course not. Why would she follow us?"

"I don't know. We just wound up in the same place."

"Maybe so, but she certainly didn't follow us. She's been here since yesterday."

"Really?"

"Yes, of course, really."

"Then what was she doing at Champney Falls?"

"Hiking."

"Yeah, but—"

"But what?"

"You mean she went there to hike?"

Alice looked at me. "Yes, of course," she said. "So did we. What's so hard to understand?"

"I'm sorry," I said. "It's just we went there because we were driving by. So, in my mind, I didn't think of it as something important enough to actually drive to. See what I mean?"

"Yes, I see what you mean," Alice said. "You have the most convoluted thought process. Tell me something, what could it possibly matter?"

Our waitress suddenly materialized, slid salads in front of us, and stalked off without a word. That was the only problem with the booth—the side partitions acted like blinders, allowing people to sneak up on you.

I picked up my fork, said, "Damn."

"What's the matter?"

"She forgot to ask us what dressing?"

"Stanley, it's house salad. Comes with house dressing."

"Yeah, but I bet they have others."

"It looks good. Try it."

I tried it. As expected, it was some sort of vinaigrette. It wasn't half bad. Still, given a choice, I would have opted for something more along the lines of blue cheese.

Alice's scampi hit the deck a moment later, accompanied by the admonition, "Don't touch it!" from the Miss Congeniality of the serving set. I'm sure she just meant it was hot, still I couldn't suppress the image of me reaching out for a shrimp and her smacking my knuckles with a ruler.

"What are you smiling at?" Alice said.

"Just a thought. What do you suppose her name is?"

"What do you mean, what do I think her name is?" Alice said. "You want me to guess her name?"

"I mean, how does she strike you? From her attitude."

"As a rather hassled waitress. What's your point?"

"No point. I was just playing a game. Like it occurred to me maybe her name was Olga and she used to moonlight as the head of a concentration camp."

"Nice guy," Alice said. "Is this just because she wouldn't let you have the barbecue ribs or put cheese glop on your salad?"

"Not at all," I said. "It's just if you were writing a murder mystery, she'd be the chief suspect."

"And therefore innocent," Alice said.

"Huh?"

"If she were as suspicious as you say, she'd have to be innocent. Otherwise there'd be no mystery. It would be too easy."

"Aha," I said. "But that's the double twist. You think it's too easy because she looks so guilty. So you figure she couldn't possibly be. But in point of fact she is."

"No good," Alice said.

"Why not?"

"Too convoluted. The double twist is the same as no twist at all. You wind up with the person who looks guilty being guilty. Wow, what a surprise."

"It is if you're led to think otherwise."

I was grateful the conversation had moved into a nonserious discussion of murder mysteries. I munched on my salad, and cast covetous glances at Alice's scampi. It was cool enough for Alice to eat, but I wasn't about to risk the ruler.

Our entrées arrived just then, and I found myself hard-pressed any longer to wish our waitress ill. Alice's shark was indeed a small portion, but my prime rib was an inch and a half thick and filled the plate. I kid you not. The potato and mixed vegetables came in side dishes. The beef stood alone.

I had just begun sawing into my mountain of meat when I heard, "Oh, to die for."

Alice had just tasted the shark. Evidently it was to her liking.

"Oh, Stanley, you have to try this. The sauce is magnificent."

To be honest, tasting shark is not a high priority in my life. I also had a mouthful of meat. Still, I was trying to be a good sport. I chewed, swallowed, took a sip of water.

Alice dipped a bit of shark in the sauce, held the fork out to me. I accepted it rather tentatively on long teeth, but had to admit it was quite good.

"See?" Alice said. "It's the sauce. The sauce is to die for."

I wouldn't have gone that far, but it was rather tasty. Still, I was happy enough to return to my prime rib. I attacked it vigorously, and polished it off about the same time Alice finished her shark.

"And how was everything?" demanded our waitress.

It struck me as a perfunctory and practically rhetorical question. I couldn't help wondering how the woman would react to anything but abject praise. On the other hand, I couldn't think of a single thing to complain about.

And Alice was still sky-high. "The shark was to die for." she said. "That sauce. What is in that sauce?"

"It's our chef's own recipe. Isn't it good?"

"It's to die for. I don't suppose . . . ?"

"What?"

"Would it be possible to get the recipe?"

She shook her head. "The chef does not make a policy of giving out his recipes."

There was something in the way she said it, and she and Alice exchanged a look. At least, that's how it seemed to me, but maybe I just imagined it, because a second later she said, "Would you care for dessert?"

"What do you recommend?" Alice said.

"The cheesecake is quite good. But if you prefer chocolate . . ."

"Yes?"

"Our chocolate cake is very popular. It's all chocolate, and very moist. It's so rich it has no frosting."

"I'll try it," Alice said.

"And I'll have the cheesecake," I said.

Alice and the waitress exchanged looks, as if to say, "How predictable." I must say, I felt somewhat picked on. What was wrong with having cheesecake?

I was about to voice that very thought when the blond hiking couple hoved into view. They were escorted across the dining room by the other waitress, and seated at a table right in our line of fire.

The young man was dressed in sneakers, shorts, and a white polo shirt, and looked as if he might have just stepped off center court at Wimbledon. The young woman was dressed in a two-piece pink sunsuit. While not nearly as revealing as her swimsuit, it still looked pretty good.

At any rate, it was impossible not to note their entrance.

"Ah," Alice said, "the floor show has arrived."

Having already taken a ribbing about talking to the girl by the pool, I was not looking forward to going through it again.

"Yes," I said. "And don't you find it a little strange?"

That caught Alice up short, and at least postponed whatever remarks she'd been about to make about the young lady's attire and my possible appreciation of it. She frowned, said, "What?"

"I mean, that they're here. Don't you find it strange that they're here? I mean, they're here, we're here, the woman with the dog is here. We were all at Champney Falls, and we're all here. It's like a bad mystery novel that's full of coincidences, where all the people in it keep bumping into one another for no apparent reason."

"I'm sure they have a reason."

"That's not the point. The point is, how did we all wind up here together? The girl says they checked in yesterday. But that doesn't have to be true."

Alice stared at me. "What are you getting at?"

"Well, did *they* follow us here?"

"Oh, for goodness' sakes."

"No, they couldn't have. When we left, she was still crying behind a rock. But what about the woman with the dog. They could have followed her here."

"Stanley . . ."

"See what I mean? They're not involved with us, but they could be involved with her."

"Stanley, what do you think you're doing?"

What I was doing was kidding around and trying to forestall any more husband-bashing.

"Shhh," I said. "Here comes the waitress. Don't let on. Just act natural."

Fortunately, that had the desired effect. Alice wasn't about to let a total stranger in on how goofy a moron she'd happened to marry. She just smiled and said, "Thank you," when the chocolate cake was slid in front of her.

Alice took a bite, and suddenly all was forgiven. Or at least forgotten. The look on her face approached ecstasy.

"Oh, my god," Alice said. "I don't believe this."

Alice's dessert was so moist and soggy it looked almost more like pudding than cake.

"Good?" I asked.

"Good? Stanley, I don't believe this cake. It's heaven."

It was, indeed. It had rescued me from the conversation. I took a bite of cheesecake—which wasn't heaven, but wasn't bad, either—and enjoyed a brief respite while the two of us drank our coffee and ate our dessert.

Unfortunately, having placed her order, the young woman got up and headed in the direction of the ladies' room, which of course led her right past our booth.

Alice watched her go, turned back, and said, "You were saying?"

"I don't remember what I was saying."

"Oh, yes, you do. You were advancing some insane theory

about how that young woman happened to be here. Probably to cover up the fact that she's actually here to see you."

"Oh, I'm sure she is. I just thought you might find that hard to accept."

"Not at all," Alice said. "I'm sure she *isn't*. Although you probably *think* she is."

"Thanks a lot."

"Anyway, do tell me your fascinating theory—what was it?— that they're here because they followed the woman with the dog. And just why would they do that?"

"Why, I have no idea. I was just saying they had the opportunity. When we left, the woman was still crying behind the rock. The woman with the dog was still up at the falls. By the time she came down, the boyfriend could have showed up, and the two of them could have followed her."

Alice looked at me. "What is this, a busman's holiday? You're a detective and you're on vacation, so you're going to make up a mystery wherever you go?"

"I'm just kidding around, Alice. All I'm saying is it's quite a coincidence, all of us winding up at the same place."

"Exactly," Alice said. "And that's all it is, coincidence. We came here because the other inn I called was full. I don't know why our friend with the dog came here, but I can certainly find out.

"And as for them," Alice said, jerking her thumb in the direction of the young woman, who had just walked by on her way back to her table, "they are probably staying here because they stayed here before, because it's a cheap place to stay, or because the other inns were full. All right, we all happened to be at Champney Falls. It's a coincidence, and that's all it is. And there's no reason to make anything more of it than that."

"Yeah, I know," I said.

And in walked the grumpy, overweight hiker with the bald head.

SEVEN

WHEN WE GOT back to the room after dinner, I suggested that since there was no television we find some other means by which to amuse ourselves.

To Alice, who knows me well, this was none too subtle a suggestion. She gave me her there-he-goes-again look, designed to make me feel like a moronic, sexist pig, incapable of controlling his base, primitive urges. But, as I pointed out, this was the first time in years we'd been vacationing alone, and it was somewhat like a second honeymoon. And I was gentle and romantic and suave and tender and caring and loving, and in every way, shape, and form, the epitome of a perfect gentleman, and the long and the short of it was Alice was moved by the sentiment, and before you know it she was in my arms, and I was nuzzling her hair, and things were looking awfully good.

And someone in the next room coughed.

You couldn't mistake it. It was as loud as a pistol shot.

Alice stiffened and pulled away, and I knew I was dead.

"Did you hear that?" she whispered. "The walls are paper-thin. You can hear everything. *Everything.*"

I whispered something about how I could be quiet, but it was a lost cause, Alice was having none of it. And just like that, our romantic evening went down the drain. And, I realized, so did all of them. Good lord, how many nights were we staying here? And I thought not having a TV was bad. Say it ain't so, Alice. Say it ain't so.

Unfortunately, it was so, and after a few more whispered arguments, entreaties, and pleas, I gave up the fight and accepted Alice's invitation to go for a walk. A walk wasn't exactly what I had in mind, but anything beat hanging out in a room so devoid of creature comforts.

First off, we stopped by the inn to see if anything was going on. Surprisingly enough, there was. From the tinkle of glasses and silverware coming from the door of the dining room dinner was still being served. And the bar was absolutely jumping with two, count 'em, two patrons sitting on bar stools sipping drinks, two young men who sat there chatting happily as if no one had told them sitting at the bar simply wasn't done. On the other hand, the middle-aged couple I'd previously seen on the porch was back on the porch, demonstrating the approved method of sipping drinks at the Blue Frog Ponds.

As if that weren't enough, a sign by the front desk announced that at nine o'clock there was a movie in the game room.

"Where's the game room?" I said.

"Right out back between East and West Ponds," Louise said.

Once again, I hadn't noticed she was there, and had no idea where she came from. I made a mental note to ask Alice about that later.

"How do you show movies?" I asked.

"There's a big-screen TV and a VCR."

"You mean you have *another* TV?" I said.

"Yes."

"On the cable?"

"Of course."

"Nice to know," I said.

Alice and I went to check out the game room. It was in a small building that I hadn't noticed before, probably because someone had neglected to put a frog on the door. Inside was a single room with a pool table, a ping-pong table, and a big-screen TV.

As an attraction, the game room was only slightly less popular than the swimming pool. Alice and I were the only ones there.

Of course, it was only eight-thirty, and the movie wasn't scheduled to start until nine. Still, aside from the dining room, I was beginning to feel like I was in a ghost town.

"Well, Fast Alice," I said, doing my best Jackie Gleason as Minnesota Fats, "whaddaya say you and me shoot a game of eight ball for ten cents a game?"

Alice has seen *The Hustler* too. She cocked her head at me, à la Paul Newman, and said, "I hear you're a big hustler, Fats. Whaddaya say we make it twenty cents a game?"

"Now I know why they call you Fast Alice," I said, and racked up the balls.

By the time people started showing up for the movie, Alice was up forty cents. I had won one game and lost three. Not that Alice is that much better than I am—actually, we're pretty evenly matched—but two of the games I'd been ahead and lost by scratching on the eight ball.

Anyway, the people who showed up to watch the movie were three women, including the one with the dog. Of course, the dog wasn't with her, that's the only way I know to describe her.

"Hi," she said. "Who's winning?"

I jerked my thumb. "The hustler."

She smiled. "Why am I not surprised?"

"He's setting me up," Alice said. "He lets me win a few games and then raises the stakes."

"Won't you have to stop playing when the movie starts?"

"Well, I'm not the brightest of hustlers," I said. "I'm Stanley, this is my wife, Alice."

"I'm Florence," the woman said.

"Really," I said. "You should have your own room."

She blinked. "I *have* my own room."

"No, I mean your name starts with *F.* You could have your own frog, like Frankie or Freddie."

"Stanley has a strange sense of humor," Alice said.

The woman smiled. "I hadn't thought of that. But now that you mention it, I'm in Fenwick."

"Fenwick?" I said.

She smiled again. "I guess they were running out of *F* names. But, yes, I have Fenwick frog on my door."

"We're in Frankie," I said.

She frowned. "I don't think I've seen Frankie."

I jerked my thumb. "East Pond, second floor."

"Oh, that's why. I'm in the inn."

"Where's Prince?" Alice asked.

"Up in the room. He didn't want to watch the movie."

Neither did I. The movie that night was *Bridges of Madison County,* which was probably why the customers were all women. In my present mood, it was a movie I seemed unlikely to enjoy, so when Louise showed up and slid a videocassette into the VCR, I excused myself and slipped out the door.

I had no idea what I was going to do. There was no Red Sox game, since they'd already played that afternoon, but it occurred to me there might be something on TV, so I wandered back to the inn to check it out.

The young hiker was standing on the front porch. Ordinarily, I'm shy at initiating conversations with people I don't know, but having talked to the girl, I didn't want to avoid talking to him.

So I walked up on the porch and said, "Hi."

If I'd made his day, you wouldn't have known it. He looked at me as if I couldn't possibly be speaking to him. In spite of the fact there was no one else there.

He said, "I beg your pardon?"

That was a conversation killer. As I say, I'm not particularly outgoing. And I'm certainly not one to force a social situation. I had ventured "Hi." As to his response, "*I beg your pardon*" was about as cold as one could get. *Hi* is not ambiguous. *Hi* is relatively simple and straightforward. *Hi* does not require an explanation. Under the circumstances, *I beg your pardon* could be translated as "I don't know you. Why are you talking to me? Leave me alone."

His body language said so also. He seemed fidgety, impatient. He never really focused on me, and kept looking around.

He was obviously waiting for the girl. Impatiently waiting. Which bothered me. I kept remembering the sound of the slap.

Which prompted me to ease my way out of the situation as quickly as possible.

"Anyone in the TV room?" I said.

His slight pause told me what a stupid question that was. He smiled coldly, said, "I have no idea."

I mumbled something about checking it out, gave him up as a lost cause, and went inside.

The dining room was just closing. I saw the young man who had served us our drinks go by with a tray of dishes. So he wasn't the bartender, just the busboy, which certainly made more sense. Unless he *was* the bartender, and in an establishment this small everyone helped with everything.

"He's my son," Louise said, startling me both by her presence and by reading my mind. "It's a family affair, and we all pitch in."

"Oh, really?" I said.

"Yes," she said. "We've only been open for two years, but we're doing very well. The dining room's the key. You run a good dining room, the rest takes care of itself."

And there I was, suddenly stuck in the dreaded bed-and-breakfast personal account of "how I came to buy the place." The crowning blow. The last straw.

Still, I couldn't be out-and-out rude. Something was called for. "That's very interesting," I said. "Who's your chef?"

Louise's eyes narrowed. "Why do you ask?"

I blinked. Because I'm inept in social situations, and I'm trying to make polite conversation was the actual point in fact, but probably wasn't about to charm her. "Because the food was so good," I said.

"Oh? What did you have?"

"I had the prime rib, and my wife had the shark."

"You must try the barbecued ribs," she said. "They're famous. Excuse me, I have to help out."

And she disappeared through the door of the dining room.

I stood there, somewhat bemused. On the one hand, I was pleased to have missed the how-we-came-to-buy-the-place lecture. On the other, it occurred to me the woman had avoided discussing the chef.

I shook my head. Good god, Alice was right. I was getting a little stir crazy, making mysteries out of everything. It occurred to me I'd better find myself something to do.

I checked out the TV room. The six-year-old girl wasn't there, but the middle-aged couple I'd observed earlier having drinks on the porch was. They were watching a TV movie of a fairly predictable variety—just a few minutes were enough to assure me it either had something to do with date rape, incest, or sexual harassment, or else someone's wife, mother, or daughter would turn out to be a call girl.

"Care to join us?" the woman on the couch asked, when the exciting drama paused for a commercial.

"Just checking out the room," I said. "My wife's watching *Bridges of Madison County.*"

"Seen it twice," the woman said. "I could see it again, but Johnny thought twice was enough."

Johnny, who was somewhat pudgy faced, smiled what I took to be a rather long-suffering smile. I must say, my heart went out to him—not being able to stand the movie a third time, he'd been paid back with this.

"Yeah, well I'm just looking around," I said. "Tell me, are there any other things here that aren't in the guidebook?"

"Guidebook?"

"I don't mean guidebook. You know, that little brochure about the inn. It listed the swimming pool and this TV room, but it didn't say anything about the game room. You know, where they're showing the movie. So I'm wondering if there's anything else at Blue Frog Ponds the brochure neglected to mention."

"Can't think of anything," the woman said.

"There's the pond," Johnny offered.

Johnny's wife was rather small and thin compared to him. Still, there was little doubt as to the pecking order. She turned on Johnny now. "The *pond,* for goodness' sake?" she said. "That's not what the man means. The man doesn't mean the pond."

"Well, now, how do you know what he means?" Johnny said.

"Well, didn't he just say so? The brochure didn't mention the game room, what else did it leave out? The man is talking about features of the inn."

"The pond's not a feature?"

"The pond's not even on the property. And what do you think about that?" the woman said. "They call the place the Blue Frog Ponds, and the pond's not even theirs."

"Where is the pond?"

Johnny jerked his thumb. "On the other side of the road. The stream widens out, forms a little pond. There's a path down to it from the parking lot. You can't miss it."

"Hush, now," Johnny's wife said. "It's starting again."

If that wasn't an exit cue, I never heard one. The movie was indeed starting again, and I didn't want to see it. I beat a hasty retreat outside.

The cranky young man was gone, and the front porch was deserted. I stood in front of the Blue Frog Ponds and looked around. The sun had just gone down, and there was an orange glow over the top of the mountains in the west. Farther east, you could see the crescent of the moon in the sky, and the stars starting to come out.

I enjoyed looking at the sky, which I guess labeled me as a tourist—if you live in New York City, it's a big deal to look at the sky.

I looked at the parking lot across the road where we'd left our Toyota. Johnny'd said there was a path leading from it. I crossed the road and took a closer look.

There it was, down by the far end. A dirt path leading off through the trees. It didn't appear to be overgrown, and it wasn't really that dark. And the stream couldn't be that far away. In fact, I could hear the sound of running water. So I figured, *what the heck, it's an adventure,* and set off down the path.

After a couple of minutes I came to the stream. It was a narrow stream, not more than ten to twenty feet wide, which came twisting and turning down the hill through a series of rocks. In spring it might have been a raging torrent, but it was quite tame now. It looked shallow enough to wade across, if one had a mind. I wasn't about to get my feet wet. I set off downstream, looking for the pond.

It didn't take long. It was right around the first bend. I came through the trees, and there it was. An actual pond, no doubt about it, a good forty to fifty feet wide, just off the far side of the stream.

When the stream was high it probably fed the pond. At the moment it was separated by a little bank of mud and rocks. It was just dark enough that the moonlight reflected off the pond made the little grove in which it stood seem like an entirely romantic setting.

Or maybe it was the young couple embracing in the shadow of the pine trees beside the stream. I didn't see them at first, and they clearly didn't see me, because they went on about their business as if I wasn't there. But some movement or other caught my eye, and suddenly there they were, necking to beat the band.

I couldn't see them clearly, and I had no idea who they were. Nor did I care. All I wanted to do was get out of there as quickly as possible, before I embarrassed them by my presence.

Then they turned slightly, and moonlight fell on the young woman's hair.

It was blond.

A blond page-boy cut.

Just my luck. And what did I do to deserve it? Here I am, minding my own business, and I happen to stumble over the Swedish hiking couple and wind up spying on their love life. What was Alice going to make of that?

I'd just had that thought when the young couple swung around sideways and light fell on their faces.

It was indeed the Swedish hiking beauty, she of the infinitesimal swimsuit.

But the young man kissing her didn't have blond hair.

His hair was dark.

Uh-oh.

He was the young man who had brought us our drinks.

The busboy.

Louise's son.

EIGHT

I DREAMED SOMETHING was treading on my chest. It was one of those dreams where you're afraid you're going to wake up and find out it's true.

I opened my eyes.

Blinked.

A large, orange, striped cat was kneading up and down on my chest with its paws, clearly tromping down a spot on which to lie. While I gawked at it in amazement, the cat completed its task, made a 360-degree turn as if screwing itself in, and plopped down on my chest and proceeded to purr.

The door opened, and Alice came in.

"You have a cat on your chest," she said.

"I see that."

"Why do you have a cat on your chest?"

"I'm not entirely sure. I guess I left the door unlatched. Was it open just now?"

"Yes, it was."

"Then I must not have closed it all the way. Either that, or this cat has mastered doorknobs."

"How long has he been there?"

"I woke up, and he was tromping on my chest. He lay down, and you came in."

"You look adorable."

"I'm glad to hear it. How was the movie?"

"You wouldn't have liked it."

"Yeah, I know. Thank you."

"For what?"

"Not making me see it. Johnny's wife made him sit through it twice."

"Who's Johnny?"

"The couple having drinks on the porch. They didn't go to the movie because they'd already seen it twice."

"Really?" Alice said. "You actually introduced yourself to them?"

"Not really. I just went in the TV room, and they were there. Watching some god-awful movie of the week."

"You watched with them?"

"Not if you paid me. I'd have rather watched your movie. Boy, is this strange."

"What?"

"You ever try talking with a cat on your chest?"

"Not that I recollect."

"Well, he's vibrating with my voice box, and the effect is a little weird. Anyway, that's not what I did tonight."

"What did you do?"

I told Alice about my adventure finding the pond. It was not easy with the cat on my chest, but I did my best.

"You found her necking?" Alice said. "Stanley, what is it with you and this girl? Are you following her around?"

"Don't be silly. I had no idea she was there."

"And yet she turns up everywhere you go."

"I wasn't the one necking with her, Alice."

"So who was?"

"The busboy," I said. It was my trump card, and I played it casually. "Louise's son."

Alice's eyes widened. "Randy?" she said. "She was making out with Randy?"

So much for my victory. I gave Alice a pained look. "His name's Randy?" I said. "How do you know that?"

"Don't be silly," Alice said. "Louise's son is named Randy. He went to Dartmouth two years, dropped out for a year, and bummed around, but he's going back in the fall. In the meantime he's living at home, helping out at the inn."

I snorted in disgust. The cat raised its head, gave me a dirty look, then got to its feet and stretched and yawned, digging its claws into my chest. It was not painful, just annoying. I cocked my head at the cat, said, "Is that really necessary?"

In answer, the cat swung a one eighty and managed to smack me in the face with its tail, in the process of going through the whole stretching routine again. Then, thoroughly satisfied with itself, it climbed down off me, curled up in a ball next to me, and began purring loudly.

"You have such a way with animals," Alice said.

"I didn't do anything," I said. "I'm just lying here. Would you mind telling me how you know all about Louise's son?"

"Everyone knows about Louise's son," Alice said. "Jean and Joan told me, but Florence knew it too."

"Jean and Joan?"

"Yes. The two women who came in together. To the movie."

"What two women who came in together?"

"Stanley, we were shooting pool, and Florence came in with those other women. That was Jean and Joan."

"Oh?"

"You didn't notice the women who came in?"

"Not particularly. Was there any reason that I should?"

"Absolutely not," Alice said. "None of them were young and attractive and practically naked. So there was no reason for you to notice them at all."

"Give me a break."

"So Randy was making out with Christine. How interesting."

"Her name's Christine?"

"You didn't know that? Yes, her name's Christine, and her boyfriend is Lars."

"Boyfriend?"

"More than likely. Of course some married women retain their last names. But they're registered as Lars Heinrick and Christine Cobb."

I blinked. "How in the world do you know all this?"

"Are you kidding?" Alice said. "An attractive young couple like that, you think people aren't going to notice them?"

I opened my mouth, closed it again. After all the grief I'd been getting for noticing them, what could I possibly say to that?

"Anyway," Alice said, "Jean snuck a peek at the registration book—Jean's the nosier of the two, even before I knew she did that, you could just tell—and that's how they're registered." Alice cocked her head. "Would you like their room number?"

"I'd prefer their frog."

Alice frowned. "I don't know their frog. It's not listed that way in the register. I think to find out, you'd have to go and see. Anyway, their room's in the main building. Room four."

"I'd go look, but I don't want to disturb the cat."

"Of course not."

"You wouldn't know its name, would you?"

"I didn't even know there was a cat."

"I'm surprised. What about the chef?"

"What about him?"

"You happen to know who he is?"

"That's rather sexist."

"What?"

"Assuming the chef is a man."

I blinked. "Alice. You said, 'What about him?' "

"So?"

"*You* assumed he's a man."

"No, I didn't."

"What?"

"I didn't assume he's a man. I *know* he's a man. It's not sexist to call the chef a man if you know he's a man."

"You know who the chef is?"

"Of course I do."

"Why am I surprised?"

"I don't know. I don't even know why you were asking."

"Because I asked Louise about the chef, and she changed the subject."

"You asked Louise about the chef?"

"I wasn't prying. She asked me about dinner. I had to say something. I asked who the chef was, she didn't answer and excused herself."

"He's her husband."

"Oh?"

"They're not getting along. That's why she didn't want to talk about him."

"Alice."

"Well, it's common knowledge. You can tell just to look at her, that is not a woman in a happy relationship. Anyway, Charlie's the cook."

"Her husband's named Charlie?"

"Didn't I just say that? And there's no way she'd divorce him, because his recipes are to die for."

I sat up a little too quickly for the cat, which sprang to its feet and arched its back, its tail lashing furiously.

"Alice," I said. "How could you say something like that?"

"Well, it's true. The only reason they're making a go of it is the dining room. Without that, the whole place goes under."

"You're suggesting Louise stay with a husband she doesn't love just to keep a business venture afloat?"

"You think she should divorce her husband?"

"I don't think anything of the sort."

"Then what are you talking about?"

"About what you said."

"I didn't say anything."

"Yes, you did. You said she couldn't divorce her husband."

"So?"

"What do you mean, so? That's the whole point. You're the one who brought up divorce."

"I didn't bring it up. I said it was out of the question."

"For financial reasons?"

"Of course."

"Alice, you can't admit that. That's the whole argument."

"What argument?"

I had no idea. My mind was mush, and I couldn't keep anything straight in my head. Which usually happens when I try to argue with Alice. After years of marriage, you'd think I'd know better.

I sighed, scratched the cat under the chin. It regarded me suspiciously a moment, then, mollified, lay down, and curled up again.

I looked at Alice. "So," I said, "here we are, once again, in our TV-less room with nothing to do."

"I'm going to bed," Alice said.

"My thought, exactly."

"I'm going to sleep. We have to be up early in the morning."

"Why?"

"We have a seven-thirty breakfast reservation."

"Seven-thirty?"

"Sure. We don't want to sleep all day. It's not like in the city. We're in the country. When the light comes in the window, you're going to want to get up."

"I'll get up," I said. "I promise you, I'll have no problem getting up. Whether I go to sleep right now, or just a little bit later."

Alice smiled and slipped out of her hiking shorts, which I thought was a promising sign.

It wasn't.

She went in the bathroom, emerging minutes later in her flannel pajamas.

"Good night," she said, getting into bed.

I made one last feeble attempt, which earned me nothing but a reminder that the walls were paper-thin, after which Alice rolled over and went right to sleep.

It's amazing how she can do that. I have trouble falling asleep. Usually, what helps me go to sleep is watching television.

I sighed, got up, trying not to disturb the cat, and rummaged through the suitcase for my book. It was a murder mystery I'd brought along at Alice's urging—when we were packing she said, "Bring a book," so I'd brought a book. But I hadn't expected to read it, so I'd just plucked it off the shelf almost at random. It was an Agatha Christie that I'd probably read before, but didn't really remember the title.

As soon as I began reading I realized why. The paperback had been published with its British title. I knew it under its American one. So *4:50 from Paddington,* which I thought was a Hercule Poirot novel I had never read, was really *What Mrs. McGillicudy Saw!,* a Miss Marple novel I had not only read before, but also remembered who did it.

Oh, well. At least it ought to put me to sleep.

Only it didn't. I have trouble adjusting to new surroundings, and my first night in a new bed I usually have a devil of a time.

Tonight was no exception. I tossed and turned, fussed with the blankets, readjusted the pillows, apologized to the cat, and worried about whether I should leave the door open so it could go out.

And reread Agatha Christie. Every now and then looking over at Alice and cursing the paper-thin walls.

Unfortunately, the state of the walls was a fact I could not dispute. When our next-door neighbors returned twenty pages later, I could hear them quite clearly. I could hear them moving around the room, washing up, and getting into bed.

I could hear them in bed.

And they either had no inhibitions whatsoever, or else they were totally unaware they could be heard.

It was so distracting, I couldn't read. All I could do was listen. And hope they wouldn't wake the cat.

As I lay there, next to my attractive-yet-sleeping wife, listening to their nocturnal activities, which seemed to be going on for quite some time, it occurred to me that Frankie, the frog on my door, had his hands in his pockets and a rueful smile, while Freddie, on their door, was winking and signaling, A-okay!

NINE

"I HAVE A cat in my room."

"An orange, stripey cat?" Louise said.

"That's the one."

"That's Max. He's a sweetheart. Is he bothering you?"

"No. I was just afraid someone might be missing him."

"Don't worry. He's not that type of cat. Very independent. Likes to hang out with the guests. If you get sick of him, throw him out. He'll show up at the kitchen door when he's hungry."

"He's your cat?"

"In a manner of speaking. He belongs to the inn. Oh, here's your wife."

Alice came in from the porch where she had stopped to talk to two women on her way to breakfast. As usual, I had misread the situation. Like a fool, I had assumed that people on their way to breakfast intended to eat breakfast. At the door to the inn I had gone inside, only to watch Alice veer off in the other direction. This had left me inside the inn but outside the dining room. Hence the conversation with Louise about the cat.

"Good morning, Mrs. Hastings," Louise said. "Seven-thirty breakfast reservation, right this way."

She led us into the dining room and sat us at a table. "Your waitress will be right with you."

When she left, I jerked my thumb in the direction of the porch. "Jean and Joan?"

"Uh-huh."

"Which is which?"

"Jean's thinner."

That did it for me. Jean was the one with leathery skin and short, frosted hair. Joan was the plump one with the glasses and curly, blond permanent.

"Uh-huh," I said. "Am I to assume you stopped to gossip about what I observed last night by the pond?"

"Gossip?" Alice said. "My, what a rude word."

"I'm sorry," I said. "You mean you didn't tell them?"

"I may have mentioned it," Alice said. "In passing. But I don't see the big deal. It's the sort of thing you'd comment on. After all, you told me."

"You're my wife."

"Exactly," Alice said. "If it's something you'd tell your wife, it's certainly worth repeating."

"Certainly," I said. "So that's Jean and Joan. Do you know there's a song about them?"

"There is?"

"Well, not about them. But there's a Jean and Joan in a song. As I recall, the chorus goes, *You've got to change your evil ways, baby.*"

"You're just making that up."

"No, I'm not. Don't you remember the song. It goes—"

"No. Don't sing. Not at the breakfast table."

"Just a chorus."

"Stanley."

Our waitress appeared. She couldn't sneak up on us the way she could when we were in a booth, still there was something in the way she approached our table that made her seem like something out of an old movie. Something furtive. A spy, perhaps, or secret agent.

I chided myself for having such a vivid imagination.

She set a pot of coffee down on the table.

Then, to my utter amazement, she glanced left and right, palmed a piece of paper from the pocket of her apron, and surreptitiously slid it under the corner of Alice's plate.

"I'll be back to take your order," she said, and hurried off to another table.

"What in the world?" I said.

"Shh," Alice said. "Act natural."

I got it. Of course. Alice was getting back at me for the way I'd acted at dinner last night. How she'd gotten the waitress in on it I had no idea, but somehow she had, and now she was playing it for all it was worth, opening and reading the paper under the table.

"Okay, I'll bite," I said. "What's the secret message?"

"You can see it. Just don't make a big deal out of it. Here, take a look. Just don't let anyone else see."

I took the paper Alice handed me and unfolded it.

It was a Xerox copy. There was writing on it in longhand. I squinted to make it out.

MIRIAM'S CHOCOLATE CAKE

1 can of Hershey syrup

4 eggs

1 cup self-rising flour

¼ pound butter
⅔ cup sugar

Cream butter and sugar. Add eggs, syrup, and flour, and stir. Pour into greased 9" square. Bake at 375° for 35 to 40 minutes.

Serve unfrosted.

I looked up at Alice. "A recipe?"

"Shh. You don't have to shout it all over the place. Of course it's a recipe. For the cake I had last night."

"I thought you couldn't get the recipe."

"You can't. I slipped Lucy ten bucks to get it for me."

"Lucy?"

"Our waitress."

"You paid ten bucks for the recipe?"

"Stanley. Did you taste that cake?"

I had, and it was rather good. Still, ten bucks is ten bucks.

Lucy returned to take our order. She made no reference to the recipe. Indeed, there was nothing in her manner to indicate anything out of the ordinary had occurred.

Nor was there in ours. We merely placed our orders. Alice had waffles, and I had the French toast.

Lucy went out, and Johnny and his wife came in. They must have missed Louise somehow, because they came in alone. With no one to show them to a table, they stood and looked around. After a few moments they spotted us and came over.

"Good morning," Johnny said. "You find that pond all right?"

"As a matter of fact, I did. Ah, this is my wife, Alice."

"Pleased to meet you. I'm Johnny. This is my wife, Clara."

"So," Clara said to Alice, "you went to the movie last night?"

"Yes."

"I wanted to go, but stick-in-the-mud here wouldn't see it."

"Seen it twice," Johnny said.

"We've already ordered, but would you care to join us?" Alice said.

"Oh, we wouldn't want to intrude," Johnny said.

Clara sat right down, said, "Thank you so much," and proceeded to pour herself a cup of coffee.

I couldn't quite believe that Alice had offered or that Clara had accepted. I'm not sure Johnny could either, but he sat down, and his wife poured him a cup of coffee too.

Lucy returned with our orders. Alice's waffle was covered with berries—strawberries, raspberries, blueberries, and even had a slice of melon. My French toast was thick and cinnamon-sugar glazed.

"That French toast sure looks good," Johnny said. "I'll have that."

"You will not," Clara said. "Look at that sugar glaze. You want to drop dead on me, you go ahead and eat like that. Now, I'll have the waffles and berries. There's a sensible meal."

After a moment's hesitation, Johnny sheepishly ordered the waffles too.

I didn't know whether to gloat. After all, I had the French toast. On the other hand, when I'd ordered it, Alice hadn't seen what it was like.

Florence came in with the two women I now recognized as Jean and Joan. Louise seated them at a table across the room. Florence, who was facing us, smiled and waved.

"You know Florence?" Clara said.

"We met her yesterday," I said. "On a hike. At Champney Falls. Nice woman."

"Yes," Clara said. "But she has that awful dog."

"Prince?" Alice said. "Oh, he's a sweetheart."

"Yes, but he's not trained. And he sheds. And drools. And he's a terrible beggar. God forbid you should give him any food."

"Did you hear that, Stanley?" Alice said. "Stanley gave him a sandwich." She managed to make it sound like a crime.

"Excuse me," I said, "but I'm going to eat this while it's hot."

I cut off a piece of French toast, dipped it in maple syrup.

"Gee, look who's here," Alice said.

I looked over my shoulder to see Louise ushering in the Swedish hiking couple. It took me a second to realize I knew their names. Another second to realize I wasn't quite sure what they were. Oh, yes, he's Lars. Not that surprising. She's Christine. Though I'd imagined her more an Inga.

Louise seated them in one of the booths. They must have reserved it. It occurred to me if we'd only had the foresight to do so, we would have escaped dining with Johnny and Clara.

Once Lars and Christine were seated in their booth, they were out of sight. Which should have put them out of mind.

Except.

A pot of coffee was delivered to their booth.

And it wasn't the waitress who brought it.

It was the busboy.

Louise's son, Randy.

Whom I had seen kissing Christine last night by the pond.

That certainly made for an interesting dynamic. A glance at Alice showed that she thought so, too, but wasn't about to mention anything in front of Clara and Johnny.

The table across the way was far less restrained. Jean, Joan, and Florence had their heads together whispering furiously, and every now and then one of them would glance in the direction of the booth.

Lucy returned with Johnny and Clara's waffles, then headed to the booth to take the young couple's order. There was a lull in the conversation while Johnny and Clara dug in. I accepted it gratefully, settled back, sipped my coffee, and surveyed the room.

The dining room was not as crowded as it had been for dinner. I assumed breakfast was primarily for the guests. At any rate, aside from those I've already mentioned, the only other people in the room were the men I'd seen last night in the bar. This morning they looked more like tourists, in shorts and hiking boots. They sat in the corner, finishing up breakfast and reading the paper. I wondered where they'd gotten the paper, which appeared to be *The New York Times*.

I also wondered if they were gay. And chided myself for the thought. Surely two men could travel together without being gay. On the other hand, maybe they were.

I wondered what their frog looked like.

Prompted by the thought, I turned to Johnny. "Who's your frog?"

He stopped with a forkful of waffle halfway to his mouth. "Huh?"

"The frog on the door of your room. What's his name?"

"Name?"

"Yeah. All the frogs have names. Ours is Frankie. What's yours?"

Johnny looked at Clara. "What's our frog's name?"

She stopped sawing her waffle and impaled him with a look. "Well now, Johnny McInnerny, how would you expect me to know that?"

Well, I guess that told me. Granted, Clara'd felt far more free to smash her husband down than if I'd been the one asking her, still the original question was mine.

Which sort of drew the line in the sand. So, don't care to know the name of your frog, eh? Well, Clara, baby, you and Johnny just lost a chance to go on my list of the all-time great fun couples.

Nonetheless, part of her answer I liked—calling her husband by his last name. Now, instead of constantly saying Johnny and Clara, I could refer to them as the McInnernys. It occurred to me what minutely small satisfactions I was managing to glean from this vacation.

Out of the corner of my eye I saw Lucy usher another couple in. They came right by our table, and I got a closer look. I was impressed. They were a most attractive couple. Not as young and perfect as the one in the booth, but still. The man was maybe thirty-five, but his face was smooth and unwrinkled, and his hair was jet-black, and all in all he looked like he'd just stepped out of high school.

The woman looked equally young, but gave the opposite impression—that the bright eyes and curly brown hair belonged to the vice president of something. Something big, like an airline or movie studio.

Anyway, the pair looked mismatched. It occurred to me, maybe they *were* mismatched. That this man and this woman were having an affair.

I looked at Alice, to see if this had registered.

Alice had indeed noticed the couple. To the McInnernys she said, "Who is that?"

"I have no idea," Clara said. "I haven't seen them before."

"Me, either," Johnny said. "You suppose they just got here?"

"Either that or they don't get out much," I said.

It had just occurred to me, maybe they were the couple I had heard next door. I hadn't mentioned them to Alice. I figured it would just give her more ammunition for invoking the passion-free zone.

I'd just had that thought when a little girl came bounding into the dining room, and went bubbling up to their table, squealing, "Mommy! Daddy!" and establishing the fact that what we were observing was your basic stable family unit.

"They didn't just get here," I said. "That's the kid who was in the TV room yesterday when I wanted to watch the Red Sox game."

"You should have thrown her out," Johnny said.

"Absolutely," Clara said. "People have no business bringing children to a place like this."

That did it. That was the last straw. I had had it with the McInnernys. They didn't like children, and they didn't like dogs. Well, I didn't like them.

I was not about to be rude, you understand. Or even start an argument. I just made a mental note to be sure to tell Alice never to invite them again.

Not that there was any danger of that. Alice was clearly as eager to get away from the McInnernys as I was. She attacked her breakfast at what had to be a record pace, and said, "Well, we better be going if we're going to get any hiking done."

"Start at Pinkham Notch," Johnny said. "They'll fit you out with everything you need."

"Where's that?"

"Pinkham Notch Visitors Center. It's on the way to Mount Washington. You can't miss it. A great big lodge by the side of the road. Information center, dining room, lodge, what-have-you. Everybody starts out there."

"Uh-huh," Alice said. "And that's right on the way to Mount Washington?"

"Uh-huh. Can't miss it. As a matter fact, we're going there ourselves, we could show you the way."

"Oh, that won't be necessary," I said.

"Don't be silly," Clara said. "We're hiking there ourselves. Johnny, we should show them Pinkham Notch."

"Absolutely," Johnny said. "We know the best trails to hike. Stick with us, and you can't go wrong."

"But you've already hiked those trails," Alice said. "You wouldn't want to do it again."

"Oh, that's no problem," Clara said. "Some of those trails are beautiful."

"See," Johnny said. "She's willing to see that stupid movie three times, you think she can't hike a trail again?"

"So, it's settled," Clara said. "Johnny and I will show you Pinkham Notch."

I looked at Alice for help, saw she was at a loss.

I looked at Johnny, smiled weakly.

Kill me now, vengeful gods. Kill me now.

TEN

SAVED BY THE dog.

In the nick of time, Prince saved the day. A true hero, just like Lassie or Rin-Tin-Tin.

You see, Florence and Jean and Joan came along to Pinkham Notch. And Florence brought Prince. And the McInnernys didn't like dogs.

What a relief.

As they made their excuses and scuttled down some trail or another, I could hardly keep from cheering. Florence and Prince were lifesavers. I even felt a fondness for Jean and Joan. I didn't know them at all, but compared to the McInnernys they had to be saints.

So, having dispensed with our would-be guides, we were now left to happily work things out on our own.

Alice, Jean and Joan, and I went into the visitors center and came back armed with instructions on what were described as easy but fun hikes.

The first one was across the highway just beyond the far end of the parking lot. We crossed the road with Prince on a leash, and found a narrow trail leading off into the woods. For a while it was easygoing. Then about a hundred yards in, the trail began to slope up, first gradually, then steeper and steeper, and before you know it we were scrambling over rocks, bracing ourselves against tree trunks, and climbing from one ledge to another.

Prince seemed to have no trouble with the terrain, but I found it hard going. I wasn't about to complain, though, what with Jean and Joan scampering up the hill as happy as clams. I gritted my teeth, and scampered along with 'em, wondering just how high this damn mountain was.

Not very. At least, not where we were going. In about twenty minutes we emerged from the woods on the top of a cliff.

"Wow, look at that," Alice said.

Alice, of course, was well ahead of me and had reached the edge of the cliff. I stepped out gingerly—heights are not one of my favorite things.

Prince rocketed by me, and I nearly jumped a mile. I was pretty far back from the edge, still I had a moment of panic as I envisioned the dog taking a flying leap and sailing off into nowhere. Fortunately, Prince skidded to a stop and proceeded to look out with all due caution. I made my way to the edge of the cliff, where Jean and Joan had already joined Florence and Alice.

Wow. Even for a skeptic, I had to admit it was pretty impressive. Below the cliff, the mountain we had just climbed fell away as a slope of rocks dissolved into a slope of treetops that leveled off into a sea of green that stretched out and eventually reached the road. Across the road, and a little to the right, was the sprawling Pinkham Notch recreation center. And behind it, rising majestically up to the sky, was the Mount Washington mountain range.

I'd seen it, of course, from below, but not like this. At Pinkham Notch you were surrounded by mountains towering around you, too close to see. Here, from the perspective of height and distance, was an entire panorama.

"Hey," I said, "this is spectacular."

"Worth the climb?" Alice said.

"Absolutely," I said. I was rather cocky, knowing how much easier the trip down would be.

We enjoyed the view a little longer, then moved back from the edge and sat down on the rocks for a drink.

Joan had a water bottle on her waist, and she and Jean drank out of that. They drank right from the bottle.

Alice and I had a bottle in the backpack, and paper cups.

Florence had a paper cup for herself, and a plastic bowl for Prince. He lapped his water gratefully and sloppily, spilling as much as he drank.

After that, we packed up our gear and headed out, which seemed sensible to me. It was a spectacular view, but we'd seen it, so on to something else.

"So, what's next?" I said, after we'd clambered down the rocks and were back on level ground.

"Glen Ellis Falls," Alice said.

"Uh-huh," I said. "And that's listed as . . ."

"Short, easy, ideal for the grumpiest husband," Alice said.

Florence, Jean, and Joan laughed. I realized in this group I had lost my identity, been subjugated to the role of Alice's husband, a notorious stick-in-the-mud, to be humored and gotten around.

It was a bit of a surprise to realize I didn't really mind.

Glen Ellis Falls was just a mile down the road. We pulled into the parking lot, piled out of our cars, and took the tunnel under the highway to the trail.

It was the easiest hike yet. A gravel path twisted down into the ravine. We followed it about a quarter of a mile, and suddenly we were there, at the top of Glen Ellis Falls.

Which was a mighty impressive sight. It was a high falls, formed by a stream of water flowing between two boulders and cascading down the mountain into a pool below. I whipped out the guidebook and was able to announce that the falls was sixty-four feet high, and had been originally called Pitcher Falls because the rock formation at the top made it look like water flowing out of a pitcher.

As I made these announcements, I realized I was losing my audience. Prince had not stopped at the top of the falls, and the women were now following him down the stone steps toward the bottom. I stuck the guidebook in the backpack and tagged along.

At the base of the falls, we climbed out on the rocks. This is one of the attractions of Glen Ellis Falls. In good weather, you can leave the stone steps and scramble around on the flat rocks surrounding the pool. Everyone else seemed to be doing it, so we did too. Alice climbed out, followed by Jean and Joan. Florence even brought Prince. She kept him on the leash, but let him climb. He seemed more surefooted than I would have given him credit for.

Not wanting to be an old stick-in-the-mud, I stashed the backpack behind a rock, and climbed out too.

It was fun scrambling from rock to rock. I could see why this falls was such a tourist attraction. Aside from the great view, you really felt you were part of it. Leaving the path. Climbing around. It had just the right sense of adventure, of doing something you weren't really supposed to do. Although, of course, you were. Scrambling on the rocks was even advertised in the guidebook.

Be that as it may, Glen Ellis Falls was a pretty good time, and I sort of hated to leave.

I hated to leave for another reason. The path was up. When we started back to the car, that was the main thing in my mind.

The fact we were going up. The other falls we'd climbed up to, and then come down. Not this time. This time we'd climbed down to the falls, and had to go up. Which was really a shame, and put a damper on what was otherwise a perfectly enjoyable outing.

The thing is, that was in my mind, but I wasn't saying it. And I was making a very conscious effort not to say it. Because it certainly seemed a normal thing to say, but seemed too grouchy even for the old grouch role I'd been reduced to playing.

Anyway, the point is, I had all that in my head when we left the falls.

Preoccupying me.

Distracting me.

Making me careless.

Which is why I felt like such a fool when we finally reached the top of the hill and headed for the parking lot and Alice said, "Where's the backpack?"

Uh-oh.

I knew where the backpack was. Right there at the base of the falls where I'd taken it off to go scrambling around on the rocks. I hadn't given it a second thought.

I explained the situation to Alice with as much dignity as I could muster, and hurried off down the path, trying to ignore the laughter and comments emanating from Florence and Alice and Jean and Joan.

At least going down to the falls was easy. Though it didn't seem easy, with the foreknowledge of what the climb back up was going to be. Still, going down was a breeze. I reached the bottom in no time at all, came around the corner into the alcove where I'd left my backpack.

And bumped right into her.

Like a fool, I hadn't been looking where I was going, I'd been looking at my backpack.

I stepped back, put up my hands, said, "Excuse me."

She said, "You."

I blinked.

It was her. My nemesis. The Swedish hiker. What's-her-name. Not Inga. Christine.

Good lord.

Christine.

"Yes," I said. "I'm sorry. I left my backpack. I wasn't looking where I was going."

She kept looking at me. "It was you, wasn't it?"

"Huh?"

"Last night. By the pond."

"Oh."

"It *was* you," she said. "I thought so. You saw me, didn't you? Didn't you?"

What could I say? "Yeah, that was me."

"I knew it. Promise me something. Promise me you won't tell anybody. You won't, will you? Promise me you won't."

"Okay," I said. "I won't."

All right, so it wasn't an exact truth. But what was I going to tell her? That half the people in the place knew anyway? That her romance with Louise's son was probably the number-one gossip topic at Blue Frog Ponds? That certainly seemed a little harsh. All she'd asked me was not to tell anybody. Well, I certainly wouldn't tell anybody.

Else.

ELEVEN

GRILLED MAKO SHARK WITH MANGO SALSA

2 mako shark steaks, approximately ½ pound each

1 tablespoon extra-virgin olive oil

MANGO SALSA

2 ripe mangoes, peeled and diced into ¼ inch pieces

3 tablespoons chopped red onion

2 cloves garlic, finely chopped

1 tablespoon jalapeño pepper, roasted and chopped

¼ teaspoon kosher salt

3 tablespoons lime juice

3 tablespoons chopped fresh cilantro

Makes 2 cups

To prepare the Mango Salsa: Seed and derib the jalapeño. Roast at 500° for 10 minutes. Peel off skin and chop. Combine with remaining ingredients.

To prepare the fish for grilling: Coat with 1 tablespoon of extra-virgin olive oil on each side. Salt and pepper. Grill to taste approximately 4 to 5 minutes on each side.

Garnish fish with a slice of lime and a sprig of cilantro. Serve with Mango Salsa.

Serves 2.

I looked up at Alice. "You paid ten bucks for this?"

She frowned, glanced around the dining room. "Please. Be a little discreet."

"I don't understand. Why do you want this recipe?"

"Stanley. Did you taste that sauce?"

"It was good."

"It was to die for."

"Whatever. The point is, when are you ever going to cook shark?"

"You don't understand." Alice turned to Florence. Smiled. "He doesn't understand."

"What's to understand?" I said. "You either cook shark or you don't. If you don't, why pay ten dollars for a sauce."

"Five dollars."

"Huh?"

"Florence and I are splitting it."

"Oh, is that right?"

"That's right," Florence said.

"You mean you cook shark?"

Florence smiled. "You don't understand."

I certainly didn't. But then I was approaching the problem from the warped male viewpoint of one used to buying things one intended to use. Even so, I probably wouldn't have made such a big deal of it if I hadn't been subjected to rather unmerciful husband-bashing all day long.

"So," I said. "Let me be sure I understand this. The two of you have joined forces to purchase a recipe for a dish you have no intention of ever preparing. Just because you happen to like the recipe."

"See, he does understand," Florence said.

I blinked. "No, no. I wasn't being serious. I was ridiculing the concept."

"And very amusingly too," Alice said. "Now, if you could just do so in a slightly lower voice."

I don't know if I might have pursued the topic, but at that moment my girlfriend came in with her boyfriend. I use the terms loosely. My girlfriend was of course Inga/Christine, my bathing companion and confidante. The boyfriend I was referring to was Lars, cranky Swedish hiking companion. Not unhappily married Louise bed-and-breakfast owner's busboy son, Randy.

They were shown to their booth by the younger, less severe-looking waitress, who to the best of my knowledge was not augmenting her income by peddling Xerox copies of pilfered recipes of Louise's husband, the chef's specialties to the guests.

Anyway, she showed the happy couple to a booth directly behind me, for which I was eternally grateful. I didn't want to be constantly glancing at the young woman, wondering if she was glancing at me.

You see, I hadn't had a chance to tell Alice yet. About our meeting by the waterfall. Because when I got back to the parking lot, Florence and Jean and Joan were there. And I'd promised. Given my word. And I couldn't see telling everybody after I'd promised. Even though they already knew, still, it didn't seem right. It was like compounding a felony, adding insult to injury, rubbing salt in the wound. I don't know exactly, but the point is, I didn't feel comfortable telling people.

Except Alice. I had to tell Alice. I meant to tell Alice. I intended to tell Alice. And I was going to tell Alice.

I just hadn't had a chance to tell Alice.

So, since I hadn't been able to tell Alice about the waterfall rendezvous, I certainly didn't want her to catch the young lady in question trying to flash me secret, unspoken messages with her eyes.

If you can't understand that, you are undoubtedly single.

"Are you ready to order?" Lucy said.

I hadn't even realized she was there. She'd disappeared earlier, after slipping the recipe under Alice's plate.

"Yes," I said. I wasn't about to blow it this time. I went right for the appetizer. "I'd like to start off with the barbecued ribs."

"Uh-huh," Lucy said. "You mean the special, or off the menu?"

Good lord. She'd told us the specials, and I hadn't heard a word. I'd been too preoccupied with other things. But it probably wouldn't be prudent to admit that now.

"From the menu," I said. "The ribs on the menu. The ones you said were famous."

"Uh-huh," she said. "And for the main course?"

"I'll have the petite filet mignon," I said, with complete confidence. It was a small portion, described as lighter fare, and would not open me to ridicule, like ordering the prime rib.

Lucy blinked. "But that *is* the special," she said. "The barbecued ribs and petite filet combination. Of course, you can order it à la carte if you want, but it's exactly the same thing, and it'll cost you about six dollars more."

"I'm sorry," I said. "I misunderstood you. Yes, of course, that's exactly what I want. I'll have the special."

"Space cadet," Alice said, shaking her head.

Fortunately, she and Florence still had to order, which kept them from giving me too much grief. Florence had the salmon filet. Alice had some sort of veal dish I had a feeling we'd wind up with the recipe for tomorrow.

When Lucy left, the husband-bashing got a little heavy, so I excused myself to go to the bathroom.

The minute I got up, I realized I'd forgotten where the bathroom was. That's not exactly right. I knew where it was. I'd forgotten who I had to walk by to get there. Fortunately, when I went by their booth, they were being served drinks, so no one noticed me.

But I certainly noticed them. Particularly since the one again serving them was none other than the busboy, Louise's son, Randy. It still made for an interesting dynamic. Of course I couldn't see much, what with the booth being semiprivate and all, but in my split-second window of opportunity as I passed by, I could swear I saw boyfriend Lars looking suspicious and Inga/Christine looking concerned.

Then I was by them and out the door of the dining room, and I couldn't for the life of me swear if I was making the whole thing up.

I stood there a second, laughed, and shook my head. The two guys traveling together whom I thought might be gay were back in the bar, and looked up. I smiled a completely impersonal, noncommittal, meaningless smile, turned and beat a retreat to the men's room.

I went in, splashed water on my face, had a little talk with myself. I'm not sure exactly what I told me, but I seem to recall a somewhat sarcastic observation that it was a good thing I hadn't opted for a job in the secret service.

On my way back into the dining room I had to pass by their booth again.

Oh, boy.

They were having a fight. Or at least an argument. Or at least a disagreement of some kind.

Not that I heard anything. They weren't loud. In fact, they weren't even talking. All I saw was the tableau.

The girl sat up straight, staring ahead with a blank look, as if seeing nothing. A tear ran down her cheek. Or had run down her cheek—it had stopped now, suspended in the hollow of her cheek-bone. She looked like she had just lost her last friend in the world.

The young man sat glaring at her. His chin set, his eyes hard. He looked positively murderous.

Neither moved.

Well, so much for my little attempt to compose myself.

I went back to my table, sat down, said, perhaps a little too heartily, "How's tricks?"

No one noticed.

"Did you see?" Alice said.

"See what?"

"When you were going out." She lowered her voice. "Randy serving them drinks."

I didn't have to ask who *they* were. "Is that right?" I said.

"Uh-huh," Alice said. "I wish the angle were better. You can't see into that booth at all."

"Aren't they entitled to a little privacy?" I said.

"If they kept to themselves, they'd have it," Florence said. "If they're going to run around with the staff . . ." She waggled her hand.

There was no way I was coming out of the conversation a winner. Fortunately, our appetizers arrived just then, driving all other thoughts from our minds.

Oh, my goodness.

When I saw the barbecued ribs, I understood why Lucy had advised me against ordering them with the prime rib. I must ad-mit, most of my experience with spare ribs comes from Chinese takeout. Still, I have had barbecued ribs on occasion, and knew generally what to expect.

But not this. This was a huge basket of ribs, piled high in three to four rows—that's right, rows—of thick, meaty ribs in a sauce that smelled absolutely sensational.

Florence and Alice, accepting comparatively modest portions of shrimp cocktail and soup, regarded the ribs with raised eyebrows.

"Good lord, Stanley," Alice said. "How can you possibly eat all that?"

"Are you telling me you'd like a rib?"

"I'm worried about your health. I mean, look at all that food."

"Uh-huh," I said. "How about you, Florence? Care for a rib? There seems to be plenty to go around."

"And then some," Florence said.

We all proceeded to eat our appetizers. Florence and Alice, despite numerous disclaimers, consented to sample the ribs. Alice had two, and Florence had at least three.

While all this was going on, the dining room was filling up. The two guys from the bar came in and were shown to a table. And the man and woman from breakfast, once again minus the little girl, were seated at a table next to Jean and Joan, who had sat down before us, and were already on their main course.

It was somewhere in there, and long about the time Alice and I were negotiating over some sparerib or other, though whether it was one I felt she should eat or one she felt I should not, I couldn't say, the bald, overweight hiker from Champney Falls came in. From my seating position, I couldn't see where he went. He walked behind me out of my line of sight, and never reappeared. So, unless I wanted to turn around and look, I was out of luck.

Not that I cared, you understand. Still, as far as I knew, he wasn't staying at the inn, so I had to wonder why he was always here. Of course, it could have just been the food.

"You know who that is?" I said.

"Who?" Florence said.

"The man who just came in."

"What man?"

"Bald. Overweight. He was here last night."

"Uh-huh. And where is he now?"

"I assume he's right behind me. I hate to turn and stare."

"There's no one behind you," Florence said.

"I don't mean *right* behind me. He came in, walked behind me, and I assume he sat down."

"Well, he's not there now."

"Alice, help me out here. The hiker from Champney Falls—where is he?"

"I have no idea."

"Didn't you see him come in?"

"No, I was talking to Florence. I wasn't watching who was going in and out."

"And he's not here now?"

"No, he's not."

That did it. Rude or not, I turned my head to look.

And he wasn't there.

To my right was the table with the two men from the bar. To my left was the table with the man and woman minus the little girl. Along the far wall, slightly at an angle, so, as Alice said, you couldn't see in, was the booth with the Swedish hiking couple, Lars and Inga/Christine.

At that moment, Lars came out of the booth. He did not look happy. He glanced back inside, as if to say something, but didn't. Then he turned and walked purposefully out the door.

I wondered if she would follow him. Somehow I hoped she wouldn't. I think in the back of my mind I was recalling the sound of that slap at Champney Falls, and then seeing her crying behind the rock. At any rate, I hoped she'd stay put.

She did. At least in the few seconds before I felt compelled to turn back to my table before I made a complete moron out of myself.

Even so, Alice said, "Stanley, what are you staring at?"

"I was looking to see where that man went."

"Well, he must have gone out, because he's clearly not here."

"Uh-oh," Florence said. "Look who's coming."

I looked, and quite agreed. The McInnernys were bearing down on us. And while there wasn't room for them at our table, they looked inclined to talk.

"So," Johnny said, "how did it go? You manage to get along without us?"

"Of course they did," Clara said. "My goodness, Johnny McInnerny, you think you're the only one knows how to read a map?"

"Nothing of the kind," Johnny said. "It's just we've done it before. So, what did you guys see?"

Florence, whose tolerance of the McInnernys was even less than ours, said, "Excuse me, I have to check on Prince," and got up.

I had a moment of panic, realizing that left two chairs free, but the McInnernys made no move to sit down.

"We did a few easy hikes," Alice said. "Square Ledge Trail. Glen Ellis Falls."

"You should try Mount Willard," Johnny said.

"Not Mount Washington?"

"Not for hiking. You do that in the van. Mount Willard you can climb."

"That's a good tip," I said, and let the conversation lie there, hoping they'd move on.

Fortunately, Louise arrived just then, functioning as the maître d', and ushered them to a table.

"That was lucky," I said.

"Luck had nothing to do with it," Alice said. "Louise is very sharp. I'll bet she read the situation, and that was a rescue."

"Oh, come on."

"You don't think so? A very smart woman. It takes an awful lot to run a place like this."

"You give her all the credit?"

"Huh?"

"Isn't her husband responsible for some of it?"

"He's the cook. It's a full-time job."

Of course. Louise's husband was the cook, which was a full-time job, and therefore he couldn't have anything to do with running the inn. On the other hand, it occurred to me if Louise was the cook, Alice would be telling me how remarkable it was the woman was able to run the inn and do the cooking too.

Florence came back to the table.

"How's Prince?" I said.

"Just fine. How are the McInnernys?"

"Same as ever," I said. "Well, that's too bad."

"What's too bad?" Alice said.

"We didn't get our entrées. Florence is back, and we didn't get served yet. Usually, if you leave the table, your food arrives."

Alice said to Florence, "He's not always like this."

"But I know what he means," Florence said. "It's like hopping in the shower when you're expecting a phone call."

"Yeah, but that works," Alice said, and the two of them laughed.

I picked up the last rib.

"You're not going to eat that," Alice said.

"I certainly am."

"You won't have room for your steak."

"I'll have room," I said, taking a bite. "Aren't these good, though?"

"They're all right," Florence said.

"Say," I said, "why don't we get the recipe for these?"

"Don't be silly," Alice said.

"Why is that silly?"

"You want a recipe for ribs? Everyone knows how to cook ribs."

"Not like this."

"You think I can't cook this?" Alice said.

"I didn't say that. I just said you didn't have the recipe."

"Stanley, I don't need a recipe for ribs."

"You're telling me you'll cook me these ribs when we get home?"

"Absolutely."

"You've never cooked barbecued ribs."

"No, but I can. It's perfectly easy."

"Uh-huh," I said. "You're saying that barbecued ribs is something that you *would* make?"

"Yes."

"On the other hand, shark is something you wouldn't."

"Are you going to start that again?"

"So, it makes sense to get a recipe for something you wouldn't cook, but no sense to get a recipe for something you would?"

"Don't be silly," Alice said. "You just don't understand."

Previously that had been Florence's cue, but fortunately she didn't seem to be picking up on the banter this time around. I was glad. I didn't want to have to excuse myself to go to the bathroom a second time.

Yeah, I know. This time I'd started it, asked for it, and brought it on myself. But those ribs sure were good.

Lucy came into view with a tray of serving dishes, and expectations were high, however, like everyone else, she veered off and passed behind me and out of view. That was depressing—our food couldn't possibly arrive until Lucy had served whoever it was she was serving.

A couple of minutes later she passed by, heading for the kitchen again. I kept an eye out hopefully, the last rib now but a fond memory. Unfortunately, the next person to emerge from the direction of the kitchen was the other waitress, so the tray of food she was holding couldn't possibly be ours. Nevertheless, I watched her as she took the route behind me out of sight. I even turned slightly in my chair to watch the tray go.

I saw her stop in front of the booth where Inga/Christine was waiting for boyfriend Lars. So, they were getting served, and he hadn't come back yet. His food would be getting cold. Somehow, that pleased me.

"What are you smiling at?" Alice said.

I hadn't realized I was smiling. "Oh, nothing," I said. "It's just sometimes things work out."

There came an ear-splitting scream. You read about them in books all the time, but it's something else to encounter one in real life.

For a second I had no idea what was going on.

Then I realized.

I jumped up, wheeled around.

The waitress who had just brought the food to the booth was shaking and crying hysterically.

It was easy to see why.

Inga/Christine was slumped half in, half out of the booth, her head loose, her blond hair dangling, her eyes glassy.

She was clearly dead.

TWELVE

THE POLICEMAN DIDN'T seem in any hurry. He stood in the middle of the dining room, cocked his head, and said, "Tell me again."

"There's nothing to tell," Louise said. "The young lady and her boyfriend are guests at the inn."

"Boyfriend?"

"Yes. They've been staying with us for three days."

"No problems up till now?"

"None whatever."

"No suspicion anything was wrong?"

"I don't think anything *is* wrong. The poor woman just had a heart attack."

"That's not what the doctor says."

So I gathered. The doctor, a rather prissy-looking little man with gray hair and a tiny mustache, had arrived within minutes, which I guess is one of the advantages of living in a small town. He'd come bustling in and taken charge in a manner which I initially thought of as efficient, an assessment I had later changed to officious. Because the man, for no apparent reason, had deemed this a suspicious death and called in the police. Which would have been all right in itself, had he not gone further and closed the dining room. Or, rather, the kitchen. The dining room was still open, in fact we were still in the dining room. We just weren't eating.

I know that's a cold and callous thing to say under the circumstances. But if we were going to be held captive by an overzealous cop, it would have been nice to have our food.

The cop in question was a human traffic jam. The type of person who could walk up to a man on fire and say, "What seems to be the trouble?" It could be he only gave that impression because he was keeping me from my meal, but I don't think so. I think it was just him.

He had a way of moving that suggested that part of his body was probably asleep. Or perhaps underwater—maybe that was it—he moved as if underwater.

The cop, whose name I didn't know, and didn't seem likely to find out, was probably my age, if not younger, a horrifying thought. He was a large man with a gleaming bald head, and ears that stuck out on each side of his head like the handles of a pitcher.

A pitcher of molasses.

"Just one more time," he said.

Louise frowned.

The doctor came in, took the cop aside and whispered to him. The cop listened patiently, then asked the doctor something. Probably to repeat what he'd told him just one more time. The doctor frowned, whispered some more. When he was finished, he straightened up and stepped away. That left the cop with the choice of talking out loud, or conceding the conversation was over.

He did neither. He raised his hand, and, slowly with one finger, gestured to the doctor to come closer again. The doctor did, though, it appeared to me, rather reluctantly. This time when he was finished, he straightened up and went out the door.

The cop lumbered over to Louise. "So," he said, "let's go over this one more time."

Louise never got a chance because Lars came in. He wasn't weeping, but he was certainly distraught. He came in the door, fighting off the young police officer who was attempting to restrain him, and barreled up to the cop.

"Please, please," he said. "Tell me what's going on. They won't let me see her. They won't tell me anything. They keep holding me in that room and telling me to wait. I'm tired of waiting, and I want to know what's going on."

"Well, now," the cop said, "I can understand you're upset. Anyone would be. Terrible thing."

"A terrible thing? That's what you call it, a terrible thing? She's dead. Christine is dead. Oh, my god, I can't believe it."

"Try to get a hold of yourself."

"Stop telling me to get a hold of myself. That's all anyone's told me since it happened. First the doctor and now you. Tells me she's dead, and won't let me near her. Do you understand? Stood in front of me and wouldn't let me near her. Then they take her away and hold me here, and no one tells me what's going on. Doesn't anyone care about my feelings at all?"

"We most certainly do. And I'd like to make this as painless as possible. Unfortunately, I have to do my job. You do understand what's going on here?"

"Understand? What's to understand? Christine is dead."

"Yes, she is. And we have to find out why. I don't mean to upset you further, but you have to understand there's every indication her death was not from natural causes."

"What are you saying?"

"Simply that. I'm sorry, but the medical findings seem to indicate that she was killed."

"Killed!"

"It's preliminary and only a suspicion until proved by the autopsy. But for the moment, we have to go on the assumption that she was killed."

"Killed? How?"

"That's something I prefer to go into in private."

The cop turned and looked over to where two officers who apparently comprised the local crime scene unit had been processing the booth. "You guys about done?"

"All yours if you want it. We're just packing up."

"Fine," the cop said. "If you don't mind, we'll talk in there." He turned and addressed the room. "Ladies and gentlemen, I'm sorry to hold you here, but you understand what's happened. You are all witnesses to an apparent crime. A young woman has been killed. Apparently. But it is unlikely that this was a natural death. It might be accidental, it might be self-inflicted, it might be murder. It's up to us to sort it out, which is why you're here. Do you understand?"

We certainly did, since the cop had made the identical speech shortly after he'd arrived and ordered us all to resume our original seats. All except Lars, of course, whose seat was part of the crime scene, and who'd been held incommunicado in the TV room, once the cops had managed to pry him away from the body.

The cop gestured to the booth. "Mr. Heinrick," he said.

Lars blinked at him. "You want me to sit in there?"

"Yes, I do. I understand why that might make you uncomfortable. But the fact is, I would like you to sit exactly where you were sitting during dinner, and describe for me what happened."

"I don't understand."

"You don't have to. That's my job. Come along now. Let's get it over with."

The cop put his arm gently but firmly around Lars' shoulders and led him over to the booth. After a moment's hesitation, while Lars looked at the cop, they sat down.

Of course, as soon as they did, they disappeared from our line of sight.

And, like unruly students when the teacher leaves the room, everyone began talking at once.

"Damn," Alice said.

"What's the matter?"

"What's the matter? We're not going to be able to hear what he says."

We most certainly weren't. And I couldn't help wondering whether that was the whole idea, if that was why the cop had assembled us here, instead of holding us like Lars in some other room. That we were there merely to provide background noise, to make sure his interrogations were not overheard.

"It's all right," I told Alice. "I happen to know what he's saying."

"What's that?"

"He's asking Lars to tell him what happened just one more time."

THIRTEEN

ALICE WENT FIRST.

I don't mean first after Lars. I mean first from our table. She was maybe the tenth, overall.

The interrogation of Lars took no time at all, maybe ten minutes, though it seemed like an hour and a half. When he was done, he was consigned to the TV room again, in the company of a young cop. While that certainly didn't look good, it was a notch above being hauled off to jail in handcuffs.

After Lars, a parade of witnesses was summoned to the booth. The cop who fetched them had a droopy mustache and a droopy face, giving him a sad-sack look. He also had an irritatingly polite manner, ending almost every sentence with, "If you wouldn't mind." Since we were in effect being held in police custody, minding was hardly an option.

Anyway, the first witness summoned had been the busboy, Randy. This caused considerable comment in certain circles, notably our table and that of Jean and Joan. In short, all those who knew of his liaison with the deceased. The fact that he'd been summoned first led to speculation—had the police learned of the affair?

Apparently not, since he was out in five minutes.

Next up was Louise's husband. I'd never seen Louise's husband, but I recognized him instantly. I took no credit, however, as he was hard to miss in his chef's apron and hat. Other clues were the fact that he came from the kitchen, and was protesting to the sad-sack cop that his food was going to burn. I was right with him there—if the man was still cooking, he should return to the kitchen and look out for my steak.

He was in twice as long as the busboy. Which seemed to confirm the theory—Randy's liaison was not yet known, they were merely concerned with who prepared the food.

This concept was not lost on the guests. The word *poison* began to reverberate throughout the room.

Next up was the waitress who found the body. Followed by our waitress, Lucy. Their interrogations were equally long, which made no sense. While the waitress who found the body might have something to say, Lucy knew nothing at all.

Which confirmed my worst fears.

The cop just loved to talk.

Next up was Louise, who hadn't even been in the dining room, and should have had nothing to say at all.

She said it for six-and-a-half minutes. By then I had taken to timing them.

After Louise, they started in on the guests. First up were the McInnernys, who objected to being taken one at a time. At least Mrs. McInnerny objected—I'm sure Johnny didn't mind. In fact, going alone was probably a relief. At any rate, we had four minutes of him and eight minutes of her. More than ten minutes of the McInnernys, who in all likelihood knew absolutely nothing at all.

After that were a couple I didn't know, a man and woman who presumably had stopped in for dinner and weren't even staying at the inn. They were followed by the two men who could be gay, another couple presumably just there for dinner, and the man and woman with the little girl.

The little girl herself was not interrogated. That struck me as a wise, humane move. It also occurred to me, when the dust had cleared and the case was finally solved, it would probably turn out that she had had the key clue all along.

After that came Alice.

She set a record, sixteen and a half minutes.

I sat there feeling most uncomfortable. Not that I was worried about what she was saying. It's just as the interview stretched on, the grumbling in the dining room became less and less restrained. The sentiment was abundantly clear—who the hell was *she,* and why was *she* so all-fired important?

Finally Alice emerged, which meant Florence would be next— at all the tables Sad Sack had been observing ladies first, part of his annoyingly mannered Emily Post routine.

I hoped Florence would be quick. Though, from what I'd observed, she seemed even more likely to gossip than Alice.

However, I was not to find out.

"Mr. Hastings?" Sad Sack said. He smiled and gestured toward the booth. "If you wouldn't mind."

FOURTEEN

EVEN THOUGH I had not yet said a word, somehow I expected the cop to begin with "Just one more time."

He didn't.

He said, "You're a private detective?"

Oh, dear. I'd been afraid of that. Alice had bragged about me.

"Is that what my wife told you?"

"Among other things."

"I see," I said. "Did she tell you what *type* of private detective?"

"I beg your pardon?"

"Did she mention I work for a negligence lawyer?"

"No, I don't believe she did."

I groaned. "Then I'm afraid you've got the wrong impression."

"Oh?"

"I work for a personal-injury lawyer who handles negligence cases. Mainly trip-and-falls. I drive around New York City interviewing accident victims and photographing cracks in the sidewalk." I smiled. "Now, if Alice has told you I have an expertise in murder cases, you have to take it with a grain of salt. It's really a matter of circumstance, and not me. I must say, I have always found the police to be much more clever and resourceful than I am. If Alice has been telling you not to worry because I'm here to solve your murder case for you, I assure you it's just a case of a wife being somewhat overzealous in praising her husband's professional skills. I'm really no expert, and my accomplishments are minimal. So I hope my wife hasn't been boring you with tales of my exploits."

The cop cocked his head, looked at me sideways. "Actually, she hasn't, Mr. Hastings. She *did* mention you did negligence work—in fact, she told me all about it. She just didn't say you worked for an attorney. I believe she described you as being self-employed." He frowned, squinted at me. "But the idea that you have a knack for solving murder cases—and, do I understand you correctly, that you might help me with this one?—that certainly is a fascinating premise. Though your wife didn't mention it at all."

I rubbed my head. Oh, dear. That ought to teach me to lead with my chin.

"I'm sorry," I said. "I should have let you do the talking. Please, go ahead."

"No, no. I find this immensely interesting. Would you care to illuminate on how you've managed to be of use to the police?"

"I'd rather be shot dead."

"I beg your pardon."

"I was trying to *downplay* my worth as an investigator. I'd assumed my wife had been in here singing my praises."

"Well, she wasn't. At least, not in that manner. I don't mean to imply your wife is not proud of you. She just never made that particular suggestion."

"I get the point."

"Good. Then, please, fill me in. How did you come to acquire such a working knowledge of police procedure that you were afraid your wife might be inclined to brag about it?"

I took a breath. "My detective work has sometimes led me into criminal cases. Not often, but enough that I've become acquainted with a few homicide cops."

"Really? And you've helped them solve crimes?"

"I'd say I've *watched* them solve crimes."

"Excellent," the cop said. "And now you'd like to watch me solve this one?"

"Is it a crime?"

"It is indeed. I'm Chief Pinehurst, by the way. You'll want to know that, of course, the next time you're listing your accomplishments."

I took a breath. Refrained from comment.

"Anyway, getting back to what your wife said. She wasn't promoting you so much as an investigator as a witness."

"Oh."

"Yes. *Oh.* Do you suppose you could elaborate on that?"

"I assume my wife has done a fairly good job."

"That she has. Still, we do prefer eyewitness accounts to hearsay."

"I understand."

"Good. Could you tell me what you saw?"

"I saw the decedent kissing a young man."

"Decedent?"

"Yes."

"You're not in court, and no one's taking this down. You don't have to be so formal. You can call her by name."

"I'm blanking on her name."

"You're blanking on her name?"

"I have trouble with names."

"And you're a private detective?"

Good lord. No wonder the interrogations had taken so long.

"I'm not a private detective by choice. It's a job. I admit I'm not as qualified as I might be."

"And yet you manage to assist the police. How extraordinary." Chief Pinehurst consulted his notebook. "The young woman's name is Christine Cobb. Was that the young woman you observed kissing someone?"

"Yes, it was."

"And who would that person be? The person she was kissing?"

"That would be the busboy, Randy. Who, I understand, is the son of the people who run the inn."

"Louise and Charles Winthrop. Well, that certainly is interesting. You observed Christine Cobb and Randy Winthrop having a romantic encounter?"

"I saw them kissing."

"And that's all?"

"That's all I saw. And only for a moment. I withdrew immediately."

"What do you mean by immediately?"

"A matter of seconds. As soon as I saw who it was, I left."

"Why?"

"So as not to embarrass them."

"I see. How come you say only a few seconds?"

"That's all it was. I saw them there. I recognized her first. I thought she was with her boyfriend. Then the light fell on his face, and I saw who it was."

"Which is when you left?"

"That's right."

"To save them embarrassment?"

"Yes."

"Because she was kissing another man?"

"Yes, of course."

"So, if it was her boyfriend, Lars, she'd been kissing, you would have stayed?"

"No, of course not."

"But you just said the reason you left was because she was kissing another man."

I said nothing.

"Was that statement false?"

"It was not."

"That statement was true?"

"Yes, of course."

"So, if you left because she was kissing another man . . ."

"It does not imply I would have stayed if she wasn't. It's faulty logic. The one thing does not imply the other. I left because she was kissing another man. I would have also left if she had been kissing Lars."

"But you didn't leave until you saw who she was kissing. Is that correct?"

"I saw who she was kissing."

"And not at first. Isn't that what you said? You recognized her first. Then the light fell on his face, and you saw him."

"That's right."

"That's right?"

"Yes, of course."

"That doesn't jibe with your current statement."

I blinked. "I beg your pardon?"

"You maintain it makes no difference to you who she was kissing, you would have left in any case. If that were true, you would not know who she was kissing, because you would have left before you found out."

"Oh, for goodness' sakes."

"You have a quarrel with that logic?"

"I find it hard to follow."

"Oh? Well, let's go over it one more time."

I put up my hand. "Let's not. I see the point you're making. It's a good one. Possibly even a great one. It may well crack the case. I admit I am incapable of explaining my inexplicable tardiness in leaving the scene of the decedent's assignation."

"Well said." Chief Pinehurst nodded approvingly. "Very impressive. You rattled that off quite expertly. The only slight fumble was forgetting the victim's name and having to refer to her as *the decedent.*" He rubbed his head, pursed his lips, frowned. "Though I can't say I join you in characterizing your behavior as inexplicable. There is indeed a perfectly logical explanation that springs to mind."

"What's that?"

"Natural curiosity. You saw the woman kissing someone, you wanted to know who. While it did not matter who she was kissing, with regard to your intention to leave, still you wanted to know who it was before you did."

"If that's so perfectly obvious, I don't see why you're making such a big deal of it."

"Because you did. I asked for your reason, and you couldn't give me one. If you'd just said, I wanted to see who it was, I would have found that perfectly natural. And we wouldn't be discussing it now. But you, perhaps embarrassed by your own natural curiosity, decline to do so."

I took a breath. "Tell me, Chief, are you punishing me for being a private detective?"

"Not at all. I'm just trying to get your story. It's always difficult when a witness is evasive."

I took another breath. "Believe me, I'm not trying to be evasive. In fact, if I could get a word in, I'd like to volunteer something."

"Oh? What's that?"

I told him about talking to Christine/Inga at Glen Ellis Falls. Of course, I didn't call her Christine/Inga—explaining why would have sent the investigation off on another unproductive tangent. But I told him everything else.

"Interesting," Pinehurst said. "So the young lady was actually aware that you had seen her."

"Yes, she was."

"Somewhat extraordinary, considering what a brief time you were there. At least, according to your account."

"It was a brief time."

"Yet long enough to be seen. And Miss Cobb asked you not to tell anyone?"

"That's right."

"Which you promised to do. Although, at the time, you had already told everyone."

"That's not true. I'd told my wife."

"Which had the same effect." He cocked his head, raised an eyebrow. "Your wife didn't mention this incident."

"That's because she didn't know about it."

"You withheld this from your wife?"

"I didn't withhold it. I hadn't had an opportunity to tell her."

"Oh? When did the incident occur?"

"Early this afternoon."

"Uh-huh. And you say you left your backpack and had to go back and get it?"

"That's right."

"So, you went back down the hill, found your backpack, and encountered Miss Cobb. She recognized you as the person who had seen her kissing Randy Winthrop. She asked you not to tell anyone. Which you promised to do. Although, in point of fact, you had already told. You then returned to the parking lot, encountered your wife, and refrained from telling her of the incident."

"I didn't want to tell her in front of Jean and Joan."

"Why not?"

"Because I'd promised I wouldn't tell."

"But Jean and Joan already knew."

"Not from me. If my wife told them, what difference does that make? I promised I wouldn't tell. I wasn't going to rush up the hill and immediately tell."

"Yes, but they already knew."

"That's not the point. Well, it *is* the point. I felt bad about that, and I didn't want to discuss it."

"That's why you withheld it from your wife?"

"No. That's why I withheld it from Jean and Joan. I was going to tell my wife at the first opportunity. I just never got one."

"Uh-huh. And is that the only thing you kept from your wife?"

I found myself taking a breath again. "It was the only thing I had not had an opportunity to tell her. I am confident that every-thing else I observed, she knew."

"And what else *had* you observed? With relation to the young woman?"

"I assume my wife told you about the incident at Champney Falls?"

"You can assume anything you like. I'd rather hear it from you."

"Okay. I'll tell you this as if you knew nothing. On the day we arrived here, which was yesterday, on our way we stopped off at Champney Falls. Christine Cobb and Lars Heinrick were there. They passed us on our way up. While we were stopping to rest. When we got to the falls we did not see them. However, there was an incident where we thought we heard the sound of a slap."

"Coming from where?"

"Somewhere in the woods. It was impossible to tell."

"But you and your wife both heard the slap?"

"Yes, we did. Didn't she tell you?"

"I'm concerned with what you're telling me. Did anyone else hear the slap?"

"Yes. Florence. The woman at our table."

"She was also at Champney Falls?"

"Yes."

"You went there together?"

"No. We met her there. Quite by accident. We didn't know her, didn't know she was staying at the inn. We began talking to her because of her dog, which was attracted to my sandwich."

"Uh-huh. And is that the only incident? The sound of the slap?"

"No, it wasn't." I told him about seeing Christine Cobb crying behind the big rock with the tree on it.

"So," Pinehurst said, "at some time after you heard the sound of a slap, you saw the decedent, Christine Cobb, crying behind a big rock. When was the next time you saw her?"

I put up my hand. "Before you get to that, there's one other significant thing about Champney Falls."

"What's that?"

"There was a hiker there who later turned up at the inn. Although he doesn't appear to be staying here."

"Yes, your wife mentioned him too. He was here tonight?"

"Yes, and I don't think he ate. Because he's not here now. He came in, and must have gone right back out."

"But you didn't see him go?"

"No, I didn't. He came in, walked behind my chair out of my line of sight. That's the last I saw of him."

"Uh-huh. And can you describe this man?"

"He was bald and overweight." As I said it, I realized the description fit Pinehurst.

If that offended him, he didn't show it, just said, "Would you care to elaborate on that?"

"On the trail he looked out of place. Like hiking wasn't a natural thing for him to do."

"Uh-huh. You think overweight people shouldn't hike?"

"Not at all. I thought *he* shouldn't hike. At least, he gave the impression he wasn't enjoying it."

"And what was he wearing?"

"On the trail, a T-shirt and shorts. Either a blue or dark gray suit at the inn."

"I see."

"Does that jibe with what my wife told you?"

"Actually, I think it does. Let me see." He flipped through the notebook again. "Let's see. Bald on top. Fringe of light brown hair. Sideburns to middle ear, short, barber cut, recently trimmed. Hazel eyes, thin eyebrows—lighter than hair. Thick lips, bulbous nose. Pale blue, Lands' End pocket tee. Tan shorts, cuffed, brown leather belt."

Pinehurst flipped a page. "And in the dining room, dark blue suit, light blue shirt, red patterned tie with gold diamond studded tie clip." He looked up from his notes. "I would assume we were discussing the same man."

"My wife is far more observant than I am. I would credit anything she tells you."

"Thanks for your opinion. But getting back to my question."

"What question?"

"The one I asked you before you chose this particular tangent. Not that it's not important, and not that I didn't want you to tell me about this man. However, right now I'm concerned with Christine Cobb. Could we go back to the time you saw her crying behind the rock? My question was, when was the *next* time you saw her?"

"Later that day at the swimming pool."

"Swimming pool?"

"Yes. The one here at the inn. My wife and I came here and checked in. We went up to our room and got settled. I went out to the swimming pool to swim, and she was there."

"Oh?"

"What do you mean, *oh?*"

"I don't mean anything. I just said *oh*. Why did you think I meant something?"

"You said *oh* as if you didn't believe me."

"Not at all. I was merely surprised. That is, if I understand you correctly. Are you saying the woman was there when you got there?"

"That's right."

"Well, that's certainly interesting. You leave the woman crying behind a rock, drive here and check in, go out to the swimming pool, and there she is. The woman seems to magically pop up wherever you go."

"Not at all. I admit I was surprised to find out she was staying here."

"Were you?"

"I certainly was. But coincidences happen."

"Yes, but at the speed of light? The way you tell it, you left the falls, drove straight here, checked in, went out to the pool, and there she was. Now, does that make any sense to you?"

"Of course not. That's not what happened. When we got here, we had to check in. Then we had to go upstairs and unpack. Discuss what we were going to do. As a matter of fact, I didn't go swimming right away. I went to watch TV. There was a ball game on. There's no TV in the rooms here. So I had to go to the TV room in the main building—" I broke off, looked at him. "But why are we talking about this? What does it matter?"

"It's important that things make sense. When something doesn't make sense, it needs to be explained. And if it can't be explained, there must be a reason why it can't be explained, and that in itself may be important. At the moment, I'm trying to establish your relationship with Christine Cobb."

"I didn't *have* a relationship with Christine Cobb."

"And yet she shows up everywhere you go. Who else was also at the swimming pool at the time?"

"No one."

"No one?"

"That's right. When I got there, she was sunbathing in one of the deck chairs."

"Sunbathing?"

"Yes."

"She was nude?"

"No. She was wearing a bikini."

"You recognized her as the woman from the falls?"

"Not at first. She was lying on her stomach, and I couldn't see her face. I went for a swim, later I saw it was her."

"Did you speak to her?"

Oh, dear.

I didn't want to talk about it. I'm not sure why. Maybe I still felt guilty about the fact I'd had a conversation with her without mentioning Alice. Or maybe I didn't want to talk about it because it was totally unimportant. Or maybe I didn't want to talk about it because it was only a one-minute conversation, but I knew we'd be talking about it forever.

Already my interrogation was running even longer than Alice's had.

And we hadn't even gotten around to discussing the murder yet.

FIFTEEN

"YOU WENT OUT?"

"I went to the bathroom."

"You went to the bathroom?"

"That's right."

"Why?"

"Chief, I wouldn't want to accuse you of overintellectualizing, but this doesn't require that much thought. I had to go to the bathroom, so I went."

Well, we'd finally gotten around to discussing the murder. Not that it made any difference. Since I didn't really know anything, I had little to contribute.

Not that Pinehurst was willing to leave it at that. Naturally, he wanted to know every little thing.

"When was it that you went to the bathroom?"

"I don't know."

"You don't know."

"I'm not in the habit of consulting my watch on such occasions. Doubtless there are people who are."

"I'm not concerned with your watch. I was hoping you could tell me relative to your meal."

"That I can do. I went to the bathroom after we placed our orders."

"See. That wasn't so hard. And on your way to the bathroom, did you happen to pass by this booth?"

"Yes, of course."

"Why *of course?*"

"Don't be silly. Look where my table is. The bathroom's out there. To get to it you walk right by."

"And as you went by did you look in the booth?"

"Actually, I couldn't see in the booth."

"Why was that?"

"The busboy was in the way. He was serving the drinks."

"The busboy, Randy?"

"That's right."

"Whom you'd observed kissing Christine Cobb?"

"That's the only busboy Randy I know."

"Uh-huh. And did that register with you at the time—I mean who all those people were?"

"Yes, it did."

"So you are absolutely certain it was the busboy, Randy, you saw at their booth?"

"That's right."

"He was serving them drinks?"

"Yes, he was."

"You saw that too?"

"Yes, I did. He had a tray with drinks. He was placing them on the table."

"And did you notice what those drinks were?"

"No, I did not."

"You don't know what Christine Cobb was drinking?"

"No, I don't."

"Or Lars Heinrick?"

"Or Lars Heinrick."

"Were they both in the booth when the drinks were being served?"

"Yes, they were."

"How can you be so sure?"

"As you say, I was aware of who these people were. I saw who it was who was serving them drinks. The significance was not lost on me. I took note of it. If Lars had *not* been there, that would have been very interesting, and I would have taken note of *that*. But I didn't. I did not see the busboy, Randy, *alone* with Christine Cobb at the booth. I saw him serving drinks to the two of them."

Pinehurst nodded. "Very convincing. I'm sure that you're right. Now, when you returned from the bathroom, what did you see then? Assuming you went by the booth?"

"Yes, I did."

"So what did you see?"

I told him about Lars Heinrick glaring at Christine Cobb, and about seeing the tear running down her cheek.

"Interesting," Pinehurst said. "Particularly in terms of the sequence. The busboy serves them drinks. They immediately have a fight. Lars is angry, and she's tearful. Can we conclude he was aware of what was going on?"

"Of course not," I said. "It could have been any number of things."

"Yes, yes," Pinehurst said. "That question was rhetorical, still I thank you for answering it. Anyway, after that you went back to your table?"

"Yes, I did."

"And immediately told your wife and her friend what you saw?"

"No, I didn't."

"I didn't think so. Or your wife might have mentioned it. Why didn't you tell your wife what you'd just seen?"

"I told you that."

"Don't be silly. How could you have told me that? The subject just came up."

"No, no. I mean the other thing. Seeing her at whatjamacallit—Glen Ellis Falls. I hadn't had a chance to tell my wife about that, and I didn't want to bring up the subject."

"What subject? This is an entirely different matter. Talking to her at Glen Ellis Falls and seeing her at dinner in the booth."

"Even so. I didn't want to talk about her at all. I simply didn't mention it."

"But your wife did. At least she says she did. She said the three of you noticed and commented on the fact it was the busboy, Randy, who was serving them drinks."

"Yes, I guess we did."

"So there you are. Wouldn't that have been the perfect time to have mentioned that right after that you'd seen the young woman with a tear in her eye and the young man looking somewhat less than pleased?"

"If I'd wanted to get into it. As I say, I was avoiding the topic until I had a chance to talk with my wife."

"You felt you needed to explain?"

"No. I *wanted* to explain. I wanted to tell my wife exactly what the young woman said, so she'd realize the position I'd been put in."

"You thought you were in a bad position?"

"Haven't I said that? The woman asked me to keep a secret. One that had already been told. It was a very uncomfortable position."

"And that's all there was to it—this uncomfortable feeling of yours?"

"What do you mean?"

"Your only real concern with this woman was keeping or not keeping her secret? She wasn't a threat to your relationship with your wife?"

"Don't be silly."

"Why is that silly? An attractive young woman like that. If she were to make a play for you . . ."

"Yes, but she didn't. She barely noticed me at all. She was involved with the busboy."

"So you say."

"What do you mean by that?"

Pinehurst shrugged. "Well, we only have your word for it. Everyone else, it's all hearsay. They're all repeating stories told by you. You're the only one who actually saw anything. So, in the event you were mistaken . . ."

"I'm not."

"Or in case you didn't happen to be telling the truth . . ."

"I beg your pardon?"

"No offense meant, but I'm a policeman. And I can't take anyone's story at face value. All these things have to be checked. Now, your story is not corroborated. Other people may know of it, but you're the only source of the information. So what if this rendezvous never took place? What if the busboy wasn't there? What if you were the man Christine Cobb was kissing?"

"Are you serious?"

"Works for me. You see her at Champney Falls. You're immediately smitten—and who could blame you. An attractive young woman, and crying, too. A damsel in distress. You arrive at the inn, spot her at the swimming pool. Sunbathing alone. You can't resist. You go out, strike up a conversation. Your wife arrives to interrupt, but not before you've established a relationship, leading to your rendezvous later that night."

"Oh, for goodness' sakes."

"You have a problem with that? It certainly works for me. Here you are, your first night at the inn, and yet you leave your wife and go stumbling around in the dark. One would think a man would have to have a motive."

"One would be wrong. I did not leave my wife. My wife left me. She went to watch *The Bridges of Madison County* in the recreation room. I did not wish to see *The Bridges of Madison County*. If that's a crime, I plead guilty as charged. I did not wish to go back to my room alone because it is somewhat cheerless and does not have a television. I went in there, to the TV room—where you're holding Lars Heinrick now—I went in there to see what was on, but there were some people watching some dreadful TV movie. It was the McInnernys, that couple at the table over there. If you want to check, they were the ones who told me about the stream and the pond. That's why I went out there to take a look, and that's how I happened to see the busboy, Randy, kissing Christine Cobb."

"Uh-huh," Pinehurst said. If he was convinced, you wouldn't have known it.

"The McInnernys will confirm everything I've just said."

"By that, I assume you mean they will confirm telling you about this pond. So," Pinehurst said, "you leave your wife at the movie. You come back to the inn, looking for Christine Cobb. You look in the TV room, but she's not there. Of course you can't tell the couple watching TV you're looking for Christine Cobb, so you become involved in a brief conversation with them about the grounds, during which they tell you about the pond.

"You leave the TV room and encounter Christine Cobb. Naturally, you want to take her someplace you won't be seen. You've just been told about this pond across the road. It sounds romantic to you. You tell the young woman about it, suggest you check it out. Which you do."

"Chief?"

"Yes?"

"Not to tell you your business, but have you considered *asking* the busboy if he was involved with Christine Cobb? If he admits it, you're done. Even if he denies it, I can't imagine a callow youth like that fooling you for long."

"Thanks for your vote of confidence. I certainly intend to question the busboy again. It's on my list."

"Your list?"

"Yes, of course. At the moment, I'm concerned with you. Now, you admit you passed by the booth twice. The time you got up and went to the bathroom."

"Admit?"

"You did pass by the booth twice, didn't you?"

"Yes, I did."

"There you are. Now, was that the *only* time you got up from the table during the meal?"

"Yes, it was."

"Well, that's something I can check with your wife. And with the other woman at the table. But say it's true. Say you only got up that one time. On your way out of the dining room the busboy was serving the drinks. That's fairly well established both by you and by your wife. So let's assume that that's true.

"So, on your way *back* from the bathroom the drinks have already been served. They're there on the table. Now, according to your story, as you pass by the booth, you see the young man glaring at the young woman and a tear running down her cheek. Is that right?"

"Yes, it is."

"Yet, here again, we have only your word for that. There's no corroboration of any kind. In this case, it's *worse* than your story of her kissing the busboy by the pool. Because you didn't even tell your wife. You didn't tell anyone. So here's a story you chose not to tell until after the crime. After the murder, questioned as to what you did, you suddenly spring this tale. That on your way back from the bathroom, this is what you saw.

"Well, it could have happened like that. What you describe is certainly in keeping with the situation. Not too inventive, of course, but seeing the woman crying is what you've described before. If you're making something up, it's hard to be artistic. It's better to be sound. The soundest thing is something that fits in with what's gone before. One would describe something similar to, or identical to, a past event, in order to give the story validity, make it seem real.

"So, you say you saw a tear running down her cheek. And the boyfriend glaring at her. Like the incident from Champney Falls. The fact she was crying and the sound of the slap. You put that together in your head, and you create the scene you describe in the booth."

"Oh, is that right? And why do I do that?"

"To cover what you actually did. Which was to stop at the booth and put poison in her glass."

"Poison?"

"Surely you've guessed that poison was involved. Assuming you're guessing. And don't know for sure because you did the deed. But, yes, that is the apparent cause of death."

"There was poison in her glass?"

"That's what I suspect. Of course, I have to await the report from the lab. But, let us assume for the sake of the discussion the young woman was poisoned. And let us assume that you stopped by her booth to put poison in her glass."

"And why would I do that?"

"Because she's a woman."

"I beg your pardon?"

"I'm sorry. That was a sexist remark. I was generalizing, and one should not generalize. But say you were having an affair with her. And say she was not willing to leave it at that. Say she wanted you to leave your wife, which you weren't willing to do, so she threatened to tell her. You can see the whole sorry pattern begin to emerge."

"I certainly can." I rubbed my head. "Chief, is there any way we could move this along? We could always come back to the matter, should any of these unfounded suspicions pan out."

Pinehurst pursed his lips. "So, you're somewhat touchy on the subject of poison."

I took a breath, exhaled. "I'm somewhat exasperated by the suggestion I might have administered it."

"Uh-huh. Well, help me out then. Show me a reason why you couldn't."

"How about this? When I returned from the bathroom, both Lars Heinrick and Christine Cobb were in the booth. If I had stopped by to drug her drink, don't you think Lars might have wondered why?"

"Sure, if your story's true. If Lars was indeed in the booth at the time."

"But he was."

"According to who?"

"There's no according to who about it. He *was*."

"How do you know?"

"Because I saw him get up and go out."

"When was that?"

"Later. After I'd returned to my table."

"And who saw him go out?"

"I did."

"There again, we have your unsubstantiated word."

"Didn't anyone else see him go out?"

"Actually, people did. But no one's that accurate on the time. And, as to whether he went out before or after you came back, well, I don't think anyone can help us there."

"Try my wife."

"Oh?"

"I'll bet she'd remember."

"Perhaps. But then a wife will alibi her husband."

"Alibi?"

"Yes, of course."

"But, but, but—"

"But what?"

"But you say my motive for killing her was to keep my wife from finding out. So why would my wife give me an alibi for the killing?"

Pinehurst shrugged. "I could be wrong. You could have another motive entirely. And you and your wife could be coconspirators."

"Give me a break."

"But let's not get off on a tangent," Pinehurst said.

I blinked. I couldn't quite believe he'd said that.

"The point is, so far no one can confirm the time Lars Heinrick went out. So it's entirely possible you could have had a moment alone in the booth with Christine Cobb. Long enough to lean over, whisper something in her ear, and administer the poison."

"Are you telling me I have to find someone who remembers when I came back, *and* who saw Lars Heinrick go out?"

"That would be nice. Though it wouldn't solve your problem."

"Why not?"

"Because you could have done it anyway. Say Lars Heinrick hasn't left yet when you come back. You stop by the booth under some guise of talking to the *two* of them. You distract their attention in some way, and slip the poison in the glass."

"Yes, but Lars Heinrick is alive."

"Yes, of course. You only poison one glass."

"No, no. You miss the point. He's alive, so you can ask him. If I stopped by the booth while he was there, he will remember it. Ask him if I came by the booth. Ask him if I had any opportunity to put the poison in that glass."

"Are you sure you want me to do that?"

"Yes, I'm sure. Why do you ask?"

"I thought you were a private detective. Well, I guess it takes all kinds. Perhaps you haven't had time to think this over. But

122

try the concept on. As good a murder suspect as you happen to look right now, Lars Heinrick looks better. He's the one with the best motive, and he's the one with the best opportunity.

"Now, assuming that he's guilty—or assuming that he's intelligent enough to realize that he *looks* guilty—his natural reaction would be to pin the crime on someone else.

"So, if I put the idea in his mind—if I suggest to him that the police might suspect you of this crime by asking him whether you stopped by the booth and had an opportunity to tamper with the glass—well, wouldn't that make it awfully tempting for the young man to say yes? Particularly, if he suspected you of being the one who had alienated the young lady's affections?"

I tried to keep my exasperation from showing. It was difficult, talking through clenched teeth. "Couldn't you manage to ask him a question somehow without tipping your hand?"

"Actually, not very well. If he's guilty, he knows what's up. Even if he's innocent, he suspects what's going on. He'd be apt to grasp at straws."

"Then don't *give* him one. Ask him if *anyone* stopped by the booth. If he names me, I'll buy you dinner."

"Sporting of you," Pinehurst said. "I assure you I will try to eliminate that as a possibility. Not the dinner, the chance he saw you in the booth. But even if I can, that leaves the much more likely possibility that when you stopped by he wasn't there."

"I don't suppose you could manage to eliminate *that* possibility?"

Pinehurst smiled. "In all good time, Mr. Hastings. In all good time."

That's what I was afraid of.

SIXTEEN

"THAT COP IS not too bright."

"Why do you say that?"

"He thinks I did it."

Alice smiled. "That would certainly account for your opinion."

"That's not what I mean."

"What do you mean?"

"He sent me back here. To sit with you. If he really thinks I did it, he's giving us a chance to compare notes and patch up our stories."

"Stories?"

"In case we were in it together—one of his scenarios. The other is I did it alone. In that case, I would now have a chance to cloud your recollection."

"As if you could."

"Yeah, but he doesn't know that. Leaving me alone with you is a bad move, if he seriously thinks I did it."

"Well, obviously he doesn't."

"Don't bet on it. And even so, it makes no sense leaving us alone."

Alice and I were alone at our table because Pinehurst was questioning Florence. If leaving us alone made no sense, questioning Florence made even less. I mean, fine, maybe the guy had to take everybody's statements and eventually he'd get to Florence, but surely there are priorities. And from what I just told him, he had to want to talk to Lars or the busboy.

But, no, that would be too easy, that might lead somewhere. That could get us out of the dining room before midnight, which wasn't apt to happen. Dawn seemed much more likely.

"So what is it we shouldn't be comparing notes on?" Alice said.

I sighed, shook my head. "You wouldn't believe me."

I told Alice about meeting the girl at Glen Ellis Falls, seeing the tear running down her cheek in the booth, and Chief Pinehurst's assessment of all that.

Alice was understandably shocked. "Oh, dear," she said when I was through.

"Yeah," I said. "What a horrible situation."

"I'll say. And the worst part is, it sounds so logical."

"Oh?"

"Well, you were alone with her at the swimming pool. And you were the only one who saw her kissing the busboy. And then you meet her at the waterfall and don't even tell me about it."

"I explained why."

"Yes, but it's an explanation that wouldn't convince a cop. You promised not to tell, so you didn't want to tell, although you'd already told. That's too convoluted reasoning for most people. As for me, I know you, I know that's exactly how you think. But a policeman?" Alice shook her head. "You're lucky you're not on your way to jail."

"I certainly am. I'm clearly his chief suspect. With the possible exception of Randy or Lars."

"Randy couldn't have done it," Alice said.

"Why not?"

"Are you kidding? Just look at him."

"He's in the kitchen."

"You know what I mean. You've seen him. Can you imagine him killing that girl?"

"Why not?"

"Why not? Are you kidding me? He was absolutely infatuated with her. Killing her was the last thing on his mind."

"Yeah, but you don't know his story."

"Story, schmory. He didn't kill her."

"What about Lars?"

"What about him?"

"Could he have killed her?"

"Sure."

"Why? Because his mother doesn't run a bed-and-breakfast?"

"It's an inn."

"Don't start that, Alice. Do you see the point I'm making? Here's Randy and Lars. Two nice, clean cut–looking young men. Nothing much to choose between 'em. But you flat out tell me Randy couldn't have done it and Lars could."

"That's just my opinion."

"Yes, but you have it. And you also have a tendency to state your opinions as facts.

"Well, that's a nice thing to say."

"You know what I mean."

"I suppose I'm responsible for making you the number-one suspect?"

"No, I seem to have done that on my own. Anyway, since the cops made the mistake of letting us confer, you think you could help me with my alibi?"

"I beg your pardon?"

"The theory is I put poison in her glass on my way back from the bathroom. My argument is how could I have done that while Lars was still there? Unfortunately, no one knows when Lars went out. Relative to when I returned from the bathroom."

"It was after."

"How do you know?"

"I saw him go. And it was a long time after you came back to the table."

"That's not good."

"Why not?"

"If it was a long time, he could have gone out and come back in the meantime. You see what I mean. He could have been out when I went by his table. Come back shortly after that, and then left again when you saw him."

"What are you doing, trying to break your own alibi?"

"Actually, yes. Because if I can do it, he can do it. I'm trying to find answers to all his objections."

Something hit me on the cheek. It bounced off, fell to the table. It was a green pea.

I looked at it, then at Alice. Then in the direction from which it came.

At the far table, either Jean or Joan was waving at us—at the moment I was blanking on which was which—but the thinner of the two was trying surreptitiously to attract our attention.

I say surreptitiously because she was obviously trying to do so without also attracting the attention of the sad-sack cop with the droopy mustache, who seemed to have appointed himself in charge of maintaining discipline in the dining room. Talking was permitted, and all the people at the tables certainly were. But intercourse *between* tables was something Sad Sack simply wouldn't allow. Whether those were Pinehurst's orders, or whether this was something Sad Sack had decided for himself was not entirely clear, but at any rate talking between tables was strictly forbidden.

Once again, I had the feeling of being in school—the teacher's back was turned, and one of the students had just hit me with a spitball.

Once she had our attention, Jean/Joan looked a question and pantomimed a kiss. When I looked puzzled, she repeated the sequence.

Alice got it. Nodded yes.

Then Sad Sack turned around, and suddenly we were all on our best behavior again.

"What was that?" I said.

"She wanted to know if we told them about Randy kissing Christine."

"You mean if we hadn't she wasn't going to bring it up?"

"How should I know?"

"Otherwise, what's the point in asking?"

"Don't be silly."

"Why is that silly."

"You think a person wouldn't just want to know?"

"Sure. But communicating behind a policeman's back is probably not the smartest move to make in a murder investigation."

"How could it hurt?"

"What if he saw you and wanted to know why?"

"I'd tell him. I mean, it's not like there's anything we're withholding from the police. Is there?"

"No, I guess not. Who is it who waved at us, by the way?"

"Stanley. You don't know who that is?"

"I know who it is. But is that Jean or Joan?"

"It's Jean."

"Oh."

Alice shook her head. "You're hopeless."

"I know. You think you could discourage Jean from further attempts at communication. She's only going to get us in trouble."

"How much trouble can we be in? You're already the prime suspect."

"That's just my point. The police already suspect me of murder. Let's not make them angry."

Alice shook her head, pityingly. Obviously I had once again proved myself to be an old fuddy-duddy.

Fortunately, Jean gave up trying to communicate, so there was no harm done.

Florence emerged from the booth. Instead of returning to our table, she looked around, caught Sad Sack's eye, and went over to him.

With the noise in the dining room I couldn't hear what she was saying, but she was talking animatedly and gesturing and pointing, and once I thought I heard the word *dog*.

I did.

Florence returned to our table with a chip on her shoulder.

"He won't let me walk Prince," she said in disgust. "If they're going to keep us here all night, the dog has to go out."

"Did you ask Pinehurst?" I said.

"Who?"

"The cop who questioned you. His name's Pinehurst. Didn't he tell you that?"

"I don't believe he did."

"He only tells the chief suspects," Alice said.

"Huh?"

"Stanley's a suspect. Couldn't you tell from the questions he was asking?"

"He mentioned the two of you. But I didn't get that impression."

"Oh? So who did it sound like he suspected?"

"It wasn't like that?"

"What do you mean?" I said.

"It wasn't like he suspected anyone. It was like he just wanted to ask questions."

"Exactly my impression," I said. "Except in my case, he acted as if he suspected me."

"Maybe that's just his way," Florence said.

"Oh, yeah? Didn't he ask you what I told you?"

"Yes, of course."

"About seeing her and Randy by the pond—did he ask you about that?"

"No, he just asked me what I knew."

"Did you tell him that?"

"Of course."

"Did he ask you any questions, try to break the story down?"

"Break it down?"

"Yes."

"No. Why would he do that?"

"Under the theory I made it up."

Florence blinked. "What?"

"That's the theory," Alice said. "Stanley made up the story about the busboy kissing her to cover up his own affair."

"Are you kidding me?"

"That's the theory," I said.

Florence exhaled, shook her head. "Poor Prince."

"Prince?" I said.

Florence nodded. "Uh-huh." She shrugged. "Looks like we'll be here all night."

SEVENTEEN

IT WAS NEARLY one o'clock before Chief Pinehurst was done. By then he had questioned everybody in the room, and had a second helping of Randy and Lars. What he had learned from all that was not entirely clear, but the bottom line was when he was finished no one was in custody, but all residents of the Blue Frog Ponds had been instructed not to check out.

My heart sank when I heard it. I felt like a man in a shaggy dog story, trapped forever in a cheerless, sexless, TV-less room in an inhospitable bed-and-breakfast, while a painstakingly pedantic policeman slowly and methodically sifted an endless spiral of clues, never drawing one whit closer to any solution.

That seemed to be Alice's assessment of the situation also. "You have to solve this," she said, when we finally got back to the room.

"I beg your pardon?"

"Come on, Stanley. You can see how it is. That cop hasn't got a clue."

"I admit his style is not reassuring."

"Reassuring? It's positively frightening. He doesn't know what he's doing. If he were to arrest Randy, it would break Louise's heart."

"I don't think he's about to do that."

"Oh, yeah? The guy questions everyone in the room. Then he asks for Randy and Lars. Well, Lars is the grieving boyfriend, but who is Randy? Who is he possibly except suspect number one."

"I thought I was suspect number one."

"Don't be dumb. Anyway, the whole thing's ridiculous. The only real suspect is Lars."

"Why?"

"Because he's the only one with a motive. He's the only one involved with her who could possibly want her dead."

"What about Randy?"

"Why would he want her dead?"

"I don't know. To shut her up?"

"Shut her up about what? The affair? Why would he care about that? What's the worst that could happen? Mommy gets miffed and gives him a lecture about keeping his hands off the guests? Would he kill to protect against that?"

"Of course not," I said. "But what about Lars?"

"What about him?"

"I would think his motive's pretty thin. He found out the girl was seeing someone else, so he killed her? I don't think so. Packed up, drove off, and left her stranded here I could buy. But took her out to dinner and slipped poison in her drink? It simply doesn't make it. If this is a crime of passion, poison just isn't that passionate. Shoot her, stab her, strangle her, that fills the bill. But poison doesn't. You don't poison someone in the heat of passion. It is a cold-blooded, premeditated crime."

"Exactly."

"What do you mean, *exactly?* That destroys your argument."

"No, it doesn't. It casts some doubt on the fact he killed her because she was having an affair with Randy, but that doesn't have to be his motive."

"So what does?"

"I have no idea. All I said was they're the ones with the relationship, so he's the one most likely to *have* a motive. But that's not important right now. What's important is keeping the cops from arresting Randy."

"You want to keep your voice down a little? The walls are thin, and this is not the type of thing I want to spread around."

Alice waved it off. "Oh, they're not back yet."

My eyes widened slightly. "Hey, you're right. They aren't."

Alice looked at me reprovingly. "Stanley. How could you even think that at a time like this?"

"A time like what? You just pointed out our neighbors aren't home."

"I don't believe you. A woman has been killed."

"Yes, but—"

"And it's one in the morning, and we have to get to bed."

"Exactly."

"Stanley. Don't joke. A woman has been killed, and someone close to us did it. That's pretty scary."

"Yeah, I know."

A floorboard creaked.

Just outside the door.

I immediately turned to look, then looked back at Alice.

Her eyes were wide.

I put my finger to my lips.

She nodded. Gestured toward the door.

I was closer. I took two steps on tiptoe, trying not to make a sound. I stretched my arm out, reached the doorknob.

Looked to Alice.

She nodded.

I twisted the doorknob, stepped back, swung the door wide.

And—

Nothing.

There was no one there.

Then Max the cat came walking in, his tail swishing proudly back and forth like a windshield wiper. He padded right by me, dropped his hindquarters, and sprang lazily onto the bed. He stretched, inspected the bedspread, then gave Alice and me a critical stare, as if reprimanding us for not warming the bed for him.

I closed the door, went over, and scratched Max under the chin. After a few moments he lay down and began purring, though, it seemed to me, rather reluctantly, as if not willing to seem readily appeased. I sat on the bed next to Max, scratched him behind the ears.

"Now then," I said. "Before we were so rudely interrupted."

Alice put up her hand. "Don't start. I'm not in the mood."

"I can see that."

"I mean for joking. This is serious. A woman has been killed. A young man is under suspicion. And the cop in charge doesn't seem to know what to do."

"I wouldn't worry about it."

Alice looked at me. "Why not? What are you saying? Is there something you're not telling me?"

"I just don't think you have to worry about the cop."

"Why not?"

I smiled. "Think about it. Here we are in a New England bed-and-breakfast—fine, call it an inn if you want to, that's not the point. Anyway, here we are in this bed-and-breakfast inn sort of place. Someone's been poisoned, the local cop's been brought in, and he's a bumbling sort of fellow. And he's ordered us not to leave, so we're all stuck here together, all the suspects under one roof—yes, I know, they're separate buildings here, I was speaking metaphorically. But you see what I'm getting at?"

"No, I don't," Alice said. "What are you talking about?"

I pointed to the Agatha Christie on the night table. "Well," I said, "we would appear to have all the elements of your basic, cozy crime novel."

"So?"

I shrugged. "Isn't it obvious?"

I scratched Max behind the ears, smiled at Alice.

"The cat will solve the crime."

EIGHTEEN

"WHAT'S THAT?"

"What?"

"That."

"Nothing."

"Alice. What's that paper in your hand?"

"Oh, that," Alice said. She brought it up from under the table rather reluctantly. "It's really not important."

"Uh-huh," I said.

I held out my hand. Alice passed the paper over. I unfolded it, read:

SUMMER GARDEN SOUP

1 *spring onion*
2 *cloves finely chopped garlic*
2 *tablespoons unsalted butter*
2 *Yukon Gold potatoes*
10 *spears asparagus*
2 *cups chopped spinach*
2 *cups chicken broth*
1 *cup water*
Reggiano Parmesan
Salt and pepper to taste
rinds of Parmesan (optional)

Snap off the tough ends of the asparagus and discard. Cut spears diagonally into 2 or 3 pieces. Sauté onion and garlic in 2 tablespoons of butter until translucent. Add 2 cups of chicken broth, 1 cup of water, and Parmesan rinds, if you wish.

Peel and slice the potatoes, add to the soup mixture, and simmer for 20 minutes. Then add the chopped fresh asparagus, simmer for 5 minutes. Be careful not to overcook. Add 2 cups of chopped spinach. Simmer 2 minutes. Remove Parmesan rinds. Salt and pepper to taste. Puree.

If served hot, drizzle with *extra-virgin olive oil* and grated Reggiano Parmesan.
If served cold, garnish with *plain yogurt* and *fresh chopped chives*.

Serves 2–4.

I looked up from the paper. "I don't believe this."
"Stanley."

"There's a murder investigation going on, and you're still buying bootleg recipes?"

"So what? One thing has nothing to do with the other."

"It's the principle of the thing."

"Now we're talking principles?"

"How about priorities?"

"What priorities? Life doesn't stop because there's a murder investigation."

"I just don't see how you could even think of a recipe."

"Did you taste that soup?"

"No."

"Case closed."

Alice and I were talking in low tones. As was everyone else in the dining room. In addition, eye avoidance was at a max. Granted, neither Florence, Jean, Joan, nor the McInnernys were there—in short, all the people we knew and might have acknowledged—still, of the people in the dining room, no one was looking at anyone else. That is, anyone at any other table. Those at the tables were, as I say, conversing in low tones.

Which was to be expected. It was eerie sitting in the dining room. Knowing a young woman had died there just the night before.

Ordering food was downright spooky.

When Lucy arrived to announce the special was blueberry pancakes, I had to stifle the urge to say, "With or without poison?" Alice and I ordered them, however, on Lucy's high recommendation.

She had just left with our orders when Louise swooped down. For a moment I thought she was going to bust us for the recipe. Naturally, that was the last thing on her mind.

Louise actually sat down at our table, leaned over, grabbed me by the arm, and said, "You have to help me."

It was so abrupt I could only blink. "I beg your pardon?"

"I hear you're a detective. My son is in trouble. Serious trouble. He needs your help."

"I'm not a lawyer."

"He doesn't need a lawyer. He needs a detective. Someone to get the facts."

"Why?"

"Why? That policeman thinks he had something to do with it."

"Why would he think that?"

Louise blinked. "I don't know. But he obviously does."

"What does your son say?"

"I don't know. He won't tell me."

"Uh-huh," I said. "So, you have no idea why he might be a suspect?"

"Well . . ."

"Well what?"

"What if he knew the girl?"

"What makes you think he did?"

Louise grimaced. "Please. One hears things. One wonders if they're true."

"And what does one hear?"

"You're not making this easy for me."

"I'm sorry. But I need to know what you want. If your son isn't talking to you, and you're asking me to help you based on what other people are saying, then I need to know who those other people are."

Louise hesitated a moment, then said, "Actually, Florence hinted there might be a connection."

"Uh-huh. And did she hint what that might be?"

"You should know."

"Oh?"

"She said you saw something."

"Did she say what?"

"Yes."

"Then you don't need to ask, do you?"

"Are you saying it's true?"

"Is that what you want—when you say you need my help—just to confirm whether the story is true?"

"Is it?"

"Ask him yourself. You expect me to rat a guy out to his mother?"

"It's for his own good."

"It always is. If it's a family affair, I'm keeping out."

Louise took a breath. Sighed. "Fine. Keep out," she said. "Don't tell me anything. Leave me in the dark. All of that's fine, if you'll just do one thing."

"What's that?"

"Talk to him. Talk to my boy. He won't talk to me, maybe he'll talk to you. He has to talk to someone."

"What about the cop?"

"What about him?"

"What did he tell the cop?"

"I don't know. Don't you understand? That's the whole point. He won't tell me."

"Then he's not going to tell me, either."

"He might."

"Why?"

"You're not his mother."

"True."

"Then there's the other thing."

"What's that?"

"What you saw. If what I hear is true, you're the one who saw it. So he'd have a hard time denying it to you."

The McInnernys arrived just then, boisterous, brash, and overbearing, just as if there hadn't been a crime. They descended on our table with their usual lack of tact.

"There you are," Johnny said. "Are you doing Mount Washington today? We are. It's crystal clear. You won't get a day like this two or three times a season. You'll see a hundred miles. You'll see five different states. You'll see Canada."

"Canada?"

"It's the day to go. You want to reserve a space?"

"Reserve?"

"In the van. We're going at ten o'clock. Want us to sign you up?"

"I don't think so," I said. "I can't guarantee we'll make it. Can we, Alice?"

"I'm not sure what we're doing," Alice said. "Maybe we'll see you up there."

"That would be nice," Mrs. McInnerny said. It occurred to me her name was Carla or Clara, though I couldn't recall which.

At any rate, that completed the conversation and left the McInnernys with nothing more to say to us. They stood there, smiling awkwardly to fill the silence, until Louise finally realized they were waiting on her, and got up to show them to their seats.

Florence came in while Louise was still seating the McInnernys. She hesitated a moment, seemed ready to select another table, but Alice waved her over. She came, I thought, rather reluctantly. I wondered if she felt guilty for having finked on me to Louise.

"Good morning," I said. "If you can say that under these circumstances."

"Yeah," Florence said. "What a night."

"How's Prince doing?" Alice asked.

"I just walked him. He seems none the worse for wear. Of course, he has no idea what's going on."

"I bet he knows something's going on," Alice said. "Animals pick up a lot."

"Sure," I said. "From your manner. He can tell from your manner you're acting different."

"I'm not acting different."

"I'm not saying you're acting different. But this had to affect you. It's affected all of us. And the dog can sense that. See what I mean?"

Florence rubbed her head. "What a nightmare."

"Yes," I said. "But it doesn't concern us. We're just observers, watching it all go by."

As if on cue, Lars came in. He stopped in the doorway and stood there, a blank look on his face.

It was hard not to feel sorry for him in that moment. He was practically a parody of a man in despair. He was unshaven, and his hair was uncombed. His shirt was buttoned wrong. His shoe-lace was untied.

He looked oblivious to his surroundings. There was no chance of him finding a seat. Indeed, it was obviously a miracle he'd managed to find the dining room at all.

Louise, who had finished with the McInnernys, went over and took him by the arm. As she guided him into the dining room, I saw her hesitate as she approached the booth, then guide him to a table on the opposite side of the room.

It was not until he was seated that I was aware of what had happened.

It was quiet. There was a dead silence in the room. All talk had stopped. Even the McInnernys held their tongues. Everyone had stopped talking, and all eyes were on Lars. If he was aware of it, it must have been living hell.

Louise was aware of it. She turned away from his table, looked around. Seemed embarrassed by the shared spotlight. She hurried back to us.

Louise must have been really upset, because she didn't ever acknowledge Florence, just bent down, grabbed my arm, and said, "Please. He's in his room out back. He won't come out. He won't talk to me. You have to help me, and—Oh!"

I looked around to see Chief Pinehurst bearing down on us. That did not bode well. Since he had chosen our table over Lars' he was undoubtedly about to order Louise to produce Randy.

He didn't.

He stopped at our table, drew himself up formally, and announced, "Alice Hastings?"

NINETEEN

RANDY WAS LYING curled up in bed, the covers pulled up under his chin. His blanket was old and worn, a security blanket, perhaps, from when he was a boy.

"Hi," I said. "May I come in?"

Randy's room was in back of the kitchen with its own outside entrance. It was a small room, and gave the impression of having once been a shed. Indeed, the door had a latch rather than a knob. I had knocked, got no answer, and stuck my head in.

I got no answer again. Not even an acknowledgement of my presence.

I was in no mood for such behavior. I stepped in, closed the door behind me. "All right, look," I said. "You can talk to me or not. That's entirely up to you. But you would do well to listen.

"The police suspect you of a crime. I don't know what you've told them, and I don't really care. I doubt if they care, either. They've got their information anyway, so they don't need much from you.

"You were having an affair with the victim. You served her the drink that killed her. The cops know that. Doubtless they've asked you about it.

"If you've admitted the affair, it's bad. It makes you suspect number one.

"If you've denied it, it's worse. Why? Because the cops know about it anyway, and they know that you're lying.

"They know because they have a witness. I'm the witness. I saw you kissing her down by the pond. Now you can deny that if you like, but in the cops' eyes that establishes only one thing—it means you're a liar. And when a chief suspect lies in a murder investigation, it is not good. Not when it's a transparent lie that wouldn't fool anyone. That is not the way to go. That is not the prescribed method for beating a murder rap."

Randy rolled over, faced the wall. "Get out," he said.

Aha. The clever detective had elicited a response. It occurred to me I'd nearly broken him. Could a confession be far behind?

"Your mother's worried about you, Randy, because you won't talk to her. I can understand that. It must be hard discussing your affairs with your mother. But that's no reason to clam up on everyone. Particularly the police."

Randy lay still, said nothing.

"Okay, if you don't want to talk, you don't want to talk. But I have to report back to your mother. So what am I gonna tell her? I guess I'm gonna tell her that there's nothing I can do. Because you're not talking, period.

"Well, that's fine. If that's the way you wanna play it, that's the way to go. But if you're gonna do it, do it right. Get a lawyer. Act on his advice. Let *him* be the one telling you not to talk. That takes the onus off of you. The cops can't regard your silence as an admission of guilt. So talk to a lawyer now. You're gonna need one anyway, to make statements for you at the time of your arrest. So get a good attorney, and let him take charge."

Again Randy said nothing.

"You ever have her here? In this room—in this bed, I mean? The cops are gonna go over it, and when they do, they're gonna use a fine-tooth comb. A single hair, that's all it will take. You wouldn't believe the things they can do nowadays with DNA.

"On the other hand, I'm sure they'll be watching to see if you try to wash the sheets. So dashing out to the laundry would probably not be the swiftest move."

Randy offered no reaction whatsoever, continued to ignore me.

"On second thought, you probably didn't bring her here. Not a particularly romantic setting. No, I would imagine you had more of a taste for the great outdoors. So examining the sheets would be a waste of time. The police would do better looking for grass stains on your clothes."

"Shut up."

"See," I said, shaking my head, "you're no good at this. The things that aren't true don't bother you, but the things that are touch a nerve. You might as well have a sign on your forehead that flashes CORRECT every time I get something right."

Randy rolled over, glared at me. "Why don't you get out of here. Go on. Get out."

"I'll tell you why, Randy. That cop came back to talk to my wife. He's talking to her right now. And you know what they're talking about? Me. They're talking about me. And do you know why? Because I'm the one who told them about you. So he's checking on my story. He wants to find out if it's true. And guess what's gonna happen if it is? Go on. Take a guess."

Whether Randy would have risen to the bait I was not to know, for at that moment the door swung open, and his father, Louise's husband, the cook, whose name for the life of me I couldn't remember, stuck his head in and said, "Randy. Come on. Get up. I need help. The dishes are stacking up. There's coffee to be served. Your mother can't do everything. You've gotta help. I don't have time to argue. The pancakes are on. Just get up."

And with that he was gone again.

"You see how it is?" I said. "If you just lie here feeling sorry for yourself, your problems aren't going to go away. In fact, they're just gonna increase, because everybody's gonna wanna know why you're doing it. You may not be guilty, but you sure look guilty. And it's not gonna take much more to convince that cop. Yes, he's slow, but he's putting it together piece by piece. And what you're doing only helps him. Why don't you give yourself a break?"

The door swung open again.

I turned to look, but there was no one there. And the door had not opened very wide.

Before I had time to think, there was a flash of orange, and Max sprang up on the bed. He climbed on Randy's chest, treaded down a spot, curled up, and began purring.

Randy let him, which said something for the boy. Most men as hassled as he was would have brushed the cat aside. Randy let him lay, actually reached up, stroked his fur.

It was a bizarre scene, the prime murder suspect lying there, refusing to talk, petting a cat.

I admit to being somewhat disconcerted, losing my train of thought. What had I just been talking about?

I realized whatever it was, it was the same old song. Randy was doing himself no favor by refusing to talk. So now I had to snap him out of it.

"Come on, Randy," I said. "You are this close to going to jail. When my wife gets done talking, you are going to be under arrest. And I hate that. I don't want your arrest on her head, or on mine. But there's no help for it if you refuse to explain. So why don't you tell me what you know? You're gonna have to tell your story to the cops. A little rehearsal might help. Whaddya say?"

Once again, I was not to know, for at that moment the door swung open, and Chief Pinehurst walked in.

I felt bad. I'd done everything I could to warn Randy, but it hadn't worked. I'd failed him, failed his mother. With him not talking, this was the inevitable result.

"All right, let's go," Pinehurst said.

Randy said nothing, just lay there petting the cat. He looked as if he were about to cry.

"Come on, Randy," I said. "It's better not to resist."

"I'm glad to hear you say that," Pinehurst said. "But I don't want him." He put his hand on my shoulder. "All right, Mr. Hastings. Let's go."

TWENTY

"I DON'T UNDERSTAND."

"Of course you don't. It's not your case. You don't have to understand."

"No. I don't understand why you want to question me."

"You don't?"

"No, I don't. I already told you everything I know."

"Well, that's a trifle broad. I think you'll find that isn't quite the case. Particularly after what your wife said."

"My wife?"

"Yes, of course."

Pinehurst and I were in the TV room: I guess he'd gotten sick of the booth. Either that or Louise had refused to let him have it during breakfast. At any rate, Pinehurst was sitting in an over-stuffed chair, and I was sitting on the couch, right where I'd found the little girl watching TV my first day there. I wondered vaguely if there was a Red Sox game today. If so, I wondered if I'd be free to watch it.

"I beg your pardon," I said, "but what could my wife have possibly said that made you suspect me?"

"Now, now," Pinehurst said. "Did I say I suspected you? I don't recall ever saying that."

"Actions speak louder than words," I said. And grimaced. Good god, the man had me talking in clichés.

"I'm sorry if I gave you that impression. Well now, what do you say we kick this around some, and I'll let you go. Your wife indicated a desire to see Mount Washington. I'd hate to hold you up."

"What was it you wanted to kick around?"

"Getting back to the scene of the crime. I find myself interested in your movements during dinner."

"We went over that."

"Yes, we did. But it certainly is interesting. Sifting through the varying accounts. It's yours now I'd like to pin down. How many times did you get up from your table during the meal?"

"Once."

"Are you sure?"

"Absolutely."

"And that's the time you went to the bathroom?"

"That's right."

"And when was that?"

"If I recall correctly, it was after I'd placed my order and before my food arrived."

"If you recall correctly?"

"When we discussed it last night it was fresh in my mind. If I should forget some trivial detail this morning, I hope you will not pounce on it as if you'd cracked the case."

"That was not my intention," Pinehurst said. "These questions are preliminary. Perhaps if we could speed things along."

Pinehurst speeding things along? The word *oxymoron* hung unspoken in the air.

"Fine," I said. "What do you want to know?"

"To the best of your recollection, you left the dining room after you placed your order and returned before your food arrived?"

"That's right."

"And that is the only time you got up from your table until after the body was discovered?"

"That's right."

"When you first arrived at your table, were Christine Cobb and her boyfriend already there?"

"No, they were not."

"How are you so sure?"

"Because I saw them come in."

"You are certain of that?"

"Yes, I am."

"Why did you note their arrival?"

"I told you that. Because I had the conversation with her by the waterfall that I hadn't had a chance to discuss with my wife. So I had reason to note her entrance."

"Uh-huh. That would seem to be convincing. Now, as to the rest of dinner. I believe you said that Florence got up to walk her dog?"

"That's right."

"And how long was she gone from the table?"

"I don't know. Five minutes, maybe. She just went to walk the dog."

"Uh-huh. Now, your wife—when did she leave the table?"

"She didn't leave the table."

"She didn't?"

"No."

"You mean she didn't leave the table while you were there?"

"She didn't leave the table at all. She came in with me, sat there the whole time."

"But you went to the bathroom."

"So?"

"So, how do you know what your wife did while you were out of the room?"

I blinked. "I beg your pardon?"

"You certainly can't vouch for your wife's whereabouts while you weren't there."

"Vouch for her whereabouts? What are you talking about?"

Pinehurst frowned, shook his head. "See, that's the problem with people's recollections. Everybody remembers something slightly different. Your wife remembers that you got up. And you remember that Florence got up. And Florence remembers your wife got up."

"What?"

"Which you don't remember. So, can I assume that this was something that happened while you had left the room?"

"What do you mean, my wife got up?"

"Your wife got up from the table. Moved around the dining room. According to the woman who was sitting with you. And, according to your wife, by the way. She remembers getting up, going over and talking to two women at another table. The women you'd been hiking with that afternoon. Which is certainly interesting when you consider where the tables are."

"What do you mean?"

"Do you recall where you were sitting? In relation to the room? To get to the other table you have to pass right by the booth. If your wife actually conferred with these women, she would have walked right by. Which she obviously did, since both of them confirm the conversation."

I put up my hands. "Wait a minute, wait a minute. What has this got to do with anything?"

"We're talking opportunity here. Opportunity and motive. You had the opportunity because you left your table. The woman with the dog had the opportunity because she left the table. And your wife had the opportunity because she left the table."

"Why are you talking about my wife?"

"I'm talking about everybody. She's just one of the people I'm talking about. No reason to get upset." Pinehurst shrugged. "On the other hand, when we start comparing motives, you must admit your wife had more than most."

I stared at him. "What?"

"If we are to assume that you and the girl were involved. That you were making the story about her and the busboy up. Now, if you were the one who was involved, which seems likely when you start adding up all your personal connections—swimming with her, meeting her by the pond and the waterfall—well, if you're the one with the connection, it doesn't necessarily give you that good a motive.

"But your wife. Well, your wife might want to kill that woman very much."

"Are you accusing my wife—"

Pinehurst put up his hands. "Please. No one is accusing anyone. We're examining possibilities. Jealousy is certainly a motive. A woman scorned."

I took a breath. "I am going to try to be calm and discuss this rationally. Which is a little difficult under the circumstances. Because I hate to dignify this with a response. But I would like to point something out. If my wife did indeed leave the table to go over to talk to Jean and Joan while I was in the bathroom, well that was long before Lars left the room. So, if my wife passed by their table, they were both there. And Lars would certainly remember if she had stopped to talk."

"I'm sure he would. On the other hand, we have the same problem that I pointed out when it came to you. Lars is no dope. He may have a convenient memory when it comes to such things."

"What do you mean, *may have?*"

Pinehurst grimaced. "Ah, well, you got me there. That's one of the problems with murder investigations. People who are the most likely suspects tend to take offense." When I opened my mouth, he said, "Not that I am suggesting that you are taking offense. No, no. I was referring to Lars."

"What about him?"

"As I say, he's taken offense. At least to the point where he's withdrawn his cooperation."

"You mean he's not talking?"

"That's right."

I blinked. "Your chief suspect isn't talking, and yet you're still questioning all of us?"

Pinehurst shrugged. "This is America. A man is innocent until proven guilty. He also has the right to remain silent. Lars Heinrick is exercising that right."

"Does he have a lawyer?"

"Not yet. Though I assure you he has been made aware he has that option. But for the moment he's merely declining to talk."

"I see."

"I'm sure you do. And I'm sure you understand the implications. With Mr. Heinrick not talking, I've been unable to corroborate the claims of the various witnesses. For instance, your claim that you did not stop by his booth. Or anyone else's claim for that matter. Which includes both your wife and the woman with the dog."

I rubbed my head, exhaled. "Fine. For the moment, you have no conclusive proof. I'll grant you that. Will you grant me the concept of reasonable doubt? Not in a legal, courtroom sense, but just in terms of *common* sense. Won't you concede that it is *unlikely* that someone stopped by the booth and put poison in the glass while Lars was still there?"

"Of course," Pinehurst said. "I'm a perfectly reasonable man.

For instance, I would be the first to admit that between your wife and the other woman at your table—Florence, the woman with the dog—your wife had less opportunity. Because when Florence went to walk the dog, Lars, by most accounts, had already left the dining room. Whereas, when your wife went by the booth, Lars was presumably still there."

I exhaled. "Thank you for that assessment."

"That is correct, is it not?" Pinehurst said. "That when the woman went to walk the dog, Lars Heinrick had already left the booth?"

"To the best of my recollection, that's true."

"And it's also true that Lars Heinrick and Christine Cobb arrived in the dining room together, prior to the time you went to the bathroom, so that at the time your wife went by their booth, Lars was presumably there?"

"Absolutely," I said. "Of course, I have no knowledge of what happened when I was out of the room, but if Alice got up then, it was at a time when Lars Heinrick was there. Because I know for a fact he was there when I left the room."

"I'm glad to hear it," Pinehurst said. "And while I'm not ready to concede the point, I have to admit it seems entirely likely. In which case your wife's opportunity is certainly lessened. Which should undoubtedly knock her down a few notches on my list of suspects. Unfortunately, her motive is rather strong."

I opened my mouth, closed it again. Talking to Pinehurst was immensely frustrating. I began to sympathize with Lars Heinrick for declining to do so.

"And if your wife got up at that time, to visit the women at the other table, she would have walked right by the booth. Isn't that right?"

"I suppose."

"And she did do that. By her own statement. So, I put it to you. If your wife saw the busboy serving them drinks, and was curious, and wanted to take a closer look, is it possible she might have chosen that moment to talk to the two women at the other table, just so she'd have a chance to go by the booth?"

I frowned. While that seemed entirely possible, it also had nothing to do with the investigation. "Maybe so," I said. "In which case when she passed by the booth, not only was Lars there, but the busboy would have been there also."

"On the way *to* the women's table, perhaps. But not on the way back. The busboy would have been gone. And it's entirely possible Lars was gone also."

"No, it isn't. I saw him in the booth. On my way back in."

"So you say. But, as I've pointed out, I only have your word for that. And if you were lying to protect your wife . . ."

"Oh, is that what we've come to? Now I'm lying to protect my wife?"

"I said *if*. The hypothetical. I'm trying to prove things here. A fact is not a fact, if it can be contradicted by a hypothetical. Anyway, your wife did not mention the fact that she'd been to the other table to talk to the two women?"

"No. Why should she?"

"No reason. But the fact is, she didn't. She didn't mention it to you, and she didn't mention it to me."

"I beg your pardon?"

"When I first questioned her. Last night. We talked about many things, but that wasn't one of them. She completely neglected to mention the fact that she got up."

"Did you ask her?"

"I asked her if she left the room. She told me she had not."

"And she hadn't. Her answer was absolutely correct."

"Yes, as far as it went. But that would have been an excellent opportunity for her to tell me she got up. Which she neglected to do. It was not until I jogged her memory this morning that she mentioned it at all."

I put up my hand. "Whoa. Hold on, here, Chief. Just hold on.

There's a huge, *huge,* difference between forgetting to mention something, and lying to the police. Which is the inference you seem to be drawing here. My wife did not lie to you. She did not mislead you. She did not attempt to trick you. If she didn't mention the fact that she talked to Jean and Joan, it is only because you didn't ask her. And because it was an irrelevant, trivial detail that totally slipped her mind."

"I never said it wasn't," Pinehurst said. "As I say, I am merely assembling facts. The fact is your wife didn't mention it. And might not have, if the other woman hadn't remembered it when I questioned her. At any rate, your wife did get up. Did leave the table. Did pass by their booth. Did refrain from mentioning this, either to you or to me the first time I questioned her. And seemed inordinately interested in what was going on in the booth when you returned from the bathroom.

"Now, can you point out any inconsistency in any of those statements?"

I blinked.

Groaned.

Rubbed my head.

TWENTY-ONE

"THIS ISN'T SO bad," Alice said.

I'm glad she thought so. We'd just careened around a hairpin turn. I don't know how it looked from Alice's side, but from where I sat, the outer wheels couldn't possibly have been on the road.

We were on our way up Mount Washington in the van. The Auto Road, as the narrow, winding road up the mountain was called, was open to private cars, but their use was discouraged by a vehicle-use fee of sixteen bucks per car and driver, plus six bucks per passenger. Since we'd come with Jean and Joan, it would have cost us thirty-four dollars just to drive up the road.

Instead, we were paying twenty-two bucks a head to take the van. Which might not seem very bright. But when we checked in at the Glen House visitors center at the base of the mountain, we were hit with a barrage of propaganda stressing the danger of the road and warning against private cars. I didn't think we needed any more tension just then—I voted for the van.

So, here we were, being driven up the mountain by a pimply faced young man, who looked as if he were probably driving on his learner's permit. Every time he turned a corner, I held my breath.

"I could have driven this," Alice said.

"I'm sure you could," I told her. And secretly wished she had, as our van lurched around another hairpin turn. I closed my eyes, wondered how much longer it could last.

The McInnernys weren't with us, by the way. Though the van was full, they were not among the present. This was, to the best I could determine, the sole benefit of Chief Pinehurst's lengthy questioning—by the time he was finished with us, the McInnernys were long gone.

Florence wasn't with us either. She begged off, saying Prince wouldn't have been allowed in the van. We were trying to talk her into leaving him behind, when the sad-sack cop showed up to say Chief Pinehurst wanted to talk to her again too. That had tipped the scale, and she told us to just go on ahead.

A noble sentiment.

On the other hand, as I viewed the narrow, curvy incline we were about to ascend, it occurred to me Chief Pinehurst might well have saved her life.

The young man who was piloting our van with such wild abandon accentuated the fact by keeping up a running commentary on the road, the conditions, the weather, the history, and what we could expect to see. Occasionally, he would spice this up by pointing out a place where people had been killed driving off the road. Somehow, this was more than I needed to know.

And the most disconcerting thing about what he was saying was the fact that his voice didn't appear to have changed.

"There's the timberline," he announced cheerily, pointing out the driver's side window to the left, while the van appeared about to launch itself off an embankment to the right. "I hope you dressed warm. It's cold on top."

That we knew. The summit temperature was almost as well publicized as the danger of the Auto Road. Alice had a sweater and I had a windbreaker. We were ready for anything.

"And to your right, down in the valley, that puff of smoke is the Cog Railway. We're gonna beat it up there, so you'll be able to watch it arrive."

"How long is the track?" Alice asked.

I had to stifle an impulse to elbow her to be quiet. No need to distract the man. Just let him drive.

"Three miles from the base station at Marshfield up to the summit. The train does it in about an hour and ten minutes."

"How come it's shorter than the road?"

"For one thing, it's more of a straight line. The road winds around."

It certainly did. And at each sickening bend, the driver was careful to note every point of interest. When we reached the summit, I practically leaped from the van in relief.

But what a view.

The McInnernys were right. There was not a cloud in the sky. The air was crystal clear.

You could see forever.

We poured out of the van, walked to the edge. Gawked like children.

It was wonderful. Below us, you could see the road on which we'd come, making its way down the mountain. At the very base was the highway, and across from it the parking lot where we'd left our car, and the Glen House visitors center where we'd signed up for the van.

Beyond it were mountains. And more mountains. And more mountains. And on and on, into the distance.

"Which way is which?" I said.

"What?" Alice said.

"I mean which way is north?"

Alice and Jean and Joan had a good deal of fun about that. I dug the binoculars out of the backpack, and we passed them around. And after determining which direction actually was north, I'd have been willing to bet it really *was* Canada we were seeing.

We were all having a perfectly good time until the McInnernys walked up.

"There you are," Johnny said. "Better late than never. Did I tell you, or what? Is this clear, or is this clear?"

"It's clear," I said.

"You'd better believe it's clear," Johnny said. He pointed. "You know, that's Canada up there. That last range of mountains is Canada."

Exactly what I thought. Though, somehow all the joy went out of it when he said so.

"You see," I said. "I told you that was Canada."

"That's right," Johnny said. "And over there's Vermont. And New York State as well. And over there's Connecticut and Massachusetts."

"Well, now you can't see Connecticut," Mrs. McInnerny said.

"You can today," Johnny said. "It's probably the only day of the year you can."

"Well, now how would you know?" his wife said. "It's not like they had borders on the states. Like here's Massachusetts, here's Connecticut. How would you know, Johnny McInnerny, which was which?"

"Didn't you hear what our driver said?"

"I heard what he said. And I also heard him say to get back in the van."

"They're not gonna leave without us."

"No, they're just gonna get mad. You want all the other passengers to get mad?"

"Oh, for goodness' sakes," Johnny said, but they were already walking back toward the parking lot.

"Check out the Summit Building," Johnny called over his shoulder. "Nifty souvenirs."

The Summit Building was a combination restaurant/souvenir shop, which also housed a publicly funded, nonprofit observatory, not to mention rest rooms and telephones. Jean and Joan went to check it out.

I forestalled Alice.

"Let's take a stroll around the summit first," I said. Alice looked at me quizzically. We had not been alone together since our talks with Pinehurst. "I think we'd better compare notes."

"Oh?"

"Yeah. Chief Pinehurst seems to have a new theory of the case."

"What's that?"

"You wouldn't believe."

I told Alice what Pinehurst had told me. She listened with an ironic deadpan.

"That's his theory of the case?" she said. "That I killed her in a fit of jealous rage?"

"Or coolly and deliberately to eliminate a rival."

"That's hardly any better."

"Actually, it's worse. It shows premeditation. The heat-of-passion defense doesn't work."

"But he's not serious."

"He sounds serious."

"Stanley, don't be dumb. The man's compulsive; he questions everything. That doesn't mean he believes it."

"Yes, but he does make good points."

"Like what?"

"Like you withheld it during your first interrogation."

"Withheld it? Talking to Jean and Joan? Would you mind telling me why I should have remembered that?"

"Didn't he ask you?"

"If I talked to Jean and Joan? He most certainly did not. He asked me if I left the room. I didn't leave the room. End of story."

"You didn't remember you got up?"

"Stanley, it wasn't important I got up. When he asked me if I got up, I told him I got up. It wasn't important until he asked me."

"Uh-huh. And the reason you went over to talk to Jean and Joan?"

"They're friends."

"Yes, but at that particular moment—why did you want to talk to them then?"

"Why are you asking me this?"

"Because Pinehurst did. Trying to make something of it."

"Well, that's stupid."

"But the man doesn't know you, so he's trying to make a case. His point is, the way he sees it, the reason you went over to talk to Jean and Joan was because of the girl."

"Oh, come on."

"No, it's true. Here's how he figures: You saw Randy serving them drinks. From where our table was, you couldn't see into the booth. You wanted to see into the booth. So you went over to talk to Jean and Joan so you'd pass by the booth and would be able to look in."

Alice frowned. "That's hardly fair."

"Fair? Alice, it's not a question of what's fair, it's a question of what's true."

"Yes, of course. But there's degrees of everything. I mean, how could I walk past that booth without seeing in?"

"What did you see?"

"Nothing. Randy was serving them drinks. Neither one of them was paying any particular attention to him."

"Which was interesting in itself, right? If she's involved with him and is elaborately pretending not to notice?"

168

"Uh-huh," Alice said. "Anyway, that's all it was. No big deal."

"What about on your way back?"

"What about it?"

"What did you see then?"

"Nothing. Randy was gone. The two of them were just sitting there together."

"Sipping their drinks?"

"Not when I went by."

"So what were they doing?"

"I think they were talking. But I couldn't really see. I couldn't hear, either. I told all this to the cop."

"The second time around."

"What's that supposed to mean?"

"It's given him a reason to suspect you."

"Oh, for goodness' sakes. He doesn't really suspect me. It's just the way he is."

"I know. But the problem is, you give him ammunition. He's able to say, Why didn't she tell me this the first time? And he's able to say, She got up to talk to the women because of what was going on in the booth. And when I ask you, it *was* because of what's going on in the booth. You wanted to talk to them about that, and you wanted to get a better look."

"Is that a crime?"

"Not at all. But this cop has an overactive imagination, and—"

"You want to discuss this with Jean and Joan?"

"No."

"Well, here they are."

"The train's coming," the plumper of the two said.

The thinner one pointed. "Around the other side."

We walked over to where we could see the train track. A puff of smoke was coming from the valley below. I took out my binoculars, located the train. It was a short little affair, with an engine and open passenger car. The car was full. I wondered if that was normal, or due to the exceptionally clear day.

I passed the binoculars around, but soon there was no need. The train came chuffing up the track, slow and steady, The Little Engine That Could. It clanked to a stop, and the passengers got out.

I scanned the faces getting off the train, looking for people I knew. Not expecting to find any, of course.

To my surprise I did. The family with the little girl, of TV-watching fame. She and her parents got off the train and went into the Summit House.

I continued to watch, though the chance of seeing someone else I knew seemed positively nil.

I didn't, but Alice did.

She nudged me in the ribs, said, "Look at that."

I looked at the man getting off the train, a large man in a parka and fur hat. The clothes were somewhat excessive—it wasn't *that* cold. Still, it hardly seemed worthy of notice.

"So?" I said.

"So?" Alice said. "You know who that is?"

"No."

"Take off the hat."

"Huh?"

"Imagine him without a hat."

I stared at him.

Blinked.

My eyes widened.

It was the bald, overweight hiker from Champney Falls.

TWENTY-TWO

I FOUND A pay phone in the Summit House, called the Blue Frog Ponds.

"Louise, it's Stanley Hastings. I need to talk to Chief Pinehurst."

"Oh, he left."

"Left?"

"Yeah. About a half hour ago. I saw him getting into his car."

"Where'd he go?"

"I have no idea. He didn't say anything, he just took off."

"I need to reach him. It's important."

"Well, he probably went back to the police station. You want the number?"

"Please."

Louise gave me the number. I didn't have a pencil to write it down, but I repeated it to Alice, who dialed it for me once I got off the phone with Louise.

I got a busy signal.

A busy signal?

No way.

The police station only has one line?

I hung up the phone.

"What's the matter?" Alice said.

"Busy," I said.

We gawked at each other. To New Yorkers, the concept of a police line being busy did not compute. Being put on hold would have been more in our realm of experience.

I retrieved the quarter from the coin return, dropped it in again.

"Still remember it?" I said.

Alice gave me a look and punched in the number.

Still busy.

"Maybe Louise gave it to me wrong."

"You wanna call information?"

"You call information. I'm gonna check on the train. See if I can get a seat."

I went out, inquired about the Cog Railway.

No luck. The return trip was sold out.

"When does it leave?" I asked.

"Forty-five minutes."

"And it takes an hour and ten minutes to go down?"

"More or less."

"Thanks."

I went back inside to find Alice. On the way I kept an eye out for our friend.

I spotted him sitting on a rock, one of a pile of rocks off to one side of the Summit House where people liked to climb. He was talking to a young man with long, blond hair, wearing jeans, work boots, and an army jacket. What the two of them had in common, I couldn't imagine.

But I sure meant to find out.

I went back inside to Alice. She'd been joined by Jean and Joan.

"Still busy," Alice said.

I raised my eyebrows.

"Oh, I told them," Alice said. "How could I not tell them?"

"We'll be discreet," Jean/Joan, the plumper one said.

"It's exciting, isn't it?" said the other.

I'm sure my smile was forced. The last thing I needed was people who found the whole thing exciting.

"Any luck?" Alice said.

"No. I can't get on the train. But it's all right. In fact, it's probably better."

"Why?"

"It doesn't leave for forty-five minutes, and it takes over an hour to get down. Our van takes half the time, and leaves before. So I can get the car, drive around, and be there when the train arrives."

"Terrific," Jean/Joan said. The thin one. "You mean we're gonna follow him?"

"I'm going to follow him. You can get a cab back."

"Don't be silly," Alice said. "You're not going to leave us."

"Well, you can't come along."

"Why not?"

"He'll spot us."

"How will he spot us? We'll be in the car."

"Exactly. He'll see the car following him."

"Stanley. You're not making sense. The car will be following him in any case. What difference does it make if we're in it?"

"If he see four people following him—"

"He will think we're out for a drive. Stanley, use your head. What is the man going to find more suspicious, a lone man tailing him in a car, or a man and three women out for a drive?"

As usual, there was no arguing with Alice. Much as I would have liked to. Not that I would have minded having her along, but I certainly could have dispensed with the presence of Jean and

Joan, who had never been involved in anything of the sort before, and found it fun, which was almost more than I could bear.

In the end I gave in with as good grace as possible, while stressing the need for being discreet and not discussing this in the van on the way down.

They didn't, but I did. Halfway down the mountain it occurred to me I had no idea where the base of the Cog Railway was. I was torn between not wanting to waste the time inquiring at the Glen House visitors center, and not wanting to distract our driver, who treated the journey down as if it were a roller-coaster ride, and seemed to get a kick out of freewheeling around the hairpin turns. I waited for a fairly straight and level stretch to ask directions.

"The Cog Railway," he said. "You're just comin' down, and you wanna go up again?"

"We just thought we'd like to take a look."

"It looks the same at the bottom as it does at the top. It's not like they change the train on you halfway down. You seen one train, you seen 'em all."

"Uh-huh. Well, could you tell us how to get there?"

"You meetin' someone on the train?"

"No. We'd just like to take a look."

"Well, if you wanna take a look, it's a free country, you gotta right to take a—Boy, that curve came up on us fast!"

Somehow we got to the parking lot with directions and without being killed, a long-shot parlay under the circumstances.

As soon as we got in our car, Alice was quick to find fault.

"So," she said. "You make us all promise to be discreet, and then you blow it yourself."

"I didn't blow it."

"Oh, no? Whaddya wanna bet that young man's in there calling the police right now?"

"In that case," I said. "They'll be on the lookout for a man and three women, and I'd better leave you behind."

"Here?" Alice looked at Jean and Joan, rolled her eyes. "Stanley, the driver is here. If you drive off and leave us, he'll wonder why. He might even ask. What would you suggest that we tell him then? The Cog Railway didn't really interest us, but you happen to be nuts for trains?"

"No, but—"

"Come on. Let's get out of here before they arrest us on the spot." Alice smiled. "Besides, you'd never find it alone."

While that wasn't exactly true, I did almost make one wrong turn before Alice pointed it out. Jean and Joan found that terribly amusing.

We got to the base of the Cog Railway, parked our car in the parking lot, and did not buy tickets. And then stood around and tried to blend in with the other people waiting for the Cog Railway, all of whom *had* bought tickets.

"Let's pretend ours are in my purse," Alice said. "What do you think, girls? Wouldn't that be a clever subterfuge, pretending the tickets are in my purse."

"I don't think that's fair," the plumper Jean/Joan said. "There's no reason to emasculate your husband. Let's let him pretend he has them in his jacket pocket."

And all three giggled.

The humor continued at about that level for the next forty-five minutes, until the train finally hoved into view. It was packed. As it came chuffing toward the station, Alice said, "Better get the car."

I blinked. Alice was right. The parking lot was nearly full. The minute passengers got off, there was going to be a monster traffic jam.

"Get the car, pull up to the front gate," Alice said.

She turned, headed for the platform the train was approaching. Jean and Joan tagged along, leaving me behind.

Great. Suddenly, they're the detectives, and I'm the chauffeur. I went and got the car, drove around the parking lot.

It was a good thing I did, because it took a while to get to the gate, even with the only traffic being cars circling looking for parking spaces. Once the train let out, it would be chaos. But I'd already be at the gate.

Or so I thought. It turned out other people had the same idea. Half a dozen cars were lined up at the exit with their motors idling. I had to either drive on out or get in line. If I drove out and waited on the highway, I'd be conspicuous on the one hand, and the women might not find me on the other. I got in line.

Or at least tried to. The end of the line turned out to coincide with an intersection of one of the rows of the parking lot. The minute I got in position, a car honked for me to let it through. I backed up, let the car go by. Wondered if I was close enough to the gate to do any good.

There was nothing I could do about it. I threw the car into park, turned, and looked out the back window for the train, which was still a good ways away. I sighed, settled back, tried to relax.

It was hard to do. Here I was, following my first solid lead of the investigation. One I was most eager to have pan out. Most eager.

It occurred to me, I was unduly anxious about what was going on. I mean, surely following this guy was not going to be that hard. Even with the women along. Even though I greatly would have preferred to be alone. If Alice hadn't insisted.

Alice. That was what was bothering me. Yes, it was rubbish what Chief Pinehurst suggested. But still. To have your wife a suspect in a murder case. And to have the facts laid out so carefully and logically in front of you.

All right, fine, so I'm getting to the age where a man's head is naturally turned by a younger woman. And his wife would certainly resent this and wish the woman ill. And Christine Cobb did turn up everywhere I went, and even asked me to share a secret with her. A secret I hadn't managed to tell Alice.

And Alice did get up from her table and pass by their booth. For an admittedly trumped-up reason. While I was out of the room.

I shook my head, smiled. On my way here it had occurred to me our real-life mystery involved a train, the Cog Railway, just like the Agatha Christie mystery I was reading, *The 4:50 from Paddington.* But what I was feeling right now came from another Agatha Christie novel, *Curtain,* the last case of Hercule Poirot, in which his trusted friend and my namesake, Hastings, comes to suspect a family member of having committed the crime.

No, I did not suspect Alice. It just made me very uncomfortable to think that someone else did.

I was roused from my musing by a car driving out. I glanced in the rearview mirror. Sure enough, the train had reached the platform, and people were streaming off.

So where was the man? I couldn't see him. Had he already left the train?

While I strained my eyes, three doors of the car opened simultaneously, and the women piled in.

"There's a blue Ford coming up from your left, be ready to pull out," Alice said. "Just be sure you have room to go."

"I have room," I said.

"He's gonna cut you off!" Jean/Joan screamed from the back—I couldn't see which one.

A Jeep wagon had just pulled in front of me from the right. Another car was inching along behind it.

"They're cutting you off," Alice said. "Don't let them cut you off."

"Coming up on the left," Jean/Joan said. "It's him, it's his car. Coming up on the left."

"Don't let 'em cut you off," the other Jean/Joan said.

"You're getting boxed in," Alice said. "Those cars are not gonna move."

"Pull out," Jean/Joan said. "Here he comes."

"He's passing us."

"He's going by."

"He's getting away."

The top of my head was coming off. I had the feeling if I attempted to drive in any direction, I was going to smash into the side of a car.

I took a breath, gritted my teeth, spun the wheel. Cut off a mother with two young boys and a kid in a car seat. She hit the horn and the brakes and gave me the evil eye.

I swerved into the outer lane, headed for the gate. Without the faintest idea of where our quarry was.

"Where is he?" I said.

For a second, no one knew.

Then Alice pointed. "He's behind you."

A glance in the rearview mirror told me Jean and Joan were pointing too.

"Could we all not point at the man we're trying to follow?" I said. I said it as nicely as possible, still I think the underlying irony shone through.

"He's two cars behind us," Alice said.

"Great," I said.

There was no easy way to get out of the lane of traffic. I drove out the gate, turned right, pulled up on the shoulder of the road. Popped the glove compartment, pulled out a map, and opened it up on the steering wheel.

"Good move," Alice said. "You look just like a man who's lost."

"I feel like a man who's lost," I said. "Just let me know which way he goes."

"He's turning left," Alice said.

"Figures," I muttered.

I passed the map to Alice, put the car in gear, and sized up my chances of a U-turn on this road. Actually, they weren't bad. With my quarry turning left, the same sort of traffic break that would work for him would work for me too.

Practically.

He hung a left by cutting off a truck coming up from the right. There was no way to get between them. I was lucky to make the U-turn and come up behind the truck.

"He's getting away!" Jean/Joan cried. "Look! He's getting away!"

The man was indeed speeding away from the truck. With a stream of cars coming from the other direction, there was no room to pass.

If I wasn't clear on what to do, it was not for lack of advice.

"Give 'em the horn!"

"Flash your lights!"

"Pass him on the right!"

Suggestions rang out in rapid succession. It was all I could do to separate out those that would not get me killed.

Luckily, as we rounded a turn, a passing zone appeared. There was a car bearing down on us, but from a fair distance. I pulled out, floored it, swept on by. The oncoming car was never really in danger, though the driver certainly had a good chance to test his brakes. I rocketed up the road after the blue Ford.

Which was nowhere to be seen.

"You lost him," Alice said.

Which seemed a pretty unfair assessment of the situation. *I* had lost him? This whole thing was my fault?

Around the next curve a car appeared in the distance. It was too far to tell, but it might well have been our blue Ford.

"There he is!"

"That's him!"

"Step on it!"

I already had the pedal to the floor. The ancient Toyota was giving its all. It seemed to me we were slowly gaining ground. As we whizzed around a particularly sharp curve, it occurred to me I was doing a fairly good impression of the pimply faced young man. It also dawned on me, after many years as a private detective, I was finally in a car chase.

With three backseat drivers.

"Look out!"

"Be careful!"

"Watch the road!"

Sound advice, that never would have occurred to me. I considered thanking the various parties involved. But sorting out just who had said what would probably take too much time. Particularly if I wanted to make the next curve.

I swung the car into a screeching left, wondering if there was any way the man we were following could possibly avoid spotting us. I mean, how often does a carload of sightseeing tourists cruise the road at ninety miles an hour?

The driver of the blue Ford was no slouch himself, because we didn't seem to be really gaining on him.

Until he hit the truck. I don't mean hit it. He didn't hit it. I mean, got stuck behind it. He evidently came up on it where there was no place to pass. Because we came around a curve and there he was. Smack-dab behind a tanker truck, crawling along at twenty miles an hour.

"There he is!"

"Slow down!"

"Don't get too close!"

Thanks to this advice, I was able to avoid driving straight up the back of the car in question. I slowed down, tagged along behind.

"He's gonna spot us," Jean/Joan said.

"I can't help that. At least he doesn't know who we are."

"But if he knows us from the inn . . ."

"Right," I said. "If he knows us from the inn. And if he knows about the murder. And he *must* know about the murder. Particularly if he's a suspect. Particularly if he did it."

"Then he'll know why we're here."

"No, he won't," Alice said. "All he'll think is we're stuck behind the truck just like him."

That assessment seemed to satisfy everyone, and led to a debate over whether we should try to get close enough to get the license number. Before we could, we hit a straightaway, and the blue Ford pulled out to pass.

Jean/Joan split on what I should do next.

"Follow him!"

"No, stay put!"

"He's getting away!"

"He'll know we're after him."

"No, he won't," Alice said. "Who'd want to stay behind the truck?"

I sure didn't. I pulled out, zoomed on by. The question now was, how fast did I want to drive to keep up?

It turned out to be a moot point. Half a mile down the road, the blue Ford signaled a turn to the left.

For once, there was no dispute. All three women said, "Look, he's turning left."

I turned left, too, without putting it to a vote. If that alerted the guy, it was just too bad. If I'd kept going straight, I'd have lost him completely.

If the man was on to us, he gave no sign. He drove more slowly down the narrow side road, and after a mile and a half, turned into a driveway of a two-story red frame house.

I checked the mailbox as we went by. There was no name, just the number 154.

"Okay, gang," I said. "We did it. There's no car in the driveway but his, so we can assume he lives there. Number one five four. All we gotta do is find a street sign and phone it in."

Of course, there wasn't one. We drove three miles without finding any sign, at which point the road came to an end in front of a dilapidated farmhouse. I turned around, headed back to the highway, though I did not recall having seen a sign.

I hadn't. There was no sign whatsoever. Our quarry lived at a known address number on an unidentifiable street. To be truthful, I wasn't sure of the town, either.

"It doesn't matter," I said. "The point is, we could find it again."

The *we* was charitable and conciliatory, including them in the investigation. Not that it had much effect. Jean/Joan the thinner was all for staking out the place, and seemed to resent the fact that I was not. An offer to let her out of the car if she really felt that way was not met with good grace.

Aside from that, I was pleased. We'd actually accomplished something. Tracked down the man from Champney Falls. The man I'd been talking about from the beginning. Pinehurst would finally have to pay some attention to him. He couldn't ignore his existence now.

I stopped at the next gas station we came to, and called the police.

And got no answer.

I blinked.

A busy signal was bad enough, but no answer?

The police station does not answer.

We all had a good laugh over that. I must say, it was nice to have the women laughing with me instead of at me for a change.

We got in the car, drove back to the Blue Frog Ponds.

You could tell at once something had happened. There were people in the yard, standing, talking among themselves. True, it was a small community, and everyone could be reasonably expected to know everybody. But these conversations were not casual. The first impression I got was of neighbors observing a fire.

We headed for Louise, who was up near the porch. Unfortunately, the McInnernys cut us off.

"Isn't that something," Johnny McInnerny said. "Imagine, there we are up the mountain, with no idea."

"No idea of what?" I said. "What happened?"

"What do you mean, what happened? Didn't you see?"

"We just got here."

"Yeah, but didn't you see the police driving off?"

"Police?"

"Of course they didn't," Mrs. McInnerny said. "Johnny Mc-Innerny, when will you stop thinking of yourself? Just because you know something, doesn't mean everybody does. If they just got here, then they don't know."

"Know what?" Alice said.

Mrs. McInnerny tried to look stern. But her eyes were gleaming. "The police have made an arrest."

My first thought was Randy. I didn't want to voice it. Instead I said, "Was it the boyfriend? Was it Lars?"

"Nope," Johnny said.

My heart sunk. Poor Louise.

"So who was it?" I said.

Mrs McInnerny could not keep the note of triumph out of her voice. "It was her," she said.

"Her?"

"Yes." Mrs. McInnerny nodded. "The woman with that awful dog."

TWENTY-THREE

THE POLICE STATION was in the middle of the road. I'm not exaggerating. The road ran right up to the front door. Then turned ninety degrees to the right, ninety degrees to the left, ninety degrees to the left again, and ninety degrees to the right, continuing on where the road would have gone if the building hadn't been there.

The result was disconcerting. Park Avenue makes a square around Grand Central Station, but that's a big building. The police station was small. The road didn't have to aim at it, it easily could have gone by. But, no, it was a dead-on hit.

For my part, I was glad. I'd been given the usual kind of directions to the police station, that is, being told I couldn't miss it. For once, however, it turned out to be true. I braked to a stop, got out, went in the front door.

The sad-sack cop was sitting behind a desk. The one with the droopy mustache. The cop, not the desk.

"Where's Pinehurst?" I said.

"He's in the kitchen."

I blinked. "The kitchen."

"Yeah. He's making coffee."

"He's not with the prisoner, he's making coffee?"

Sad Sack tugged at his mustache. "You got a problem with that? We happen to be out of coffee."

"I need to see him."

"Sure thing." He pointed. "Right through there."

I went through the door indicated, down a short hallway, into a kitchen alcove on the left.

Pinehurst was pouring water into an electric drip percolator. He was bent over, squinting to make sure he filled it up to the line.

"I hate these things," Pinehurst said. "I don't mind making the coffee, it's washing the pot every time. And then, before you know it, you run out of filters, and what do you do then?"

I was in no mood for a lecture on coffee making. "You arrested Florence," I said.

"Yes, I did, and I'm glad you're here. She's been asking for you."

"Oh?"

"Yeah. I was going to have to send Henry to get you, but he wouldn't have wanted to go until he'd had his coffee. Now he won't have to."

"Why does she want to talk to me?"

"I have no idea. She wouldn't say. She just asked for you."

"I don't understand. Why is she under arrest?"

"For the murder of Christine Cobb."

"Yes, yes, of course," I said, impatiently. "*Why* is she under arrest for the murder of Christine Cobb?"

186

"Well, now," Pinehurst said. "I would rather not prejudice you until you've talked to the woman. Go have a talk, get her side of the story, then we can compare notes."

"You mean with what she told you?"

"I mean in general. But by all means, go have a talk with her."

"Fine, I'll do that," I said. "But that's not why I'm here."

"Oh?"

"I found the man I told you about. The hiker from Champney Falls. The one who was there that night."

"Well, that's interesting," Pinehurst said. "And I certainly want to hear about it. But since I have a suspect in custody, it's slightly less urgent. So why don't you hold that thought until you've talked to her. After that, it may not seem quite so important."

"Where is she?"

"Yes, do let me set you up," Pinehurst said. "Right this way."

He led me back down the hallway and through the police station proper, where Sad Sack gave us a sour look, probably because we did not come bearing coffee.

We went through another door to a lockup in the back, which consisted of four small cells. Two were empty. One housed what appeared to be a sleeping drunk.

In the fourth was Florence. She was sitting on the bed with her head in her hands. She looked up, saw us, got to her feet. Her eyes were red, her face was caked with tears. She looked at me, and her lip trembled.

We stood there, looking at each other, not knowing what to say.

"Well," Pinehurst said, "I'll leave you two together. I'm going to pat you down. I'm going to assume you're too intelligent to try to help her escape. When you're done, just come back down the hall."

Pinehurst left.

When the door closed behind him, I turned back and said, "Florence, what's going on?"

Her eyes were wide. "I have no idea."

"Why'd he arrest you?"

"I can't say."

"You don't know?"

"I'm not allowed to talk about it. My lawyer's on his way. He told me to be quiet."

"You called a lawyer?"

"Well, wouldn't you? They arrested me for murder. For *murder*, for goodness' sakes!"

"Yes, but why?"

"I can't talk about it. I called my lawyer in Boston. He's driving up. He made me promise not to talk. You know how frustrating that is, not to be able to talk?"

"Then why did you send for me?"

"Oh. The dog. Can you take care of Prince? He's got to be walked. He's got to be fed. He's in my room. They took me away and left him there. It's so awful. But he likes you, he'll go with you. Could you walk him, please?"

"Yes, of course."

"Thank you." She sighed. "At least I don't have to worry about that."

"But, Florence. What's this all about?"

She shook her head. "I can't talk. I can't. I'm sorry. I really am."

I went back to find Chief Pinehurst, who was sitting at a desk across from Sad Sack. The two of them were holding coffee mugs.

"Want some coffee?" Pinehurst said.

"No, thanks, I'm fine. You mind telling me what's going on?"

"You mean she didn't tell you?"

"Her lawyer advised her not to talk."

"That's a fine state of affairs," Pinehurst said. "You try to conduct a murder investigation, and the suspects decline to talk."

"You knew that when I went in there."

"So?"

"You sent me in anyway, hoping she'd spill something to me she wouldn't tell you."

"Did she?"

"That's hardly ethical."

"Ethical?" The coffee mug stopped on the way to Pinehurst's lips. "The woman asked to talk to you. I let her. If she told you anything interesting, then it would be your ethics whether you wish to withhold it from the police. Am I to gather she didn't?"

"That would be a good gather," I said. "The woman is sitting tight and waiting for her lawyer. She only wanted me to walk her dog."

"That's disappointing," Pinehurst said. "So, you want to tell me why you're here? Some other suspect you'd like me to run down?"

"I told you what other suspect. The man from Champney Falls. The one who's not staying at the inn, but keeps showing up there."

"Uh-huh. What about him?"

"I saw him today on the Cog Railway. I followed him to where he lives."

"And where is that?"

"I don't know."

"You don't know?"

"I don't know the address. I can find it, though."

"You don't know the address?"

"It's one five four something road. Only there's no sign for the road."

"In what town?"

"I'm not sure."

"What about the license plate?"

"I couldn't get close enough to see."

"This is an excellent lead you're bringing me."

"I can show you the house. You will know the street and town."

"That's very interesting. You will understand why I'm not as thrilled as I would have been had I not made an arrest?"

"What if you're wrong?"

"Then I will apologize. And probably get slapped with a suit for false arrest. Though that will be just a gesture, and won't hold up when the lawyer fails to establish malice."

"What I meant was, if you're wrong, this man could be the answer you're looking for."

"He could, and I will certainly check him out. At the moment, I'm more concerned with my prisoner's request. She would like you to walk her dog?"

"That's right."

"So would I. Like you to walk her dog, I mean. We have a warrant to search the room. I'm reluctant to do so while the dog is there. Perhaps if we were to take a run over, we might kill two birds with one stone."

"Could we stop by my friend's on the way?"

"Your hiker suspect? Does it happen to be on the way?"

"More or less."

"Then I suppose we could swing by. Not to talk with the gentleman, you understand, just to verify the address." He looked at me. "Would that satisfy you?"

"I don't think *satisfy* is the right word. But I'd certainly like you to do that."

"Then I'd be happy to," Pinehurst said. "Just let me finish my coffee, we'll take a run over. How's that?"

"Wonderful," I said. "Now that we've got that out of the way, would you mind telling me why you've arrested this woman? Surely it wasn't on a whim."

"I assure you it was not. I arrested her on the basis of the evidence."

"What evidence?"

"Unfortunately, it is not physical evidence, merely circumstantial. That's why I want to search her room. I don't think she'd be stupid enough to hang on to the poison, but if it had been in some container, there might be a trace left. That would certainly nail it down."

"Nail what down? What do you have on her?"

"Well, you will admit she had the opportunity, won't you? Because just before the murder, she got up and went out to walk her dog. At exactly the critical time. The drinks had already been served and were sitting there on the table. Including the fatal one. And, yes, it *was* the fatal one—that's come back from the lab. Christine Cobb died of cyanide poisoning. The poison was administered in her drink. The drink was a stinger, which is some god-awful sweet-tasting concoction young people seem to like. Ideal for disguising the poison.

"Anyway, she went out and came back during the time of optimal access. When Lars was presumably not in the booth. Which, we all agree, is when it probably happened."

"So what? So she went out to walk the dog. Anyone actually see her at the booth?"

"So far, no one did."

"So far?"

"In the first round of questioning, we didn't know what we were after. So some things slipped by. Such as your wife getting up from the table, which she didn't mention the first time around. But we hear about later on. Prompted, the witness' recollection improves. So it's entirely possible someone saw her and failed to mention the fact."

"Fine. It's entirely possible, but so what? So far, no one did. So what have you got? Yes, she was up from the table, but so was everyone else. I was. My wife was. Half a dozen other people were. And the waitresses, the busboy, and even Louise. So why pick on her?"

"Well, there's the motive."

"The motive?"

"Yes. She's the one with the motive. It took a little doing, but

I finally ran it down. Not that easy to do over the phone, but sometimes you get lucky."

"Florence had a motive? Are you kidding? She didn't even know Christine Cobb."

"Maybe not, but her husband did."

"What?"

"Florence's husband. He knew Christine. Knew her well." Pinehurst shrugged. "As a matter of fact, they had an affair."

TWENTY-FOUR

PRINCE NEARLY KNOCKED me down. He came bounding out the door, leaped up, put his paws on my shoulders, and licked my face. Before I could grab him he hopped down and took off, his paws skidding a mile a minute on the wooden floor like a cartoon dog, before finally gaining traction and rocketing around the corner and down the stairs.

"Better get him," Pinehurst said.

"Leash. I need the leash."

"Yes, yes. Get the leash."

It was hanging on the inside doorknob. Pinehurst found it first, thrust it at me before I had a chance to look around. I caught a glimpse of a bare room not dissimilar to mine, before Pinehurst shoved me out and slammed the door in my face.

I had no time to take offense. The dog was on the loose. I turned, hurried down the steps.

Prince was cavorting downstairs. He came out of the TV room and shot by me, heading for the front desk. By the time I got there he was in the dining room, where dinner was not yet being served—thank goodness for small favors. Prince circled the room once, then went through the swinging kitchen door. I heard a yowl and a spat, followed by furious barking. I gritted my teeth, sprinted through the kitchen door.

It was quite a tableau.

Max the cat, up on the windowsill, appeared twice his normal size. His back was arched, his teeth were bared. His orange fur was standing straight up all over his body. He looked like malevolent marmalade.

Prince the dog was barking at him ferociously. Yet there was a somewhat plaintive, hurt, surprised quality to his bark. And on closer look, his nose appeared to be scratched.

Between the two of them, and protecting the cat, stood Louise's nameless husband, the cook. He was dressed in his chef's apron and hat, and stood, meat cleaver in hand, poised and ready, if need be, to behead the dog on behalf of the cat.

I didn't want that to happen. I slipped up behind Prince, snapped the leash on, turned and pulled him away. It took all my strength to get him out the kitchen door. Fortunately, Prince seemed to believe in "out of sight, out of mind." Once we were in the dining room he gave up tugging, his tail began to wag, and in no time at all he was leading me outside.

Alice was waiting on the front lawn. She'd seen us drive up and tried to tag along. Pinehurst hadn't let her, which, in terms of endearing himself to her, probably ranked right up there with being willing to consider her a murder suspect.

"What's happening?" Alice said.

"I have to walk Prince."

"I know you have to walk Prince. What's happening with Florence?"

"Let's take a walk." The McInnernys were on the porch, along with the two businessmen who might be gay—it occurred to me I had to learn their names so I could stop thinking of them like that. "Let's get out of earshot, shall we?"

"Is it that bad?"

"Worse."

I dropped the bombshell on her. Alice took it about as hard as I'd expected.

"Florence's husband had an affair with Christine Cobb?" she said, incredulously.

"That's right. Before the divorce too. The way Pinehurst tells it, Christine Cobb was responsible for breaking up the marriage."

"It doesn't mean she killed her."

"No, but it sure looks bad. I mean, here she is, following the woman around."

"That has yet to be proved."

"Alice, what's to prove? She follows them to New Hampshire, checks in at the same bed-and-breakfast."

"You don't *know* she followed them," Alice said. I could tell she was upset because she didn't issue her usual disclaimer that the Blue Frog Ponds was really an inn.

"What do you mean, I don't know she followed them? She's *here*."

"Yes, but she didn't have to follow them. Maybe she's just here."

"You mean it's coincidence?"

"Why not?"

"Because it's too much coincidence. If two people happen to vacation in the same place, that's coincidence. When one of them hates the other, and the other one dies, that's too much coincidence. You see what I mean?"

"I suppose."

"You'll recall she was also at Champney Falls."

"So?"

"So? Here she is, dogging the woman's footsteps, following her everywhere she went."

"But she didn't follow her to Champney Falls. Don't you remember? When we got to the top, she was already there."

"Yes, but so were they."

"Yes, but they passed us on the way up. Florence didn't pass us on the way up. She and Prince were already there. Now, you have to admit that. Bad as you are with faces, you would have noticed if a woman had passed us with a dog."

"Fine. She didn't pass us on the way up. But that doesn't prove anything. Say Florence is following them. The minute they drive into the parking lot, she knows where they're going. So she parks the car, and she and Prince go up the mountain. While they're fussing with their gear. Or packing their backpacks. She goes on up and waits for them at the top."

"Why?"

"Huh?"

"Why would she do that. I mean, what does she plan to do to them at the top of Champney Falls?"

"She didn't have to have anything planned. If she's an obsessive stalker, she just wants to be there. She can follow them for days before taking action."

"I think that's stretching."

"Stretching? Alice. Pinehurst found the motive. Just who is stretching things here?"

"Pinehurst found the connection. It doesn't have to be the motive."

"So now we're into semantics? Alice, look how far you have to go even to plead your case."

We had reached the road. Two figures coming back from the direction of town called out and waved their arms.

"Uh-oh," Alice said. "Jean and Joan. They're gonna want to hear."

I knew they would. And I didn't feel like going through it again. "You tell 'em," I said. "I gotta put the dog away."

I headed for the Blue Frog Ponds. The McInnernys came down off the porch and cut me off.

"What's going on?" Mrs. McInnerny demanded.

I was in no mood for them, either. "You know as much as I do," I said.

"Well, now, that can't be true," Johnny said. "We don't know about the affair."

"The affair?"

"Yeah. From what I hear, that woman was having an affair, and—Hey, watch that dog, willya?"

Prince had started to sniff Johnny McInnerny's crotch. A bad move if ever I saw one. I tugged him away, and he aimed at Mrs. McInnerny, with an unexpectedly fortuitous result. When she said, "Get that animal away from me," I was happy to comply, and guided Prince in the front door.

Lars was coming down the stairs. I had to admit, I'd forgotten all about him. The fact that he was there, I mean. The grieving boyfriend, former suspect. Living right there in the main building. But seeing him come down the stairs reminded me that, not only was Florence staying at the same bed-and-breakfast, she was right there on the same floor. The odds of winning the lottery began to appear *better* than the odds that this was just coincidence.

While I was thinking that, Prince took off for the kitchen. He was still on his leash, but it didn't mean anything except that he pulled me right through the dining room door. I stopped him, turned him around, and walked back out, just in time to see Lars leave by the front door.

Prince and I went on up the stairs. When we reached the landing, I realized I didn't have Florence's room key. Pinehurst was gone, the door was closed, and I couldn't get in. A fine state of affairs.

Just on the off chance, I tried the knob, but of course it was locked.

I looked ruefully at the door. Looking back at me was Fenwick Frog. Fenwick was a happy-go-lucky sort, depicted flipping a coin in the air, à la Cyd Charisse and Gene Kelly in the "Gotta Dance" number from *Singin' in the Rain*. Looking at Fenwick Frog, one wouldn't expect the occupant of his room to be in jail for murder.

Florence's room was number three. The door across from it was number four. They were the only two doors on the landing. So rooms one and two must have had a separate staircase.

And room four must have been Christine Cobb's.

I looked at the door for no other reason than to check out her frog. Silly, I know, but I was curious. I wanted to know who the decedent's frog was.

It was Felicity.

Felicity was a decidedly female frog, with a pink bow on her head, and long eyelashes. If you've never seen a frog with long eyelashes, it's impossible to describe the effect. But trust me, this was one attractive frog.

I swear I had not had the intention, and I don't know what it was that possessed me, but I had just tried Florence's doorknob and found it locked, and now unconsciously I found myself trying Christine's.

It was locked. Thank goodness. I mean, what was I thinking? Had it clicked open, what would I have done? Taken the dog in and let him sniff around? Somehow, I don't think so. It had been a long day, I was tired, I was not thinking clearly, I needed to put the dog away and get out of there.

I went downstairs, found Louise, asked her for the key. Tried to forestall the barrage of questions she wanted to ask me. Louise was naturally excited by the arrest. Not that she had anything against Florence, I'm sure, it was just the thrill of having her son in the clear.

"It's a relief," she said. "You can't imagine what a relief."

"I know how you feel."

"Do you? I don't think so. Unless it's your son, you just can't know."

"Maybe not, but I'm glad it's off your mind. Anyway, could I have the key?"

"Yes, of course," Louise said. She popped behind the desk, checked the board. "Let's see, room three? No, it's not here. That's funny. There should be one here."

"There has to be," I said. "The police were just there. I took out the dog."

"And they're not still here?"

"No. They're gone. I was just up there. The door is locked."

"Then they must have the key," Louise said. "They must have forgotten to turn it in."

"There's only one key?"

"No, there's two. Florence has one."

"You mean both keys are at the police station? Great. So what do I do with the dog?"

"Don't worry. I'll give you a passkey."

"You have a passkey?"

"Sure. For emergencies like this. Let's see. Here it is. Just don't lose it. And be sure to bring it back."

"Thank goodness," I said. "He's a nice dog and all that, but we hadn't planned on keeping a dog, and he doesn't really get along with the cat."

"No, Max isn't big on dogs," Louise said.

I took the passkey upstairs, unlocked Florence's door, and let Prince in.

And remembered I had to feed him.

His water and his bowl were on a newspaper near the bathroom door. Dry and canned dog food was on the floor beside it.

Florence hadn't told me how much to give him. I guess she must have had other things on her mind. I put dry food in the bowl, opened one of the cans, scooped about half of it out on top. Looked critically at Prince, added the other half.

Prince was not one to stand on ceremony. While I was still filling the bowl he nosed his way in, and began chomping the dog food down.

I stood up, looked for a place to get rid of the can. I rinsed it out in the sink, and put it in the wastebasket. I washed the spoon, put it back next to the canned food. Prince was still merrily chomping. I stood there and surveyed the room.

What, if anything, had the police found? I had no idea. The room looked exactly as it had when we'd first entered it. There was no indication anyone had even been there.

Oh, well.

I told myself it was for Florence's own good. I went over to the dresser, began pulling out drawers.

Found nothing. Just clothes.

The closet yielded only more clothes and an empty suitcase.

The bathroom only cosmetics.

Nothing in the end table. Nothing under the bed. Nothing under the chair.

Nothing.

Had the police taken it?

Taken what?

The vial with the poison?

Had I been reading too many mystery stories?

No, there was nothing here. It was time to go.

I debated turning out the light. Would Florence leave Prince in the dark? I figured she wouldn't sleep with the light on. But she wouldn't turn it off this early, either. I finally compromised by turning off the overhead light and leaving the bedside light on.

Prince was still eating. Had I overfed him? The least of my worries.

I let myself out, took out the passkey, and locked the door.

Turned and looked.

Across from me was Felicity Frog. She of the long eyelashes. She whose occupant was dead. One of whose occupants was dead. The other I'd seen going down the stairs.

Had Lars come back? No, surely I would have heard him. Surely he was still gone. Surely the room was empty.

The passkey. I held it in my hands. What Louise had described as a passkey.

Uh-oh.

Don't be a fool.

I walked to the door, put the passkey in the lock.

It fit.

Of course it fit. It was the passkey. That's what they do.

I turned it. The lock clicked back. I turned the doorknob, and the door opened. Had a moment of absolute panic that I hadn't heard Lars come back, and when I opened the door he would be standing there.

He wasn't. The room was empty. I hesitated a moment, and stepped in.

Next decision—did I close the door for privacy, or leave it open so I could hear him coming? I decided to leave it open. So I'd at least have a chance of getting out. Short of diving out of the second-story window.

All right, enough thinking. This had to be done fast.

I marched to the closet door, threw it open.

Felt a pang. The clothes in the closet were largely hers. There were a jacket and pants that belonged to Lars, as well as a dress shirt. But mostly there were dresses, skirts, shirts, sunsuits, pullovers, and shorts that had belonged to Christine. Lars hadn't packed them up, and why would he? Why would he want to, why would he care, and how could he bring himself to do it?

Poor man.

I realized it was the first time since the murder I had thought of him in that way. As a poor man. Whether it was the sound of the slap, or the tears on her face, or the look in his eyes when I'd passed the booth, or whether I was just projecting all that, but up till now I had never once felt sorry for Lars.

And it bothered me. Not that I hadn't felt sorry for him. But that I did now. Because it occurred to me the only reason I did now was because mentally I had taken him off my list of murder suspects. And the only reason I would have done that was if I thought I knew who did it. And in the present state of the evidence, the only one I could possibly make a case for thinking they might have done it would be Florence.

And I had *not* let myself believe that. Despite the evidence. Despite what I'd said to Alice. Despite everything else, I still clung to the hope that Florence, the woman with the dog, was not guilty. Was not the one who had done it.

My sudden feeling for Lars showed me just how hollow was that particular hope. How much I had been deluding myself.

I shook my head angrily. *Get a grip. You're in here, risking discovery, for a purpose. Go to it.*

I went through the clothes in the closet, searching the pockets. Christine's held nothing. Indeed, her clothes had few pockets to search.

Lars' jacket was another story. I found a comb, a pen, a handkerchief, and a half-dozen business cards from an insurance firm in Boston. In the lower right hand corner it read LARS HEINRICK, SALES EXECUTIVE. A fancy name, to be sure.

I put one of the cards in my pocket. I don't know why, I just found it interesting. Maybe the fact he was from Boston. Of course, they had to be from Boston for Christine and Florence's husband to have gotten involved.

Or maybe it was the fact Lars sold insurance for a living. I wondered what that meant. Was a sales executive just someone who ran around trying to sell people insurance? Did he work on commission and, if so, just how successful was Lars?

Believe me, I hadn't been standing there thinking all that. I, in fact, had moved on to the dresser, was pulling open drawers.

The top one held her underwear. It was sheer. I felt a number of conflicting emotions. Here I was, snooping through the lingerie of this very attractive woman, who had appealed to me for help before becoming the centerpiece in this murder I felt I now had to solve.

Second drawer, more clothes. Of the T-shirt variety. Plus the bathing suit she'd been wearing by the pool. Another disturbing mental image.

Bottom drawer, just a couple of pairs of pants.

I started to close the drawer, noticed a bulge.

Stopped.

Lifted the pants.

A case. A small leather case. The size a man might use to carry his toiletries.

Oh, boy.

I cocked my ear to the door.

Heard nothing.

Looked at the case.

It had a zipper that went three quarters of the way around.

Enough hesitation. I pulled the zipper, lifted the top.

Inside was just what I'd expected. A comb. A hairbrush. A safety razor. A toothbrush.

Perfectly normal.

Except.

Even from where I stood, I could see all those items laid out on the shelf over the bathroom sink.

So why the case?

There was a zippered compartment in the lid. I unzipped it, pulled out a nail clipper. Some Q-tips. Some Band-Aids. Some Tylenol.

And . . .

A small, glass, screw-top bottle half full of white powder.

Good lord.

The poison?

Had I actually found the poison?

I was beginning to sweat. Too many things were open. The open door. The open drawer. The open case. The open compartment.

The open vial?

I felt in my pocket for a piece of paper. Found a stick of gum. Wrigley's Doublemint. Double your pleasure, double your fun. I pulled the wrapper off, unfolded it. Set it on the floor. Unscrewed the top from the little glass bottle, tilted it over the gum wrapper, tapped some powder out.

And heard a step on the stair!

What a chill.

What a rush of adrenaline.

What a moment of sheer, unadulterated panic.

I screwed the top on the bottle, zipped the bottle in the compartment, zipped the case shut, slid the case in the drawer, flipped the pants over it, closed the drawer, bolted out of the room.

Before I could slam the door, a voice demanded, "What are you doing?"

I turned around to find Lars Heinrick. He'd stopped a few steps from the top of the stairs. He was looking up at me, a scowl on his face.

I blinked at him. Said the first thing that came to mind. Which turned out to be, "Huh?"

Lars Heinrick came up the last few steps. "Just what do you think you're doing?"

"Walking the dog."

He blinked at me. "Huh?"

"The woman's in jail. They asked me to walk the dog."

Lars Heinrick blinked again. I could practically see his mind struggling its way through the non-sequitur. "That's my room."

"I beg your pardon?"

Lars pointed. "That's *my* room."

I pointed too. "That's *your* room?"

"Yes."

"I was wondering where the dog was."

"How did you get in my room?"

"I wasn't going in your room. I was just gonna walk the dog."

"How did you open the door?"

"Oh. I have a key." I held it up.

"You have the key to my room?"

"No. I have the passkey. They gave me a passkey to walk the dog. So, this is the wrong room." I pointed across the hall. "Is that room hers?"

"Yes, of course."

"Oh. My mistake. Sorry to bother you."

I crossed the hallway, put the key in the lock, unlocked the door.

"Here, Prince," I called.

I was afraid Prince would be too busy eating to care, but he came bounding right up. I grabbed him by the collar, pretended to find the leash on the inside doorknob.

"Right where she said it would be," I said, although it was actually right where I'd left it.

I snapped the leash on the collar, closed the door, smiled at Lars, said, "Come on, Prince," and followed the dog down the stairs.

My heart was pounding. Had I really gotten away with it? Had Lars bought the story? Or had he seen me with Prince earlier, when he was coming down the stairs? And even if he hadn't, would something else trigger his memory? Make him suddenly realize I'd already walked the dog?

Well, there was nothing I could do about it, but thanks to Lars, Prince was getting a double dip. I took him out on the front lawn, ran him around a while. Just long enough to seem reasonable, in case Lars noticed me bringing him back.

He didn't. At least, as far as I know, he didn't. He might have been listening just inside the door. But, in that case, I realized, it made little difference, since his suspicions would be already aroused.

At any rate, I didn't see him. I put the dog back in the room, went downstairs, and returned the passkey to Louise.

"You walked him twice," Louise said.

I was afraid she'd noticed. "Yeah. After I fed him, he needed to go again."

"Maybe you should feed him first."

I nodded. "Now I know."

Moments later I was out the front door.

With the evidence in my pocket.

TWENTY-FIVE

PINEHURST WASN'T IMPRESSED.

"You stole this from his room?"

"I uncovered some evidence."

"Is that what you call this?"

"You think this isn't evidence?"

"It doesn't matter what I think. It matters what a judge does."

"A judge, Chief? Let's not get sidetracked here. The point is not whether this evidence will stand up in court. The point is what it means."

"It means you're guilty of criminal trespass."

"Fine. Arrest me. Put me in jail. But that's another tangent. The point is, if this is poison, you've got your killer."

"I've already got my killer."

"You just think you do. But what if you're wrong?"

"Then I will need to catch another killer. Which I can only do by legal means."

"Fine. Do it by legal means. Just do it."

"Unfortunately, you've rendered that impossible. By an illegal search and seizure."

"Wrong. Absolutely wrong. I am not a policeman. I'm a private citizen. I cannot violate Lars Heinrick's rights. I might lay myself open to criminal prosecution or a civil suit, but that's another matter. And that's way off the subject. The point is, Lars Heinrick had this powder. It might be poison. Now, you want to analyze it or not?"

"Of course I want to analyze it. Otherwise I won't know what it is."

"Fine. Then we have no problem."

"That will depend on what it is. If it's poison, we have a big problem."

"No, we don't. If it's poison, you know who the killer is. So you get a warrant, you search his room, end of case."

"And if it turns out that warrant was obtained on the basis of information found during an illegal search, any evidence I find during my own search is contaminated and cannot be used in court."

"Fine, Chief. Split hairs all you want." I pointed to the Doublemint gum wrapper full of powder I had laid on Pinehurst's desk. "If this is poison, never mind what it means legally, at least you'll know who did it."

"But I won't."

"What?"

"I won't know. You give me this powder. You say it's from his room. It could be. But I have only your word for it."

"So you search his room and find the vial."

"That wouldn't change a thing. For all the same reasons. If you're making the story up, the question then is how much of your story is true. The part that sounds true is the part about you getting a passkey. If you did, what's to stop you from planting the poison in his room?"

"Oh, come on."

"Come on? Why is that any different than you lying in the first place?"

"Why would I lie?"

"Are you kidding? If the woman is innocent, as you maintain, then you yourself are a suspect. Not to mention your wife. You'd have every reason to lie."

I looked at him narrowly. "You know, Chief, it occurs to me the way you're belittling this, maybe you got something better. You find anything in Florence's room?"

"I was not aware that you were a party to this investigation."

"I'm not. I'm that insufferable amateur detective that's always messing around with the evidence. However, if you want me to go away, your best bet is to give me what you've got. Because I'm not inclined to fly in the face of logic. If you found something that nails down the case against Florence, I'll feel stupid about my gum wrapper full of powder."

"And it would be worth telling you just for that," Pinehurst said. "Unfortunately, I can tell you nothing. Because we found nothing. Not that we expected to. And not that it weakens our case. I wouldn't expect her to hang on to the murder weapon. If she had, I would have found it suspicious." He pointed to the Doublemint wrapper. "Just as I find this somewhat suspicious."

"Beware of Greeks bearing gifts, Chief?" I said. "Anyway, when you get this analyzed, you mind telling me what it is?"

"You'll be one of the first to know. If it's poison, you'll probably be under arrest."

"I beg your pardon?"

"For trying to frame Lars Heinrick. And that's just for starters. You might be under arrest for murder."

"What?"

"Well, why not? If you had the murder weapon in your possession."

"Which I brought to you."

"Yes, of course. The colossal double bluff. The killer, arrogantly overconfident, walks into the police station and hands over the murder weapon to the poor, bumbling investigator, all the time laughing in his sleeve."

"I think that's a misplaced modifier, Chief."

"Huh?"

"Wasn't it the *murderer* who was laughing in his sleeve?"

Pinehurst frowned. "You think I'm kidding?"

I exhaled, shook my head.

"I sure hope you're kidding."

TWENTY-SIX

WE HAD DINNER with Jean and Joan. After the events of the day, I suppose that was inevitable. They were eager to pump me for information.

So were the McInnernys. They descended on our table before Louise could stop them, and demanded to know what was going on. I was torn between wanting to be rid of them, and not wanting to be outright rude. Fortunately, they didn't know how much I knew. In fact, they didn't know much at all.

"An affair, that's the rumor," Mrs. McInnerny said. "That's the story going around."

"Well, let's not spread it any further," I said. "If we could at least keep our voices down."

"As if everyone didn't know," Mrs. McInnerny said. "That woman was having an affair right under her boyfriend's nose."

Ah. That affair. The one with Randy. The McInnernys knew nothing about Florence's husband. In terms of the murder investigation, they were a good two steps behind.

"One shouldn't speak ill of the dead," Jean or Joan said. The plumper one. It occurred to me I had to ask Alice which was which again.

"Don't be silly," Mrs. McInnerny said. "It's a murder case, and the facts are the facts. But they have to make sense. What could this possibly have to do with your friend with the dog?"

"Absolutely nothing," I said. "It's my opinion the police made a mistake."

"But they must have *some* reason," Johnny said. "You spoke to them, what did they say?"

"Florence isn't talking on the advice of her attorney."

Anyone wondering about the actual effectiveness of the concept of innocent until proven guilty and the right to remain silent should have seen the look on the McInnernys' faces. From their reaction, I might as well have told them Florence had confessed.

"I can't believe it," Mrs. McInnerny said. "She seemed like such a nice woman."

I resisted adding, "With an awful dog."

"She *is* a nice woman," Jean/Joan the thinner said. "The police made a mistake."

It was nice to see her standing up for Florence. Particularly since she was better informed than the McInnernys. Jean and Joan knew about Florence's husband's affair.

As I sat there, trying to figure our how to get rid of the McInnernys, it occurred to me what a complicated dynamic there was at the table, in terms of levels of information.

The McInnernys were at the bottom of the food chain. They knew about Christine's affair with Randy, and not much else.

Jean and Joan, on the other hand, knew about Christine's affair with Florence's husband. But they didn't know about my discovery in Lars Heinrick's room.

Alice knew that. I told her as soon as I got back. Actually, I told her before I left. What I'd found and was talking to Pinehurst about. Then when I got back, I told her Pinehurst's reaction. Which was frustrating as hell. And not just his reaction. But her reaction to it. Because Alice, in her infinite contrariness, saw nothing wrong with Pinehurst's point of view.

"But I *didn't* plant the evidence," I told her.

"Of course not," Alice said. "You don't have to convince me. But I can see why it wouldn't convince him."

See? Totally exasperating. Anyway, there I was, sitting at the table, dealing with a who-knew-what-when scenario potentially more complicated than Watergate. So it was a relief when Louise showed up to guide the McInnernys away.

When she did, it seemed to me they were regarding her differently. I wondered if that was because they had identified her as the mother of the person with whom they had heard Christine had had the affair.

The minute they were gone, Jean/Joan the thinner took up the attack.

"So, what's the story?" Jean/Joan the thinner said. "Has he traced him yet?"

The *he* and the *him* had been gone over before the McInnernys' interruption. Jean/Joan was asking if Pinehurst had found out who the hiker was. Jean and Joan knew I'd gone back to the police station. They did not know I'd gone back there to deliver evidence that might be poison. They had assumed—and Alice and I had not contradicted the assumption—that I had gone there to follow up on the investigation we'd begun. To see if the police had traced down our man.

"Not yet," I said. "He assures me it's being done, but claims he hasn't had the time."

"How long could it take?" Jean/Joan the plumper.

"Longer than usual, because he doesn't know what road it is, either."

"What?"

"He doesn't know the name of the road, any more than we do. There's no signpost, so he doesn't know."

"What about the license plate number?"

"He doesn't have it."

"Why not?"

"Because there's no way to get it without tipping the man off."

See what I mean about complicated? What I was telling Jean and Joan now was a complete fabrication. What I *assumed* was Pinehurst's assessment of the situation. In actual point of fact, Pinehurst and I hadn't discussed the hiker from Champney Falls at all. At least not when I'd gone there to give him the poison.

It was long about then that Lucy passed by and slipped a piece of paper under Alice's coffee cup. I couldn't quite believe she'd done that. I snatched it out, opened it up, read:

CHICKEN DIJONNAISE

2½–3 pound whole free range chicken

sprigs of fresh tarragon

2 tablespoons Dijon mustard

1 cup dry white wine

2 tablespoons olive oil

2 tablespoons crème fraîche

1 teaspoon lemon juice

kosher salt and pepper

Preheat oven to 375°. Wash and dry chicken thoroughly.
Prepare the chicken by rubbing kosher salt and pepper on the skin and in the cavity. Stuff the cavity with fresh tarragon sprigs. Coat the chicken with Dijon mustard and let sit at room temperature for 1 hour.

214

On top of the stove in a heavy Dutch oven, brown the chicken on all sides in 2 tablespoons of olive oil. Add 1 cup of dry white wine. Bring to boil. Cover with a lid and place in the oven for 1¼ to 1½ hours.

Remove the chicken from the pot. Skim fat from cooking liquid. Remove the tarragon, chop and return to the pot liquid. Add the crème fraîche, stir in lemon juice and simmer 1–2 minutes until thickened slightly.

Divide the chicken into serving pieces and top with sauce. Serve with small steamed new potatoes.

Serves 4.

"Alice," I said.

Alice looked somewhat defensive. After all, a friend of hers was in jail. "I couldn't help it," she said. "That chicken was to die for."

Jean and Joan were in complete agreement that Alice's actions were totally justified. What a surprise. I wondered cynically if their support had been purchased by the promise of Xerox copies.

While we were bantering about the recipe a hush fell over the dining room. It was sudden and unmistakable. I knew without looking that Lars Heinrick had walked in.

I took a sip of water, which allowed me a sideways glance over my shoulder. Lars Heinrick was plodding along behind Louise. He was taking no apparent notice of his surrounding. If I'd aroused his suspicions by searching his room, you wouldn't have known it. He followed Louise to a table on the far side of the dining room and sat down.

"I don't know why he's here," Jean/Joan the thinner said.

"Who?"

"Lars. I don't how he can stand to be here."

"The man has to eat."

"Yes, but here? With everyone staring at him? You think he doesn't notice everyone stops talking when he enters the room?"

"Well, he can't leave," I said. "The police ordered everyone to stay."

"That was before they made an arrest," Jean/Joan the plumper said. "Do they really expect us to stay now?"

"I hadn't thought of it."

"Then you must be staying the week. Jean and I were checking out tomorrow."

Aha. Jean and I. Thank you, Joan the plumper, for that valuable bit of information.

"Are you going to make an issue of it?" I said.

"We would," Jean said. "Except . . ."

"Except what?"

She shrugged. "Well, how could we leave now?"

"Yes," Joan said. "With poor Florence in jail."

I stifled a grin. So that was how they had worked it out in their minds. Poor Florence, indeed. Jean and Joan weren't checking out, and it had nothing to do with Florence or Pinehurst's instructions. They couldn't bear not to see how this turned out. Jean and Joan had signed on for the duration.

As if on cue, Louise arrived at the table. I had a premonition—she somehow knew what we'd been discussing and was about to inform us that, in light of Florence's arrest, the police were now allowing the guests to leave. This, of course, proved to be entirely wrong.

"Excuse me, Mr. Hastings," she said. "You have a phone call."

"Oh?"

"Yes. You can take it at the front desk."

"Who is it?"

Louise lowered her voice. "The police."

I got up and left the room, leaving three very curious women at my table.

The receiver was lying next to the phone on the front desk. I picked it up, said, "Hello?"

"Stanley Hastings?"

"Yes. Chief Pinehurst?"

"Yes. Sorry to drag you away from dinner, but I thought you'd want to know. I got the results back from the lab."

"So soon?"

"You'd like them to take longer?"

"No, no, Chief. I'm glad. Just surprised. So, what was it?" I lowered my voice. "Was it poison?"

"No."

"No?"

"No. At least, not officially. It's poison in my book. But it isn't cyanide."

"So what is it?"

"Cocaine."

"What?"

"Cocaine. Evidently you stumbled upon a stash of drugs."

"Oh."

"Disappointed?"

"Well, it's not what I was hoping."

"I understand. But the facts are the facts. The sample is cocaine. Now, however you may feel about that, it is *not* what killed Christine Cobb."

"So what are you going to do about it?"

"Me? Absolutely nothing. I'm not about to make a drug bust on the basis of an illegal search and seizure. Life is too short. That type of aggravation one simply does not need."

"Oh, good lord."

"Well, now, don't be too upset. We follow lots of leads. Not all of them pan out."

"No kidding. So, I don't suppose you got anything on our friend?"

"Who?"

"The hiker from Champney Falls. You get anywhere with him?"

"Why do you ask?"

"Why do I ask? What kind of question is that?"

"I'm just wondering why you chose to ask that now."

I took a breath. "I'll tell you why, Chief. You just had me paged in the dining room. I've got three women at my table dying to know why the police wanted to talk to me. What could possibly be so urgent. When I get back to the table, I am going to have to answer questions. My wife knows about the sample I gave you, but the other women don't. And I don't particularly want to tell them. So when they ask me what you had to say, I have to come with something else."

"And that's the reason for your interest?"

"Frankly, yes. I'm grasping at straws. I didn't expect you to have anything by now."

"Oh, but I do."

"I beg your pardon?"

"I have the information you've been bugging me about. That's partly why I called."

My patience with Pinehurst was wearing awfully thin. "Then why couldn't you just say so?"

"I *am* saying so. I wasn't withholding anything. I was merely curious why you would be asking now."

"I'm asking now because I've been asking all along. What are you talking about?"

"I'm talking about the connection."

"Connection?"

"Exactly. No pun intended. But there you are. The man you refer to as the hiker from Champney Falls is Delmar Hobart. That is confirmed both by his address and the registration of his car. The license plate number of which I have still not gotten close enough to read. But which I now possess. And it was issued to a blue Ford that matches the description of the car in the gentleman's driveway."

"And what has this man got to do with the case?"

"Absolutely nothing. However, he happens to have a record. Guess what for."

I blinked. "Drugs?"

"Very good, Mr. Hastings. Very good, indeed. Of course, this is just circumstantial, but putting two and two together, and considering the fact that Delmar Hobart came to the Blue Frog Ponds but did not eat there, I would think we can conclude why he was there."

"I see," I said.

"I know you're not happy to hear that. You would have preferred some bizarre murder plot. And not just to get your friend off the hook, either. You strike me as the type of man whose taste gravitates toward bizarre murder plots. If that's an unfair assessment, I can only say I'm sorry."

I sighed. "What about Florence?"

"What about her?"

"Has her lawyer showed up yet?"

"No, but don't hold your breath. If you were expecting her back, I mean. Because it isn't going to happen. I know the judge. He's not about to set bail in a case like this. No matter what some smart city lawyer says."

"Smart city lawyer? Chief, did a prejudiced observation just cross your lips?"

"Prejudiced? Don't be silly. Which word were you objecting to? Smart, city, or lawyer? I assure you, all three apply."

"Never mind, Chief," I said. "Nice talking to you."

"My pleasure," Pinehurst said, and hung up the phone.

The line did not immediately go dead. After the click of Pinehurst hanging up, the line stayed open.

A moment later there was another click.

The sound of someone hanging up a phone.

TWENTY-SEVEN

I STOPPED IN the door of the dining room, looked around.

Alice and Jean and Joan were at our table.

At the next table was the family with the little girl, all of whom were present.

Behind them was the McInnernys' table. Johnny McInnerny was there, but his wife was gone.

Next to them was a table at which sat one of the two possibly gay businessmen. The other was nowhere to be seen.

Neither was Lars. I wasn't sure exactly what table Louise had shown him to, but wherever it was, he wasn't there.

I strode back to my table, sat down, leaned in, and lowered my voice. "Who went out right after I did?"

"Huh?" Alice said.

"Someone listened in on the call. Keep your voice down, don't spread it around, and don't point. But who went out right after me?"

"Lars Heinrick," Jean said.

"Are you sure?"

"Sure. He left right after he placed his order."

"Anybody else?"

"Mrs. McInnerny," Alice said. "She left right after you did."

"Before Lars?"

"Absolutely. She left right after you."

"Anyone else?"

"No."

"How about the businessman over there?"

"He came in after you went out. I haven't seen his brother."

I blinked. "His brother?"

"Yes, of course," Alice said. "Didn't you know they were brothers?"

"It never occurred to me."

Alice rolled her eyes. "You're hopeless. You can't see the resemblance?"

I was in no mood for a lecture on my powers of observation. I spotted Louise in the doorway, got up, intercepted her, led her outside.

"Anything wrong, Mr. Hastings?" she said.

"No, not really," I said. "I was just wondering."

"What?"

"About the phone. The one at the desk. Where I just took the call. Is there any extension to that phone?"

"Extension?"

"Yes. Could I have taken that call in another room?"

"Yes, if it was important. Is anything wrong?"

"I'm just trying to understand the mechanics. Where is the extension?"

"Actually, there are two. One in the kitchen, and one in the den."

"The den?"

"Yes. Just off the living room. There's a small reading room we call the den."

"With an extension phone?"

"That's right."

"I don't understand. You mean any guest could go in there and make a call?"

"No. It's locked."

"Locked?"

"Yes."

"The room?"

"No. The phone."

"The phone?"

"Yes."

"Show me."

"Now?"

"Please."

I followed Louise down the hall through the living room into the den. It was a small room, boasting a bookcase, a desk, and two overstuffed chairs.

There was a phone on the desk. A black rotary phone. Almost an anachronism in the day and age of Touch-Tones.

A metal lock protruded from one of the holes in the dial.

"See," Louise said. "It's locked. You can't dial it. There's no way to call out from here."

"But I could have taken my phone call?"

"Of course. That's why it's here. I'm not always at the desk. If I'm working on this side of the house, I'll answer the phone here."

"And if you're not?"

"They'll get it in the kitchen. Though I prefer that not to happen."

"Uh-huh," I said. I noticed she'd said *they*, rather than referring to her husband.

Louise was looking at me closely. "Can you tell me why you're so interested?"

I smiled enigmatically. "Just getting the lay of the land."

I reached for the phone. And felt a thrill. It was stupid, I know, but it occurred to me if this were a mystery story, the phone would be warm, so the detective could tell it had been used. Or cold, so he could tell that it hadn't.

I picked up the receiver.

It didn't tell me a thing.

TWENTY-EIGHT

"WHAT'S THE REAL story?" Alice asked.

"Real story?"

"Don't be dumb," she said as we went out the front door. "I heard what you told Jean and Joan. Now what really went on?"

"Let's take a walk," I said.

"Where?"

"Down by the swimming pool."

"I thought it was closed after dinner."

"It is."

We went down to the pool, sat in deck chairs. As expected, we were the only ones there. We watched the sunset and discussed the crime.

I had told Jean and Joan that Pinehurst had identified the hiker, but not as a drug dealer. I told Alice now.

"Interesting," she said. "So the man was Lars' connection. I wonder if he appreciated having a rendezvous at Champney Falls."

"He certainly didn't look like it," I said.

"No, he didn't," Alice said. "And I apologize."

"You do? For what?"

"What I said. When we saw him on the path. You pointed him out as a hiker grumpier than you. I said, maybe so, but at least he was a volunteer. No one was forcing him to do it. It now appears that wasn't the case."

"If Lars did indeed set it up. Which would seem likely. On the other hand, the guy shows up on the top of Mount Washington. Where I saw him talking to a young man. Who, in all likelihood, was buying drugs. At least, that would seem a reasonable assumption. So, maybe it's the hiker who had a penchant for conducting drug deals outdoors."

"A penchant?"

"I used the word wrong?"

"No. You just used it. Do people really say penchant?"

"Alice, I've had it up to here with Pinehurst. Don't you start digressing on me too."

"Okay. Sorry. Say the man did like to deal in the great outdoors. How come he shows up here?"

"The first time he ate here. Which might have been coincidence. I don't like coincidence, but you can't rule it out. The second night he popped in and out, undoubtedly a sale. I would imagine Lars had gone through his stash."

"So, he leaves the dining room, buys some dope, and then what?" Alice said. "Hides it in his room?"

"I would tend to think so," I said. "One, because that's where I found it. And, two, because the cops didn't. After the murder, I mean. I didn't ask Pinehurst, but I would assume the police searched Lars. In which case, he could not have been carrying drugs."

"Does that make sense?" Alice said. "That he would buy the stuff, and immediately hide it in his room?"

"Why not?"

"He's in the middle of dinner. Why wouldn't he just put it in his pocket?"

"I don't know," I said. "I'm not sure where this transaction took place. Say it was in or around the men's room. That's right near the stairs. It would only take a minute to pop up to his room, stash the stuff, and return to the booth. Which he might do if he were at all uneasy about making the buy in a semipublic place. Just in case he was seen, he might feel better not having it on him."

"Thin," Alice said. "But, since you found it there, you're probably right. So, what do we do now?"

"What do you mean?"

"We have a major problem here. The click on the phone line—if that was Lars, listening in on the conversation, then he knows you found the cocaine." She looked at me. "He *would* know that, wouldn't he? Did you discuss that with Pinehurst—the fact it was your sample he was testing?"

"I'm not sure. I would tend to think so."

"So would I. And, even if you didn't, he can put two and two together. The drugs came from his room. He caught you opening his door. So, even if he doesn't remember seeing you earlier on the stairs—and you don't think he did?"

"He looked totally oblivious. And if he *had* seen me with the dog, he would have *known* what I was telling him couldn't be true."

"Right. So we have to assume he didn't. But he knows you opened his door. So, if he overheard the conversation, that would give him enough. So, if it was him listening in on the line, what's his first move?"

"To get rid of the drugs."

"Or to get rid of you."

"I beg your pardon?"

"We can't be too careful here. Christine Cobb was killed. You have got to be very careful here not to fall into a trap."

"What do you mean?"

"You're used to big-city crime. Now you're here on vacation. This is not all fun and games. You've got to be sure you don't take this too lightly just because you're in a New England bed-and-breakfast."

"You realize you just said bed-and-breakfast?"

"Stanley, I'm not kidding. I don't like the idea this man may have seen you going into his room."

"So, whaddya wanna do, follow him? We shouldn't be here now, we should be back at the inn, waiting for him to come out of the dining room?"

"You realize you just called it an inn?"

"Alice, I'm very upset I got caught in his room. I said the first thing that came to mind, which was a very stupid thing to say if he had seen me earlier with the dog. But I don't think he did. He came down the stairs walking like a zombie. And the dog took off for the kitchen. So we didn't pass him. I saw him from a distance, and I don't think he saw me.

"And it really didn't register when I told him I was going to walk the dog. Yes, he was skeptical. Yes, he thought my behavior was strange. But that's what he was reacting to—the fact it was odd. *Not* the fact it was a complete fabrication, an absolute, obvious falsehood. *That* did not register."

"I'll keep an eye on him," Alice said.

"I don't think we should follow him."

"I'm not going to follow him. I'm just going to see where he goes."

"Most likely, it will be back to his room."

"Okay, what are you gonna do?"

"When dinner's over, I thought I'd check up on the kitchen phone."

"Sounds good. Let's go back inside, see if anything's happening."

Nothing was.

In the dining room, Lars was still at his table, waiting for coffee and dessert. The McInnernys were on their way out, and were arguing about the evening movie. Johnny McInnerny wanted to see it, and his wife didn't.

"You can see it if you want to," she said. "I've seen it a million times."

"So have I," Johnny said. "But it's always good."

"What's the movie?" I said.

"*Arsenic and Old Lace*," Mrs. McInnerny said.

"The old Cary Grant version," Johnny said. "You know, with Peter Lorre."

"Oh, so there's a new version?" Mrs. McInnerny said.

"What new version?" Johnny said.

"Exactly," Mrs. McInnerny said. "If there's a new version, I never heard of it. And neither did you. So what sense does it make to say the old Cary Grant version? That's the only version there is."

"Well, these people might not know that," Johnny said. "It doesn't hurt to say who's in a movie. Now how could that hurt?"

"Well, it's a questionable choice, if you ask me," Mrs. McInnerny said. "What with everything that's going on. To show a movie about poison."

"Well, let's not give away the plot," Johnny said.

"Now, Johnny McInnerny, you think these people don't know *Arsenic and Old Lace* is about poison?"

"Oh, well, I suppose."

"Come along now. You can see the movie if you want. It doesn't mean I have to."

The McInnernys went out the front door. A moment later I heard, *Pssst!*

Alice and I looked around.

Jean and Joan were gesturing to us from the direction of the TV room. Alice and I went over and joined them.

"What are you doing?" I said.

"Waiting for Lars to get finished," Jean said. Then looked around to see who might be overhearing us, though we were alone.

"Now, look," I said. "You can't follow Lars."

"You said to keep our eyes open," Joan said.

"Yes, I did. And that's fine. Go about your business, keep your eyes open, see what happens. But don't hide in corners and spy on people. Because if someone sees you doing it, the result could be very bad."

"So what should we do?" Jean said.

"I don't know. The movie tonight is *Arsenic and Old Lace*."

"Oh, I love that movie," Joan said.

"Then maybe you should check it out. See who's there. You might try to sit where you can watch their reactions."

"Why?" Jean said.

"Because it's a movie about poisoning people. Someone might be uneasy about the subject."

"Gotcha."

"Meanwhile, leave Lars alone. There's no need to put him on his guard."

Jean and Joan gave in, though with somewhat bad grace.

"I feel like the Grinch Who Stole Christmas," I said as they went out the door.

"They'll get over it," Alice said. "Besides, I can't wait to hear their reports on how Johnny McInnerny reacted to the poison in *Arsenic and Old Lace*."

"It will make my day," I said. "Let's see how dinner's coming."

We strolled back past the dining room. Lars Heinrick was the only one left. He sat sipping his coffee, his back to the door.

Most of the other tables had been cleared. Randy the busboy was working on the last one.

"I think I'll try the kitchen," I said.

"Fine. I'll hang out here," Alice said. When I raised my eyes, she added, "Discreetly."

"Just be careful," I said. I turned toward the kitchen, turned back. "What's the chef's name?"

The look Alice gave me might have been appropriate if I had asked her for *her* name. "Charlie," she said.

"Right. Charlie. Thanks."

I pushed through the swinging doors into the kitchen.

The chef, Louise's husband and Randy's father, was at the sink.

He heard me, turned his head, did a double-take, wheeled around and said, "Oh! You don't have the dog?"

"No."

"I don't want him in here, that dog."

"I got that impression."

He seemed surprised when I didn't turn and go. "Did you want something?"

"I'd like to ask you a couple of questions."

"I don't give out recipes."

"Yes, I know. Not that the food isn't very good. But that wasn't it. I have some questions about the girl."

"The girl?"

"The dead girl. Christine Cobb."

"I don't know anything about that."

"I know. But I'm looking into it, and there are some things I need to ask."

"You're looking into it?"

"Yes."

"Why?"

"Actually, your wife asked me to. On account of your son."

As if on cue, Randy came through the swinging door with a tray of dishes. He carried them over to the dishwasher, began loading them into racks to go into the machine.

His father and I stood there looking at him. As if we couldn't talk while he was in the room.

Randy finished unloading the tray into the rack, went back out through the swinging door.

His father turned to me. "You're not making any sense. My son has nothing to do with this. The police made an arrest."

Yes, they did. Your wife asked me to help before that happened. Because she did, certain things were set in motion. Now they need to be tied up."

"What things?"

"Nothing that should concern you. You, or your son. When you hear my questions, you'll see what I mean."

"What questions?"

"You have a phone in the kitchen?"

"I beg your pardon?"

"Your wife said there was a phone."

"Sure. Over there on the wall."

I could see it from where we stood. In a small alcove with shelves of canned goods. A black wall phone with a rotary dial. This one did not appear to have a lock.

"I see," I said. "So you can call out from here?"

"Or take calls, sure. What's the idea?"

"Did anyone use that phone tonight?"

"Tonight?"

"Yeah. During dinner. Did anyone use the phone?"

"I have no idea. I didn't. Randy didn't. The waitresses, I'm not sure."

"The waitresses?"

"Well, they're in and out all the time. I can't pay attention, I'm cooking the food. They're not supposed to make phone calls when dinner's being served. But if one of them did, just a short call, how could I possibly notice?"

"And you didn't notice?"

"No. If I did, I would say so. But the fact is, I didn't."

"And you didn't notice anyone else in the kitchen tonight?"

"Anyone else?"

"Yeah. Who wouldn't normally be here. Like one of the guests."

"Now, *that* I would notice."

"You're saying it's impossible one of the guests slipped in here and made a phone call?"

"Without being seen? I would say so. Sure, I'm busy cooking. But it's not just me. There's the waitresses. Any guest who comes through that door's gonna be asked what they're doing here."

"And no one was?"

"As far as I know."

"Where are the waitresses now?"

"On their way home. They don't have to clear. Last dessert served, and they're gone."

Randy came back through the swinging door with a coffee cup and a dessert plate. He took them over to the dishwasher, put them in the racks, began feeding the racks into the machine.

Which meant Lars was done.

I wondered where he'd gone.

I wondered where Alice was.

Randy fed the last rack into the machine, took a broom and dustpan, and went back out the swinging door.

"What's this got to do with the crime?" the chef said. "I thought it was solved."

"The police made an arrest. It's not the same thing. The case is yet to be proved."

"And you're looking for proof?"

"In a manner of speaking."

"What does that mean?"

"I'm looking for evidence."

"That this woman committed the crime?"

"Or that she didn't."

"I'm not sure I like that."

"I can see why you wouldn't. But please understand. I was doing this on behalf of your son. That job doesn't end just because the police made an arrest. In the event that they're wrong, they'll come looking for someone else. It would be nice if the facts indicated it wasn't him."

"And do they indicate that?"

"That's what I'm working on now."

The sweeping up either wasn't that big a job, or Randy wasn't very careful about it, because he came back through the swinging door, dumped the dustpan, put the broom away, and, without a word to his father, went out the door to the back.

When Randy went out, Max came in. He hopped up on the kitchen table, strolled between the pots and pans, climbed up onto the butcher block right next to the carving knife, and meowed loudly.

"Hello, Max," the chef said. For the first time his eyes lit up.

It was kind of sad. He showed only minimal interest in his wife and son. But he seemed to care about the cat.

"Hungry, Max?" he said. "Want some fish? Is that what you'd like?"

Max meowed loudly, which was disconcerting. It was as if he'd answered the question.

The chef certainly took it that way. He said, "Sure you do. Well, look what I've got here."

He went to the refrigerator, took out a tin wrapped in a plastic sandwich bag. He slid the bag off the tin, held it up.

"Sardines," he said. "His favorite. Drives him nuts."

He looked at me and his eyes were bright. "Watch this," he said. "A Stupid Pet Trick. Like on the Letterman show. Here. I'll show you."

Near the coffee urn was a stack of foam cups. He took three cups off the stack, brought them over to the butcher block, where Max was waiting impatiently, licking his lips and swishing his tail.

"Ready, Max?" he said. "Let's do your trick."

As if on cue, Max yawned and stretched, as if to show his complete indifference in the proceedings.

The chef knew better. He smiled, took the three Styrofoam cups, turned them over, and set them in a row upside down in front of the cat.

"There you are," he said. "The old shell game. Guess which cup the pea is under. Ever see it played by a cat? Watch this."

He took a sardine out of the tin, put it under the center cup. Then, he began switching the cups around, sliding them on the butcher block, faster, faster, faster, just like a con man playing the old shell game.

The cat never moved a muscle. He sat there, staring at the cups.

The chef finished. The three cups sat in a row. He'd gone so fast I had no idea which was the right one.

But Max did. He stretched out a paw, tipped the cup over, grabbed the fish.

The chef smiled, did a *ta-da!* gesture. "And there you are. A Stupid Pet Trick." He shrugged. "It's the smell, of course. He can't watch the cup. He goes by the smell. But people don't think of that. A dog, they credit with a sense of smell. But not a cat. Well, Max smells just fine. He can find the fish."

"I see that," I said.

We watched the cat tear apart the small fish.

The chef nodded in agreement with himself. "It's like catnip to him," he said. "Drives him wild."

He nodded again. Then his face sobered. "About what you said."

"I beg your pardon?"

"What you said before. If they let the woman out."

"Yes?"

"Protect my boy." He exhaled, looked at me. "That's what you said you were doing, right? That's what she asked you to do?

Well, can you do it? Will you promise me that? Will you protect my boy?"

He looked at me with anxious eyes. A father, concerned for his son. It occurred to me I knew his name. For all the good it did me. I wasn't about to call him Charlie.

I took a breath. "I'll do my best."

TWENTY-NINE

I FOUND ALICE in the living room. She was sitting in an overstuffed chair reading a magazine. Or at least pretending to. If the latter, it was for the benefit of the two brothers formerly known as the businessmen I wondered if might be gay, who were drinking at the bar.

I sat in a chair next to Alice. "What's up?" I said.

"Nothing. Lars finished his meal, went back to his room."

"That's boring."

"I'll say. Whaddya wanna do now?"

"Shall we check out the movie?"

"When's it start?"

"About five minutes ago."

"Why not."

Alice and I went up to the game room. The lights were out,

and on the big-screen TV Cary Grant was finding out the neighbors had been complaining about Teddy blowing his bugle again.

Enjoying the movie were Jean and Joan, Johnny McInnerny, the family with the little girl, and a man and woman I hadn't seen before, who must have just checked in today and for some reason dined somewhere else.

And Lucy.

Our waitress sat in the dark, watching the movie. I nudged Alice with my elbow, pointed to her.

Alice nodded.

Gratefully.

I leaned close, whispered, "This is not a chance to buy recipes, this is a chance to find out if anyone used the kitchen phone."

Alice nodded impatiently, as if the idea of obtaining recipes had never crossed her mind.

While this was going on, the two brothers from the bar came in and sat down. That left Alice and me as the only people still standing.

I gave Alice a look.

"I'll stay," Alice whispered.

I had a feeling recipes had more to do with her decision than she would like to pretend. Still, that was fine with me.

I said, "Okay, I may be back," and slipped out the door.

I stood outside of the recreation room and looked around. It was dark out, and lights were on in all the buildings. East Pond. West Pond. The main house. And there was a light over the sign by the road.

Across the road, I could see the path into the woods, the path I'd taken on another night just like this, when I'd decided not to see the movie and wound up spying on Christine. I wondered how much it mattered—if it did at all—the fact that I had seen them, and that I had told people. Had that not happened, would she be alive?

I didn't think so. I didn't want to think so. I mean, surely it couldn't be all me. If I hadn't seen them, we might not know about Randy. But what would that mean in the general scheme of things? What I mean is, had someone else known? Would the police have known? Would Randy have even been a suspect then?

I had no idea. And it occurred to me, the more I learned in this particular case, the less idea I had. Because the only thing that made sense, the only thing that was logical at all, much as I hated to admit it, was that Florence had done it, that Florence was guilty, that the killer was indeed the woman with the dog.

I roused myself from this melancholy musing, went for a walk around the grounds. East Pond and West Pond seemed quiet enough. So did the main house, for that matter. I walked around it, looking at the lights. That light there, for instance—was that Lars' room? No, his room was on the other side. That must be someone else's room. The McInnernys', perhaps. Or perhaps the family with the little girl.

How about Jean and Joan? Were they in West Pond? Did Alice say that? Why did I think that?

It occurred to me, aside from Lars and Florence, I had not sorted out where anybody lived.

I wondered if that mattered.

I continued walking around the inn. Reached the back. I could see a light on in the kitchen window. I wondered if that meant the cook was still there. Surely he would turn the lights out at night, and—

I froze.

Randy's door was open. And someone was standing in it. I could see the person's back. Not clearly, just a shadow, a silhouette.

Who could be calling on Randy at this time of night? Did he have a girlfriend? A lover? Someone who might be jealous of Christine?

I shrunk back into the shadows, began to creep around to where I could get a better look.

239

There. I could see the light from the door, and there was Randy standing there, talking to the woman. Yes, it was a woman. So why didn't he invite her in? If it was a lover, surely he'd invite her in.

Unless there was friction.

Tension.

Caused by Christine.

Could that be it?

I had to move a little farther. I was only seeing the woman's back. I crept through the shadows and—

Felt like a total fool.

The woman calling on Randy was Mrs. McInnerny.

But of course. The gossip. The snoop. Who had only just heard of the affair. The wrong affair. The affair with Randy. Not the affair with Florence's husband. Yes, it was poor old Mrs. McInnerny, a good two steps behind. No wonder she'd begged off the movie. She was all gung-ho to go detecting.

With yesterday's clues.

I'm sure Randy'd had many lectures about not being disrespectful to the guests, still, I wondered how long it would be before he slammed the door in her face.

I didn't stay to find out. I continued around the building.

On the far side there were two lights on on the second floor. The one on the right would be Florence's room. I'd left the bedside light on for Prince.

The one on the left would be Lars. Who should be there now, since Alice told me he'd gone back to his room.

What was he doing, I wondered? Was he lying in bed with his thoughts? Was he reading a book? I knew he didn't have TV.

TV.

I wondered if anyone was in the TV room. What with *Arsenic and Old Lace* being so popular and all.

I completed my circuit of the building, went inside. There was no sign of Louise or her husband. In fact, there was no one there.

240

The bar was unattended. It was also open and unlocked. Anyone could walk right up and pour themselves a drink. In New York City that would happen. A bar like this wouldn't last a day. But in New Hampshire, no one gave it a thought.

I glanced into the dining room. The lights were out, and the moonlight coming in the window cast dark shadows on the walls.

I looked over at the booth where it had happened. I couldn't see it clearly. Because of the darkness and the angle.

An impulse seized me. I walked over to the booth and sat in it. In her seat. Sat where she sat. Looked to see what she could see.

Not much. Her back was to half the dining room. As to the other half, Lars' side of the booth cut off her view of most of it.

She could see the door. The angle was just right for that. She could see anyone who walked in. She would have seen the hiker. Lars' connection. The man from Champney Falls. She would have seen him come in, and Lars wouldn't have. Because his back was to the door. She would have had to tell him he was there. Otherwise, the man would have had to find them. Stop at their booth. Which I didn't think he'd done. So she must have told him.

Did that matter?

I had no idea.

I got up from the booth, looked around.

There was light coming from under the bottom of the kitchen door. No surprise there. I'd seen the kitchen light was on from outside. Did that mean the chef was still there, or was the light left on all night? For Max, perhaps?

I went to the swinging door. It wasn't locked. I pushed it open, looked into the kitchen.

There was no one there. Just the ovens and refrigerators and hanging pots and pans. There was the dishwasher Randy had filled, silent now, the trays having emerged from the other side. And there was the butcher block where Max had done his Stupid Pet Trick.

And there was the phone in the alcove. With no lock on the dial, and no lock on the kitchen door. A phone any guest could use in the dead of night to call Australia, if they saw fit. Apparently, that was not a problem.

I left the kitchen and the dining room, went by the front desk, which was unmanned. Anyone could use that phone, too, right after fixing themselves a free drink at the bar.

Well, it wasn't my concern. I went into the TV room. As expected, there was no one there. I sat down on the couch, picked up the remote control. Clicked the TV on. Flipped through the channels.

And found the Red Sox game.

All right, I admit, I'd had it in mind when I'd seen everyone watching the movie. And there didn't seem to be much I could do in the way of detection. There really didn't. And this vacation had just been one disappointment after another—I realize that's an insensitive word to use under the circumstances. But still, could you blame me for taking time out to enjoy a baseball game?

Go ahead and blame me, because that's what I did.

The Red Sox were playing the White Sox, and it was the top of the first inning, and there were runners on first and second, and Nomar Garciaparra was up, and on a three and one count he hit the ball up the gap in right center, driving them both home, and I for one could not have been happier at finally getting to watch my game.

It got rained out in the top of the third. The Red Sox were leading seven to one. If play ever resumed, they had the game well in hand. But this wasn't a shower, it was an absolute gale, and despite the announcers' attempts to be upbeat, it was easy to tell that there wasn't a prayer.

I switched off the TV and went out.

The place was still deserted. I saw no one inside, no one outside.

I walked by the rec room. The movie was still going on. I considered going in, catching the end. Decided against it. There was no one I really wanted to talk to. Alice could give me a report. It had been a long day, and I was tired. I went back to my room. Kicked off my shoes, got in bed, and began reading *4:50 From Paddington.* Or, *What Mrs. McGillicuddy Saw!*

I had trouble finding my place. I hadn't used a bookmark, and I wasn't sure of the page. I kept reading stuff I'd read before. Which didn't always register, because, of course, I'd read the book years ago, so all of it was vaguely familiar. It was a question of separating what was *recently* familiar.

Which was difficult with what had happened lately. Too much input. I mean, which crime are we dealing with, the real one or the fictional one? What the woman saw on the train, that's the train in the book, not the Cog Railway. What we saw on the Cog Railway was the drug dealer, who may have had nothing to do with the murder. So just what is it I'm reading here?

I wasn't sure. So I was glad ten minutes later to hear voices in the hallway and footsteps on the stairs.

One voice was Alice's. I wondered who she was talking to. I got up, opened the door.

Just my luck. She was talking to Johnny McInnerny about *Arsenic and Old Lace.*

"Oh, and there's my stick-in-the-mud husband," she said, "who missed the whole show."

I groaned. I didn't want to go through the seen-it-before routine again with Johnny McInnerny. I had also hoped Alice would have something interesting to report. Obviously not, if she'd wound up discussing the movie with Johnny McInnerny. I was certainly glad I'd been spared that, and—

Good lord.

Johnny McInnerny?

I have to admit, what with everything that had happened, I was so stressed out that things were slow kicking in.

Johnny McInnerny had come upstairs with Alice.

Johnny McInnerny was standing in front of the room with Freddy Frog on the door.

Johnny McInnerny and his wife were the couple whose amorous adventures I'd envied through the paper-thin wall.

The McInnernys?

The mind boggled.

That revelation having hit me, I found myself incapable of speech. I stood there like a lump, grinning moronically.

However, Johnny needed no prompting. "Well, you missed a good show. And it's so much better with an audience. I must have seen that movie on TV a dozen times. But it's not the same thing, watching it alone. It's so much better with an audience laughing at it."

I quite agreed. I just had no wish to prolong the conversation. "Absolutely," I said. "Wish I'd been there. Well, good night, now."

I took Alice by the hand and practically pulled her into the room.

"Are you kidding me?" I whispered the minute the door closed. "The McInnernys live next door?"

"So it seems."

"The McInnernys are the reason we've been keeping quiet?"

"Stanley," Alice said, reprovingly.

From next door came a horrifying scream. We would have heard it even if the walls hadn't been paper-thin. As it was, it might as well have been in the same room.

Alice and I looked at each other, bolted for the door. Alice, who was closer, got there first, ripped it open, dashed out into the hall. I followed.

The McInnernys' door was open. Inside, Johnny McInnerny was kneeling next to his wife.

Mrs. McInnerny lay sprawled out on the floor.

A large carving knife protruded from her chest.

THIRTY

PINEHURST SEEMED IRRITATED. Which didn't seem quite right. Don't get me wrong. I'm not saying he should have been pleased. Still, his reaction went beyond what one would expect. The man was definitely annoyed.

Alice and I were outside, where access to East Pond was being denied by the cop with the droopy mustache. Aside from the police, the only one allowed inside was the medical examiner, who was currently plying his trade. I, for one, was not holding my breath waiting for his report. There was really nothing the man could tell me. Mrs. McInnerny had been stabbed in the heart with a knife somewhere between eight and ten o'clock. I doubt if the doctor could do better than that.

Also outside on the lawn was practically everybody from Blue Frog Ponds. Pinehurst had come whipping in with his siren. By then everyone was already outside, but just in case anyone was inclined to sleep through the action, that sort of sealed the deal. They were all out here now, even the six-year-old girl, who wore a pink flowery nightgown, and was yawning and rubbing her eyes as she snuggled up in her father's arms.

I knew how she felt. With Pinehurst in charge of the operation, it was going to be a long night.

He came out of East Pond, looked around, spotted me standing with Alice and Jean and Joan. He strode over to us and addressed Alice.

"You were with Mr. McInnerny when he found the body?"

"We both were," I said.

"Yes, yes," Pinehurst said. "But you were with him before, at the movie. You came back from the movie together and were there when he found his wife."

"That's right," Alice said.

"Mr. McInnerny was at the movie the whole time?"

"Yes, he was," Alice said. "I can vouch for his whereabouts from eight o'clock on."

"So can we," Jean said.

"Oh?"

"Joan and I were at the movie too. And she's absolutely right. The man never left."

"And you didn't either?"

"No, of course not."

"None of you?"

Jean frowned. "What do you mean, none of us?"

"Mrs. Hastings too?"

"We were all there the whole time," Jean said.

"Uh-huh," Pinehurst said. He turned to me. "But you were not?"

"No."

"Why not?"

"I'd seen the movie before."

"Who hasn't?" Pinehurst said. "Everyone's seen that movie before. Most people decided to see it again. Why not you?"

"You want me to discuss this in front of everyone?"

Pinehurst frowned.

So did Alice.

So did Jean and Joan.

I realized I had suddenly made myself unpopular with everyone.

"If you'll excuse us," Pinehurst said.

He led me off in the direction of the road.

"Now then," he said, when we were presumably out of earshot, "what was so all-fired important that you decided to miss the movie?"

"It wasn't like that. I wanted to look around, and I wanted to watch the game."

"The game?"

"There was a Red Sox game on television. With everyone in the rec room, I figured the TV room might be free."

"Was it?"

"It was. I saw three innings of the Red Sox–White Sox."

"Three innings?"

"It rained in Chicago."

"Oh." Pinehurst cocked his head. "You didn't feel you could tell me this in front of the others?"

I almost said, "Don't be dumb." I took a breath, exhaled. "Before I watched TV, I went for a walk. I happened to see the victim."

"Mrs. McInnerny? Where?"

"In back of the main house. In the door to Randy's room."

"Randy?"

"Randy the busboy. Louise's son. The one who was having an affair with Christine Cobb." I looked at Pinehurst. "Is this an interrogation technique? Or have you *really* forgotten who these people are?"

"It was conversational, merely," Pinehurst said. "So, you saw Mrs. McInnerny in the busboy Randy's room?"

"Not in his room. In the doorway."

"In the doorway?"

"Yes. Like she'd knocked on the door and he'd opened it."

"But had not invited her in?"

"Well, would you?"

"And he didn't?"

"As far as I know."

"You didn't stay to see?"

"No. It was old news. Mrs. McInnerny had just found out about the affair. Between Randy and Christine Cobb. She told me so this afternoon. I knew that's why she was talking to him."

"You didn't think it was important?"

"It was yesterday's news. My only interest in Mrs. McInnerny was she was out of the room when I got the call."

"The call?"

"From you. Telling me about the cocaine. She was out of the dining room at the time."

"What's that got to do with it?"

I told him about the click on the line.

"Interesting," Pinehurst said. "So you think someone may have overheard the call?"

"It's the obvious explanation."

"And you thought it was her?"

"She was one possibility. Another was Lars Heinrick. Then there's the cook, the waitresses, and the busboy."

"Why them?"

"Because there's an extension in the kitchen. As well as one in the reading room."

"Uh-huh," Pinehurst said. "Well, that's certainly something to take into consideration. For the time being, I'd like to concentrate on this murder. What time was it you saw Mrs. McInnerny talking to the busboy?"

"Around eight-fifteen, eight-twenty."

"How do you fix the time?"

"The movie started around eight. Alice and I got there late, after it had started. Say between five and ten after. She decided to stay, I decided not to. I left there, walked around the grounds. By the time I got to the back of the main house it was probably eight-fifteen to eight-twenty. Somewhere along in there. I saw Mrs. McInnerny, but did not stay to watch. I finished checking out the building and went inside."

"To watch TV?"

"That's right. I watched three innings of the ball game."

"When you turned on the TV, was the game already on?"

"Yes. It was in the first inning, with two on and nobody out."

"The first inning?"

"Yes."

"The game was only in the first inning?"

"They're playing in Chicago. The game had an eight-thirty start."

"Eight-thirty?"

"Yes."

"And the game was already in the first inning and there were two runners on?"

"Yes. Why?"

Pinehurst shrugged. "Well, I'm not a huge baseball fan, but I do watch the game. And you know, they start five minutes late. An eight-thirty game starts at eight-thirty-five. Some papers even list them that way. A seven-thirty-five start. A seven-o-five start. That's when the first pitch is thrown, as opposed to when the broadcast starts."

"So?"

"So, if you turn on the game and there's two men on base, it's gotta be around eight-forty. And you just saw Mrs. McInnerny around eight-fifteen."

"I said eight-fifteen to eight-twenty."

"It's still a good twenty minutes. If you went inside to watch TV, there's no way you'd miss the beginning of the game."

"I didn't go straight to the TV room."

"No? What did you do?"

"I circled the house. I remember seeing the lights on in Lars' and Florence's room. I knew he'd gone back to his room, and I wondered what he was doing. And I remembered I'd left the light on in her room for the dog.

"Anyway, I did that. Then when I went inside, I didn't go to the TV room, I went to check out the dining room first."

"Why?"

"I don't know. It was there. It was dark. Everyone had left. It was quiet. I went and sat in the booth, where Christine Cobb had sat, and tried to put it all together in my mind."

"Any luck?"

"The only thing I came up with was from where she was sitting she would have seen the drug connection come in the door. And Lars wouldn't. So she would have had to tell him he was there."

"Uh-huh," Pinehurst said, without enthusiasm. "And that took twenty minutes?"

"I also checked out the kitchen."

"The kitchen?"

"Yes."

"Why?"

"Like I said. One of the extension phones was there."

"And what did you hope to learn from the kitchen?"

"I don't know. But there was a light on. I could see it under the door. I wondered if anyone was there. I also wondered if I could get in."

"Could you?"

"Sure. The door was unlocked. I pushed it open, went right in."

"The door was unlocked at that time?"

"Yes. Why?" My eyes widened. "The knife?"

"It appears to have been from the kitchen, yes."

"Oh, no."

"Oh, no, what?"

"I think I saw it."

"The knife?"

"Yes."

"Then?"

"No. Earlier this evening."

"How is that?"

I told him about talking to the chef and seeing Max's Stupid Pet Trick.

"The knife was on the butcher block then?"

"Yes. I remember seeing it."

"And when you checked out the kitchen later, somewhere around eight-thirty?"

"I don't know."

"You don't remember seeing it?"

"No."

"But you don't remember *not* seeing it?"

"No, I don't."

"It's somewhat important."

"I'm aware of that."

"Are you? Good. Then should anything jog your memory, please be so kind as to let me know. Anyway, you went in and watched the ball game. Or at least three innings of it."

"Until it started to rain."

"And what time was that?"

"Around nine-thirty."

"An hour later. That figures. That's how slow ball games are these days. At which point you went back to your room."

"That's right."

"You got back to your room some time around nine-thirty?"

"Say nine-thirty, nine-thirty-five."

"And what did you do?"

"I got in bed and read a book."

"Until your wife came home with Johnny McInnerny?"

"That's right."

"And during the time you were reading, did you hear anything, anything at all?"

"Not a peep."

"Is it possible that the murder happened then, during that time while you were reading—that someone came up the stairs, knocked on the door, stabbed Mrs. McInnerny dead?"

"Not at all. The walls are paper-thin. I would have heard the footsteps, I would have heard the knock on the door, I would have heard the body fall."

"So that pins it down. The murder had to happen between eight-fifteen and nine-thirty. Which is probably better than the doctor can do. Fine. Thanks for your help."

Pinehurst turned, strode away.

I was puzzled by Pinehurst. Not only did he seem peculiarly annoyed, somehow he had become practically animated. Unlike his ponderous questionings in the Christine Cobb affair, his interrogations now were far less formal. As I watched, he descended on the clump of people clustered outside East Pond, buttonholed Randy, and led him away from the group, very much in the manner of a sheep dog, singling out a lamb from the flock.

As I walked back to the others, Louise came rushing up.

"What did you tell him? What have you done? Now he's after my boy."

"It's all right. He's only concerned with the time element."

"What?"

"Mrs. McInnerny saw Randy tonight. In his room."

Her eyes widened. "You told him that?"

"Relax. He's not a suspect. The fact is Mrs. McInnerny was snooping around. She'd heard your boy was involved with Christine Cobb. She wanted to know if it was true."

Louise looked even more distressed. "That sounds like a motive."

"Not at all. It's old news. Trust me, all Pinehurst wants to know is when she left."

Louise didn't look convinced, but at that moment Pinehurst left Randy and headed back our way. He veered off, however, to intercept Sad Sack, who was coming back from the direction of the main house. Sad Sack spread his arms, shook his head. "Still no luck," he said.

Pinehurst frowned, turned, surveyed the group.

Lars Heinrick was standing off to one side, alone as usual. He appeared absorbed in his thoughts. Pinehurst swooped down on him, attracted his attention, led him aside.

"See," I said. "There's your real suspect. No one really thinks it's your boy."

"No one *did*," Louise said. "They arrested that woman. And everything was all right. I know that's a terrible thing to say, but that's how I saw it." She spread her arms. "And then this. It's awful. They know *she* didn't do it now."

Of course. Louise had just put into words what I myself had known, but hadn't quite processed. No wonder Pinehurst was so upset. His whole theory of the case had just blown up in his face.

Florence was in jail. Florence hadn't killed Mrs. McInnerny. And unless these were separate crimes committed by two separate murderers—the probability of which I figured somewhere around a million to one—Florence hadn't killed Christine Cobb.

So Pinehurst's bad mood was suddenly quite understandable indeed.

The medical examiner came out of East Pond. Pinehurst went to meet him, and the two of them conversed in low tones.

Louise swooped down on Randy. He brushed her off, walked away. I wondered if Sad Sack would let him go, or head him off and herd him back to the group. However, Randy stopped of his own accord, circled away from his mother, and hung out on the edge of the crowd.

I felt a hand on my shoulder, looked around to find Alice. She didn't look pleased.

"So," Alice said, "what was so important you couldn't talk about it in front of me?"

"Not you," I said. "Jean and Joan. We haven't told them everything, and I'm going nuts keeping straight who knows what. All I was telling him about was Mrs. McInnerny calling on Randy. But other stuff came up. About the cocaine. That I didn't want to go into in front of them."

"Fine. But you cut me out."

"I'm sorry."

"And I have something to say."

"I beg your pardon?"

"About the movie. He was asking if Johnny left the movie. Which he didn't. Or if I left it. Or Jean and Joan. Which we didn't."

"So?"

"Someone else did."

I looked at her in surprise. "Who?"

"Lucy."

"Lucy?"

"I know," Alice said. "I don't suspect her for a moment. But she's a waitress. She did have access to the kitchen phone. And she left in the middle of the movie."

"You mean she went home?"

"She's here now. Didn't you see her?"

"Yes, I did. So what do you mean?"

"She went out and came back. She left the movie in the middle, came back and saw the end."

"Maybe she went to the bathroom."

"Not for that long," Alice said. "She was gone long enough

that I assumed she'd gone home. It was a surprise when she came back."

"You should tell Pinehurst."

"I was about to when you led him away."

"I'm sorry. How was I to know?"

"Not that I suspect Lucy, you understand. I don't for a minute think she did this. But we do have to report the facts. The police are never going to get anywhere without the facts."

It occurred to me Chief Pinehurst was unlikely to get anywhere, even *with* the facts. So far all he'd managed to do was arrest an innocent woman.

"So you think I should tell him about Lucy?" Alice said.

"In good time. I don't think it's particularly urgent. The woman's here, he can question her if he likes."

When I said that I naturally looked over to where Lucy was standing.

And she wasn't there. Right where she'd been a moment before. It was like a magic trick. As if talking about her had made her disappear.

I glanced around, spotted Lucy heading in the direction of the inn.

I turned back to Alice. "There goes Lucy now. I wanna see where she's going. If you get a chance, tell Pinehurst. I should be right back."

I walked hurriedly across the lawn after Lucy. She was already in the driveway, heading for the front door of the main house. I hung back, not wanting her to hear my feet crunch in the gravel. I circled around in the grass, waiting for her to go up on the porch. As she did, I was across the driveway on little cat feet, heading up the steps the minute she went through the front door.

The lights were on in the building. Through the glass door I could see her pass by the front desk heading for the dining room. I waited a few seconds, slipped in the door. Tiptoed swiftly past the front desk. Reached the door to the dining room.

The room was dark, but the light in the kitchen was still on. It was flickering through the swinging kitchen door. I crept to the door, pushed it open a crack, peered in.

Sure enough, Lucy was headed for the phone.

I tried to tell myself it didn't have to mean anything. It was late, and she was calling her husband, her brother, her mother, her friend, or whatever to say she'd been detained.

Nonetheless, I couldn't help feeling excited. I had caught her sneaking off to the phone.

Only she wasn't. She stopped right next to the phone and opened a cabinet in the cupboard beside it. She reached in, took something down, brought it over to the kitchen table, right next to the butcher block where Max had done his Stupid Pet Trick. When she brought it into the light, I could see what it was.

It was a file. A brown cardboard accordion file. The type with alphabetical divisions. The type you might use to file important papers if you didn't have an actual file cabinet.

Lucy set the file on the table. Then opened her purse and proceeded to rummage through it. It was a large, drawstring purse, wide enough that she was able to take out a stack of unfolded sheets of paper.

Lucy took one page from the top of the stack and set it aside. She took the rest of the stack, straightened the edges, fished a paper clip from the bottom of the file folder, and clipped them together. She then took the stack of papers, riffled through the file for the right alphabetical listing, and inserted them into the file folder.

From the same space in the file folder she extracted a single sheet of paper, looked at it, put it down on the table. She rummaged through her purse, found a pen, marked something on the paper, and returned the paper to the file. She put the pen back in her purse, closed the file, and returned the file to the cabinet.

And headed for the door.

I had a moment of panic. There was no way I could get out

the dining room door before she came through the kitchen one. She was going to catch me spying on her.

I was not standing there thinking this. Futile or not, I was fleeing as quick as I could.

Halfway across the room I was seized by inspiration. Prompted largely by the kitchen door starting to swing open. Quick like a bunny, I slipped into the booth.

And suddenly, there I sat, heart pounding fiercely, right in the seat where Christine Cobb had died.

From where I sat I could not see the kitchen door, which was good, because it meant Lucy couldn't see me. But I could see the dining room door. I could see when she went out.

Which she did.

Without seeing me.

I heaved a sigh of relief, then waited in the booth until I heard the outside door bang. Even so, I went to the door of the dining room to look out to make sure she was gone.

She was. There was no one there.

As soon as I had assured myself of that fact, I went back to the kitchen. I went straight to the cabinet and took out the file.

It was too dark in the alcove by the phone to examine it. Like Lucy, I found myself bringing it over to the butcher block. Where I would have no way to hide it if someone came in. Well, it couldn't be helped. This was a murder investigation.

The file was tied shut with string. I untied it, pulled the file open.

It was, as I'd assumed, an alphabetical file, with compartments for each letter.

I tried to judge which compartment Lucy had used. It seemed to me it was about two thirds of the way through.

I tried the compartment marked R. Pulled out a stack of papers.

The one on top was a chart of some kind. In the form of a grid. Like an accountant might use.

Down the left side was what proved to be a vaguely alphabetical listing. Reading down the row I found such entries as "Raisin Cake," "Raspberry Tart," "Ratatouille," "Relish—Antoine's," "Relish—Carl's," "Relish—Victor's."

Across the top of the grid were the months of the year. There was a total column after each month. Under the months, and after the names, were check marks, which were then totaled up. For instance, in January, under "Relish—Victor's," were four check marks. In the total column was the figure *$40*. "Ratatouille" had two check marks for twenty dollars. The "Raspberry Tart" had seven for seventy.

I pulled the top sheet off the pile. Underneath was a recipe for ratatouille. At the top of the recipe was a paper clip. Taking the paper off the stack, I saw that the paper clip held three of four pages together. I flipped through them. They were all Xerox copies of the same recipe for ratatouille.

Beneath them, attached together by a paper clip, were a number of copies of the recipe for the raspberry tart.

I riffled through the rest of the stack, found nothing but Xerox copies of recipes.

I took the stack of papers, squared it up, and started to put it back in the proper slot in the file. To do so, I spread the slot open with my left hand.

Something yellow near the bottom caught my eye. I reached in, pulled it out.

It was a small, crumpled piece of paper. I unfolded it, smoothed it out. It was a yellow Post-it, the type people use to write short messages on.

There was a message on this one, scrawled in pen. It was almost illegible. I held it up to the light, tried to make it out. It began *L—*, which made sense, since I assumed it was a note to Lucy.

I squinted at the note.

Blinked.

The first word appeared to be *cop*.

Cop?

What had I stumbled on?

What cop?

The next word was hard to make out. I deciphered it as *restart*.

The next two words were easy. *Check others.*

It was signed *C—*.

That made the whole message: *L—Cop restart check others C—*.

Obviously a note to Lucy from the cook, who signed it C either for *cook*, *chef*, or because his name began with C. Alice had told me his name. Charlie. Which clinched it. Clearly a note to Lucy from the chef.

Cop restart check others? What sort of warning was that?

I peered closer. Discerned a squiggle after *cop*. And a slight break in *restart*. I also realized what I had thought was an *e* was really an *a*.

Which allowed me to revise my translation of the message to: *L—Copy ras. tart Check others C—*.

Undoubtedly instructions from the chef to have Lucy Xerox more copies of the raspberry tart recipe and check the other recipes to see if anything else needed duplicating.

So I had not indeed cracked the murder. Instead, I had learned the chef was not at all reluctant to give out his recipes, he just wasn't giving them out for free.

I wondered how Alice would take that news.

I folded up the file and put it back in the cabinet. It occurred to me, every investigation I'd undertaken in this case had led to a dead end. Or at least a lesser crime. First I'd unmasked a cocaine dealer. Now I'd penetrated a phony blackmarket recipe ring.

I wondered if Pinehurst had to hear about this. I realized if Alice had told him about Lucy leaving the movie he probably would.

I was not a happy camper as I left the main house. From up on the porch I could see the people gathered around East Pond. I had no real wish to return to them. In particular, I was not eager to report my findings to Alice. Not that she wouldn't find it fascinating, it was just there was no way I was going to be able to tell her without seeming to gloat.

I felt like I needed to clear my head. Just relax and not talk to anyone for a few minutes. So instead of joining the group around East Pond, I walked down to the road.

It was dark. The moon was behind some clouds, and the street light was burned out. I could barely see the outline of the fence around the swimming pool.

I stood there a few moments, letting my eyes grow accustomed to the dark. Shapes became slightly more distinct. I walked down to the pool, unhooked the gate, went inside, and sat in one of the chairs.

I had to think it out. Somehow or other, I had to think it out. Because, as Louise said, with Florence out of it, the cops would pick on someone else. And while Lars seemed the likely suspect, Randy wasn't a bad guess. But, aside from him and Lars, who else was there?

Of course, one name loomed larger than the rest. Johnny McInnerny. The husband is always the prime suspect in a case like this. Only Alice said he never left the movie. And Alice was surely right. So Johnny McInnerny could not have done it. He had an ironclad alibi.

So did Florence. That was the other given. Florence was off the hook, because Florence was in jail.

So who could have done it? Lars. Randy. Louise. The chef. Lucy. The other waitress, who wasn't there, and had presumably gone home.

And . . .

The man from Champney Falls.

What if that was it? What if it had been about drugs all along? Granted, the man from Champney Falls hadn't been here tonight. But that was just as far as I knew. All I really knew was that no one had seen him. But if everyone was in the movie, no one would have seen him. He could have driven up, approached Mrs. Mc-Innerny.

Why?

Small stumbling block there. Somehow putting Mrs. Mc-Innerny together with a drug dealer just didn't compute.

Except for the phone call. If she'd overheard the phone call, it could work just fine.

Had it?

I had no idea.

Across the road in the distance, I could see the activity around East Pond. Not clearly, just indistinct shapes milling around in the light flickering through the windows.

As I watched, two of the shapes detached themselves from the general mess, and headed in the direction of the main house. As they drew nearer, I could see it was Louise and Sad Sack. I wondered what they were after. It occurred to me, most likely coffee. They came up on the porch and went in the front door.

I could have used a cup of coffee just then. I wondered if they were making it for everyone, or just for the cops. I had to laugh at myself. There was no reason at all to assume they were making coffee. In all likelihood, they weren't. I just thought they were because I wanted some.

I heaved a sigh and got to my feet. It was time to take the bull by the horns and go back and join the group. I was also curious as to what was going on. Though, with Pinehurst in charge, that was very likely nothing. It occurred to me this was the only murder investigation I could imagine that, with the police on the scene and the body not yet removed, I could take ten minutes out to sit down, kick back, and collect my thoughts.

That thought amused me. Made me decide, perversely, to give it one more minute. I lay back down in the deck chair, gazed up at the stars. Which I couldn't see for the clouds. Which didn't mean they weren't there. Just like the solution to this crime.

How profound.

Maybe I'll solve this yet.

A door banged. I looked up to see Sad Sack and Louise come out on the porch. They looked animated, and Sad Sack had something in his hand. They came down the steps, hurried off in the direction of East Pond.

I sprang from the deck chair, went out the gate and across the road. I was walking briskly across the lawn when I heard a jangling sound behind me. The next thing I knew something banged into me and knocked me down.

I instinctively rolled over, and put up my hands to protect myself from my assailant.

And felt something wet on my face.

Licking me.

A voice said, "Prince! Stop it, now!"

I blinked.

Reached up, grabbed his collar, pushed him off. Struggled to my feet.

It was Prince, all right.

And the person whose voice I'd heard, the woman who'd just stooped down to retrieve the leash, was Florence.

"I'm sorry," she said. "He's just so excited to be out at night. And he really does take to you."

I gawked at her, incapable of speech.

I was dimly aware of people approaching us. I looked around, saw Pinehurst and Sad Sack, followed by what appeared to be practically everyone.

Sad Sack was holding a plastic evidence bag. Inside was something white and bloody.

They marched straight up to Florence.

"Florence Baker," Pinehurst said. "You're under arrest for the murder of Clara McInnerny."

THIRTY-ONE

"WE HAVE HER dead to rights," Pinehurst said. He didn't seem particularly happy about it. He leaned back in his desk chair, took a sip of coffee.

Pinehurst and I were in the police station. Florence was in her jail cell, waiting for her lawyer to drive up from Boston. Or rather from someplace halfway between here and Boston—the lawyer had a car phone, and Florence had reached him on his way home. The lawyer had driven up earlier in the day and arranged for bail. Which was, of course, the real reason Pinehurst looked so grim. He'd fought vigorously against her release, only to have another murder occur not two hours later.

"There must be some mistake," I said.

Pinehurst grimaced. "Yes, you would think that."

"Can you tell me what you've got?"

"Might as well," Pinehurst said. "She's not talking until the lawyer gets here, and I doubt if she will even then."

He jerked open his desk drawer, took out a plastic evidence bag. "What we've got are these. A pair of bloody gloves. We can match the blood type to the victim's, then nail it down with DNA."

"You've done that?"

"No, but we will. And it will match. Why? Because Christine Cobb was poisoned, and there is no other bloody crime it could be."

"Which doesn't mean it couldn't be something else."

Pinehurst put up his hand. "I don't want to argue it. Odds are it will match. Even if it doesn't, the woman gets out of jail, silences the prime witness against her."

"*What* prime witness? Mrs. McInnerny didn't know anything."

"Ah, but she did."

"How do you know?"

"Because she's dead."

"That's circular logic, Chief. It doesn't mean anything."

"Maybe not to you, but it does to me. Anyway, she was snooping around. According to the busboy, Randy. She came around asking prying questions."

"Indicating she was way off base."

"Not really. Randy and Christine Cobb *were* having an affair. That information was accurate."

"But irrelevant. And shows the woman was on the wrong track."

"Yes, but she must have gotten on the right one, because she's dead."

"Fine," I said. "You wanna tell me about the gloves."

"I thought I did."

"No, you just showed them to me. Where did you get them?"

"Oh, well, that's the thing. They were in her wastebasket."

"You're kidding."

"Not at all."

"You arrested her on the basis of a pair of bloody gloves found in her wastebasket?"

"Why not?"

"Why not? Give me a break. Your theory is this woman went out and killed Mrs. McInnerny. She was smart enough to wear white gloves so she wouldn't get blood on her hands. Then she's dumb enough to leave the white gloves in her room?"

"Undoubtedly what her lawyer will argue."

"That doesn't bother you?"

"Everything bothers me. The stupidity defense—which is what you're arguing—how could the woman be that stupid?—I don't go for it. Criminals always do something stupid. I can't go around apologizing for them."

"Uh-huh," I said. "And the time element?"

"What about it?"

"How does that work out? Did Florence have time to kill this woman?"

"Absolutely," Pinehurst said. "Her lawyer showed up right after I talked to you. He called ahead, had a judge waiting. Slapped me with a habeas corpus, told me release her or take her before a magistrate. The judge in question is off my Christmas list. He grants her bail, and she commits another murder."

"Is there any possibility of an overlap?"

"What do you mean?"

"Any possibility Mrs. McInnerny was killed before Florence was released?"

"Not according to you."

"Huh?"

"By your own statement you saw Mrs. McInnerny alive as late as eight-fifteen. She was out of here by then."

"This works for you?"

"It works just fine. The McInnerny woman was a snoop. She stumbles on something that's dangerous to the killer."

"What about the murder weapon?"

"What about it?"

"Was it from the kitchen like you thought?"

"It appears to be. The chef admits it looks like his. Rather reluctantly, I might add. Of course, he still thinks he's protecting his son. Plus, no one's ever too eager to claim ownership of a murder weapon."

"So your theory is the killer took the knife from the kitchen, which was unlocked?"

"Yes, of course."

"Then this might interest you."

I told him about following Lucy and discovering the recipes.

"Interesting," Pinehurst said. "Your wife told me she left during the movie. Your theory is she went out to make copies?"

"I think so. There's a copier behind the front desk. I figure she went to the kitchen, got the things she needed to copy, went to the front desk, copied them, and went back to the movie."

"And returned later to put them back?"

"Exactly."

"Why would she do that?"

"I assume because of the crime."

"I beg your pardon?"

"I mean because Mrs. McInnerny was killed."

"Oh, really?" Pinehurst said. "I was going to point out it seemed strange to me she'd bother to put them back with all that going on."

"I can give you a theory."

"By all means do."

"I would say Lucy had no intention of putting the recipes back, and she would have gone home after the movie and brought them in tomorrow. When the body's discovered, she hangs around like everybody else. So she's hanging around with the copies in her purse. And she knows there's going to be a police investigation.

She doesn't want to have to explain the copies, so she puts them back."

Pinehurst frowned. "I suppose that could be it."

"I can only think of one other explanation."

"What's that?"

"That she's guilty of the crime. Of the murder, I mean. She left the movie, not to make copies, but to go to the kitchen, get the knife, and kill Mrs. McInnerny." I shrugged. "Either that or it's both."

"Both?"

"Yes. Lucy goes to the kitchen to make copies. Mrs. McInnerny finds her, demands to know what she's doing. She kills her to shut her up."

"Over a bunch of recipes?"

"Stranger things have happened."

"Not in my lifetime. Not if you tie it in to the murder of Christine Cobb. Then you have two, separate, unrelated murders in one week at the Blue Frog Ponds, which I cannot credit. Or, Christine Cobb was also killed over these recipes. Which I credit even less. I'm very glad you told me this, however."

"Why?"

"It makes talking to Lucy my next order of business. It wasn't important when your wife told me. Not with Florence on the loose. Now she's important, not as a suspect, but as a witness. If she really went to the kitchen when she left the movie, there are only three possibilities. The knife was taken before she got there. After she left there. Or while she was there. It becomes very important whether she saw that knife."

"It's also possible she saw the killer."

"Maybe, but I don't think so."

"Why not?"

"Because she didn't mention it. Everyone thought Florence was in jail. If Lucy had seen her, she'd have said so."

"You're assuming the killer is Florence."

"Yes, I am."

"If you're wrong, and the killer was someone else, Lucy might have seen them and not have mentioned it."

"I'll certainly ask her. Not that a response is likely to vindicate the suspect. Still, if anyone was prowling around, I would certainly like to know."

"I'm glad to hear it. Might I ask if you've pursued any *other* avenues that might tend to vindicate the suspect?"

"Such as?"

"How about the phone call?"

"The phone call?"

"Yes. Your phone call to me. Someone listened in on the line. That person obviously wasn't Florence, because she was in jail at the time. So, are you assuming that was Mrs. McInnerny?"

"It would seem likely."

"Maybe so, but have you any positive indication that it was?"

"Only that after dinner she began snooping around."

"By that you mean talking to Randy. Aside from that, the only indication she was snooping around is the fact she wound up dead. Or is there something you're not telling me?"

"No, that's really all I have."

"What did Randy say?"

"Just what you'd expect. Mrs. McInnerny wanted to know about him and Christine Cobb."

"And that's all?"

"What do you mean?"

"Did she ask about anything else?"

"Not according to him. Of course, the boy's not particularly forthcoming. Just getting him to admit she was there at all was like pulling teeth."

"But he admits she was asking about him and Christine Cobb?"

"Rather grudgingly. And only when specifically asked."

"Did you specifically ask about anything else?"

"Like what?"

"Did you ask him about drugs?"

"Drugs?"

"Yes."

"No."

"Well, wouldn't that be a logical question? I mean, if we're taking the premise Mrs. McInnerny began snooping because of the phone call, the phone call was about drugs."

"True."

"You didn't ask him about that?"

"It's a side issue."

I smiled. "You'll pardon me, but that's never stopped you before."

"I admit to taking great pains to see which suspect to arrest. Having made that determination, I do not hesitate to act on it."

"I suppose that's commendable. But just on the off chance that you're wrong, you want to follow this thought process through? If Mrs. McInnerny overheard our conversation, and started snooping because of it, then we both agree Randy was the wrong track. She got on the right track and she got killed. Well, that conversation she overheard was about drugs. They were Lars Heinrick's drugs. So, if she got on the right track, it would lead to Lars Heinrick, and not Florence."

"Yes, but how would she know?"

"I beg your pardon?"

"How would she know that? About Lars Heinrick, I mean. She didn't find out from our phone conversation. I am rather careful talking on the phone. I am sure I didn't mention his name."

"You mentioned Delmar Hobart's."

"That I did. And if you would like to point out to me how Mrs. McInnerny could trace the drugs from Delmar Hobart to Lars Heinrick, I would be delighted to listen. She overheard the phone call during dinner, right after dinner she's out talking to

Randy, right after that she gets killed. Now, how did she manage to track this down? Even if Delmar Hobart is listed in the phone book—I'm not sure he is, but let's say so just for the sake of argument—well, then she gets him on the phone, says, 'Excuse me, I'm sorry to bother you, but could you tell me just who you sold drugs to at the Blue Frog Ponds?' " Pinehurst shook his head. "I'm sorry, but it just doesn't fly."

"You wanna make the connection to Florence work?"

"I don't have to. The connection is there. The woman's a busybody, she's snooping around. In the course of her investigations what does she find? The person the police have accused of the crime. You think she's not going to ask some probing questions? Maybe insinuate she knows something the police might like to know?"

"That's all speculation. You're making it up."

"Yes, but it's certainly logical."

"Maybe so. Tell me something, Chief. Aside from the bloody gloves, is there anything to connect Florence to the crime?"

"You mean aside from the fact it was committed to cover up *another* crime I have her dead to rights on?" Pinehurst's smile managed to seem both smug and pained. "No, probably not."

THIRTY-TWO

THE NEXT MORNING we did not hike. Alice woke up with a severe headache, and right after breakfast she went back to bed. Not that we would have hiked in any case. What with everything that had happened, no one was in the mood. Nonetheless, there I was, on a beautiful sunny morning, with a sick wife, and nothing to do.

Except walk the dog. With Florence back in jail, that duty had once again fallen on me. After breakfast I got the passkey from the desk, went up to the room, and let him out.

He nearly knocked me down again, but this time I saw him coming. I was able to sidestep him, grab his collar, and attach the leash. He actually pulled me down the stairs in his eagerness to get out the door.

We walked everywhere. Around the grounds, along the road, and down to the stream.

Randy was there, sitting on a rock. I gave Prince his head, let him pull me along. He bounded to the rock, dog tags jangling, looked up at the boy.

"Hi," I said. "How you doing?"

As usual, Randy didn't answer.

"It must be rough," I said, "to have this happen on top of everything else."

"A lot you care," Randy said.

"Huh?"

"You're the one who told him. Again. You told him again."

Randy was right, of course. I'd told Pinehurst about seeing him with Mrs. McInnerny. Just like I'd told Pinehurst about seeing him with Christine. I'd seen him with both of the victims. Reported it to the police. It was a little much.

But totally irrelevant.

"Don't be silly," I said. "No one thinks you did it. No one suspects you of either crime. It's just you happen to be the last person to see Mrs. McInnerny alive. Usually that's suspicious to a cop, but not in this case, because he's already made an arrest. Yes, you're important, but as a witness, not a suspect. Don't you understand?"

"Sure, I understand. They let that woman out of jail. The woman who killed Christine. And what does she do, she kills someone else. Is that supposed to make me happy, that it wasn't me? Well, guess what? This is not big news. I *knew* it wasn't me."

"What if it wasn't her?"

"What?"

"What if it wasn't her, either? What if the woman happens to be innocent?"

"You trying to pin this on me?"

"Not at all. I'm trying to keep you out of it. But if the case against Florence blows up, the police will pick on you. I'd like to head that off. I promised your mother. Besides, the person who did this should pay. The police think they know who did it. They're not going to look any further. I am. So I put it to you. Do you want the killer caught?"

"Don't be silly."

"That's not silly. You might have reasons to want the killer to get away."

"Oh, yeah? Why would I want that?"

"What if it was someone you knew?"

"It isn't."

"Are you sure?"

"Yes, of course."

"Then you must want the killer caught."

Randy refused to dignify that with an answer.

"If you do, help me."

He didn't answer that either. I let it lay there, waited him out. After a while he said, "How?"

"Tell me about Mrs. McInnerny. When she called on you last night, what did she want?"

"What do you think?"

"Yes, I know. You and Christine. I don't care about that. I mean aside from that. Did she mention anything else?"

"Like what?"

"You tell me. What did she ask about?"

"Nothing," Randy said.

But his eyes shifted.

I shook my head. "Randy, you're no good at this. Every time you lie, I can tell. And if I can tell, the police can tell. Did you lie to Chief Pinehurst when he asked you?"

Randy looked away, refused to answer. I could see him set his jaw.

"Right. You didn't tell him anything. Because he didn't ask you. He asked you about Christine Cobb. And that's what you told him. Mrs. McInnerny wanted to know about Christine Cobb.

So that's all you talked about. With Pinehurst, I mean. The other subject never came up.

"And you weren't going to bring it up, were you?" I smiled, lobbed it out there. "It's hard to talk to a policeman about drugs."

Bingo.

Bull's-eye.

Randy's eyes widened, and his mouth fell open. He turned and stared at me as if I were some weirdo psychic who could read his mind.

"She asked you about drugs, didn't she? Specifically, she asked you about cocaine. That must have freaked you out, particularly if you've ever done any."

Randy's lip quivered. His eyes blinked rapidly. "Who are you?" he said.

"And there," I said, "is another indication of your being poor at this. You *know* who I am. Asking that question is the same as saying, 'How did you know that?' Which confirms that it's true. But, to answer your question—the one you didn't ask—Mrs. McInnerny was a snoop. She found out cocaine was involved in the case. But she didn't know whose cocaine. So she was asking around. That's why she asked you. Not that she had anything to go on. But that's why she asked about drugs. Maybe even asked about Delmar Hobart."

He frowned. "Who?"

I raised my finger. "Now, there's where it's good to be bad. I can tell from your reaction you've never heard the name."

"What are you talking about?"

"I'm trying to get your story. It would be easier if you just told it. You wanna fill me in?"

Randy looked away, set his jaw again. "I have nothing to say."

Maybe not, but it didn't matter. He'd already confirmed what I wanted to know. Mrs. McInnerny had asked him about drugs. Mrs. McInnerny had listened in on the phone line.

I walked Prince back to the inn. I didn't run into anyone on the way. I took him upstairs, put him back in his room.

When I came out, I looked over at Lars' door. Felicity Frog smiled back at me, she of the long eyelashes. She seemed to be batting them at me. Enticing me. Luring me in,

I resisted manfully. Which wasn't easy. Had Mrs. McInnerny been up here last night? Somehow followed the trail to Lars? Or had she, as Pinehurst assumed, followed the trail to Florence?

I stood there, the passkey clutched in my hand.

Then, like a good boy, I walked down the stairs and returned the key to the front desk.

Louise wasn't there, so I went behind the desk and hung the passkey on its hook.

I stood there a moment, looked around. There was the Xerox machine, where Lucy had presumably made the copies. And there was the register, where Jean or Joan had snuck a peek and found out Lars and Christine weren't married, not that hard to do with the front desk so seldom manned.

I looked around some more. In the corner was a tall plastic wastebasket, from the top of which protruded the handles of several golf clubs. I walked over, looked in. Discovered it was putters and golf balls for the putting green.

Why not? That was just the sort of mindless activity I needed to clear my head. I took a putter and ball and went outside.

The putting green was next to the swimming pool. It wasn't that big, but it was gently sloped, and featured nine numbered holes, the numbers on the nine metal flags sticking up from them. Which allowed me to play it as a nine-hole miniature golf course. I figured each hole was a par two. So par for nine holes was eighteen. That was the score I was trying to beat.

I am not a good golfer, but I had beginner's luck. My first putt, a twenty footer, stopped inches from the hole. I tapped it in for a two.

The second hole, about as long with a sharp break to the left, I ran the ball three and a half feet by, and sank the return putt.

The third hole, maybe fifteen feet with a slight break to the right, I started the ball wide to the left and watched it curl neatly into the cup.

Unbelievable. I had done the first three holes in five strokes. One under par. With that kind of a start, I was on my way to a record round.

I fished the ball out of the hole, lined up my putt on four. Took back my putter.

A ball rolled across the hole. Just as I swung. Whether it was that or the high-pitched giggle that accompanied it, I couldn't quite say, but for a moment I was completely unnerved. My hands tensed on the putter, my arms jerked forward, and I nearly lost my balance. The ball, struck with far more force than I'd intended, shot by the hole and rolled right off the green into a clump of tall grass.

So much for my record round.

I turned my gaze from the hopeless lie to the one who had caused it.

Smiling up at me was the six-year-old girl. That figured. First she rained on my Red Sox, then she ruined my golf.

Not only that, from the look on her face, she had finally concluded I wasn't the enemy. I had become, instead, another grown-up she felt free to annoy.

"Hi," she said. She couldn't have been more chipper if she'd been auditioning for *Sesame Street*.

I took a breath, smiled, and said, "Hi."

She giggled, pointed at my ball. "You missed."

I smiled, ruefully. "Yes, I believe I did."

I looked around for the girl's parents, but didn't see them. I couldn't help wondering what they were thinking, letting her out alone like this. After all, there'd been two murders at the inn. For all they knew, I could be the killer.

The girl didn't seem to think so. In her mind I had somehow made the transition from loathsome stranger to her best friend. "I bet I can get closer than you can," she said.

I didn't doubt it. Her ball had rolled a good twenty feet by the hole, but it was still on the green. If one were making odds, she would have been an overwhelming favorite.

Not that she really meant to play. With another giggle, she ran across the green to her ball, and then, wielding her putter like a hockey stick, dribbled it toward the hole with a series of short swings, pushes, and pokes. With a final squeal of delight, she stopped it next to the hole and tapped it in.

Had it been possible to count her strokes, they probably would have numbered around nine or ten.

Which was still likely to beat me.

With another squeal of delight, the girl grabbed the metal flag and pulled it up, flipping her ball out of the hole. She rammed the flag back in the hole, looked up, smiled, and declared, "My name's Margie."

"Margie?"

"Yes. What's your name?"

"Stanley."

She burst into hysterical laughter. Then waggled her finger at me. "No. What's your *real* name?"

"Stanley."

She burst into laughter again.

It was somewhat disconcerting. As a stand-up comedian, I had never played to a better audience. Still, I was not that happy with the punch line.

"What's your name?" she demanded.

"George Washington," I told her.

Her face twisted into a happy pout. "No, it's not," she said.

"It's not?"

"No."

"What is it?"

"Stanley."

I don't know why it wasn't funny when she said it.

"Stanley?" I said.

She laughed hysterically.

Maybe it was my delivery.

When she stopped laughing, I said, "Stanley," again.

And she started again.

I don't know how long we might have kept it up. I, for one, found it more promising than attempting to hit my golf ball. But after a while she looked at me and said, "I feel sorry for the man. Do you feel sorry for the man?"

If the little girl, who I had to remind myself was named Margie—I almost couldn't remember, having repeated Stanley so many times—really felt sorry for the man, you would not have known it from her face. Still, I was willing to give her the benefit of the doubt.

"Yes," I said. "I feel sorry for the man."

"Me too. It's so sad. He lost his wife."

I nodded. A forgivable euphemism, I suppose, for a six-year-old. Lost his wife, as if Mrs. McInnerny had somehow been mislaid, instead of been stabbed in the heart with a carving knife.

"Yes," I said. "Poor Mr. McInnerny."

She wrinkled up her nose. "Who?"

"Mr. McInnerny. You were saying it was sad about his wife."

"No, I wasn't."

I almost said, "Yes, you were." I stopped myself. Just because you're dealing with a child, doesn't mean you have to get into a childish argument.

"You weren't talking about Mr. McInnerny?" I said.

"No, not him," she said. Then added, as if in complete explanation, "He's old."

If Mr. McInnerny was old, I wondered what that made me.

"Who were you talking about?" I said.

"The *young* man. I was talking about the young man."

Oh. Lars Heinrick. I wondered if she just assumed he was married, or if her parents had told her that to account for Lars and Christine living together. In any event, if she was feeling bad about it, it seemed kinder to disillusion her.

"If you mean Lars Heinrick," I said, "she wasn't his wife. They weren't married."

"Yes, they were," she said.

She seemed quite positive. So her parents must have told her. I can't say I approved of the practice, lying to children in an effort to make things easier to comprehend. It occurred to me male-female relationships were hard enough for the young to understand without an underlying layer of deceit.

"Oh," I said. "Is that what your parents told you?"

"No."

"So how do you know they're married?"

"I just know."

So. The other possibility. The six-year-old mind simply decides something is true.

"So," I said, "no one told you that?"

"Yes, they did."

"Oh, is that right? Someone told you Lars and Christine were married?"

"Uh-huh."

"Oh?" I said. "And who told you that?"

"She did."

THIRTY-THREE

PINEHURST WASN'T CONVINCED. No surprise there. Chief Pinehurst was *never* convinced.

Which was totally frustrating. He had started off with a completely open mind. Then he'd arrested Florence. And his mind had closed. It would admit no information other than that relating to her guilt.

"You're not listening," I told him.

"I'm listening," Pinehurst said. "I'm just not hearing anything."

"Oh, no? Randy confirms Mrs. McInnerny was asking about drugs."

"So you say."

"Ask him yourself."

"I most certainly will. Not that it will prove anything."

"Oh, no? It proves she heard the phone call."

"So what?"

"So what? How can you say so what? She overheard the phone call, found out about the drugs. She was asking Randy about the drugs. Trying to find out whose they were. And the next thing you know she gets killed. Wouldn't that make the person who owned the drugs a likely suspect?"

"The case is not about drugs. That's a tangent. It's coincidental. The woman may have been asking about drugs, but you and I both know she was investigating a murder."

I took a breath. "Yes, of course. She was investigating a murder. And when she started asking about drugs, it got her killed."

"That has yet to be proved."

I exhaled sharply. "Fine. Will you at least concede it can be shown by inference?"

Pinehurst pushed back his chair, got up from his desk. "I don't know why we wind up arguing about these petty issues."

"Going somewhere, Chief?"

"I need a cup of coffee. Couldn't you use a cup of coffee?"

"I suppose it couldn't hurt."

I followed Pinehurst into the pantry. The coffeemaker was still on, heating the remnants in the pot. Pinehurst took two cups, divided the coffee. It poured like mud. I added milk and sugar. Pinehurst took his black.

"How is it?" he said.

"Dreadful."

He took a sip, nodded. "Yeah. Pretty bad. But better than nothing."

He switched off the coffeemaker, and we carried the coffee back to his desk.

"Now," I said, "we've stalled and made coffee, had a chance to think it over. Would you care to consider the information I've brought you?"

Pinehurst took a sip and grimaced. I wasn't sure if it was the coffee or what I said. "I've thought over what you've brought me.

I continue to think over what you have brought me. I assure you I will not discard it. It just happens to be relatively minor in the general scheme of things."

"Lars Heinrick and Christine Cobb were married."

"According to a six-year-old girl."

"Here again, Chief, this is something that could be checked."

"And I assure you I will. It just doesn't mean as much as you think it does."

"Oh, no? You have a secret marriage. One they carefully refrained from telling anyone about. Even after her death. Does Lars Heinrick pine for his murdered wife? No. He keeps up the pretense of merely being the boyfriend."

"Oh, but he doesn't. If you'll recall, he refused to answer questions. Withdrew his cooperation. He never denied they were married. The subject never came up."

"He never brought it up, and never would. Not until someone else got hooked for the murder. Then he would quietly assert his rights.

"What rights?"

"To inherit her estate."

"What estate?"

"Again, I have no idea. But you could find out."

"Anything else you'd like me to find out?"

"Yes. How much money did the McInnernys have? Does Mr. McInnerny inherit under his wife's will? And did he have an outside interest?"

"Are you serious?"

"Absolutely." I held up my finger. "We have two separate but interrelated crimes. Your present theory is the same person committed both."

"Isn't yours?"

"I'm trying to keep an open mind. But, assuming that theory, that one person committed both, you have two suspects looming larger than the rest. Lars Heinrick and Johnny McInnerny."

Pinehurst winced. "Oh, please."

I put up my hands. "Yes, yes. I understand, Florence is your chief suspect. But, aside from that, you've got Johnny and Lars. In which case, possibility number one is Lars Heinrick kills Christine Cobb, and to cover it up, he has to silence a snooping Mrs. McInnerny.

"Possibility number two, Johnny McInnerny is the killer, the killing of Mrs. McInnerny is the main crime, and the killing of Christine Cobb is merely a ploy to divert suspicion from himself."

"Oh, for goodness' sakes."

"You don't like that?"

"Like it? Your theory is the man kills a woman he never met?"

"Exactly. In order to draw suspicion from himself. Suppose Christine Cobb hadn't died. Then Mrs. McInnerny is killed. Who is the chief suspect? Johnny McInnerny, cut and dried. No doubt about it. On the other hand, if he kills Christine Cobb first, what a master stroke. Now he can kill his wife, and no one will suspect him at all. Which is exactly what's happened. Not only do you not suspect him, you ridicule the suggestion."

"And for good reason," Pinehurst said. "*Arsenic and Old Lace.* Johnny McInnerny never left the movie. According to your wife. He returned with her and found the body. He has a perfect alibi for the crime."

"Yes, and isn't that suspicious?"

"I beg your pardon?"

"When a suspect has a perfect alibi, doesn't that raise a red flag? Like maybe he *meant* to have a perfect alibi?"

"Whether he meant to or not, the fact is he does. You can't get away from that."

"Oh, no? I'm thinking of another movie. *Strangers on a Train.*" Pinehurst's eyes widened. "Are you saying . . . ?"

"Suppose Johnny McInnerny and Lars Heinrick have a pact. You do my murder, I'll do yours. Johnny McInnerny poisons Christine Cobb. Lars Heinrick stabs Mrs. McInnerny."

Pinehurst stared at me. Blinked twice. Then shook his head. "No, it doesn't work."

"Why not?"

"Johnny McInnerny has an alibi for killing his wife. Lars Heinrick doesn't. If your theory was right, he would. Christine Cobb would have been killed in a way he could not possibly have done it. Because otherwise there is no point."

"So what if Johnny McInnerny was inept?"

Pinehurst rubbed his forehead, put up his hands. "Stop, stop, stop. Good lord. Do you have any idea how convoluted this is? How far you are stretching things, to try to make your theory hold water? The two men have a pact to kill each other's wives, so as to give each other alibis. Johnny McInnerny kills Christine Cobb, but is so stupid he *fails* to give Lars Heinrick an alibi. Lars Heinrick, being a man of his word, feels morally obligated to kill Mrs. McInnerny, even though the murder of Christine Cobb has been bungled to such a degree he might as well have done it himself."

"I admit it's not the best theory in the world."

"No kidding. Particularly since I have the killer dead to rights." Pinehurst took a sip of coffee, grimaced. "Not to put too fine a point on it, but all of these theories are somewhat irrelevant, since they happen to ignore the person who actually committed the crime. Can you give me any theory, any theory at all, to account for the fact that Christine Cobb had an affair with Florence's husband and broke up her marriage, after which Florence followed Christine Cobb to New Hampshire, registered at the same inn, and dogged her footsteps everywhere she went? You got any explanation for that?"

"Sure."

THIRTY-FOUR

PINEHURST LOOKED AROUND the dining room. "Is that everybody?"

Sad Sack referred to a list, nodded yes.

"Good," Pinehurst said. "Then let us begin."

We were once again back in our original positions where we had been sitting on the night of the murder of Christine Cobb.

With a few exceptions.

Mrs. McInnerny, of course, was no longer with us. Johnny McInnerny sat alone.

And the dinner crowd was not included. That is, those who were not staying at the inn.

That left:

Lars Heinrick.

Jean and Joan.

The two businessmen who had turned out to be brothers.

The family with the little girl.

And Alice and me.

Florence was not at our table. She sat at another table with her attorney, a rather sour-looking man in a brown suit, who gave the impression he was not at all happy to be there. Indeed, I gathered he was a divorce lawyer, and found the criminal practice somewhat distasteful.

Florence wasn't in handcuffs, which was something of a concession. She'd arrived in handcuffs, but was being allowed to sit at a table without them. Her lawyer had argued for the right.

At another table sat Louise, Randy, and the chef. I realized it was the first time I'd ever seen them together. They did not look like a harmonious family unit.

Randy looked aggrieved, among other things. Those included cocky, arrogant, sulky, sullen, insolent, and on edge. In short, your typical teenager. I had to remind myself he was actually a young man in his twenties.

His mother was a picture of concern. Louise looked as if her world was crashing down on her. Whatever relief she must have felt at learning Florence was free when Mrs. McInnerny was killed, and had been arrested for the crime, had apparently been undone when Pinehurst had called and instructed her to assemble everyone in the dining room at five o'clock. Canceling dinner was surely the least of her worries.

Evidently, she had done so at the last moment. The chef, sitting on the other side of Randy, was still wearing his apron. At least he had taken off his hat. His hair was brown, flecked with gray, and was quite full. For the first time I could see a resemblance to his son.

The two waitresses sat together. The young one looked somewhat nervous, but Lucy looked positively miffed. I wondered if that was due to missing out on the possibility of selling recipes at dinner, or if it was the defensive look of someone who expected to be accused. In any event, her expression recalled my first impression of her, my concentration-camp-commandant assessment.

As for the rest, Jean and Joan seemed positively thrilled; the two businessmen who might be brothers seemed slightly bored; and the mother and father seemed concerned for and protective of the six-year-old girl, who looked as bright-eyed and bushy-tailed as if she were on line for a ride at Disney World.

Johnny McInnerny and Lars Heinrick sat in their respective seats, Johnny at his table, and Lars in the booth. They looked dull, vague, numb, as if they could not believe this thing that had happened to them.

And then there was Alice, sweet Alice, sick this morning, recovered this afternoon, or at least feigning recovery, bundling up in sweater and slacks, clutching a box of tissues, and venturing stoically forth, despite sniffles and sneezes and a fever of 102. She sat at the table, watery-eyed, sweating, determined not to miss a thing.

Pinehurst took a breath, looked around the dining room, and said, "I'd like to go over this one more time."

There were audible groans.

"Yes, I know," Pinehurst said. "It would seem as if we've been over the ground enough. And yet, each day there are new developments, new matters that come to our attention. Matters that must be addressed.

"We are all aware of what happened last night. Mrs. McInnerny was killed. Florence Baker was arrested for the crime." He held up one finger. "However, this must not prejudice us. There is in this country a system of justice that maintains that a person is considered innocent until proven guilty. Which is why she is with us today, sitting here among us."

"Is she out on bail?" Louise demanded.

If Pinehurst was annoyed by the interruption, he didn't show it. He considered a moment, then said, "Actually, she is not. Since we are here to share information, I suppose I should tell you. In point of fact, bail was asked for and denied in this case. The judge who had previously granted bail ordered it revoked. In light of the subsequent crime."

Pinehurst put up his hand. "But that's a side issue. Florence is here today because I asked that she be here. She is here with her attorney's consent, and in his presence. So that she may hear some of the things that we are going to hear."

"Are you going to make a statement?" Louise said.

"No, I am not. As the arresting officer in the case, I feel it would be inappropriate for me to do so at this time. For that reason, I am going to turn the floor over to another type of investigator. That is, Mr. Stanley Hastings, a private detective from New York, who has been looking into the matter. Mr. Hastings?"

All eyes turned to our table.

Alice sneezed.

I handed her the box of tissues. She pulled out two and blew her nose.

I got up, walked to where Pinehurst was standing. He gave way, sat at an empty table. I stood there, surveyed the room.

I felt a sudden, overpowering urge to say, "Let's go over this one more time." I stifled it.

"Thanks for your attention. I am, as Chief Pinehurst said, a private detective. I have no official standing in this case. What I am about to tell you does not bind anyone to anything. I am merely presenting some facts and/or theories for your consideration. In an effort to clear up the crime. Or, rather, crimes.

"Let us take them one at a time. To begin with, the murder of Christine Cobb. By now, you are all aware of the background. Christine Cobb had an affair with Florence Baker's husband, who subsequently divorced her. Florence became embittered, fixated on revenge. Followed Christine Cobb on vacation, observed her in the company of a young man."

I turned, gestured to Lars in the booth. "Lars Heinrick. Young, handsome, romantic. In every way, they are the perfect couple.

"She spies on the young couple, and what does she see?" I raised one finger. "Christine Cobb does it again. She leaves the young man to run after another."

I gestured to Randy.

"As far as Florence is concerned, this is the last straw. She has brought poison with her. She uses it."

I paused, looked around the room.

"At least that is how the police construct the case. And how do they construct the second one? Mrs. McInnerny was interested in the crime. As are we all. But she was interested enough to do something about it. She began her own amateur detective work. She had learned of the affair between Randy and Christine Cobb. She questioned him about it last night. Visited him at approximately eight-fifteen, when almost everybody else was in the movie. She called on him in his room behind the kitchen."

I pointed at the boy. "Now, Randy had been admonished many times not to be rude to the guests. Just how well he took that to heart remains to be seen. The fact is, he gave Mrs. McInnerny no satisfaction and got rid of her as quickly as possible.

"Then sometime between eight-fifteen and ten o'clock, Mrs. McInnerny was killed. And we can narrow that down a bit more. Because I returned to my room at nine-thirty. And I heard nothing. And the walls in East Pond are paper-thin. Not only would I have heard the murder, I would have heard Mrs. McInnerny return to her room. So she *had* to have been killed before that.

"What is the police theory of the case? Florence, released from jail, returns to the inn. She encounters Mrs. McInnerny, who has just been rebuffed by the busboy, Randy. Mrs. McInnerny accosts Florence, springs on her some fact she has managed to dig up with her detective work.

"In all likelihood, Mrs. McInnerny did not know how devastating this information was. But Florence did. She hears it, and panics. She swears Mrs. McInnerny to silence. She tells her that though the facts look black, she can explain everything. In fact, she has evidence. She can *prove* she's not guilty. If Mrs. McInnerny will just give her the benefit of the doubt, she will show it to her. She will bring it to her room.

"So, Mrs. McInnerny goes to her room and waits. But Florence doesn't go to get the evidence, she goes to the kitchen to get the carving knife. She goes to Mrs. McInnerny's room, stabs her, rushes back to her room to get Prince, and takes him out, so if anyone asks her what she was doing at the time of the murder, she can say she was walking the dog. Her only mistake is leaving the gloves she wore to commit the crime in her room."

I paused, spread my arms. "Is there any problem with this police theory of the case? Anything about it that doesn't quite seem right?"

After a few moments, I said, "No, there is not. It's a perfectly logical interpretation of the facts. It could have happened just that way.

"So, the thing we have to ask ourselves now is, is there any *other* logical explanation. Anything else that might have happened. Or, in legal terms, can these facts be explained away by any reasonable hypothesis other than that of guilt? Or, more simply, could anyone else have committed the crimes?

"In order to consider that, we have to throw in a few more facts."

I looked around the room. "I assume you are all familiar with Agatha Christie? Even if you haven't read the books. You've heard of her Belgian detective Hercule Poirot, and Miss Marple, the little old lady who solves crimes in a small English village. Well, in one of Miss Marple's books she finds a clue at Somerset House." I looked around at utterly blank faces. "Yes, I know, it means nothing to you. But in England, that is where the marriage records are kept.

"Which brings us to fact number one. Lars Heinrick and Christine Cobb were married."

I looked over to see the sheer astonishment on the faces of Jean and Joan.

"That's right. I know you all made the assumption that they were not, as they had registered under both of their names. But, in point of fact, they were man and wife.

"Does this change things? Well, yes, it does, if you throw in fact number two. Christine Cobb had some money. Which Lars now stands to inherit. Money is always a motive for murder."

I glanced over at Lars. His face betrayed nothing. If I'd been playing poker with him, I wouldn't have known whether to raise or fold.

"Does that mean he did it? Not necessarily. But it certainly gives him a motive."

I turned to the other side of the room.

"Just as it gives Johnny McInnerny."

Mr. McInnerny, on the other hand, was transparent as glass. His face, already a picture of grief, twisted into one of horror and surprise. He gawked at me, as if unable to believe I'd said such a thing.

"I'm sorry if that upsets you, Mr. McInnerny. But it happens to be a fact. You and your wife had some money. With her death, it now comes to you."

I turned back to the room at large.

"But would he kill for it? And, if so, why would he also kill Christine? Because that is the situation here. We have two crimes. And the first question is, are they separate, or are they connected?

"That is the easiest question to answer. They are connected. Why? Because if they were separate, it would defy the laws of logic, the law of averages, and the name of reason. For the murders to be unrelated is just too fantastic to be considered.

"There is one small possibility I would grant. That the one murder was *inspired* by the other. For instance, Lars Heinrick kills his wife, Johnny McInnerny says, 'That's a good idea,' and does the same.

I put up my hands. "I am not saying that happened. I am using it as an example. But I believe it is one we can discard. It is my personal opinion the same person killed both women.

"So, let us look at our potential killers. First off, Lars Heinrick. Because his wife died first. It is what the police would call the primary crime.

"The first question is, could Lars Heinrick have committed it?"

I spread my arms.

"Absolutely. He was sitting in the booth with Christine. During the course of dinner he drops the poison in her glass. He leaves the dining room before she drinks it, does not return until he hears the screams. As far as murders go, it's easy as pie. In terms of opportunity, clearly Lars Heinrick had the best.

"Next best would be the busboy, Randy."

Louise sprang to her feet. "Now see here, I'm not going to let you accuse my son."

I put up my hands. "No one's accusing anyone of anything. I am merely laying out facts. Some of them will involve your son, just as others will involve other people. Could we all take that for granted? I am going to lay out facts involving several people in this room. There is no reason for us to take offense each time someone's name is mentioned."

Louise sat back down.

"Now, as I was saying, the person with the next best opportunity is Randy, who served them the drinks. He could easily have put the poison in the glass. Why he would *want* to is hard to comprehend, unless you are willing to grant the youthful obsessive love of the if-I-can't-have-her-no-one-can mentality."

Since both Randy and Louise seemed on the verge of springing up, I went on quickly.

"But I am not claiming that happened. I am presenting all these theories for what they're worth. Granted, some of them are not worth much.

"Where was I? Oh, yes. Who had opportunities to poison the glass? Well, the next best would be Florence. She had an opportunity to poison the glass when she left the dining room to walk the dog. What gives her a good opportunity is the timing. She left the dining room after Lars Heinrick went out. At a time when Christine Cobb would have been alone in the booth. So no one but Christine would know that she stopped there.

"Also—and this is an important point that I happen to know because she was sitting at my table—she left the table just as Mr. and Mrs. McInnerny stopped to talk to us. When the McInnernys stopped by our table, she excused herself to walk the dog."

I raised my finger. "Why is that important? It is important because the McInnernys were a distraction. To Alice and me. Ordinarily, when a person gets up and leaves your table, you would watch them go. At least to some extent. And look where our table is."

I pointed to our table, where Alice was blowing her nose. She looked out from under the tissue with pink eyes, like a little white mouse.

"If you get up from our table and go out the door, you walk by the booth. But you reach it rather quickly. It's actually quite close. So, without the distraction of the McInnernys, either Alice or I would have been likely to notice if she'd stopped at the booth. By carefully timing her exit, Florence is able to insure that that does not happen. She stops by the booth when the only witness to see her there will shortly be dead."

I raised one finger. "And what of Johnny McInnerny? Did *he* have an opportunity to poison the drink? Remember, he came in with his wife, he came in late, and he came directly to my table. This was after the drinks had been served, and after Lars Heinrick had already left. Johnny McInnerny is at my table, with his wife, talking to Alice and me, just as Florence is leaving to walk the dog."

I pointed. "After which, Louise escorts him to a table on the other side of the room. But could he, at any time, have stopped by the booth?"

I paused, looked all around the room.

Smiled.

"I can see the answer on all of your faces. You . . . don't . . . know. Not one of you can tell me whether Johnny McInnerny had an opportunity to go to the booth. And why is that? Because you never once considered him a suspect. Ever. Not until the murder of his wife. That is the first thing that involves him in any way in the crimes. Johnny McInnerny is a perfectly ordinary middle-aged man that there is no particular reason to notice at all."

I looked at him. "No offense meant, Mr. McInnerny, but you are not memorable. Not like a Lars Heinrick, who is a young, handsome man traveling with a drop-dead gorgeous woman whom everyone notices at once. So, for that reason, and that reason alone, you could get up from your table, walk over to the booth, tell Christine Cobb some innocuous fact about some hiking trail or other, drop poison in her glass, and no one would particularly notice.

"So the answer is yes, Johnny McInnerny could have committed the crime. Why would he do so?" I smiled. "Well, I explained this to Chief Pinehurst, and I can't say he liked it. But, of course, he thinks he has his killer in jail. If Johnny McInnerny planned to kill his wife, if that was the point all along, if he were to simply do so he would be the number-one suspect. But if he kills someone else first, someone he has absolutely nothing to do with—and the police investigation has shown that there is no connection whatsoever between Johnny McInnerny and Christine Cobb—well, if he can make the murder of his wife look like it's tied in to the murder of this other woman, then no one in the world will seriously suspect he did it."

I looked around the room. "Pretty clever, huh? When you think about it, it is an absolutely brilliant crime."

I paused. Frowned. "There is only one problem. Johnny McInnerny was at the movie *Arsenic and Old Lace*. And he never left. That fact is verified by several of you, including my wife."

I tried to avoid looking at Alice, though I could see several heads swiveling in her direction.

"So, Johnny McInnerny would seem to have a perfect alibi for the murder. So does that mean he couldn't have done it?" I smiled. "Well, not if my reading of crime fiction is any guide. The person with the perfect alibi is always suspect. For, while an innocent man may have an alibi, a guilty man usually goes out of his way to see he has one. So the very fact that Johnny McInnerny's alibi is so good is in itself suspicious."

I turned, pointed to the booth. "On the other hand, Lars Heinrick has no alibi at all. He was alone in his room. While almost everyone else was in the movie. Could he have left his room and killed Mrs. McInnerny? Absolutely. Particularly if she came and found him. We know she was snooping around about the crime. She had already called on Randy. Suppose she calls on Lars? Now we have the same scenario as with Florence. Mrs. McInnerny drops some information that alerts Lars to the fact she knows he committed the crime. Lars arranges to meet her in her room, goes to the kitchen, gets the carving knife, and kills her. No problem at all. Piece of cake.

"And, of course, Randy was not at the movie. Randy was in his room. Mrs. McInnerny called on him there at eight-fifteen. By his own admission, he is the last person to see Mrs. McInnerny alive. And no one can vouch for *his* whereabouts. He says he sent her away. He could also have accompanied her up to her room, and killed her."

I held up my hand. "And, thank you, Louise, I don't need you to point out that he didn't. I am merely saying he *could*. And he, of all people, would have had access to the knife.

"As would his father and mother. Neither of whom were at the movie. Either of whom could have taken the knife. Indeed, who would have had more access than the chef? As to motive, a parent will often kill to protect a child. Either one of them could have struck Mrs. McInnerny down if they saw her as a threat to their son.

"And here again we have the exception that proves the rule. I said there had to be one killer. Well, yes and no. If the killer was their son—if Randy killed Christine Cobb—well, they could kill to cover up that fact."

I spread my arms. "Well, you see, we suddenly have several suspects. Can we narrow it down? Let's go at it from another angle. Let's see who could have taken the knife."

I turned, pointed to another table. "I'm going to ask you, Lucy, if you saw it there when you went to the kitchen during the time you were gone from the movie?"

Lucy's eyes widened, and her face drained of color. "I . . . I . . ." she sputtered.

"There are many witnesses to the fact you left the movie. At approximately the time Mrs. McInnerny was killed. It becomes very important whether you saw that knife."

Lucy had regained her composure. Her face was hard. "Are you accusing me of this crime?"

"Not at all. You certainly had the opportunity. But your motive's a little thin. Even if Mrs. McInnerny had accosted you in the kitchen and wanted to know what you were doing, when all you doing was copying a recipe, well, I can't see you killing her over that."

Murmurs of "recipe" could be heard around the room.

I smiled. "I see that rings a bell. I gather some of you are aware of Lucy's sideline." I turned back to Lucy. "But so what? Even if she caught you at it, it wasn't as if she could turn you in." I smiled again, gestured to the chef. "Particularly since your employer knew you were doing it. There was nothing illegal about it. A chef has every right to sell his recipes, even if his manner of doing so is somewhat bizarre."

The murmurs this time featured both surprise and grumbling. I avoided looking at Alice.

"But that's a side issue. The point is, did you see the knife?"

Lucy's jaw had been set, but now her face showed her dismay. "No. I didn't notice."

"That's a shame, but I didn't really expect you did. And, of course, if you had seen anyone you would have said so. I take it you did not?"

"No."

"Then we must move on. One more fact is known. At the time of her death, Mrs. McInnerny was inquiring about drugs. She asked Randy about them. Specifically, she asked about cocaine. I know that's news to most of you, but it is also a significant fact.

"Oh, one more significant fact. The bloody gloves. The evidence against Florence includes a pair of bloody gloves that were found in her room. This, I must say, is the one thing that most strongly convinced me of her innocence. I don't care how stupid a murderer is, they do not leave the bloody gloves in their room.

"On the other hand, the murderer is happy to leave the bloody gloves in someone else's room. Could someone have planted the gloves in Florence's room? Absolutely. There's a passkey hanging on a hook behind the front desk. All the murderer had to do was take the passkey, open Florence's door, and plant the gloves. I happen to know this key opens Florence's door because while she was in jail I used it in order to walk her dog.

"And that's another thing. The dog. Florence got out of jail, came home, and went right out to walk Prince.

"And that's when the murderer planted the gloves. That's the only time the murderer could have planted the gloves. Because the murderer couldn't have done it while the dog was there.

"So. A picture is beginning to take shape. The murder had something to do with money. Something to do with drugs. The murderer was connected in some way to at least one of the two victims. And the crimes are related.

"Do we have a suspect? Yes. Unfortunately, we have several. The first one we must set aside. That would be Florence. I admit the evidence against her is grim. Her husband had an affair with Christine Cobb. She came to New Hampshire, registered at the inn, and appeared to dog Christine Cobb's footsteps until her death. Is there an explanation for her behavior other than guilt?"

I paused, looked around. "Unfortunately, we do not know. And the reason we do not know is because Florence has not told us. Nor has Florence told the police. Nor has Florence told her lawyer."

I paused, let that sink in. "And why not?"

I shrugged. "Because, point of fact, Florence doesn't know. Florence's biggest problem in defending herself is the fact that she is totally ignorant of all aspects of the crime. So we must take her for a moment and set her aside.

"So, what are we left with? Of the remaining suspects, we have three. Lars Heinrick. Johnny McInnerny. And Randy Winthrop. Is there any way to choose among them? Actually, there is not. Any one of them might have done it. And while we can raise inferences through deductive reasoning, there is nothing that can be proved."

I paused, looked around the dining room.

"So how can we know who did it?"

I smiled.

"Actually, it's rather easy."

I paused again, then spoke softly.

"We have a witness."

I waited for the reaction, the murmur of whispers through the room.

I smiled again.

"That's right. Ironic, isn't it? Here we drive ourselves crazy trying to develop theories of the case, and all the time there is an eyewitness. No need for guesswork, we can solve the crime.

"I'm going to solve it now. To do so, we need a lineup. That's how identifications are made. The suspect is picked out of a lineup."

I went to an unoccupied table, took three chairs, placed them in a row in the front of the room.

"I realize in a police lineup there's usually six. In our case there are only three. Randy, come here."

Randy looked up, sullen and unwilling. I walked over to his table.

"You want the killer caught, Randy? Help me out here."

Louise looked about to protest, but her husband said quietly, "Do it, Randy."

Randy looked at his father. Then got up, followed me over to the chairs. I sat him in the one on the left, then went and got Johnny McInnerny. He didn't protest, just followed me blindly to the front of the room. I sat him in the chair in the middle.

I walked over to the booth. "Come on, Lars," I said.

I took his arm, helped him out of the booth. Guided him over to the chairs, sat him in the one on the right.

"And there you have it," I said. "Our three suspects, all in a row. Your basic lineup.

"And now the witness."

I went through the swinging door into the kitchen.

I returned a minute later with Max the cat. I cradled him in my arms, stroking him, keeping him calm, a tough job, with so many people around.

"Here's your witness," I said. "Max the cat. Max lives in the kitchen, but he also hangs out in East Pond. He was there last night, and he saw the murder. He saw the killing, and he was absolutely traumatized by it. I'm trying to calm him down. I'm going to ask you all to be very quiet and not scare him. But the fact is, Max saw the murderer, and Max is going to identify him now."

I looked around. Everyone in the dining room was staring at me as if I'd lost my mind. I ignored them, talked to the cat.

"Are you ready, Max? Here we go."

I set Max on the floor in front of the three chairs.

No one moved. You could have heard a pin drop.

Max looked toward Randy.

Then toward Johnny McInnerny.

Then toward Lars.

He lashed his tail back and forth. Licked his lips.

Looked at Randy again.

Then his head swiveled around. His body followed. He padded over to Lars, dropped his hindquarters, and suddenly sprang into his lap, landing with his full weight, and digging in with his claws.

Lars sprang to his feet, hurling the cat to the floor. He glared at me, his face contorted with rage.

"You devil!" he cried. "How did you get it?"

I smiled.

A quote from Agatha Christie.

Perfect.

THIRTY-FIVE

"I CAN'T THANK you enough," Louise said.

"Don't be silly."

We were sitting on the porch of the Blue Frog Ponds. There we were, at long last, the owner and I having the dreaded bed-and-breakfast conversation. Though at least it didn't seem to be running to "how we came to buy the inn."

"It's not silly," Louise said. "I mean, look what happened. The police made a mistake. Arrested the wrong person. What if she'd gone to trial, and the case had fallen apart. And the evidence had gotten mixed up, and nothing was ever proved. All his life, there would have been a stigma on my boy."

"I'm glad there's not, but I don't think anyone ever seriously suspected him."

"It doesn't matter. There'd be talk. There still will. Particularly if they can't convict that young man."

"I think they can. Of course, I don't want to talk out of turn."

Jean and Joan came out on the porch.

"Oh, good, you're up," the thinner one said. A mental cross-reference reminded me that would be Jean. "We're checking out this morning, but we have to know. Is it over? Did he confess?"

I shrugged. "You know as much as I do. I haven't heard a word since they took him away."

"And you," Joan said, accusingly. "We looked for you last night, and you were gone."

"I'm sorry. I had to take care of my wife."

Which was true. While the police were taking Lars into custody, I had bundled Alice off to bed. Which was one of the reasons Pinehurst and I hadn't spoken.

"Oh, how is she?" Jean asked.

"Much better, thanks. Twenty-four-hour bug." I jerked my thumb. "She's calling the camp now, trying to see how our son is doing."

Jean and Joan sat down at the table.

"So, tell us," Jean said. "What's the story? How did you know it was Lars?"

"Because it wasn't Florence."

Joan made a face. "Don't be like that, or I'll strangle you. Tell us how you knew."

"I would rather not be strangled, but that happens to be the answer. Florence looked guilty. Florence had the motive and the opportunity. Her husband had an affair with Christine Cobb, and she followed her here and dogged her footsteps. Those are facts that you could not get away from. If Florence is not guilty, how could they possibly be true?"

I shrugged. "They could only be true if they were carefully engineered by someone else. In which case, there was only one person that someone else could be.

304

"Forget Florence for a minute, and think about what really happened. Lars Heinrick is an unscrupulous young man who wants money. So he marries a young woman and kills her for it. A perfectly simple crime. Of course, I don't know if it was that premeditated. He might have married her, and then decided to kill her, or he might have been planning on doing it all along. I would assume the latter, since he kept the marriage a secret. And this secret was a major factor in obscuring his motive. Not that it wouldn't have come out eventually, but, in the meantime, their ignorance of this made it all too easy for the police to develop a case against a different suspect."

"What's that got to do with Florence?" Joan said.

"I'm getting there. But it's important to understand the background. Lars Heinrick has married Christine Cobb. She has money. He wants it. His problem is how to kill her without suspicion attaching itself to him. The concealed marriage is a step in that direction. As I say, it will give the police time to suspect someone else. He has to make sure that happens. How does he do that? He frames them.

"And how does that work? Let's go back to the original problem. Christine Cobb is a attractive young woman who happens to be a bit of a flirt."

Jean snorted. "That's one way of describing her."

"Right," I said. "Some people would say she was downright promiscuous. At any rate, she's had her share of affairs, some with married men. Lars pokes around, finds a case of one man she's had an affair with who subsequently divorced his wife. That wife is Florence Baker. So Lars proceeds to find out what he can about her. Which is probably not that hard. Christine Cobb knew Florence's husband. She met him somehow. So they must have had some acquaintances in common. Through them, Lars learns about Florence Baker. Keeps tabs on her, to see what she's going to do. And what does he learn? He learns she's going on vacation in New Hampshire. He finds out where and when, and makes a reservation for the same day at the same bed-and-breakfast."

"It's an inn," Louise said.

"Of course," I said. I was glad Alice was still on the phone. "Anyway, he books a vacation at the Blue Frog Ponds. On the day in question, he leaves early, to be sure he checks in *ahead* of Florence. So it will look as if she followed him there."

I held up one finger. "Here we have a flaw in his plan, and one that will come back to haunt him. He had a reservation. And so did she. So it's not like she followed him up here. The rooms were booked in advance."

"Right," Joan said. "So how could that work?"

"The only way would be if she found out where he was going, and then made a reservation there. But in point of fact, her reservation was made first. Now, granted, it *could* have happened that way. She could have learned where Lars and Christine were *planning* to go, and made a reservation at that place before they did. But that's pretty thin. It's not the type of argument I'd be happy to make. And I'm sure Lars' attorney will not be particularly pleased, either.

"On the other hand, thin as it is, it probably would have been sufficient to convict Florence. Since everything else damning was in place, or seemed to be. As long as you take the facts at face value, here's Florence following the woman around who had the affair with her husband. It's hard to see beyond it.

"Anyway, that's what Lars did. That's why he wound up at Champney Falls." I smiled. "Here again, we overlook the obvious. Florence got there first. When Alice and I went to Champney Falls, Lars and Christine passed us on the way up. When we got to the top, Florence was there eating lunch with her dog. Obviously, she'd gone up ahead of them. The police explain it away—she overheard them at breakfast saying that where they were going, so she simply went there first.

"Actually, it was the other way around."

Louise frowned. "What do you mean?"

"Actually, it was Lars who overheard Florence saying she was climbing Champney Falls and arranged to go there too."

"How do you know he didn't just follow her there?" Joan said.

"Because Christine isn't in on it. *She* doesn't know Lars is following Florence. Lars can't get in the car with her and say, 'Let's follow the woman with the dog.' He has to say, 'Hey, I've got an idea, let's go to Champney Falls.' And if Christine isn't ready to go when Florence leaves, he has no reasonable explanation for hurrying her. Not that he can tell her. Which is why he gets there after Florence, much as he would prefer to have gotten there before."

A police car pulled up, and Chief Pinehurst got out. As he came up on the porch the women all began talking at once.

"What happened?"

"Is it over?"

"Did he do it?"

"Did he confess?"

Pinehurst put up his hands. "Please, please," he said. "I'll tell you all about it, but not so fast. I don't suppose I could get a cup of coffee?"

Jean and Joan looked at him in total exasperation, but Louise said, "Anything you want, Chief," and went in the front door.

Pinehurst pulled up a chair, sat down at the table, and deflected any questions until Louise returned. As he accepted the coffee and took a sip, it occurred to me the case was ending just as it had begun, with Pinehurst stalling and dragging things out.

"So," he said, "in point of fact, Lars Heinrick has not confessed, nor do I expect him to. But that shouldn't concern us, because we should have no problem building a case."

"How?" Louise said.

"Very much along the lines Mr. Hastings suggested. If this happened the way he laid it out—and there is every reason to believe that it did—then corroboration will not be hard to find. If Lars Heinrick made inquiries about Florence, learned of her vacation, and arranged to be here, too, that can undoubtedly be shown."

"Have you uncovered anything?" Jean said.

"Not yet, but we're just getting started. The point is, if the solution is correct, the evidence must be there."

"But you have nothing to go on?" Joan said.

"Did I say that?" Pinehurst said. "Not at all. I merely said we had not yet run down those particular leads. But as far as having nothing to go on—while Lars Heinrick hasn't confessed, Delmar Hobart has."

The name meant nothing to Louise, but Jean and Joan perked right up.

"Delmar Hobart!"

"The hiker!"

"You mean he was in on it?"

"Not the actual crime," Pinehurst said. "But he was certainly a factor. You see, Delmar Hobart was Lars Heinrick's drug connection."

Jean and Joan's eyes were wide.

"I knew it!" Jean said. "I knew there was something wrong with him."

"And we're the ones who nailed him!" Joan said.

"That's true," Pinehurst said. "Your information did help."

Joan looked positively flattered, but I could see Jean's mind going.

"Wait a minute, wait a minute," Jean said. "If Hobart was the drug connection, and Mrs. McInnerny was asking about drugs . . ." She turned to me accusingly. "And if Mrs. McInnerny overheard your phone call. The one where you learned his name . . ."

Chief Pinehurst bailed me out. "You're right," he said. "That's how she knew. I told Mr. Hastings we'd identified Delmar Hobart as a drug dealer. But I asked him to withhold the fact. You mustn't blame him for not sharing the information. At the time, there was no reason to believe it had anything to do with the case."

Pinehurst turned to me. "However, Mr. Hastings, let me fill you in. When I arrested Lars Heinrick last night, he had a vial on him, which proved to contain cocaine. On the basis of that information, we questioned Delmar Hobart. Who, as I say, has confessed. I'm sure one of the *reasons* he's confessed is we happened to catch him with a considerable quantity of drugs, but the fact is, the man is cooperating. And, according to him, Lars Heinrick purchased cocaine on several occasions. Including the afternoon at Champney Falls."

"So that's what he was doing there," Jean said.

"Absolutely. And his statement tends to corroborate our theory that Lars was following Florence around. According to Delmar Hobart, Lars Heinrick had him come to Champney Falls because he had to be there, and could not wait for him at the inn, even as much as half an hour. Why? Because he was following Florence."

Pinehurst shrugged. "Granted, Delmar Hobart doesn't know that. But it raises the inference, and, taken with everything else, it is corroboration."

"But is it enough to convict?" Louise said. "If he gets off, people will always wonder."

"I can't promise you what a jury will do. But the evidence will be there. Even if a jury fails to find him guilty beyond a reasonable doubt, there will be no doubt in the eyes of the public. That I can promise you."

Florence came around the side of the building with Prince on a leash. Jean and Joan sprang up and ran over to her, ostensibly to offer support, but more likely to relate their thrilling tale of following a drug dealer. Talking animatedly, the three women followed Prince across the lawn.

"Well, I'll be off," Pinehurst said. He gulped the last of his coffee, set down the cup. Gave me a meaningful look. "Just wanted to let you know about the cocaine."

I got it. I had without him underlining it, but it was nice to have the confirmation. Lars' connection with drugs would be established by the vial he was carrying when he was arrested. The cocaine I'd pilfered from his room would disappear.

I watched with satisfaction as Pinehurst got in his car and drove off. No, he hadn't really had to come by this morning. But it was nice to hear him go over it one more time.

Johnny McInnerny appeared, lugging two suitcases from the direction of East Pond. He plodded down to the parking lot, opened his trunk, put them in his car. He slammed the trunk, came back up to the porch.

"I'm checking out," he said to Louise. "Is there anything I need to do?"

"No, just give me the keys."

Johnny passed them over. Like the suitcases, there were two. A sobering fact.

I got up, extended my hand. "Good-bye, Johnny. I'm sorry about anything I may have said last night. About considering you a suspect. It wasn't meant to hurt you, just to fool Lars."

"I know," Johnny said. "You had to get him. I'm glad you did."

He shook my hand, nodded to Louise, turned and plodded off, climbed into his car, and drove away.

Moments later the door banged, and Alice came out on the porch.

"I got through to the camp," she said. "According to his counselor, Tommie hasn't asked for us once. He's signed up for tennis, basketball, baseball, soccer, archery, and riflery, his only problem is choosing, because he wants to do everything. He couldn't talk to me because right now he's in a canoe in the middle of the lake.

He supposedly wrote to us yesterday, so we should have a letter by the time we get home."

"We'd better write to him," I said. "But what can we say? I can't imagine explaining all this in a letter."

"You're leaving today?" Louise said.

I nodded. "As soon as we get packed. I'll stop by the front desk and settle the bill."

I half expected her to say, "Don't bother, there is no charge." I was glad when she didn't. I would have found it embarrassing. And I preferred to remember her as a shrewd businesswoman.

Max came around the corner of the porch, his tail held high. He marched up to us, dropped his hindquarters, sprang up onto the table.

"Max," Louise said, "behave yourself. And in front of the guests."

I reached up, scratched him under the chin.

"No, I think he's entitled. After all, he solved the murder."

"Yes, he did," Louise said. She smiled. "I can still see the look on Lars Heinrick's face."

So could I. Shock, terror, disbelief. The man had to be terribly disconcerted to suddenly have a cat accusing him of a crime.

Which Max wasn't, of course. He hadn't really been in East Pond, and even if he had witnessed the murder, I doubt if he could have picked out the killer.

No, Max was merely doing his Stupid Pet Trick. When I'd helped Lars out of the booth and led him to his chair I'd slipped a sardine in his jacket pocket.

Max had done the rest.

He was a truly remarkable cat. I scratched him behind his ears, and he lay down on the table and began purring.

The chef came out on the porch. Charlie. Louise's husband. As always, he seemed somewhat stiff and unnatural out of the kitchen. He smiled when he saw me petting the cat.

"I understand you're leaving," he said. "I just wanted to say thank you."

"I think it's Max that deserves the thanks," I said. "You might give him a special treat for dinner."

"I will," he said. "But anyway, I'm no good at this sort of thing, but . . . well, here."

He pulled something from behind his back. A large manilla envelope. But he didn't hand it to me, he handed it to Alice.

"Me?" she said. "What is this?"

Alice undid the clasp, opened the envelope. Pulled out a sheaf of papers. As she looked at the top one, her face lit up with a smile.

I leaned across the table to look, though I didn't need to. Alice's reaction told me what they were.

Recipes.